teach ®
yourself

cantonese

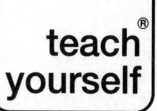

teach®
yourself

cantonese
hugh baker
and
ho pui-kei

For over 60 years, more than
40 million people have learnt over
750 subjects the **teach yourself**
way, with impressive results.

be where you want to be
with **teach yourself**

For UK order enquiries: please contact Bookpoint Ltd., 130 Milton Park, Abingdon, Oxon OX14 4SB. Telephone: +44 (0) 1235 827720. Fax: +44 (0) 1235 400454. Lines are open 09.00–18.00, Monday to Saturday, with a 24-hour message answering service. You can also order through our website www.madaboutbooks.com.

For USA order enquiries: please contact McGraw-Hill Customer Services, PO Box 545, Blacklick, OH 43004-0545, USA. Telephone: 1-800-722-4726. Fax: 1-614-755-5645.

For Canada order enquiries: please contact McGraw-Hill Ryerson Ltd., 300 Water St, Whitby, Ontario L1N 9B6, Canada. Telephone: 905 430 5000. Fax: 905 430 5020.

Long renowned as the authoritative source for self-guided learning – with more than 30 million copies sold worldwide – the *Teach Yourself* series includes over 300 titles in the fields of languages, crafts, hobbies, business, computing and education.

British Library Cataloguing in Publication Data: a catalogue record for this title is available from The British Library

Library of Congress Catalog Card Number: On file

First published in UK 1995 by Hodder Headline Ltd., 338 Euston Road, London, NW1 3BH.

First published in US 1996 by Contemporary Books, a Division of The McGraw-Hill Companies, 1 Prudential Plaza, 130 East Randolph Street, Chicago, IL 60601 USA.

This edition published 2003.

Typeset by Graphicraft Limited, Hong Kong

Printed in Great Britain for Hodder & Stoughton Educational, a division of Hodder Headline Ltd., 338 Euston Road, London NW1 3BH by Cox & Wyman Ltd., Reading, Berkshire.

Impression number   10 9 8 7 6 5 4 3 2 1
Year   2009 2008 2007 2006 2005 2004 2003

v

contents

introduction

Welcome to a new experience. If you have never tried to learn a Chinese language before you are in for a rare treat.

There are some real eye-openers: have you ever met a language where verbs have only one form and don't change according to tense or number or mood?; a language where there are no cases? (you can forget about vocatives, genitives, ablatives and their confusing brethren); where no gender differences are acknowledged? (have you noticed how Chinese people speaking English frequently get 'he' and 'she' mixed up?); where there are no agreements of anything with anything else? ('singular, third person, feminine' what's that?!); where there are no subjunctives? (Would 'twere so for English!)

Contrariwise, have you ever tried a language which has to be sung in order to be understood? Or where word orders are so crucial that if you get them wrong you will be totally unintelligible? Or where you can't count objects without first specifying what kind of objects they are? Or where almost every single syllable has a meaning? (Unlike English where the individual syllables of a word such as 'trousers' mean nothing at all.)

Cantonese is a vital living language spoken by upwards of a hundred million people in southeast China (including Hong Kong and Macau), Malaysia, Europe, Australia, Fiji, North America and many other parts of the world where the adventurous Cantonese people have settled. It is one of a large family of Chinese languages and retains many more traces of its ancient roots than do most of the other languages. By way of contrast, it is a language which seems unafraid to adopt or adapt, notably from English in the past century or so, and it invents, evolves and discards slang at a frenetic rate. As a result it is a very rich language.

The people who speak Cantonese are lively, quick-thinking, direct and fun-loving. They are tuned into their language so much that they cannot resist having fun with it – they pun all the time and often with great ingenuity. They love it when foreigners stammer out their first words of Cantonese, because there is bound to be a howler or two which can be punned into something funny. Don't be put off, you are brightening their lives and they will not despise you for it.

And if you have the chance to get help from a Cantonese you should, of course, seize it. The odds are that he or she will not want to be bothered with the romanized text which you are learning from and it is for this reason that we have supplied Chinese characters for the dialogues and new word lists. We are not attempting to teach you characters beyond the briefest of introductions at the end of the text – the reason is that it takes a great investment of time to learn to read and write Chinese characters and you will learn to speak and to understand speech much sooner if you ignore the script. You can always move on to learning it later.

Most of the units of this book follow the same pattern: two dialogues (often humorous, if you think silly jokes are humorous), each with a list of the new words used and explanations of new grammar points, and followed by some exercises. Units 7, 14, 21 and 26 are revision units, giving more material based on what has been learned but not introducing anything new. The appendices summarize the most important grammar points and refer you to the units of the book in which they are first explained and they also introduce you to Chinese writing. At the back will be found the answers to all exercises and a two-way glossary to help you find your way round the book.

A few points to note:

- Do not look for consistent characterization of the people who appear in the dialogues: there is none, the Mr Wong of one unit being a totally different person from the Mr Wong who figures in another.
- Do not be put off by the fact that in our system of writing Cantonese Mr Wong is spelled **Wòhng**, Mr Cheung is spelled **Jèung**, etc. – our system is meant to work *for you the learner*,

but the man in the street does not need to be as precise about pronunciation as you do, so we also show you the spellings which he would probably normally use.

- You may be puzzled by the numbers of words which are pronounced the same but which have quite different meanings (**daai,** for instance, means both 'to bring' and 'to wear'). Cantonese, like all the Chinese languages, is full of homophones (words pronounced the same): it is a fact of life that you will have to accept – and it is one of the reasons why punning is so common.
- When you first hear Cantonese it sounds rather ugly and even a normal chat can seem like a violent argument because of the vigour and velocity with which ideas are delivered. Fear not, you will quickly learn to detect beneath that coarse exterior melodic and beautiful cadences which can be as romantic, heart-warming or soft as anyone could desire.

We have had fun writing this. We hope you will enjoy studying it. We *know* you will get a great kick out of speaking with Cantonese people.

Symbols

▶ = material included on the recording

ℹ = information about culture, way of life etc.

pronunciation guide

A note on romanization

This note is about the sounds of Cantonese and how to represent them on paper. It should be read with the recording available so that you can hear a clear demonstration of what the sounds are.

Cantonese, like all the Chinese languages, is written in characters. As you will discover when you read the appendices of this book, characters are symbols representing ideas, while the letters of our alphabet are symbols representing sounds. Written English reproduces the sounds of speech using an economical 26 symbols, which are quite sufficient to do the job; but the Chinese writing system pays little attention to the sounds of the spoken language and tackles the massive problem of providing instead a separate symbol for most of the ideas which need to be written.

When you learn to write an English word you learn how to say it (even if the spelling is sometimes a little erratic). If you were to try to learn the basic Cantonese of this book through Chinese characters, not only would you have the daunting task of learning nearly 1,500 different symbols, but even when you had learned them you would be none the wiser about how to speak the language, because the symbols are generally dumb about how they should be pronounced.

So generations of foreign learners have struggled to find ways to 'romanize' Cantonese, that is, to represent Cantonese sounds with the Roman alphabet. Since there are very few sounds in Cantonese which are difficult for English speakers, this would be an easy task but for one thing: Cantonese is a *tonal language*, that is, each one of the sounds of Cantonese can be pronounced (or perhaps 'sung' would be a better word) in seven different ways (the *tones*). The Roman alphabet does not have any devices for representing tones and musical notations added to letters of the alphabet would be much too awkward to handle.

Romanization is only a tool to enable you to learn how to speak the language; it is useless outside the classroom, a private communication system just between us the teachers and you the learner. There is no 'official' romanization of Cantonese, and many different systems are in existence. In this new edition of *Teach Yourself Cantonese* we have chosen to use a version of the Yale system, which we believe to be helpful for the following reasons:

- It distinguishes clearly each one of the sounds and each of the seven tones.
- Only three additional symbols (the macron [¯], the grave [`] and the acute [´] accent) are required to indicate the tones.
- There are reference materials available which use the same system and the beginner will thus be able to expand beyond the scope of this book if desired.

If you intend to go really deeply into Cantonese you will certainly have to learn Chinese characters and then romanization will be largely redundant. Meanwhile, try to familiarize yourself with the principles of the Yale system as quickly as possible so that it becomes a tool and not an obstacle to your learning the language.

▶ The Cantonese tones

Cantonese has seven tones which it is essential to master for fluent and comprehensible speech. Some teachers have been known to claim that it is possible to be understood even if tones are totally ignored, but while it is true that a certain limited communication may be possible given great goodwill on the listener's part, in normal circumstances the toneless speaker would be met by blank incomprehension. The tones occur on all syllables and are located in three pitches (high, mid, low), the voice remaining level, rising or falling within those pitches. The seven tones are:

High pitch	High level
	High falling
Mid pitch	Mid rising
	Mid level
Low pitch	Low falling
	Low rising
	Low level

- Low pitch words are shown by the addition of **h** after the vowel.
- Rising tones are shown by the acute accent ['], falling tones by the grave accent [`], and the macron [ˉ] shows the high level tone.
- The accents are marked on the vowel or (where there is a vowel chain) the first vowel of the syllable.

Thus the seven tones of the sounds **ma** and **hung** would be written:

High level	**mā**	**hūng**
High falling	**mà**	**hùng**
Mid rising	**má**	**húng**
Mid level	**ma**	**hung**
Low falling	**màh**	**hùhng**
Low rising	**máh**	**húhng**
Low level	**mah**	**huhng**

Listen to how these are spoken on the recording and do your best to copy them exactly.

Every now and then a word changes its tone in a particular context: we have pointed it out when it occurs in this book and suggest that you try to accept these occurrences as the oddities they are rather than try to figure out why they change.

▶ The sounds of Cantonese

1 The consonant sounds which begin Cantonese syllables are simple for English speakers. The only exception is the initial consonant **ng-** and that is only difficult because English does not have syllables which start with this sound. You can imagine how it is done if you think of the word *singalong* and try to pronounce it without the letters *si* at the front. If you have the recording you should be able to pick up how

ng- syllables are pronounced without much difficulty. For example:

ngan nga ngok ngai ngaam

2 There are very few consonants which can appear at the end of Cantonese syllables, in fact there are only six (**-n, -ng, -m, -p, -t, -k**). Of these, the first three are completely straightforward, just as you would expect them to be if you were reading the sounds off in English. For example:

haan seun leng mong taam gam

But the other three (**-p, -t, -k**) are hardly pronounced at all, the tongue and the lips getting into position to pronounce them and then not following through. So your lips should snap together to get ready to make the **-p** at the end of the syllable **sap**, but you should not open them again to release the puff of air which has built up to make the full **p** sound. Similarly with the sound **bat**, the tip of your tongue should make contact with the hard ridge behind your upper teeth, but the air should not puff out to make a full **t** and with **baak** the flat top of your tongue should go up into your palate but not allow the air to escape to make the full **k** sound. Listen carefully to the recording examples:

sap jaap kat faat sik jek

3 The vowel sounds of Cantonese are a little more complicated. The following is a guide to the sounds based wherever possible on 'BBC English' pronunciations, but please note that this is only a rough guide. The best way to grasp them is to listen carefully several times to the pronunciation section of the recording: while your ear is getting used to hearing the sounds, your eye will be taking in the system which we use for spelling those sounds. To start with concentrate on the sound itself without being too much concerned with tone. You will get more pronunciation practice later, because each unit's dialogues and new words lists are also on the recording. And, of course, if you have the luxury of a Cantonese friend, ask him or her to make the sounds for you as well.

-aa is a long vowel sound, rather like the sound of the word *are* in English. It combines with **-i** to make a long vowel as in a drawled version of *eye*, and it combines with **-u** to make a long version of *cow*. If there is no final consonant the Yale system always uses just one **a**, but it should always be pronounced long as if it were **aa** (**ba** is pronounced *bar*). For example:

ba   baai   baau   baan   saam   laang   a   daap

-a is a shorter version of the **aa** sound, pronounced somewhere between the English b*a*t and b*u*t. For example:

jam   pan   hang   tai   tau   sat

-e is rather like the English f*ai*ry. For example:

be   che   leng   jek

-ei is like the English d*ay*. For example:

bei   sei

-eu is something like English f*ur*ther. For example:

jeun   leung   cheut   geuk

-eui is rather like h*er* *e*vening (but don't pronounce the *r*). For example:

deui   neui   heui

-i is not too different from English s*ee*, except when it is followed by **-k** when it is more like English s*i*ck. For example:

ni   tiu   tim   min   ting   lip   mit   sik

-o is somewhere between English th*aw* and g*o*ne. For example:

fo   on   bong   hok   ngoi   mou

-u is somewhere between English t*oo* and c*oo*k. For example:

fu   fun   hung   juk   mui

-yu is like the German *ü*ber or the French t*u*. In English you can get close to the sound by saying *see you* very quickly. For example:

jyu   syun   hyut   yu

4   Cantonese syllables all carry virtually equal stress and each therefore sounds more or less discrete; and Chinese characters each represent one syllable and are all written discretely. Our romanization, therefore, could spell each syllable separately, but we have chosen to use hyphens where two or more syllables are so closely associated that they may be thought of as one word or one concept, as with **pàhng-yáuh** (*friend*), **jùng-yi** (*to like*) and **Jùng-gwok-wá** (*Chinese language*).

Signs of change

Language never stands still and Cantonese is changing very rapidly. There are four important sound changes which seem to have been developing over recent decades:

1 Many people (perhaps even a majority of people) now do not use an initial **n-** sound at all and all the words which appear in this book with an initial **n-** would be pronounced by them with an **l-** instead. So **néih** becomes **léih** and **nàahm-yán** becomes **làahm-yán**. You are bound to meet some native speakers who do this constantly or who perhaps even alternate between the two.

2 Some people now do not distinguish between initial **g-** and initial **gw-**, pronouncing **Jùng-gwok** as **Jùng-gok**. This change is not so common, but you should be prepared to understand it if you do hear it.

3 The initial **ng-** sound seems to have been gradually falling out of favour over many years and some people have now dropped it altogether. So you may hear such things as **óh** for **ngóh** or **aùh-yuhk** for **ngàuh-yuhk**.

4 The distinction between the two high pitch tones seems to be less critical now than it once was and you will meet some native speakers who use only high level or who quite freely use one or the other regardless of which is the 'correct' tone.

What you hear native speakers say will affect the way you speak and you may find yourself following some or all of these changes as you go on. Meanwhile, you can be confident that if you speak in the way this book teaches you, you will not be wrong.

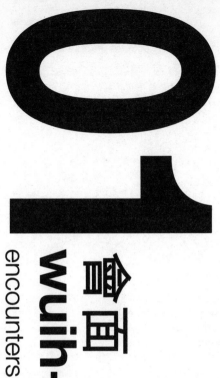

01

會面
wuih-mihn

encounters

In this unit you will learn
- how to greet and address people
- how to ask questions
- how to use descriptive words

▶ Dialogue 1

Mr Wong and his boss Miss Cheung meet in the lift on the way up to the office.

早晨，王先生。
早晨，張小姐。你好嗎？
我好好。你呢？
好好。
你太太呢？
佢都好，有心。

Cheung	Jóu-sàhn, Wòhng Sìn-sàang.
Wong	Jóu-sàhn, Jèung Síu-jé. Néih hóu ma?
Cheung	Ngóh hóu hóu. Néih nē?
Wong	Hóu hóu.
Cheung	Néih taai-táai nē?
Wong	Kéuih dōu hóu, yáuh-sàm.

早晨 **jóu-sàhn**	*good morning*
王 **Wòhng**	*a surname: Wong*
先生 **sìn-sàang**	*Mr, Sir, gentleman, husband*
張 **Jèung**	*a surname: Cheung*
小姐 **síu-jé**	*Miss, young lady*
你 **néih**	*you*
好 **hóu**	*very; well, fine, OK, nice, good*
嗎？ **ma?**	*a word that makes a sentence into a question*
我 **ngóh**	*I, me*
呢？ **nē?**	*a word that repeats the same question about a different matter*
太太 **taai-táai**	*Mrs, wife, married woman*
佢 **kéuih**	*she, her, he, him, it*
都 **dōu**	*also*
有心 **yáuh-sàm**	*kind of you to ask*

Now that you have read the dialogue, can you say whether **Jèung Síu-jé** has a husband or not? Has **Wòhng Sìn-sàang**? Are any of the three people unwell? How would you address the person that Miss Cheung enquires about?

(The answers, as if you didn't know, are no, no, no and **Wòhng Taai-táai**.)

Grammar

1 Identifying people and things

ngóh	*I, me*
néih	*you* (singular)
kéuih	*he, she, him, her, it*

Each of these *personal pronouns* can be made plural by the addition of -**deih**:

ngóh-deih	*we, us*
néih-deih	*you* (plural)
kéuih-deih	*they, them*

2 Addressing people

Unlike English, Chinese surnames are always given before titles:

Wòhng Sìn-sàang	*Mr Wong*
Wòhng Taai-táai	*Mrs Wong*
Wòhng Síu-jé	*Miss Wong*

ℹ Why does the surname come first?

As well as Mr, Mrs, and Miss, other titles, such as president, doctor, professor, ambassador, sister, are also given after the surname. Personal names follow the surname too, so someone called Mr John Smith becomes *Smith John Mr* in the Cantonese order. It all fits in with the great stress which the Chinese people have traditionally placed on the family. The surname shows your family line and so it is the surname which comes first in the Cantonese order, as with **Wòhng Gwok Méih Sìn-sàang**.

3 Adjectives or verbs? Both!

Hóu means *good, nice, well, fine, OK* and so on. Just as in English, such words (they are *adjectives*) go in front of nouns, so a *good husband* is a **hóu sìn-sàang**. But in Cantonese all adjectives can also act as verbs to describe things (*descriptive verbs*) and so **hóu** means not only *good* but also *to be good*:

Kéuih-deih hóu.	*They are well.*
Wòhng Sìn-sàang hóu.	*Mr Wong is fine.*

Remember, it is not only the adjective **hóu** which is also a descriptive verb – all adjectives behave the same. So the word for *ugly* also means *to be ugly*, *difficult* can also mean *to be difficult* and so on.

4 Simple questions

In Mandarin (now usually known as *Putonghua*, the official common language of China) you can ask a question simply by putting the little word **ma?** on the end of a statement. Sometimes you will hear Cantonese speakers do the same, but it is not common. However, in one expression you will hear this 'spoken question mark' very often, and that is in the polite question:

Néih hóu ma?   *How are you?*

The practice seems to be extending to asking after other people's health as well:

Jèung Taai-táai hóu ma?   *Is Mrs Cheung OK?*

You will meet the most common way of asking questions later in this unit.

5 Two for the price of one

When you learned **hóu** you got double value, because it not only means *good, well* etc. but *very* as well. So **hóu hóu** means *very good*.

6 Follow-up questions

A special kind of shortcut question is formed with the little word **nē?** **Nē?** asks a follow-up question without the tedium of repeating in full what went before:

Jèung Taai-táai hóu ma?   *Is Mrs Cheung OK?*
Kéuih hóu hóu.   *She's very well.*
  Wòhng Síu-jé nē?   *And how's Miss Wong?*

7 Dōu *also*

Dōu means *also, too*. It always comes just before a verb:

Ngóh hóu.   *I'm well.*
Kéuih dōu hóu.   *She's well too.*

8 And now for the good news

It may have escaped your notice: verbs only have one form! The same word **hóu** was translated as *am well*, *is well* and *are well* in our earlier examples and it was no accident. **Hóu** only ever appears like that even though the English verb *to be well* takes many guises (*am well*, *is well*, *are well*, *will be well*, *have been well*, *was well*, *were well*, etc.). Regardless of the tense, the mood, the subject or anything else, the verb will always be simply **hóu**. And, better still, this applies to all verbs, there are no irregularities to make life difficult!

▶ Dialogue 2

When she gets to the office, Miss Cheung is surprised to find a visitor waiting for her.

噢，對唔住，貴姓呀？
我姓何，你係李小姐嗎？
唔係，我姓張。何先生，你係唔係美國人呀？
唔係，我係英國人，我賣美國車：美國車好靚，你要唔要呀？
唔要，唔要。美國車好貴：我要日本車。再見，何先生。
你唔要，李小姐要唔要呀？
李小姐都唔要。再見，再見。

Cheung	Òu, deui-m̀h-jyuh, gwai-sing a?
Ho	Ngóh sing Hòh. Néih haih Léih Síu-jé ma?
Cheung	M̀h haih, ngóh sing Jèung. Hòh Sìn-sàang, néih haih m̀h haih Méih-gwok-yàhn a?
Ho	M̀h haih, ngóh haih Yìng-gwok-yàhn. Ngóh maaih Méih-gwok chē: Méih-gwok chē hóu leng, néih yiu m̀h yiu a?
Cheung	M̀h yiu, m̀h yiu. Méih-gwok chē hóu gwai: ngóh yiu Yaht-bún chē. Joi-gin, Hòh Sìn-sàang.
Ho	Néih m̀h yiu, Léih Síu-jé yiu m̀h yiu a?
Cheung	Léih Síu-jé dōu m̀h yiu. Joi-gin, joi-gìn.

噢	**òu**	*oh!* (surprise)
對唔住	**deui-m̀h-jyuh**	*I'm sorry; excuse me; pardon me*
貴姓呀？	**gwai-sing a?**	*what is your name?*
		(lit: *distinguished surname?*)
姓	**sing**	*surname; to be surnamed*
何	**Hòh**	*a surname: Ho*
係	**haih**	*to be*
李	**Léih**	*a surname: Li*
唔	**m̀h**	*not*

美國人	**Méih-gwok-yàhn**	*American person*
美國	**Méih-gwok**	*America, USA*
人	**yàhn**	*person*
呀？	**a?**	*word used at the end of a question*
英國人	**Yìng-gwok-yàhn**	*British person*
英國	**Yìng-gwok**	*Britain, UK, England*
賣	**maaih**	*to sell*
車	**chē**	*car, cars*
靚	**leng**	*pretty, good-looking, handsome, of good quality*
要	**yiu**	*to want*
貴	**gwai**	*expensive; distinguished*
日本人	**Yaht-bún-yàhn**	*Japanese person*
日本	**Yaht-bún**	*Japan*
再見	**joi-gin**	*goodbye*

You should be able to answer these questions if you have understood the second dialogue. Why did Miss Cheung not want an American car? What kind of car did she want? Could Mr Ho supply it? Was he going to have better luck with Miss Li?

(Answers: Too expensive; Japanese; no; no.)

Having read Dialogue 2 again, can you say which of these statements is/are true and which false?

a Jèung Síu-jé haih Méih-gwok-yàhn.
b Hòh Sìn-sàang m̀h maaih Méih-gwok chē.
c Wòhng Sìn-sàang maaih chē.
d Jèung Síu-jé haih taai-táai.

(Answers: All false.)

Grammar

9 People

Yàhn means *person* but it also means *people*. In fact, all nouns in Cantonese are the same whether single or plural and you can only tell which is meant from the sense of the conversation. There is usually no problem: by looking at the personal pronouns you can easily tell which is which in the following examples:

Ngóh haih Yìng-gwok-yàhn.
Kéuih-deih haih Yaht-bún-yàhn.

ℹ️ More on surnames

You have already met a number of surnames (**Wòhng, Jèung, Hòh, Léih**) and you will of course meet others. It is interesting that although there are several thousand different surnames in existence, the vast majority of the Chinese share just a few dozen of them. You will certainly meet many people with the four surnames you've just learned, but the most common surname of all among Cantonese people is **Chàhn**.

10 Negatives

The word for *not* is **m̀h**. It always comes in front of the word it refers to:

Wòhng Sìn-sàang m̀h leng	*Mr Wong isn't handsome.*
Ngóh m̀h yiu chē	*I don't want a car.*

11 Another way to ask questions

The most common way to ask a question in Cantonese is by using the positive and negative of a verb together and adding the little word **a?** at the end of the sentence:

Kéuih leng m̀h leng a?	*Is she pretty?*

What you are really doing is offering your listener a choice of answers (*She pretty? Not pretty? Eh?*) and the answer is going to be either:

Kéuih leng.	*She is pretty.*
or Kéuih m̀h leng.	*She's not pretty.*

In the same way you can ask:

Néih maaih m̀h maaih Méih-gwok chē a?	*Are you selling American cars?*

Cantonese people like to have a comfortable noise to round off their sentences with and they have a whole string of little words (usually called *particles*) which they use. **A?** has no meaning on its own, it is just used to punch home the question which has been asked in the sentence. **Ma?** and **nē?** which we have already met are other examples of particles.

12 The unspoken *if*

There are various words for *if* in Cantonese, but quite often none of them is used, the meaning seeming to flow naturally from the context. In the dialogue the sentence **Néih m̀h yiu, Léih Síu-jé yiu m̀h yiu a?** (literally, *You not want, Miss Li want not want, eh?*) should be understood to mean *If you don't want one, does Miss Li?*

Exercise 1

Here's a fine mess! The following words have got all jumbled up. Sort them out and make meaningful sentences of them. For example, **Taai-táai Wòhng leng hóu** does not make sense, but rearranged into **Wòhng Taai-táai hóu leng** it is a correct sentence meaning *Mrs Wong is very beautiful.*

a Hóu kéuih-deih hóu
b Sìn-sàang Wòhng hóu
c Dōu Jèung hóu Síu-jé

(Answers to all exercises and tests from now on are at the back of the book.)

Exercise 2

What would you reply?

a Jóu-sàhn.
b Néih hóu ma?
c Joi-gin.

Exercise 3

Fill in the blanks with words which will make sense. You will have to think a bit to work out what the sentence must mean!

a Wòhng Sìn-sàang __ yiu Méih-gwok chē.
b Chàhn Síu-jé leng __ leng a?
c Kéuih-deih haih m̀h __ Yaht-bún-yàhn a?
d Ngóh m̀h maaih Yaht-bún chē, ngóh maaih __.

Exercise 4

Translate these simple sentences into Cantonese. If you can do so, you can really congratulate yourself on having mastered this unit.

a Japanese cars aren't expensive.
b He isn't nice.
c You are very pretty.
d Do they want cars?
e He is good-looking too.
f They are Americans.
g Mr Wong sells cars.
h British people don't sell American cars.

02

個人財物
go-yàhn
chòih-maht

personal property

In this unit you will learn
- numbers
- classifiers (words which introduce different types of nouns)

▶ Dialogue 1

Mr Ho is working in his office when a woman comes in.

太太，你搵邊個呀？
我搵王國美先生，佢係中國人，係我嘅朋友。
你搵王先生有乜嘢事呀？
我要賣我嘅美國車，王先生想買。
好，我帶你去王先生嘅寫字樓。
唔該你。

Ho	Taai-táai, néih wán bīn-go a?
Lady	Ngóh wán Wòhng Gwok Méih Sìn-sàang, kéuih haih Jùng-gwok-yàhn, haih ngóh ge pàhng-yáuh.
Ho	Néih wán Wòhng Sìn-sàang yáuh-māt-yéh-sih-a?
Lady	Ngóh yiu maaih ngóh ge Méih-gwok chē, Wòhng Sìn-sàang séung máaih.
Ho	Hóu, ngóh daai néih heui Wòhng Sìn-sàang ge sé-jih-làuh.
Lady	M̀h-gòi néih.

▶

搵	**wán**	to look for
邊個	**bīn-go**	who? which person? which one?
中國	**Jùng-gwok**	China
嘅	**ge**	's (shows possession)
我嘅	**ngóh ge**	my
朋友	**pàhng-yáuh**	friend
有	**yáuh**	to have
乜嘢	**māt-yéh**	what? what kind of?
事	**sih**	matter, business, affair
有乜嘢事呀？ **yáuh-māt-yéh-sih-a?**		for what purpose? why?
想	**séung**	to want to, intend to, would like to
買	**máaih**	to buy
帶	**daai**	to lead, to bring, to go with
去	**heui**	to go to, to go
寫字樓	**sé-jih-làuh**	office
唔該（你）	**m̀h-gòi (néih)**	thank you

▶ True or false?

If you have understood the dialogue you should be able to pass judgement on the following statements about it.

a   Wòhng Gwok Méih Sìn-sàang séung maaih chē.
b   Wòhng Sìn-sàang séung maaih Yaht-bún chē.
c   Hòh Sìn-sàang, Wòhng Sìn-sàang kéuih-deih haih pàhng-yáuh.
d   Wòhng Taai-táai wán Wòhng Sìn-sàang.

Grammar

1 Question words

Question words like **bīn-go?** *who?* and **māt-yéh?** *what?* come in
the same position in the sentence as the answer to them does.
In English question and answer have different word orders, but
in Chinese they have the same word order. In the two examples
following note how the English is twisted but the Chinese is not:

Kéuih sing māt-yéh a?	*What is he surnamed?*
Kéuih sing Hòh.	*He is surnamed Ho.*
Kéuih wán bīn-go a?	*Who is she looking for?*
Kéuih wán Hòh Síu-jé.	*She is looking for Miss Ho.*

Some people say **mī-yéh?** instead of **māt-yéh?**: there is no
difference in meaning, you can please yourself which you say.
Note how **a** is used at the end of sentences which are questions.

2 Possession

The little word **ge** shows possession, like the apostrophe *s* ('*s*) in
English. So **ngóh ge** is *my* or *mine*, **néih ge** is *your* or *yours*,
kéuih ge is *his*, *her*, *hers* or *its* and **Léih Taai-táai ge** is *Mrs Li's*:

Wòhng Taai-táai ge chē	*Mrs Wong's car*
ngóh-deih ge sé-jih-làuh	*our office*
Chē haih Wòhng Síu-jé ge.	*The car is Miss Wong's.*
Jùng-gwok chē haih kéuih ge.	*The Chinese car is his.*

When there is a close personal relationship with a person, **ge** is
often left out, but the relationship term must have at least two
syllables, as with **taai-táai** and **pàhng-yáuh** here:

ngóh taai-táai *my wife*   **kéuih pàhng-yáuh** *her friend*

3 *Mh-gòi* thank you

Mh-gòi literally means *ought not*, but it is the most common
word for *thank you*. If someone holds the door open for you,
passes you the soy sauce or tells you your shoelace is undone,
you should politely say **mh-gòi** to them.

▶ Dialogue 2

Miss Cheung has found a watch and a pen on her desk. She asks Mr Ho if they are his.

噢！一個手錶，一枝筆……何先生，呢個手錶同埋嗰枝筆係唔係
   你嘅？

呢個手錶唔係我嘅：嗰枝筆係我嘅。

呢個手錶好靚，係美國手錶。你估係邊個㗎？

我估係王先生嘅。

我都估係佢嘅。我哋去問佢，好唔好呀？

王先生而家唔喺佢嘅寫字樓。

唔緊要，我遲啲問佢。

Cheung	Òu! Yāt go sáu-bīu, yāt jì bāt . . . Hòh Sìn-sàang, nī go sáu-bīu tùhng-màaih gó jì bāt haih m̀h haih néih ga?
Ho	Nī go sáu-bīu m̀h haih ngóh ge: gó jì bāt haih ngóh ge.
Cheung	Nī go sáu-bīu hóu leng, haih Méih-gwok sáu-bīu. Néih gú haih bīn-go ga?
Ho	Ngóh gú haih Wòhng Sìn-sàang ge.
Cheung	Ngóh dōu gú haih kéuih ge. Ngóh-deih heui mahn kéuih, hóu m̀h hóu a?
Ho	Wòhng Sìn-sàang yìh-gā m̀h hái kéuih ge sé-jih-làuh.
Cheung	M̀h gán-yiu. Ngóh chìh-dī mahn kéuih.

▶

一	**yāt**	*one*
個	**go**	classifier word for people and many objects
手錶	**sáu-bīu**	*wristwatch*
枝	**jì**	classifier word for stick-like things
筆	**bāt**	*a pen, any writing tool*
呢	**nī**	*this*
同埋	**tùhng-màaih**	*and, with*
嗰	**gó**	*that*
㗎	**ga?**	= **ge** + **a**?
估	**gú**	*to guess, reckon*
問	**mahn**	*to ask a question*
而家	**yìh-gā**	*now*
喺	**hái**	*at/in/on, to be at/in/on*
唔緊要	**m̀h gán-yiu**	*never mind, it doesn't matter*
遲啲	**chìh-dī**	*later on*

Grammar

4 *This, that* and *which?*

nī go yàhn	*this person*
gó go yàhn	*that person*
bīn go yàhn?	*which person?*

In English when you specify a word with *this*, *that* or *which?*, you just put it in front of the word (*this man*, *that ship*, *which pen?*), but in Cantonese you need to use a classifier word as well (*this* classifier *man*, *that* classifier *ship*, *which* classifier *pen?*). It is not necessarily easy to guess which classifier goes with which noun, although you can expect, for instance, that almost any object which is thin, straight and stick-like will be classified with jì. You will be given the correct classifier for each noun you meet from now on. The classifier for people is **go**, so:

nī go yàhn	*this person*
bīn go Méih-gwok-yàhn a?	*which American?*

The classifier for wristwatch is also **go**:

gó go sáu-bīu	*that watch*

The classifier for pen is **jì**:

gó jì bāt	*that pen*

If it is clear what is meant, it is possible to drop off the noun, but the classifier must still be used. Note the following question and answer:

Néih yiu bīn jì bāt a?	*Which pen do you want?*
Ngóh yiu nī jì.	*I want this one.*

5 How about it?

Hóu m̀h hóu a? literally means *is it good?*, but it is also used at the ends of sentences meaning *what do you say?*, *how about it?*, *OK?* (And there is **a** at the end of a question sentence again!)

▶ 6 Numbers

The Cantonese number system is very straightforward. The numbers one to ten are all single-syllable words; 11 is 10+1, 12 is 10+2, 13 is 10+3, and so on up to 20 which is 2×10; 21 is 2×10+1, 29 is 2×10+9; 30 is 3×10, 31 is 3×10+1 . . .

Memorize the numbers one to ten and then try counting up to 99 (and back again if you are really confident):

1 yāt	11 sahp-yāt	21 yih-sahp-yāt
2 yih	12 sahp-yih	22 yih-sahp-yih
3 sàam	13 sahp-sàam	23 yih-sahp-sàam
4 sei	14 sahp-sei	24 yih-sahp-sei
5 ńgh	15 sahp-ńgh	25 yih-sahp-ńgh
6 luhk	16 sahp-luhk	26 yih-sahp-luhk
7 chāt	17 sahp-chāt	27 yih-sahp-chāt
8 baat	18 sahp-baat	28 yih-sahp-baat
9 gáu	19 sahp-gáu	29 yih-sahp-gáu
10 sahp	20 yih-sahp	30 sàam-sahp

40 sei-sahp	41 sei-sahp-yāt	47 sei-sahp-chāt
50 ńgh-sahp	52 ńgh-sahp-yih	58 ńgh-sahp-baat
60 luhk-sahp	63 luhk-sahp-sàam	69 luhk-sahp-gáu
70 chāt-sahp	74 chāt-sahp-sei	75 chāt-sahp-ńgh
80 baat-sahp	85 baat-sahp-ńgh	87 baat-sahp-chāt
90 gáu-sahp	96 gáu-sahp-luhk	99 gáu-sahp-gáu

When things are counted (*one person*, *three pens*, etc.) the classifier must be used in the same way as with specifying words. So:

yāt go yàhn	*one person*
sei jì bāt	*four pens*
sahp-yih go sáu-bīu	*twelve watches*

The whole number system is nice and regular with one exception: the number *two* is not **yih** but **léuhng** when it is followed by a classifier, so:

yāt, yih, sàam, sei, . . .	*one, two, three, four, . . .* but
yāt jì bāt, léuhng jì bāt,	*one pen, two pens, three pens,*
sàam jì bāt, sei jì bāt, . . .	*four pens, . . .*

It is only the number *two* itself which plays this trick; complex numbers which end in a two are not affected, as you can see from the example of *twelve watches*. (And don't feel too hard done by: English is even crazier about the number two – think of *brace of*, *pair of*, *couple of*, *twin*, *duo-* and *bi-*!)

ℹ The magic of numbers

Cantonese people are very interested in numbers and many people believe that numbers can influence fate. Everybody loves the number eight because **baat** sounds rather like **faat** which means *get rich*. By way of contrast, four is considered an unlucky number because **sei** sounds like **séi** which means *to die*. Two and eight are good because **yih baat** sounds like **yih faat** *easy to get rich*, but five and eight are bad because **ńgh baat** resembles **m̀h faat** *not get rich*. A Chinese purchaser recently insisted on paying £280,000 for a house in the south of England rather than the asking price of £279,500, believing that the larger sum was much luckier sounding! For many years the Hong Kong government auctioned 'lucky' car registration numbers for charity: an astronomical price was paid for 8888, which adorned one of the territory's many Rolls-Royces.

Exercise 1
Try to give answers to the following questions. You cannot be sure of the answer to the second one, but common sense should help you.

a Gwai-sing a?
b Wòhng Sìn-sàang haih m̀h haih Jùng-gwok-yàhn a?
c Néih máaih m̀h máaih chē a? (Answer: No)
d Néih yáuh Yaht-bún pàhng-yáuh ma? (Answer: Yes)

Exercise 2
See if you can understand what these sentences mean. Practise saying them out loud until they come fluently.

a Sáu-bīu tùhng-màaih bāt dōu haih Hòh Sìn-sàang ge.
b Gó go sáu-bīu hóu leng.
c Hòh Sìn-sàang chìh-dī heui mahn Wòhng Taai-táai.
d Bīn jì bāt haih Jèung Síu-jé ga?

Exercise 3
Fill in the blanks to make correct and meaningful sentences.

a Nī ___ sáu-bīu haih Hòh Taai-táai ge.
b Néih haih m̀h haih Yìng-gwok ____ a?
c Ngóh gú Yaht-___ chē hóu gwai.
d Wòhng Síu-jé leng ___ leng a?
e Néih séung máaih ___-yéh a?
f ___-go haih Jèung Síu-jé a?
g Kéuih m̀h haih Yìng-gwok-yàhn, ___ m̀h haih Méih-gwok-yàhn; kéuih haih Yaht-bún-yàhn.
h Ngóh ___ Wòhng Sìn-sàang, 'Néih yáuh Yìng-gwok chē ma?'

Exercise 4
Make up your own conversation. Tell Mr Wong that you want to go to England to buy a British car. He tells you that British cars are expensive. Ask him what kind of car he's got. He says that he has a British car too.

Exercise 5

In the picture all the women are American, all the men are Chinese and all the children are Japanese. Try saying in Cantonese how many of each there are, say how many watches Mr Wong is selling and describe what the woman is doing with her money at the stationery stall.

03

家人同朋友
gà-yàhn tùhng
pàhng-yáuh

family and friends

In this unit you will learn
- one of the only two irregular verbs in Cantonese: *to have*
- some important words for family members
- some final particles

▶ Dialogue 1

Mr Ho meets Mr Wong on the street.

王先生，你去邊處呀？
早晨，何先生，我返屋企。
你返屋企做乜嘢呀？
我帶我媽媽去睇醫生。
你同媽媽一齊住吖？
係，我同爸爸，媽媽，兄弟，姊妹，七個人一齊住。
七個人一齊住……嗽樣，你哋間屋一定好大嘞。
係，都幾大。對唔住，何先生，我要走嘞，再見。
再見，王先生。

Ho	Wòhng Sìn-sàang, néih heui bīn-syu a?
Wong	Jóu-sàhn, Hòh Sìn-sàang, ngóh fàan ūk-kéi.
Ho	Néih fàan ūk-kéi jouh-māt-yéh a?
Wong	Ngóh daai ngóh màh-mā heui tái-yī-sāng.
Ho	Néih tùhng màh-mā yāt-chàih jyuh àh?
Wong	Haih, ngóh tùhng bàh-bā, màh-mā, hìng-daih, jí-muih, chāt go yàhn yāt-chàih jyuh.
Ho	Chāt go yàhn yāt-chàih jyuh . . . gám-yéung, néih-deih gàan ūk yāt-dihng hóu daaih lak.
Wong	Haih, dōu-géi daaih. Deui-m̀h-jyuh, Hòh Sìn-sàang, ngóh yiu jáu lak, joi-gin.
Ho	Joi-gin, Wòhng Sìn-sàang.

邊處、邊度 **bīn-syu** or **bīn-douh**	where? which place?
返 **fàan**	to return, to return to
屋企 **ūk-kéi**	family; home
做乜嘢 **jouh māt-yéh**	why? for what reason?
做 **jouh**	to do
媽媽 **màh-mā**	mother
睇醫生 **tái-yī-sāng**	to see the doctor
醫生 **yī-sāng**	doctor
同 **tùhng**	with, and (a shorter form of **tùhng-màaih**)
一齊 **yāt-chàih**	together
住 **jyuh**	to dwell, to live
吖？ **àh?**	a question word (that's right, isn't it?)
爸爸 **bàh-bā**	father
兄弟 **hìng-daih**	brothers
姊妹 **jí-muih**	sisters

嗽，嗽樣 gám or gám-yéung	in that case, so
間 gàan	classifier for houses and rooms
屋 ūk	house
一定 yāt-dihng	certainly
大 daaih	big
嘞、嘑 lak or la	a statement word (*that's how the case stands now*)
都幾、幾 dōu-géi or géi	quite, rather, fairly
要 yiu	must, need to
走 jáu	to run; to run away; to leave

Picture quiz

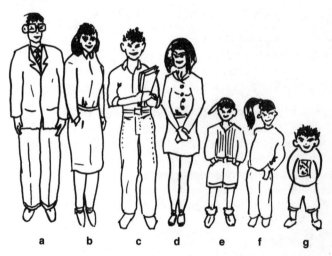

a   b   c   d   e   f   g

Here is the Wong family. How would C address A? How would D address B? How would D address A? How would you address D? How would you address B? Which one do you think is the Mr Wong who figures in the dialogue?

Grammar

1 Where?

Bīn-syu? *where?* works to the same rules as **bīn-go?** *who?* and **māt-yéh?** *what?* (See Unit 2, grammar point 1.)

| Néih heui bīn-syu a? | *Where are you going?* |
| Ngóh heui sé-jih-làuh. | *I'm going to the office.* |

Bīn-syu and bīn-douh both mean *where?* and you can use whichever of them you prefer.

2 *Fàan* to return

Fàan means *to return*. It combines easily with heui *to go* as fàan-heui meaning *to go back*, that is *to return in a direction away from me the speaker*:

Néih fàan-heui m̀h fàan-heui a?   *Are you going back?*

or in its more commonly shortened form:

Néih fàan m̀h fàan-heui a?   *Are you going back?*

Fàan also means *to go where one usually goes*:

Wòhng Síu-jé fàan ūk-kéi.   *Miss Wong is going home.*
Ngóh fàan sé-jih-làuh.   *I'm going to the office.*

3 Why?

Jouh-māt-yéh? literally means *to do what?* but it has come to mean *why?* It can be positioned quite freely in the sentence without any change of meaning: all the following examples mean *Why must you sell your car?*:

Néih jouh-māt-yéh yiu maaih chē a?
Jouh-māt-yéh néih yiu maaih chē a?
Néih yiu maaih chē jouh-māt-yéh a?

ⓘ Yes and *no*

There are no words for *yes* and *no* in Cantonese. You should use the positive or negative form of the appropriate verb, so in answer to Néih heui m̀h heui Jùng-gwok a? *Are you going to China?* you can reply heui *yes* or m̀h heui *no*. If it is not the verb itself which is the focus of the question, it is useful to use haih *it is the case* or m̀h haih *it is not the case*, as in the dialogue. Haih and m̀h haih come as close to *yes* and *no* as Cantonese gets.

4 The adverb *yāt-chàih* 'together'

Yāt-chàih *together*, *all together* is an adverb and like almost all adverbs it comes in front of the verb in the sentence. So yāt-chàih jyuh is *to live together* and yāt-chàih fàan Yìng-gwok means *to return to Britain together*.

5 That's right, isn't it?

The word **àh?** comes at the end of a sentence to ask for confirmation that what you have said is correct:

Néih haih Jèung Sìn-sàang àh?   *You're Mr Cheung, aren't you?*
Néih heui Yìng-gwok àh?   *I take it you're going to England, right?*

6 That's how the case stands now

Lak (sometimes pronounced **la**) comes at the end of the sentence to state what the current position is. Naturally enough that means that often there has been some change before that position has been arrived at:

Ngóh yiu jáu lak.   *I must be going now.*
Kéuih m̀h séung máaih chē lak.   *He doesn't want to buy a car any more.*

▶ Dialogue 2

Mr Ho hasn't seen Mr Cheung for a long while. They meet by chance.

張先生，好耐冇見。你好嗎？你而家喺邊處住呀？
我而家住喺香港花園道二十八號三樓。
花園道好唔好住呀？
好住。花園道有好多巴士同的士搭。何先生，你住喺邊處呀？
我重住喺喱啡街七十三號地下。你有時間請嚟坐喇。
你有心。你間屋有車房嗎？
我唔係住一間屋，我住一層樓啫。呢層樓唔係幾大，冇車房嘅。
好，有時間我嚟探你，再見。
再見。

Ho	Jèung Sìn-sàang, hóu-noih-móuh-gin. Néih hóu ma? Néih yìh-gā hái bīn-syu jyuh a?
Cheung	Ngóh yìh-gā jyuh hái Hèung-góng Fà-yùhn Douh yih-sahp-baat houh sàam láu.
Ho	Fà-yùhn Douh hóu m̀h hóu jyuh a?
Cheung	Hóu jyuh. Fà-yùhn Douh yáuh hóu dò bā-sí tùhng dīk-sí daap. Hòh Sìn-sàang, néih jyuh hái bīn-syu a?
Ho	Ngóh juhng jyuh hái Ga-fē Gāai chāt-sahp-sàam houh deih-há. Néih yáuh sìh-gaan chéng làih chóh lā.
Cheung	Néih yáuh-sàm. Néih gàan ūk yáuh móuh chē-fòhng a?

Ho	Ngóh m̀h haih jyuh yāt gàan ūk, ngóh jyuh yāt chàhng láu jē. Nī chàhng láu m̀h-haih-géi-daaih, móuh chē-fòhng ge.	
Cheung	Hóu, yáuh sìh-gaan ngóh làih taam néih. Joi-gin.	
Ho	Joi-gin.	

耐 **noih**	*a long time*	
好耐冇見 **hóu-noih-móuh-gin**	*long time no see*	
冇 **móuh**	*have not (negative of* **yauh** *to have)*	
香港 **Hèung-góng**	*Hong Kong*	
花園道 **Fà-yùhn Douh**	*Garden Road*	
花園 **fà-yún**	*garden (note the tone change from* **yùhn** *to* **yún***)*	
道 **douh**	*street, road*	
......號 **. . . houh**	*number . . .*	
樓 **láu**	*a flat; a high building; a storey*	
多 **dò**	*many, much*	
巴士 **bā-sí**	*bus*	
的士 **dīk-sí**	*taxi*	
搭 **daap**	*to travel by/catch/take (public transport)*	
重 **juhng**	*still, yet*	
喋啡 **ga-fē**	*coffee*	
街 **gāai**	*street*	
地下 **deih-há**	*ground floor; the ground; the floor*	
時間 **sìh-gaan**	*time*	
請 **chéng**	*please*	
嚟 **làih**	*to come, to come to*	
坐 **chóh**	*to sit*	
喇 **lā**	*a particle urging someone to agree with you or to do something for you*	
車房 **chē-fòhng**	*garage*	
層 **chàhng**	*classifier for a flat; storey, deck*	
啫 **jē** or **jēk**	*only; and that's all*	
唔係幾／好 **m̀h-haih-géi/hóu**	*not very*	
嘅 **ge**	*makes a statement more emphatic: that's how it is and that's how it's going to stay*	
探 **taam**	*to see, to visit*	

Haih m̀h haih a?

Test your understanding of Dialogue 2 by answering **haih** *it is so* or **m̀h haih** *it is not so* to the following statements.

a   Fà-yùhn Douh m̀h hóu jyuh.
b   Hòh Sìn-sàang jyuh hái yāt gàan ūk.
c   Hòh Sìn-sàang jyuh hái deih-há.
d   Hòh Sìn-sàang ge chē-fòhng hóu daaih.
e   Jèung Sìn-sàang heui Hòh Sìn-sàang ūk-kéi.

▶ **Answer the questions**

a   Hòh Sìn-sàang jyuh hái bīn-syu a?
b   Jèung Sìn-sàang jyuh hái bīn-syu a?
c   Hòh Sìn-sàang ge láu yáuh móuh chē-fòhng a?
d   Jèung Sìn-sàang séung m̀h séung taam Hòh Sìn-sàang a?
e   Yáuh móuh bā-sí heui Fà-yùhn Douh a?

Grammar

7   The verb *yáuh*

The verb **yáuh** *to have* is an oddity. It is not made negative with **m̀h**: instead the negative of **yáuh** is another verb **móuh** *not to have*. So while *Are you English?* is **Néih haih m̀h haih Yìng-gwok-yàhn a?** *Have you got an English car?* is **Néih yáuh móuh Yìng-gwok chē a?** and *I haven't got a car* is **Ngóh móuh chē.**

ℹ️ **From the general to the particular**

When Mr Cheung gives his address in the dialogue, you will see that he gives it in the order Hong Kong, Garden Road, No. 28, 3rd floor – i.e. in the opposite way to English. Chinese always prefers to work from the general to the particular, from the large to the small. We shall see later that it is the same with dates and times, so that the Chinese would translate *3.18 p.m. on 17 May 1995* in the order *1995, May, 17, p.m., 3.18*.

8 Jē or jēk

Jē (pronounced by some people as jēk) is a very useful little word which is tacked onto the end of sentences to give the meaning *only, that's all*:

Ngóh yáuh léuhng jì bāt.	*I've got two pens.*
Kéuih yáuh yāt jì bāt jē.	*He's only got one pen.*

9 Not very

The negative of **daaih** *big* is **m̀h daaih** *not big*, just as you would expect. The negative of **hóu daaih** *very big*, however, is **m̀h-haih-géi-daaih** or **m̀h-haih-hóu-daaih** both of which mean *not very big*. So you will need to remember that the verb **haih** is slipped into this *not very* construction:

Nī chàhng láu m̀h-haih-géi-gwai.	*This flat is not very dear.*
Wòhng Síu-jé m̀h-haih-hóu-leng.	*Miss Wong is not very pretty.*

10 A recap: final particles

You have now met quite a few words like jē, that is, words that are added to the end of a sentence to round it off or to give an extra meaning. They are usually called final particles and they are used a great deal in everyday speech. Before you meet any more of them, here is a reminder of those you already know.

ma? A spoken question mark. It makes a statement into a question.

nē? The shortcut question word which asks follow-up questions.

a? The final particle which is added to sentences which already contain positive–negative-type questions or question words like **māt-yéh?**

ga? The particle made when **ge** is followed by **a?**

àh? The question word which expects the listener to be in agreement: *That's right, isn't it?*

lak/la The word which shows that things were different before but this is how the situation stands now.

jē/jēk *Only.*

lā The word you use when you are trying to urge someone to do something for you or to persuade someone to agree with you.

ge Makes a statement more emphatic: *That's the way it is!*

Exercise 1
Sort out these jumbled words into meaningful sentences.

a   bàh-bā yī-sāng Hòh Sìn-sàang haih.
b   jouh-māt-yéh hái ūk-kéi Wòhng Taai-táai a?
c   tái yī-sāng ngóh heui m̀h séung.
d   ngóh-deih sé-jih-làuh yāt-chàih fàan.

Exercise 2
Fill in the blanks with words which will make sense of the sentences.

a   Wòhng Taai-táai heui tái __ __.
b   Ngóh-deih __ heui Wòhng Sìn-sàang __ __.
c   Ngóh bàh-bā haih __ __.
d   Ngóh-deih jyuh hái __ __.

Exercise 3
You have just bumped into your old friend Mr Wong in the street in Hong Kong. You haven't seen him for several months. How do you greet him? Ask after his wife and where he lives now. Apologize to him and say that you have to catch a bus to Garden Road now to visit your father whom you have to take to see the doctor.

04

食嘢
sihk-yéh
eating in and eating out

In this unit you will learn
- about 'lonely verbs'
- some more about classifiers
- some verb endings

▶ Dialogue 1

Mr Ho invites Mr Wong to his home for a meal.

何先生，你太客氣啦，煮咁多餸請我食飯。
便飯啫，隨便食喇。要唔要茶呀？
唔要，唔該。何太太呢？佢喺邊處呀？
佢喺廚房煮緊飯，唔駛等佢啦。
何太太煮嘅餸真好食嘞。好似酒樓嘅一樣。何先生你有冇幫佢手呀？
冇呀！
何太太一定用咗好多時間預備呢餐飯嘞。
佢用咗半個鐘頭啫。
只係半個鐘頭吖？我唔信。
係真㗎。啲餸都係佢去附近嘅酒樓買嘅。
哦！

Wong	Hòh Sìn-sàang, néih taai hak-hei la, jyú gam dò sung chéng ngóh sihk-faahn.
Ho	Bihn-faahn jē, chèuih-bín sihk lā. Yiu m̀h yiu chàh a?
Wong	M̀h yiu, m̀h-gòi. Hòh Taai-táai nē? Kéuih hái bīn-syu a?
Ho	Kéuih hái chyùh-fóng jyú-gán faahn, m̀h-sái dáng kéuih la.
Wong	Hòh Taai-táai jyú ge sung jàn hóu-sihk lak. Hóu-chíh jáu-làuh ge yāt-yeuhng. Hòh Sìn-sàang néih yáuh móuh bòng kéuih sáu a?
Ho	Móuh a!
Wong	Hòh Taai-táai yāt-dihng yuhng-jó hóu dò sìh-gaan yuh-beih nī chàan faahn lak.
Ho	Kéuih yuhng-jó bun go jūng-tàuh jē.
Wong	Jí-haih bun go jūng-tàuh àh? Ngóh m̀h seun.
Ho	Haih jàn ga. Dī sung dōu haih kéuih heui fuh-gahn ge jáu-làuh máaih ge.
Wong	Óh!

太......（啦）	**taai . . . (la)**	*too . . . , exceedingly . . .*
客氣	**haak-hei**	*polite*
煮	**jyú**	*to cook*
咁	**gam**	*so*
餸	**sung**	*food; a course or dish other than rice or soup*
請	**chéng**	*to invite*
食飯	**sihk-faahn**	*to eat, to eat a meal*
食	**sihk**	*to eat*
飯	**faahn**	*rice; food*

便飯 **bihn-faahn**	*pot luck, a meal of whatever comes to hand*
隨便 **chèuih-bín**	*as you please, feel free*
茶 **chàh**	*tea*
廚房 **chyùh-fóng**	*kitchen*
......緊 **-gán**	*a verb ending for continuing action, -ing*
唔駛 **m̀h-sái**	*no need to, not necessary to*
等 **dáng**	*to wait, to wait for*
真（係）**jàn(-haih)**	*truly, really; true, real*
好食 **hóu-sihk**	*delicious*
好似......一樣 **hóu-chíh . . . yāt-yeuhng**	*just like . . .*
酒樓 **jáu-làuh**	*Chinese restaurant*
幫......手 **bòng . . . sáu**	*to help . . . , to give . . . a hand*
用 **yuhng**	*to use, to spend*
......咗 **-jó**	*a verb ending for completed action, -ed*
預備 **yuh-beih**	*to prepare, to get ready*
餐 **chàan**	*classifier for food, a meal*
半 **bun**	*half*
鐘頭 **jūng-tàuh**	*an hour (classifier = **go**)*
只（係）**jí(-haih)**	*only*
信 **seun**	*to believe, to trust*
啲 **dī**	*plural classifier, classifier for uncountable things*
都 **dōu**	*all, both*
附近 **fuh-gahn**	*nearby*
哦 **óh**	*oh, really! oh, now I understand!*

True or false?

a Hòh Sìn-sàang chéng Wòhng Sìn-sàang heui jáu-làuh sihk-faahn.

b Hòh Sìn-sàang jýu-jó léuhng go sung chéng Wòhng Sìn-sàang sihk.

c Hòh Sìn-sàang bòng Hòh Taai-táai sáu jýu-faahn.

d Hòh Sìn-sàang, Hòh Taai-táai yuhng-jó léuhng go bun jūng-tàuh jýu-faahn.

e Hòh Taai-táai m̀h jýu sung, kéuih jí-haih heui jáu-làuh máaih-sung.

Grammar

1 *Chéng* to invite

In Unit 3 we saw that **chéng** means *please*. It has another meaning of *to invite*:

Kéuih chéng ngóh heui kéuih ūk-kéi.	*He invites me to go to his home.*

2 'Lonely verbs'

Some verbs feel incomplete if they have no object, so Cantonese will supply an all-purpose object to comfort their loneliness! In English we have no problem with saying *he is eating*, but the Cantonese verb **sihk** is unhappy on its own and if it is not specified what he is eating then the all-purpose object **faahn** *rice* will be added. The normal translation of *he is eating* is thus **kéuih sihk-faahn**. **Jýu** *to cook* is another verb which takes **faahn** for want of anything more definite and we will meet other such verbs and other all-purpose objects as we go on.

3 Adverbs of place

The adverb which says where an action is happening comes either before or after the subject depending on the sense, but in any case it *always* comes before the verb:

Kéuih hái ūk-kéi chóh.	*She is sitting indoors.*
Hái sé-jih-làuh néih yáuh móuh bāt a?	*Have you got a pen in the office?*

4 Two new verb endings

-gán is tagged onto a verb to emphasize that the action is actually going on at the time:

Wòhng Sìn-sàang tái-gán yī-sāng.	*Mr Wong is in with the doctor.*

-jó is tagged onto a verb in the same way to show that the action has been completed. Usually the particle **lak** is added at the end of the sentence to back it up:

Kéuih tái-jó yī-sāng lak.	*He saw the doctor.*
Ngóh máaih-jó Méih-gwok chē lak.	*I bought an American car.*

5 An irregular verb: *yiu/sái!*

Here's a rare treat, another irregularity in verbs. *To need to* is **yiu** but *not to need to* is **m̀h sái**:

Ngóh-deih yiu dáng kéuih.	*We need to wait for her.*
Ngóh-deih m̀h sái dáng kéuih la.	*We don't need to wait for her.*
Ngóh yiu máaih chē.	*I need to buy a car.*
Ngóh m̀h sái máaih chē.	*I don't need to buy a car.*

However, when **yiu** means *to want* its negative is **m̀h yiu**:

Ngóh m̀h yiu faahn.	*I don't want any rice.*

The question form for *to need to* is **sái m̀h sái**:

Ngóh-deih sái m̀h sái dáng kéuih a?	*Do we need to wait for her?*

The question form for *to want* is **yiu m̀h yiu**:

Néih yiu m̀h yiu faahn a?	*Do you want some rice?*

6 Another use of *ge*

We saw in Unit 2 that **ge** shows possession: **ngóh ge chē** *my car*. It also is used to link a descriptive phrase to a noun:

hóu gwai ge ga-fē	*very expensive coffee, coffee which is very expensive*
máaih-gán bāt ge yàhn	*the person who is buying a pen*
kéuih jyuh ge ūk	*the house that he lives in*

7 Have you done it?

To ask if an action has been completed, Cantonese (like English) can use the verb *to have* (**yáuh**):

Néih taai-táai yáuh móuh fàan-heui a?	*Has your wife gone back?*
Kéuih yáuh móuh sihk-faahn a?	*Has he eaten?*

The answer is a simple **yáuh** *yes* or **móuh** *no*.

8 More on classifiers

In Unit 2 we met classifiers used with numbers and with specifying words like *this* and *that*. Some nouns are uncountable – think of *water* and *air* for instance – and the classifier to use then is **dī**:

Nī dī sung hóu hóu-sihk.	*This food is delicious.*

Dī is also used as the classifier for all nouns when they are 'plural but uncounted'. Compare the classifiers in the following:

nī go yàhn	*this person*
gó jì bāt	*that pen*
gó ńgh jì bāt	*those five pens*
sàam go Yìng-gwok-yàhn	*three British people*
gó dī yàhn	*those people* (plural but not counted)
bīn dī bāt a?	*which pens?* (plural but not counted)

When a sentence starts with a definite noun (*the pen, the food, the Americans*) Cantonese uses the appropriate classifier where English uses *the*:

Jì bāt hóu leng.	*The pen is very nice.*
Dī sung m̀h gwai.	*The food is not expensive.*
Dī Méih-gwok-yàhn làih m̀h làih a?	*Are the Americans coming?*

9 The adverb *dōu* again

In Unit 1 we met the adverb **dōu** meaning *also*. Other meanings are *all* and *both*. **Dōu** must come immediately before a verb and it obeys a further rule that it must come after the noun it refers to. Note carefully the placing of **dou** in the following:

Néih yáuh bāt; kéuih dōu yáuh bāt.	*You have a pen, and he has too.*
Ngóh-deih dōu yáuh chē.	*All of us have cars.*
Wòhng Sìn-sàang Wòhng Síu-jé dōu fàan-jó sé-jih-làuh lak.	*Both Mr and Miss Wong have gone to the office.*
Gó léuhng go Yìng-gwok-yàhn dōu m̀h séung sihk-faahn.	*Neither of those two British people wants to eat.*

ⓘ Rice

Rice is the staple food of the south of China and is much appreciated as the superior grain in the north too. Not surprisingly, rice figures large in Chinese culture: it is offered in religious sacrifices to the ancestors; it is thrown over newly-weds to bring fertility to them; bags of it are laid on babies' stomachs to comfort them and stop them crying; the language is full of sayings about it. English has only the one word *rice* but Cantonese has many words for it. **Faahn** means *rice* only when it is *cooked rice*. There are different words for rice when growing, rice when harvested but not husked, rice husked but not cooked, and rice cooked into a gruel, as well as yet other terms for different kinds of rice such as red rice, glutinous rice and non-glutinous rice.

▶ Dialogue 2

Mr Ho tries to order a meal from a waiter.

伙記，我想要一個湯。你哋嘅湯新唔新鮮呀？
先生，你要個牛肉湯喇。好新鮮㗎。
好，我就要個牛肉湯。主菜有乜嘢好介紹呀？
龍蝦飯喇，好好味㗎。如果你要呢個飯，我哋送生果沙律俾你。
點解送生果沙律呀？
因為我哋嘅廚房昨日整咗太多，今日重有唔少，所以就送俾你食喇。
你哋昨日整嘅生果沙律今日俾我食，你識唔識做生意㗎？
先生，你唔好嬲。我再送今朝早整嘅甜品俾你，好嗎？重係好好味㗎。
乜嘢話？昨日嘅生果沙律；今朝早嘅甜品！你當我係垃圾桶吖！

Ho	Fó-gei, ngóh séung yiu yāt go tòng. Néih-deih ge tòng sàn m̀h sàn-sìn a?
Waiter	Sìn-sàang, néih yiu go ngàuh-yuhk tòng lā. Hóu sàn-sìn ga.
Ho	Hóu, ngóh jauh yiu go ngàuh-yuhk tòng. Jyu-choi yáuh māt-yéh hóu gaai-siuh a?
Waiter	Lùhng-hā-faahn lā, hóu hóu-meih ga. Yùh-gwó néih yiu nī go faahn, ngóh-deih sung sàang-gwó sà-léut béi néih.
Ho	Dím-gáai sung sàang-gwó sà-léut a?
Waiter	Yàn-waih ngóh-deih ge chyùh-fóng johk-yaht jíng-jó taai dò, gàm-yaht juhng yáuh m̀h síu, só-yíh jauh sung béi néih sihk lā.

Ho Néih-deih johk-yaht jíng ge sàang-gwó sà-léut gàm-yaht béi ngóh sihk, néih sīk m̀h sīk jouh-sàang-yi ga?

Waiter Sìn-sàang, néih m̀h-hóu nàu. Ngóh joi sung gàm-jìu-jóu jíng ge tìhm-bán béi néih, hóu ma? Juhng haih hóu hóu-meih ga.

Ho Māt-yéh wá? Johk-yaht ge sàang-gwó sà-léut; gàm-jìu-jóu ge tìhm-bán! Néih dong ngóh haih laahp-saap-túng àh!

伙記 **fó-gei**		*waiter*
湯 **tòng**		*soup*
新鮮 **sàn-sìn**		*fresh*
牛肉 **ngàuh-yuhk**		*beef*
牛 **ngàuh**		*cow, ox, cattle*
肉 **yuhk**		*meat, flesh*
就 **jauh**		*then*
主菜 **jyú-choi**		*main course*
介紹 **gaai-siuh**		*to recommend; to introduce*
龍蝦 **lùhng-hā**		*lobster*
好味 **hóu-meih**		*delicious*
如果 **yùh-gwó**		*if*
送...... 俾...... **sung x béi y**		*to give x as a present to y*
生果 **sàang-gwó**		*fruit*
沙律 **sà-léut**		*salad*
點解？ **dím-gáai?**		*why?*
因為 **yàn-waih**		*because*
昨日 **johk-yaht**		*yesterday*
整 **jíng**		*to make; to prepare*
今日 **gàm-yaht**		*today*
少 **síu**		*few; little*
所以 **só-yíh**		*therefore, so*
識 **sīk**		*to know how to, to be able to*
做生意 **jouh-sàang-yi**		*to do business, to run a business*
唔好 **m̀h-hóu**		*don't*
嬲 **nàu**		*angry*
再 **joi**		*in addition; again*
朝早 **jìu-jóu**		*morning; in the morning*
早 **jóu**		*early*
甜品 **tìhm-bán**		*dessert*
話 **wá**		*words, language, speech, saying*
當 **dong**		*to regard as*
垃圾桶 **laahp-saap-túng**		*rubbish bin*
垃圾 **laahp-saap**		*rubbish*

Grammar

10 To give

Sung means *to present, to make a gift*. It usually appears with **béi** which itself means *to give, to give to*. The word order for giving a present to someone is a comfortable one for an English speaker:

Kéuih sung yāt jì bāt béi ngóh.   *He gives a pen to me (as a gift).*

Béi is sometimes used on its own to mean *to present*, but it is more commonly found meaning just *to give to, to hand over to*:

Kéuih béi yāt jì bāt ngóh.   *He hands a pen to me/hands me a pen.*

11 Don't!

To tell someone not to do something, Cantonese uses **m̀h-hóu** *it's not good to . . .* or **néih m̀h-hóu** *it's not good that you should . . .*:

M̀h-hóu heui!	*Don't go!*
Néih m̀h-hóu máaih chē!	*Don't buy a car!*

12 Shortcuts

Cantonese is a lively quick-fire language and speakers often find ways of shortening phrases which seem to them to be too tediously long. Here is a list of shortened forms of phrases which you have met so far:

gàm-yaht jìu-jóu > **gàm-jìu-jóu** or even shorter > **gàm-jìu**
johk-yaht jìu-jóu > **johk-jìu-jóu** or > **johk-jìu**
Wòhng Sìn-sàang > **Wòhng Sàang**
Wòhng Taai-táai > **Wòhng Táai**
m̀h-hóu   > **máih** (both mean *don't* but **máih** is a bit ruder because it is so abrupt sounding)

Exercise 1
Make meaningful sentences from the jumbled words. You have done exercises like this before, but it gets more difficult now that you know more complicated patterns.

a Hòh Taai-táai séung Wòhng Sìn-sàang sihk-faahn dáng
yāt-chàih.

b chyùh-fóng hái jyú-gán faahn Hòh Taai-táai.

c ma? mahn Wòhng Sìn-sàang Hòh Taai-táai hóu-meih jyú ge
sung kéuih.

d sáu Hòh Taai-táai Hòh Sìn-sàang yáuh a? móuh bòng.

e jyú ge sung jáu-làuh yāt-yeuhng ge hóu-chíh Hòh Taai-táai.

Exercise 2

Try to answer these questions in Cantonese.

a Néih sīk m̀h sīk jyú ngàuh-yuhk tòng a? (Answer: Yes)

b Néih ūk-kéi fuh-gahn yáuh móuh jáu-làuh a? (Answer: No)

c Johk-yaht néih yáuh móuh bòng néih màh-mā sáu jyú-faahn
a? (Answer: No)

d Dím-gáai néih gàm-jìu-jóu gam nàu a? (Answer: I'm not)

e Néih jí-haih sīk jouh sàang-yi m̀h sīk jyú-faahn, haih m̀h
haih a? (Answer: It's not so)

Exercise 3

a **Hái chyùh-fóng yáuh māt-yéh a?** See how many answers
you can make up along the lines of **Hái chyùh-fóng yáuh
lùhng-hā, dōu yáuh . . .**

b **Hái chyùh-fóng yáuh móuh laahp-saap-túng a?** If your
answer is *yes*, try to explain it. If your answer is *no*, think
again but less seriously!

05

購物
kau-maht
shops and markets

In this unit you will learn
- more about classifiers and verb endings
- two different ways of saying *thank you*

▶ Dialogue 1

Miss Wong and Miss Cheung are shopping in a fashion store.

今日係禮拜一，唔係禮拜日，點解呢間舖頭咁多人呢？

呢間舖頭大減價丫嗎。我哋入去睇吓好嗎？

好呀，嘩！你睇，嗰件衫裙真係好平嚩！

係嚩。質地又好；款式又新；顏色又靚；真係好嘅。

噉，我就買呢件喇。

我都想買嗰件紅色嘅。

咦，呢處有少少爛咗嚩。

係咩？哦！係嚩！我呢件都有少少爛咗。等我睇吓其他嘅有冇爛呢。

唔駛睇啦，件件都有少少爛嘅，因為佢哋都係次貨，所以咁平。

Wong	Gàm-yaht haih Láih-baai-yāt, m̀h haih Láih-baai-yaht, dím-gáai nī gàan pou-táu gam dò yàhn nē?
Cheung	Nī gàan pou-táu daaih-gáam-ga ā-ma. Ngóh-deih yahp-heui tái-háh hóu ma?
Wong	Hóu a. Wà! Néih tái, gó gihn sāam-kwàhn jàn-haih hóu pèhng bo!
Cheung	Haih bo. Jāt-déi yauh hóu; fún-sīk yauh sàn; ngàahn-sīk yauh leng: jàn-haih hóu lak.
Wong	Gám, ngóh jauh máaih nī gihn lā.
Cheung	Ngóh dōu séung máaih gó gihn hùhng-sīk ge.
Wong	Yí, nī-syu yáuh síu-síu laahn-jó bo!
Cheung	Haih mē? Où! Haih bo! Ngóh nī gihn dōu yáuh síu-síu laahn-jó. Dáng ngóh tái-háh kèih-tà ge yáuh móuh laahn nē.
Wong	M̀h-sái tái la, gihn-gihn dōu yáuh síu-síu laahn ge, yàn-waih kéuih-deih dōu haih chi-fo, só-yíh gam pèhng.

禮拜、星期		*week*
láih-baai or **sìng-kèih**		
禮拜一 **Láih-baai-yāt**		*Monday*
禮拜日 **Láih-baai-yaht**		*Sunday*
舖頭 **pou-táu**		*shop*
大減價 **daaih-gáam-ga**		*a sale*
丫嗎 **ā-ma**		final particle, *you should realize, don't you know*
入 **yahp**		*to enter*
睇 **tái**		*to look at*
......吓 **-háh**		verb ending, *have a little –*
嘩！ **wà!**		*wow!*
件 **gihn**		classifier for most items of clothing

衫裙 **sāam-kwàhn**	*dress*
平 **pèhng**	*cheap*
嘞！**bo!**	*final particle, let me remind you, let me tell you*
質地 **jāt-déi**	*quality*
又...... 又...... **yauh . . . yauh . . .**	*both . . . and . . .*
款色 **fún-sīk**	*style*
新 **sàn**	*new; up to date*
顏色 **ngàahn-sīk**	*colour*
紅色嘅 **hùhng-sīk ge**	*red*
咦 **yí**	*exclamation of surprise, hello, what's this?*
呢處 **nī-syu**	*here*
少少 **síu-síu**	*a little bit, somewhat*
爛 **laahn**	*broken, damaged*
咩？**mē?**	*final particle, do you mean to say that . . .?*
等 **dáng**	*let, allow*
其他 **kèih-tà**	*other*
次貨 **chi-fo**	*seconds*

Picture quiz

a Wòhng Síu-jé gó gihn sāam-kwàhn pèhng m̀h pèhng a? Leng m̀h leng a?
b Wòhng Síu-jé gó gihn sāam-kwàhn yáuh móuh laahn ga? Jèung Síu-jé gó gihn nē?

Grammar

1 The week

Láih-baai means *week*: it is classified with **go**, so *one week* is **yāt go láih-baai**, *two weeks* is **léuhng go láih-baai** and so on.

The days of the week are simply numbered 1–6 from Monday to Saturday:

Láih-baai-yāt	*Monday*	**Láih-baai-sei**	*Thursday*
Láih-baai-yih	*Tuesday*	**Láih-baai-ńgh**	*Friday*
Láih-baai-sàam	*Wednesday*	**Láih-baai-luhk**	*Saturday*

Sunday is not numbered; instead the word for *sun* **yaht** is used, so **Láih-baai-yaht** is *Sunday*. Go very carefully with your tones or you will mix up *Sunday* (**Láih-baai-yaht**) and *Monday* (**Láih-baai-yāt**)!

Some people say **sìng-kèih** instead of **láih-baai** and you may do so too if you wish. Simply substitute **sìng-kèih** for **láih-baai** in any of the words in the previous list.

2 *Nē?* again

You have met **nē?** as a final particle which asks a follow-up question (see Unit 1). It is also used after rhetorical questions, that is when you do not expect an answer or perhaps when you are wondering to yourself:

Gó go yàhn haih bīn-go nē? *I wonder who that can be?*

There are two examples in the dialogue.

3 Coming and going

Làih *to come* and **heui** *to go* are often used with other verbs of movement to show which direction the movement is in. For instance:

fàan	*to return*	**yahp**	*to enter*
fàan-heui	*to go back*	**yahp-heui**	*to go in*
fàan-làih	*to come back*	**yahp-làih**	*to come in*

4 Another verb ending: -háh

In Unit 4 you met the verb endings -jó and -gán. Another one is
-háh, which gives the idea of *doing something for a bit*:

tái-háh	*have a glance at (look a bit)*
dáng-háh	*wait for a moment (wait a bit)*
chóh-háh	*sit for a while (sit a bit)*

5 *Yauh . . . yauh . . .* : both . . . and . . .

Yauh basically means *furthermore* and it is an adverb. It has to
obey the rule for such adverbs and come in front of a verb (see
dōu in Units 1 and 4), even when it is being repeated to give the
meaning *both . . . and. . . .* In the dialogue you can see that it
does obey (the three verbs are **hóu** *to be good*, **sàn** *to be new* and
leng *to be pretty*). If you bear that rule in mind you will easily
understand why the translation of *both Mr and Mrs Wong are
going* might be **Wòhng Sìn-sàang yauh heui, Wòhng Taai-táai
yauh heui.**

6 Colours

Hùhng means *red*, but it is most easily used in combination
with **sīk** *colour* as **hùhng-sīk** *red-coloured*. **Ge** is added to link
hùhng-sīk with a noun (see Unit 4):

| Kéuih ge chē haih māt-yéh
ngàahn-sīk ga? | *What colour's his car?* |
| Haih hùhng-sīk ge chē. | *It's a red car.* |

7 *Here* and *there*

In Unit 3 you met **bīn-syu** and **bīn-douh** *where?* **Bīn** means
which? and **syu** and **douh** both mean *place*, so *which place?* and
where?. Logically enough, *here* and *there* are made from *this
place* and *that place*:

| nī-syu or nī-douh | *here* |
| gó-syu or gó-douh | *there* |

8 Final particle *mē?*

If you want to express great incredulity in a question in English
(*You can speak 57 languages fluently?!*) you raise your voice

almost to a squeak at the end of the question; but, of course, it is less easy to do that in Cantonese because of the need to observe tones. **Mē?** does the job for you. It indicates great surprise, astonishment, near disbelief, *surely that's not the case, is it?*, *do you mean to say that . . . ?*. The answer given is almost always **haih** or **m̀h haih** (*it is the case* or *it is not the case*).

9 *Dáng* again

Dáng means *to wait*, as you saw in Unit 4. **Dáng ngóh** means *wait for me* or *wait for me to*, and so **dáng ngóh sihk-faahn** means *wait for me to eat*. From *wait for me to eat* to *let me eat* is not a big jump and you will find that Cantonese often uses **dáng ngóh** where English would say *let me . . .* Generally, if **dáng ngóh** comes at the beginning of a sentence it is likely to be used in the sense of *let me . . .*; and if it comes embedded in a sentence then it is likely to mean *wait for*:

Dáng ngóh bòng néih sáu.	*Let me help you.*
M̀h-hóu dáng ngóh sihk-faahn.	*Don't wait for me to eat.*

10 Double classifiers

Doubling-up classifiers and adding **dōu** *all* before the verb is a useful way of conveying the idea *every one of*, *each one of*:

Gàan-gàan ūk dōu hóu leng.	*All the houses are very nice.*
Jì-jì Méih-gwok bāt dōu gwai.	*All American pens are expensive.*
Gihn-gihn sāam-kwàhn dōu m̀h pèhng.	*None of the dresses is cheap.*

ⓘ Let me pay!

In restaurants you will often hear Chinese customers vying with each other to pay the bill, the winner gaining in 'face' what he/she loses in pocket. The standard wording used is **Dáng ngóh béi!** *Let me pay!* (lit: *let me give!*) You too can play that game, but be sure you have the money about you in case you should be (un)lucky enough to win!

▶ Dialogue 2

Miss Cheung gets a bargain (perhaps) from the fish seller in the market.

呢啲蝦幾多錢一斤呀？
八十五蚊一斤。
呢啲蝦咁細，八十五蚊一斤太貴嘞。七十蚊一斤得唔得呀？
唔得！小姐，你睇，隻隻蝦都好新鮮會游水。八十五蚊一斤唔貴嘅啦。
嗰處嘅檔口只係要七十二蚊一斤啫。點解你哋要八十五蚊一斤呀？
因為我哋係'買一送一'吖嗎。
點樣買一送一呀？
即係買一斤蝦，免費送一斤蝦喇。
好！我要一斤喇。嗱，呢處八十五蚊。
多謝。嗱，呢處兩斤蝦。
點解咁多死蝦㗎？
買一斤游水蝦，送一斤死蝦吖嗎。

Cheung	Nī dī hā géi-dō chín yāt gàn a?
Seller	Baat-sahp-ńgh màn yāt gàn.
Cheung	Nī dī hā gam sai, baat-sahp-ńgh màn yāt gàn taai gwai lak. Chāt-sahp màn yāt gàn dāk m̀h dāk a?
Seller	M̀h dāk! Síu-jé, néih tái, jek-jek hā dōu hóu sàn-sìn wúih yàuh-séui. Baat-sahp-ńgh màn yāt gàn m̀h gwai ge-la.
Cheung	Gó-syu ge dong-háu jí-haih yiu chāt-sahp-yih màn yāt gàn jē. Dím-gáai néih-deih yiu baat-sahp-ńgh màn yāt gàn a?
Seller	Yàn-waih ngóh-deih haih 'máaih-yāt-sung-yāt' ā-ma.
Cheung	Dím-yéung máaih-yāt-sung-yāt a?
Seller	Jīk-haih máaih yāt gàn hā, míhn-fai sung yāt gàn hā lā.
Cheung	Hóu! Ngóh yiu yāt gàn lā. Nàh, nī-syu baat-sahp-ńgh màn.
Seller	Dò-jeh. Nàh, nī-syu léuhng gàn hā.
Cheung	Dím-gáai gam dò séi hā ga?
Seller	Máaih yāt gàn yàuh-séui hā, sung yāt gàn séi hā ā-ma.

蝦 **hā**		*prawn*
幾多？ **géi-dō?**		*how much? how many?*
錢 **chín**		*money*
斤 **gàn**		*a catty (= 20 ounces)*
蚊 **màn**		*dollar*
細 **sai**		*small*
得 **dāk**		*OK, can do, acceptable*
隻 **jek**		*classifier for animals*
會 **wúih**		*to be able to, to know how to*

游水 **yàuh-séui**		*to swim*
水 **séui**		*water*
嘅啦 **ge-la**		*final particle giving strong emphasis*
檔口 **dong-háu**		*street stall*
點樣? **dím-yéung?**		*how? in what way?*
即係 **jīk-haih**		*that is, that is to say*
免費 **míhn-fai**		*free of charge*
嗱 **nàh**		*'there', 'here you are', 'here it is, look'*
多謝 (你) **dò-jeh (néih)**		*thank you*
死 **séi**		*dead; to die*

▶ **Answer the questions**

a Jèung Síu-jé hái dong-háu séung máaih māt-yéh a?
b Dī hā géi-dō chín yāt gàn a?
c Kèih-tà dong-háu ge hā, géi-do chín yāt gàn a?
d Jèung Síu-jé máaih-jó hā dím-gáai hóu nàu a?

Grammar

11 So much each

Note the simple formula for giving prices:

Géi-dō chín yāt gàn a?	*How much per catty?*
Léuhng mān yāt gàn.	*$2 a catty.*

The same kind of formula can be used with other terms:

Sàam-kwàhn luhk-sahp màn yāt gihn.	*Dresses cost $60 each.*
Yāt go yàhn sàam jì bāt.	*Three pens per person.*

12 *How about it?* again

In Unit 2 you met **hóu m̀h hóu a?** as a way of asking someone's opinion after making a statement. **Dāk m̀h dāk a?** is perhaps even more commonly used for the same purpose, meaning *will that do?, is that OK by you?, are you happy with that?*

13 Thank you

You have now met two words for *thank you*: **m̀h-gòi** and **dò-jeh**. They are used in different ways and it is important to try to sort them out.

M̀h-gòi is used for everyday minor politenesses, such as thanking someone for holding a door open for you, for passing you the soy sauce or for doing the washing-up.

Dò-jeh is used for more heartfelt thanks, for example in gratitude to someone for a present received, for saving your life or for finding you a job. It is *always* used when receiving money.

So, when you take the goods from a shopkeeper, you may or may not say **m̀h-gòi** (depending how polite you feel like being), but he will certainly say **dò-jeh** when he takes your money. The polite response to someone who thanks you is **m̀h-sái** *there's no need to*. The longer forms **m̀h-sái m̀h-gòi** and **m̀h-sái dò-jeh** can be used too.

ℹ️ Pidgin English

Pidgin English was developed in the early 18th century in Canton. It was a strange language which was a kind of halfway house between English and Cantonese and therefore was presumed to be equally easy/difficult for both sides to learn and to speak as they transacted 'pidgin' (*business*) together. It used English vocabulary but often in Cantonese grammar patterns. Like Cantonese it didn't really have any plural forms, tenses or agreements and it invented the word *piecee* to take the place of the Cantonese classifiers (*four piecee man, that piecee pen*). Some of its expressions have passed into regular English, such as *to have a look-see, long time no see, chop-chop* and *no can do*. This last phrase comes from the Cantonese **m̀h dāk** which you met in this lesson.

Exercise 1

Insert the bracketed element to make a sentence which is still meaningful. For example, the answer to the first question would be **Hùhng-sīk ge Méih-gwok chē hóu gwai.**

a Méih-gwok chē hóu gwai. (hùhng-sīk ge)
b Ngóh sīk yàuh-séui. (bàh-bā)
c Wòhng Taai-táai heui máaih-yéh. (pou-táu)
d Kéuih gàm-yaht m̀h sihk-faahn. (séung)
e Hòh Sàang m̀h sihk Hòh Táai jyú ge sung. (Taai-)

Exercise 2

Here is a test of your understanding of classifiers. See if you can put the correct classifier into the blank space. Be aware that *there are two trick sentences*, so you will need to keep your wits about you!

a Gó __ ūk haih Hòh Sìn-sàang ge.
b Kéuih ge __ sāam-kwàhn yáuh síu-síu laahn-jó.
c Wòhng Síu-jé ge bàh-bā m̀h haih __ Jùng-gwok-yàhn.
d Nī __ Méih-gwok bāt hóu gwai.
e Gó __ lùhng-hā dōu hóu daaih.
f __ __ hā dōu séi-jó.

Exercise 3

Now try your mathematical skills!

a Lùhng-hā sahp-sei mān yāt jek. Wòhng Táai máaih-jó léuhng jek. Kéuih yiu béi géi-dō chín a?

b Nī go dong-háu ge hā m̀h gwai: sàam-sahp-yih mān yāt gàn, máaih yāt gàn sung bun gàn. Wòhng Táai yiu sàam gàn – kéuih yiu béi géi-dō chín a?

06

交通
gàau-tùng
getting around

In this unit you will learn
- about means of transport
- how to get to places

▶ Dialogue 1

Mr Wong is a stranger in town and asks a local person the way.

我要搭飛機返英國，請問去飛機場要搭幾多號巴士呀？
呢處冇巴士去飛機場㗎。你要先由呢處搭小巴一直去，過三個街口到
　大馬路，喺巴士站你要落小巴，再轉搭十五號巴士去飛機場喇。
噉，有冇小輪去飛機場呢？
冇小輪去機場㗎。
我好想搭地下鐵路。有冇地下鐵路去機場呢？
都冇㗎！地鐵只去市區啫。
噉，我去大會堂喇！有冇地鐵去呀？地鐵站喺邊處呀？
有，地鐵站喺嗰度，但係你話要搭飛機返英國。喺大會堂冇飛機場㗎。

Wong	Ngóh yiu daap fèi-gèi fàan Yìng-gwok, chéng-mahn heui fèi-gèi-chèuhng yiu daap géi-dō houh bā-sí a?
Local	Nī-syu móuh bā-sí heui fèi-gèi-chèuhng bo. Néih yiu sìn yàuh nī-syu daap síu-bā yāt-jihk heui, gwo sàam go gàai-háu dou daaih máh-louh, hái bā-sí-jaahm néih yiu lohk síu-bā, joi jýun daap sahp-ńgh houh bā-sí heui fèi-gèi-chèuhng lā.
Wong	Gám, yáuh móuh síu-lèuhn heui fèi-gèi-chèuhng nē?
Local	Móuh síu-lèuhn heui gèi-chèuhng bo.
Wong	Ngóh hóu séung daap deih-hah-tit-louh. Yáuh móuh deih-hah-tit-louh heui gèi-chèuhng nē?
Local	Dōu móuh bo! Deih-tit jí heui síh-kèui jē.
Wong	Gám, ngóh heui Daaih-wuih-tòhng lā! Yáuh móuh deih-tit heui a? Deih-tit-jaahm hái bīn-syu a?
Local	Yáuh, deih-tit-jaahm hái gó-douh, daahn-haih néih wah yiu daap fèi-gèi fàan Yìng-gwok. Hái Daaih-wuih-tòhng móuh fèi-gèi-chèuhng bo.

The Chinese character for **séuhng** board can be seen next to the front door of the bus and **lohk** alight next to the exit door.

飛機 **fèi-gèi**	aircraft
飛機場 (fèi-) **gèi-chèuhng**	airport
請問 **chéng-mahn**	please, may I ask . . . ?
先 **sìn**	first
由 **yàuh**	from
小巴 **síu-bā**	mini-bus
一直 **yāt-jihk**	straight, directly
過 **gwo**	go past, go across, go by
街口 **gàai-háu**	road junction
到 **dou**	to arrive, arrive at, reach
馬路 **máh-louh**	road
巴士站 **bā-sí-jaahm**	bus stop
落 **lohk**	to alight from
轉 **jyun**	to turn, to change to
小輪 **síu-lèuhn**	ferry
地下鐵路 **deih-hah-tit-louh**	underground railway
市區 **síh-kèui**	urban area
大會堂 **daaih-wuih-tòhng**	city hall
地鐵站 **deih-tit-jaahm**	underground station
但係 **daahn-haih**	but
話 **wah**	to say

▶ True or false?

a Wòhng Sìn-sàang yiu daap fèi-gèi fàan Yìng-gwok.

b Wòhng Sìn-sàang yiu daap sahp-ńgh houh bā-sí heui fèi-gèi-chèuhng.

c Yáuh síu-lèuhn heui fèi-gèi-chèuhng.

d Dōu yáuh deih-hah-tit-louh heui fèi-gèi-chèuhng.

e Daahn-haih móuh deih-tit heui Daaih-wuih-tòhng.

Grammar

1 *Chéng-mahn*: please may I ask . . . ?

Chéng-mahn, a combination of *please* and *ask*, is the polite way to begin a question to a stranger and is very useful therefore when asking directions. It is also the respectful way to begin a question to someone of higher status than yourself.

2 To travel by

In Unit 3 you were introduced to **daap** *to travel by* and in the same unit you met **chóh** *to sit*. **Chóh** can actually be used like **daap** to mean *to travel by* as well, probably because when you take transport you sit on it (if you're lucky!). So **daap bā-sí** and **chóh bā-sí** both mean *to travel by bus*. Beware, however: you cannot do the opposite and get away with making **daap** mean *to sit*!

3 First this, then that

The adverbs *first* and *then* are **sìn** and **joi**. Being adverbs they come before verbs (see Units 1, 4 and 5):

Kéuih sìn heui gèi-chèuhng   *He's going first to the airport*
  joi chóh bā-sí fàan ūk-kéi.   *and then taking the bus home.*

4 More shortcuts

Hong Kong's Chek Lap Kok airport (**Chek-laahp-gok fèi-gèi-chèuhng**) is such a common feature of everybody's life that the shortening of the term was almost inevitable. People mostly reduce it just to **gèi-chèuhng**. Similarly, the full formal word for an underground railway **deih-hah-tit-louh** is far too much of a mouthful for most people, who reduce it to **deih-tit**.

▊ The Mass Transit Railway

The underground railway in Hong Kong, the **deih-hah-tit-louh** or **deih-tit** for short, is known in English as the MTR, short for Mass Transit Railway. The first section of it was opened in 1979, 43 kilometres were in service by 1989 and new extensions are constantly being added. It is air-conditioned throughout (including the tunnels), clean, fast and efficient and fares are low. Hong Kong people are noticeably proud of the system. The trains have no barriers between the coaches, so that you can stand at one end and look down the full length of the inside of the train as it snakes its way through the tunnels. For speed of travel through crowded Hong Kong it cannot be bettered. Since 1998 it has been possible to interchange onto the very fast Airport Express Line which shuttles at up to 135 kilometres an hour between the new Chek Lap Kok International Airport and the very heart of Hong Kong in Central district (**Jùng-wàahn**) next to the famous Star Ferry Pier (**Tīn-sīng Máh-tàuh**).

▶ Dialogue 2

Mr Wong visits Britain and is met by his friend Mr Chan.

老陳，我第一次嚟倫敦，請你話我聽去邊處玩好呢？
等我帶你去玩喇。我哋搭火車先向北行，去參觀劍橋大學。
好呀。劍橋大學係世界最有名嘅大學之一。
參觀完之後，我哋搭巴士去英國東部睇吓嗰處嘅鄉下。
好主意。我好中意去鄉下地方玩。
喺嗰處我有一個好朋友，我哋可以喺佢屋企住一晚。第二日請佢揸車
　送我哋去英國南部嘅漁港睇吓。
香港都有漁港，我去過好多次嘞。
我哋由漁港再搭小輪去離島。
我唔想去離島嘞。兩日之內去咁多地方，又搭咁耐車，我話好似走難
　唔似去玩嗰。

Wong	Lóuh Chán, ngóh daih-yāt chi làih Lèuhn-dēun, chéng néih wah ngóh tèng heui bīn-syu wáan hóu nē?
Chan	Dáng ngóh daai néih heui wáan la. Ngóh-deih daap fó-chè sìn heung bāk hàhng, heui chàam-gwùn Gim-kìuh Daaih-hohk.
Wong	Hóu a. Gim-kìuh Daaih-hohk haih sai-gaai jeui yáuh-méng ge daaih-hohk jì yāt.
Chan	Chàam-gwùn-yùhn jì-hauh, ngóh-deih daap bā-sí heui Yìng-gwok dùng bouh tái-háh gó-syu ge hèung-há.
Wong	Hóu jýu-yi. Ngóh hóu jùng-yi heui hèung-há deih-fòng wáan.
Chan	Hái gó-syu ngóh yáuh yāt go hóu pàhng-yáuh, ngóh-deih hó-yíh hái kéuih ūk-kéi jyuh yāt máahn. Daih-yih yaht chéng kéuih jà chē sung ngóh-deih heui Yìng-gwok nàahm bouh ge yùh-góng tái-háh.
Wong	Hèung-góng dōu yáuh yùh-góng, ngóh heui-gwo hóu dò chi lak.
Chan	Ngóh-deih yàuh yùh-góng joi daap síu-lèuhn heui lèih-dóu.
Wong	Ngóh m̀h séung heui lèih-dóu lak. Léuhng yaht jì-noih heui gam dò deih-fòng, yauh daap gam noih chē ngóh wah hóu-chíh jáu-naahn m̀h-chíh heui wáan gám.

老 **lóuh**	*elderly, aged, old*
第 **daih-**	*(makes ordinal numbers)*
	the first, the second etc.
倫敦 **Lèuhn-dēun**	*London*
聽 **tèng**	*to listen*
玩 **wáan**	*to play, to enjoy, to amuse*
	oneself
火車 **fó-chè**	*railway train*
向 **heung**	*towards*
北 **bāk**	*north*
行 **hàhng**	*to journey, to go towards*
參觀 **chàam-gwùn**	*to visit*
劍橋 **Gim-kìuh**	*Cambridge*
大學 **daaih-hohk**	*university*
世界 **sai-gaai**	*the world*
最 **jeui**	*most*
有名 **yáuh-méng**	*famous*
......之一 **... jì-yāt**	*one of the . . .*
......完 **-yùhn**	*finished*
之後 **jì-hauh**	*after*
部 **bouh**	*area, part, portion*
東 **dùng**	*east*
鄉下 **hèung-há**	*countryside*
主意 **jýu-yi**	*idea*
中意 **jùng-yi**	*to like, to be fond of*
地方 **deih-fòng**	*place*
可以 **hó-yíh**	*can, may*
晚 **máahn**	*evening, night*
日 **yaht**	*day*
揸車 **jà-chē**	*to drive (a vehicle)*
送 **sung**	*to deliver, escort, send*
南 **nàahm**	*south*
漁港 **yùh-góng**	*fishing port*
...... 過 **-gwo**	*verb ending, to have experienced*
次 **chi**	*a time, an occasion*
離島 **lèih-dóu**	*outlying island*
之內 **jì-noih**	*within*
好似......唔似	*to be more like . . . than like . . .*
hóu-chíh . . . m̀h-chíh	
走難 **jáu-naahn**	*to flee from disaster, to be a*
	refugee

Answer the questions

a Chàhn Sìn-sàang haih m̀h haih daih-yāt chi làih Lèuhn-dēun a?
b Gim-kìuh Daaih-hohk haih m̀h haih hái Lèuhn-dēun fuh-gahn a?
c Yìng-gwok dùng bouh yáuh hóu dò yáuh-méng ge yùh-góng, haih m̀h haih a?
d Chàhn Sìn-sàang hóu jùng-yi heui lèih-dóu wáan, haih m̀h haih a?

Grammar

5 *Lóuh*

Lóuh means *elderly*, *aged* and is used only for people and animals (that is, you would not describe a building or a book as **lóuh**). It is often used with the surname as a familiar or affectionate term of address to a man (rarely to a woman):

Lóuh Wóng, . . .   *Wong, old chap, . . .*

Note that when this is done the tone of the surname is changed to a mid rising tone from the original low falling tone. So the surname **Wòhng** becomes **Lóuh Wóng** and **Chàhn** becomes **Lóuh Chán**.

6 Ordinal numbers

You met the cardinal numbers (one, two, three, four, etc.) in Unit 2. The ordinal numbers (the first, the second, the third, the fourth, etc.) are formed by putting **daih-** in front of the cardinal number:

yāt go yàhn   *one person*
daih-yāt go yàhn   *the first person*

You will remember from Unit 2 that the number two obeys different rules, so that **yih** becomes **léuhng** in front of classifiers. Note that with ordinal numbers there is no such exception:

léuhng go yàhn   *two people*
daih-yih go yàhn   *the second person*

While we are on the subject we might as well look at a couple of other peculiarities of *two*. **Daih-yih** as well as *the second* can quite logically extend to mean *the next*:

Daih-yih yaht kéuih jáu-jó lak.   *He left the next day.*

It can also logically extend to mean *the other*:

Ngóh juhng yáuh daih-yih jì bāt.   *I've still got another pen.*

But you need to stretch your mind a little further to take in the notion that **daih-yih** can mean *the others*:

Daih-yih dī bāt dōu haih kéuih ge.   *The other pens are all hers.*

7 To tell

Tell has various meanings in English and they are not all translated by the same word in Cantonese. When *tell* means *tell someone about something* you can use **wah . . . tèng . . .** :

Kéuih wah ngóh tèng kéuih m̀h   *He told me he doesn't*
**   sīk jà-chē.**   *know how to drive.*

8 Directions

dùng *east*   **nàahm** *south*   **sài** *west*   **bāk** *north*

Cantonese lists the four directions in the order given here, though English speakers normally start with *north*. The intermediate directions are straightforward provided you remember that they are always the opposite way round from English, i.e. Cantonese says *eastnorth* where English says *northeast*:

dùng-bāk   *northeast*   **dùng-nàahm**   *southeast*
sài-nàahm *southwest*   **sài-bāk**   *northwest*

9 Another verb ending: -yùhn finished

Yùhn means *the end* or *to finish*. It is used as a verb ending to show that the action of the verb is all over with:

sihk-yùhn	*finished eating*
chàam-gwùn-yùhn	*finished visiting*

10 'Time when'

Time expressions which begin with *after* are translated with jì-hauh in Cantonese, but jì-hauh is placed at the end of the time expression not at the beginning:

Néih jáu-jó jì-hauh, kéuih wah ngóh tèng néih m̀h jùng-yi sihk hā.	*After you'd gone she told me you don't like prawns.*

In English the *after you'd gone* could come at the end of the sentence (*She told me you don't like prawns after you'd gone*), but with expressions which pinpoint the *time when* something happens Cantonese likes to have the information before the verb of the main statement is given, so you do not have the option of putting néih jáu-jó jì-hauh at the end. Other *time when* expressions you have met so far, such as gàm-yaht *today* and Láih-baai-ńgh *Friday*, as well as the many you haven't yet met (*at 6 o'clock; in May last year; when I got there; before he had breakfast; in 1492 AD*), all obey the same rule:

Láih-baai-luhk néih heui m̀h heui a?	*Are you going on Saturday?*
Ngóh gàm-yaht séung heui yàuh-séui.	*I'd like to go swimming today.*

11 Can, able to

You met sīk in Unit 4 and in this unit comes hó-yíh: both mean *can, able to*. They are not usually interchangeable. Sīk really means *to have learned how to* and implies that you are able to do something because you have acquired the skill to do it (speak a foreign language, ride a bicycle, eat with chopsticks, etc.). Hó-yíh operates in the realm of permission (*may*) and absence of obstacles to doing something:

Néih sīk m̀h sīk jà-chē a?	*Can you drive? (Do you know how to drive?)*
Néih hó-yíh m̀h hó-yíh jà-chē a?	*Can you drive? (Have you a licence? Is the car available?)*

Another way to say *can, be able* is by using the verb ending -dāk. This is actually the same word that you met in Unit 5, but in this use it must go directly onto a verb, as in **Ngóh m̀h heui-dāk** (*I can't go*):

Kéuih jà-dāk chē.	*He can drive.*

With -dāk there is no guidance as to whether he can drive because he knows how to, because his father says he may, because he has his full physical powers or because there is a car available, so it is a good all-purpose way of saying *can*. Do remember though that -dāk can only be put onto a verb, not onto any other part of speech.

12 'Time how long'

Time expressions which show *how long* something goes on for (as opposed to the *time when* something happens) come *after* the main verb in Cantonese:

daap gam noih chē	*travelling in a car for so long*
Ngóh-deih hai Hèung-góng jyuh léuhng go láih-baai.	*We're staying in Hong Kong for two weeks.*
Kéuih chóh-jó ńgh go jūng-tàuh fēi-gèi.	*He was on the plane for five hours.*

13 Yet another verb ending: -*gwo* to have had the experience

Gwo literally means *to go past*, as you saw earlier in this unit. As a verb ending -gwo shows that the verb has been experienced at some time:

Ngóh sihk-gwo hā.	*I have had prawns (I have experienced eating prawns).*

The following pairs of sentences illustrate the difference between the two verb endings -jó and -gwo: -jó, as we saw in Unit 4, shows that an action has been completed at a particular point in time; -gwo shows that an action has at some time or other occurred:

Kéuih heui-jó Hèung-góng.	*He went to Hong Kong.*
Kéuih heui-gwo Hèung-góng.	*He has been to Hong Kong.*
Wòhng Taai-táai gàm-yaht tái-jó yī-sāng.	*Mrs Wong went to the doctor's today.*
Néih tái-gwo yī-sāng ma?	*Have you ever been to the doctor's?*

Exercise 1

All of the following sentences are already complete, but each of them will allow one of the lettered elements to be inserted and still make sense. For example, if you insert element c into sentence 1 you create a new sentence which reads: **Gim-kìuh Daaih-hohk haih sai-gaai jeui yáuh-méng ge daaih-hohk jì-yāt.** *Cambridge is one of the most famous universities in the world.* Now try the rest.

1 Gim-kìuh Daaih-hohk haih daaih-hohk jì-yāt.
2 Yàuh Lèuhn-dēun heui Gim-kìuh Daaih-hohk chàam-gwùn yiu heung bāk hàhng.
3 Yàuh nī-syu daap bā-sí heui fèi-gèi-chèuhng yiu géi-dō chín a?
4 Nī-syu ge deih-hah-tit-louh jí heui Daaih-wuih-tòhng.
5 Néih yiu daap bā-sí heui fèi-gèi-chèuhng.
   a daap chē   b sahp-ńgh houh
   c sai-gaai jeui yáuh-méng ge d m̀h heui fèi-gèi-chèuhng
   e gwo sàam go gàai-háu dou Fà-yùhn Douh

Exercise 2

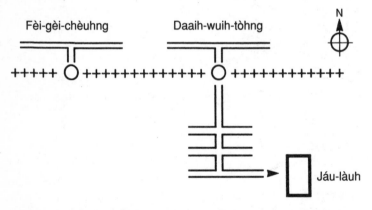

Fèi-gèi-chèuhng   Daaih-wuih-tòhng   N

Jáu-làuh

Jèung Sìn-sàang Jèung Taai-táai chéng ngóh sihk-faahn. M̀h-gòi néih* wah ngóh tèng yàuh fèi-gèi-chèuhng dím-yéung heui jáu-làuh a?

(*Note that **m̀h-gòi néih** is used here to mean not *thank you* but *please*. It is very commonly used in this way and quite often is used to attract someone's attention as well, rather as we might say *excuse me*, so it is a kind of all-purpose expression of politeness.)

07

溫習（一）
wàn-jaahp (yāt)

revision (1)

This unit gives you no new vocabulary or grammar rules. Instead it goes back over a lot of the material from the first six units, presenting it in a new way so that you can become more fluent through the extra practice. If you are stuck for any of the words, remember that there is a word list at the end of the book to help you. Units 14, 21 and 26 are also revision units, and just to make sure that you can check on your progress properly you will find translations and answers in the key at the end of the book.

Passage 1

Read this passage out loud.

Johk-yaht màh-mā mahn ngóh-deih séung m̀h séung sihk sà-léut? Ngóh-deih go-go dōu wah hóu séung sihk. Màh-mā wah, 'Hóu hóu, ngóh jauh jíng lùhng-hā sà-léut béi néih-deih sihk lā. Nàh, yìh-gā ngóh heui máaih lùhng-hā, néih-deih heui máaih dī sàn-sìn sàang-gwó fàan-làih lā.' Ngóh-deih máaih-jó hóu dò sàn-sìn sàang-gwó fàan ūk-kéi, yauh* yāt-chàih hái chyùh-fóng fàan-làih lak. Kéuih wah, 'Gàm-yaht dī lùhng-hā yauh sai yauh m̀h sàn-sìn, só-yíh ngóh móuh máaih, jí-haih máaih-jó dī daaih hā jē. Néih-deih jauh sihk daaih hā sà-léut dong lùhng-hā sà-léut lā!'

(*See Unit 5: **yauh** = *furthermore*.)

Exercise 1
True or false?

a Johk-yaht màh-mā wah kéuih hóu séung sihk sà-léut.
b Màh-mā jeui sīk jíng lùhng-hā sà-léut.
c Ngóh-deih máaih-jó hóu dò sàn-sìn sàang-gwó fàan ūk-kéi.
d Màh-mā máaih-jó yāt jek hóu daaih ge lùhng-hā.
e Màh-mā jíng ge lùhng-hā sà-léut hóu hóu-meih.

Exercise 2
Answer in Cantonese.

a Màh-mā máaih-jó māt-yéh fàan ūk-kéi a?
b Ngóh-deih máaih-jó māt-yéh fàan ūk-kéi a?
c Johk-yaht dī lùhng-hā sàn m̀h sàn-sìn a?
d Néih sīk m̀h sīk jíng sà-léut a?
e Hái néih ūk-kéi fuh-gahn ge jáu-làuh yáuh móuh sà-léut maaih a?

Exercise 3
Translate into Cantonese.

a Have you ever tasted beef salad?
b This American pen is one of the pens I most want to buy.
c This is the first time I've been to your office.

Exercise 4
Eavesdropping – you can hear one end of a phone conversation: see if you can guess what the other end might be.

X _____
Y M̀h gán-yiu. Néih yìh-gā hái bīn-douh a?
X _____
Y Òu, hái ūk-kéi. Māt-yéh sih a?
X _____
Y Hóu, hóu. Dò-jeh, dò-jeh. Hái bīn-syu sihk a?

Easy, isn't it? Try this one

X _____
Y Hóu hóu. Néih nē?
X _____
Y Kéuih dōu géi hóu. Yáuh-sàm. Néih taai-táai nē?
X _____
Y Deui-m̀h-jyuh, ngóh gàm-yaht m̀h fàan sé-jih-làuh, m̀h hó-yíh tùhng néih fàan. Sìng-kèih-sei, hóu m̀h hóu a?
X _____
Y Ngóh m̀h séung jà-chē heui, séung chóh bā-sí heui.
X _____
Y Chóh luhk houh lā.
X _____
Y Hóu, Láih-baai-sei joi-gin.

Exercise 5
Fill in the blanks.

a Wòhng Sàang haih kéuih bràa-bhā, Wòhng Táai haih __.
b Ngóh móuh bàh-bā, màh-mā, hìng-daih, jí-muih, ūk-kéi jí yáuh ngóh __ go yàhn jē.
c Chóh fèi-gèi gwai, daahn-haih chóh bā-sí __.
d Ngóh-deih Láih-baai-yaht __ sái fàan sé-jih-làuh.
e Hòh Sìn-sàang móuh chín, m̀h __ daap dīk-sí.

Exercise 6
Insert the appropriate plugs (i–v, overleaf) to create meaningful new sentences.

a Ngóh-deih nī go Sìng-kèih-luhk daap fèi-gèi heui Yìng-gwok wáan.
b Wòhng Taai-táai tùhng Wòhng Sìn-sàang làih ngóh ge sé-jih-làuh.
c Néih ge jyú-yi haih jeui hóu ge.
d Nī gàan daaih-hohk haih yáuh-méng ge daaih-hohk.
e Lèuhn-dēun haih Yìng-gwok jeui dò yàhn ge deih-fòng.
   i sai-gaai   ii sàam go yàhn   iii jì-yāt
   iv yāt-dihng   v yāt-chàih

Passage 2

Finally, here is another passage for you to read and understand. When you have understood it, read it out loud several times until it feels natural and easy on the tongue.

Gàm-yaht ngóh fàan sé-jih-làuh. Hòh Sìn-sàang wah ngóh tèng Láih-baai-luhk kéuih yiu daap fèi-gèi fàan-heui Yìng-gwok, só-yíh hái Láih-baai-sàam jì-hauh jauh m̀h fàan sé-jih-làuh lak. Hòh Sìn-sàang haih ngóh jeui hóu ge pàhng-yáuh jì-yāt, kéuih nī chi fàan-heui Yìng-gwok jì-hauh, ngóh gú jauh m̀h fàan-làih ge lak. Gám, ngóh yiu sung māt-yéh béi kéuih hóu nē? Ngóh séung-jó hóu noih dōu móuh jyú-yi, jauh heui mahn Wòhng Síu-jé tùhng Jèung Taai-táai. Wòhng Síu-jé wah, 'Ngóh-deih sàam go yàhn yāt-chàih chéng Hòh Sìn-sàang sihk-faahn lā! Hóu ma?' Jèung Taai-táai wah, 'Yùh-gwó Hòh Taai-táai hó-yíh tùhng Hòh Sìn-sàang yāt-chàih làih, gám jauh jeui hóu lak.'

Ngóh wah síu-jé tùhng taai-táai ge jyú-yi yāt-dihng haih jeui hóu ge. Néih wah haih m̀h haih a?

08

天氣
tin-hei

blowing hot and cold

In this unit you will learn
- vocabulary for talking about heat and cold

▶ Dialogue 1

A husband and wife agree about the temperature, but not about much else.

而家天氣漸漸冷嘞。我好怕冷，我最中意晒太陽嘅。天文臺話今日會
　落雨，呢個星期六重會落雪添。

我已經預備咗啲冷天衫啦。

我想聽日買個電暖爐返嚟，你話好唔好呀？

唔好。

噉，我要幾時買呀？

唔好買電暖爐啦！你買嘅嘢時時都唔實用嘅。

我唔同意，我買嘅嘢最實用嘅嘞。

你要知道買唔實用嘅嘢即係嘥錢。

你話我聽，我買咗乜嘢唔實用呀？

擠喺走廊牆角嗰個手提滅火筒，你舊年買嘅，一年之內都冇用過，
　你話係唔係唔實用吖！

Mr Wong	Yìh-gā tìn-hei jihm-jím láahng lak. Ngóh hóu pa láahng: ngóh jeui jùng-yi saai-taai-yèuhng ge. Tìn-màhn-tòih wah gàm-yaht wúih lohk-yúh, nī go Sìng-kèih-luhk juhng wúih lohk-syut tìm.
Mrs Wong	Ngóh yíh-gìng yuh-beih-jó dī láahng-tìn sāam la.
Mr Wong	Ngóh séung tìng-yaht máaih go dihn-nyúhn-lòuh fàan-làih, néih wah hóu m̀h hóu a?
Mrs Wong	M̀h hóu.
Mr Wong	Gám, ngóh yiu géi-sí máaih a?
Mrs Wong	M̀h-hóu máaih dihn-nyúhn-lòuh lā! Néih máaih ge yéh sìh-sìh dōu m̀h saht-yuhng ge.
Mr Wong	Ngóh m̀h tùhng-yi. Ngóh máaih ge yéh jeui saht-yuhng ge lak.
Mrs Wong	Néih yiu jì-dou máaih m̀h saht-yuhng ge yéh jīk-haih sàai-chín.
Mr Wong	Néih wah ngóh tèng, ngóh máaih-jó māt-yeh m̀h saht-yuhng a?
Mrs Wong	Jài hái jáu-lóng chèuhng-gok gó go sáu-tàih miht-fó-túng, néih gauh-nín máaih ge, yāt nìhn jì-noih dōu móuh yuhng-gwo. Néih wah haih m̀h haih m̀h saht-yuhng ā!

天氣	**tìn-hei**	*weather*
漸漸	**jihm-jím**	*gradually*
冷	**láahng**	*cold*
晒太陽	**saai-taai-yèuhng**	*to sunbathe*
怕	**pa**	*to fear; to dislike*
天文臺	**tìn-màhn-tòih**	*observatory*
落雨	**lohk-yúh**	*to rain* (lit: *to fall down rain*)
重	**juhng**	*in addition, furthermore*
會	**wúih**	*it is likely that* (future possibility)
落雪	**lohk-syut**	*to snow*
添	**tìm**	*as well, also, what's more* (final particle)
已經	**yíh-gìng**	*already*
冷天	**láahng-tīn**	*cold weather, winter*
衫	**sāam**	*clothing*
聽日	**tìng-yaht**	*tomorrow*
電暖爐	**dihn-nýuhn-lòuh**	*electric heater*
幾時？	**géi-sí?** or **géi-sìh?**	*when?*
嘢	**yéh**	*thing, object*
時時（都）	**sìh-sìh (dōu)**	*always, frequently*
實用	**saht-yuhng**	*practical*
同意	**tùhng-yi**	*to agree*
知道、知	**jì-dou** or **jì**	*to know a fact, to understand*
唯	**sàai**	*to waste*
擠	**jài**	*to put, to place*
走廊	**jáu-lóng**	*passage, corridor*
牆角	**chèuhng-gok**	*corner* (of house, room, etc.)
手提	**sáu-tàih**	*hand held, portable*
滅火筒	**miht-fó-túng**	*fire extinguisher*
舊年	**gauh-nín**	*last year*
年	**nìhn**	*year*
丫？	**ā?**	(particle) (triumphantly scoring a point) *didn't I tell you so!*

Have you understood?

Read the dialogue again and then select the correct phrases from the ones in brackets in the following sentences. You will no doubt feel insulted if we tell you that the answer to the first one is **dihn-nýuhn-lòuh** . . . so we won't!

a Wòhng Sìn-sàang dá-syun máaih (dihn-nýuhn-lòuh/miht-fó-túng).

b Wòhng Taai-táai wah Wòhng Sìn-sàang máaih ge yéh sìh-sìh dōu (yáuh-yuhng/móuh-yuhng/m̀h saht-yuhng).

c Gó go sáu-tàih miht-fó-túng jài hái (jáu-làuh/sé-jih-làuh/
   chèuhng-gok).
d Gó go sáu-tàih miht-fó-túng (yuhng-gwo yāt chi/móuh
   yuhng-gwo/sìh-sìh yuhng).

Grammar

1 What's more

Juhng means *furthermore, in addition* (you met the same word in Unit 3 when it meant *still, yet*). It is an adverb and therefore, as you now know, comes before the verb in the sentence. The final particle **tìm** is usually added on at the end to give additional force to **juhng**:

Ngóh juhng yáuh léuhng   *I've got two more as well.*
  go tìm.
Kéuih juhng séung heui   *What's more she wants to go to*
  Méih-gwok yāt chi tìm.   *the States once as well.*

2 When?

Géi-sí? *when?* is the question word which asks for a *time when* answer. Not surprisingly then, you will find **gei-si?** in the same place in the sentence where the *time when* answer comes. If you have forgotten the rule, refresh your memory by rereading Unit 6.

Néih géi-sí heui a?   *When are you going?*
Ngóh Láih-baai-yaht heui.   *I'm going on Sunday.*

3 More on *dōu*

You by now are well aware that **dōu** is an adverb which means *all, both, also* and that it is placed like other adverbs immediately in front of the verb. Sometimes it is used where there seems no need for it in English: for instance, in the dialogue Mrs Wong says **Néih máaih ge yéh sìh-sìh dōu m̀h saht-yuhng ge** (*The things you buy are always impractical*). What **dōu** is doing is backing up the word **sìh-sìh** *always*, and it does so because **sìh-sìh** feels like a plural idea in Cantonese – it literally means *time–time*. You first met this in Unit 5 where **dōu** was used to back up doubled classifiers. So whenever there are plural ideas (*the cows all* . . . ; *Mr and Mrs Wong* . . . ; *electric heaters* . . .) or ideas of wholeness (*the entire population* . . . ;

the whole busload . . .) you can expect **dōu** to be thrown in for good measure.

4   More about *most*

In Unit 6 you met **jeui** *most* and you will have had no difficulty in using it to make superlatives (biggest, coldest, best, etc.). Quite often you will find that the final particle **lak** is tacked onto the sentence to back up **jeui**, just as **tìm** backs up **juhng**:

jeui daaih lak	*biggest*
jeui hóu-sihk lak	*most delicious*
jeui hóu lak	*best*
Rolls-Royce haih Yìng-gwok jeui gwai ge chē lak	*The Rolls-Royce is Britain's most expensive car*

5   Tone changes

Up to now you have met no exceptions to the rule that a word is always pronounced in the same tone. Alas, Cantonese is not, in fact, quite so straightforward and, from time to time, you will come across the odd word which does not obey the rule. In the last speech of the dialogue you will notice that the word for *year* appears in two different tones. The usual tone is **nìhn** (low falling), but in *last year* **gauh-nín** it becomes mid rising. There is no obvious reason why this tone change should occur, but take heart that it only happens in the following common words:

gauh-nín	*last year*
gàm-nín	*this year*
chēut-nín	*next year*

In all other cases *year* is pronounced in the low falling tone **nìhn**.

6   Years and days

While we are talking about **nìhn** you might note that it is one of a very small number of nouns which do not need a classifier. You have learned that nouns must have a classifier when they are counted or specified with words like *this*, *that* and *which* (see Unit 2), so you know that *two pens* must be **léuhng jì bāt** and *three Americans* must be **sàam go Méih-gwok-yàhn**. **Nìhn** *year* and **yaht** *day*, however, along with one or two other nouns that you have not met, do not have a classifier; they seem to combine the role of classifier and noun at the same time. So *one day* is **yāt yaht** and *two years* is **léuhng nìhn**.

This is a convenient place to set out in clear form the words for years and days that you have met so far:

gàm-yaht	*today*	**gàm-nín**	*this year*
johk-yaht	*yesterday*	**gauh-nín**	*last year*
tìng-yaht	*tomorrow*	**chēut-nín**	*next year*

▶ Dialogue 2

Mr Chan and Mr Cheung demonstrate how buying an air conditioner can lead to a conflict of stinginess.

張先生，你好。去邊處呀？
我去買冷氣機。
係呀！天氣漸漸熱，買冷氣機係時候啦。
陳先生，你有乜野打算呢？
我冇錢買冷氣機。天氣太熱嘅時候，我會去海灘游水，飲啤酒，
　食雪糕，咁就唔熱喇。
但係如果打風就唔可以去海灘，落雨就唔可以去買雪糕……咁，
　就點呀？冷氣機唔算好貴，但係好有用：你都唔買，真係慳嘞！
我唔算慳啦！我話你太太重慳喇！
佢點樣慳法呀！
呢個禮拜二我喺百貨公司買游水褲嘅時候，見到你太太，佢好開心咁
　話我知，佢只係用咗一條你嘅舊領呔就可以改成一套'比堅尼'嘞。
　你話佢慳唔慳呢呀！

Chan	Jèung Sìn-sàang, néih hóu. Heui bīn-syu a?
Cheung	Ngóh heui máaih láahng-hei-gèi.
Chan	Haih a! Tìn-hei jihm-jím yiht, máaih láahng-hei-gèi haih sìh-hauh la.
Cheung	Chàhn Sìn-sàang, néih yáuh māt-yéh dá-syun nē?
Chan	Ngóh móuh chín máaih láahng-hei-gèi. Tìn-hei taai yiht ge sìh-hauh, ngóh wúih heui hói-tàan yàuh-séui, yám bē-jáu, sihk syut-gōu, gám jauh m̀h yiht la.
Cheung	Daahn-haih yùh-gwó dá-fùng jauh m̀h hó-yíh heui hói-tàan, lohk-yúh jauh m̀h hó-yíh heui máaih syut-gōu . . . gám, jauh dím a? Láahng-hei-gèi m̀h syun hóu gwai, daahn-haih hóu yáuh-yuhng: néih dōu m̀h máaih, jàn-haih hàan lak!
Chan	Ngóh m̀h syun hàan la! Ngóh wah néih taai-táai juhng hàan la!
Cheung	Kéuih dím-yéung hàan-faat a?
Chan	Nī go Láih-baai-yih ngóh hái baak-fo-gūng-sī máaih yàuh-séui-fu ge sìh-hauh, gin-dóu néih taai-táai, kéuih hóu hòi-sām gám wah ngóh jì kéuih jí-haih yuhng-jó yāt tìuh néih ge gauh léhng-tàai jauh hó-yíh gói-sèhng yāt tou 'béi-gìn-nèih' lak. Néih wah kéuih hàan m̀h hàan nē?

冷氣機 **láahng-hei-gèi**	air-conditioner
	(lit: cold air machine)
熱 **yiht**	hot
時候 **sìh-hauh**	time
打算 **dá-syun**	to intend; intention
海灘 **hói-tàan**	beach
飲 **yám**	to drink
啤酒 **bē-jáu**	beer
酒 **jáu**	any alcoholic drink
雪糕 **syut-gōu**	ice cream
打風 **dá-fùng**	to have a typhoon
風 **fùng**	wind
算 **syun**	to be regarded as, to be reckoned
有用 **yáuh-yuhng**	useful
慳 **hàan**	to save; to be parsimonious, stingy
重 **juhng**	even more
點樣……法？ **dím-yéung . . . -faat?**	in what way . . . ?
百貨公司 **baak-fo-gūng-sī**	department store
公司 **gūng-sī**	a company
游水褲 **yàuh-séui-fu**	swimming trunks
見 **gin**	to see, to meet
倒 **-dóu**	(verb ending) to succeed in
開心 **hòi-sām**	happy
話……知 = 話……聽 **wah . . . jì = wah . . . tèng**	to tell
條 **tìuh**	classifier for long, thin, flexible things
舊 **gauh**	old, used
領呔 **léhng-tàai**	necktie
改 **gói**	to alter, to change (usually for the better)
成 **-sèhng**	(verb ending) . . . to become, . . . into
套 **tou**	classifier for a set of, a suit of
比堅尼 **béi-gìn-nèih**	bikini

ℹ️ Typhoons

It is likely that the word *typhoon* comes from the Cantonese word **daaih-fùng** *great wind*. The summer monsoon season is the usual time for these swirling torrents of rain and ferocious winds which can exceed speeds of 160 km/h, and woe betide those who are caught unprepared. In recent years few really bad typhoons have hit Hong Kong and early warning systems mean that there is usually plenty of time to get to safety and put up shutters. During a typhoon Hong Kong comes to a standstill, creating an unaccustomed silence which even the noise of the wind cannot disguise.

Picture quiz

a   Néih wah Jèung Táai yuhng nī tìuh léhng-tàai gói-sèhng béi-gìn-nèih dāk m̀h dāk a?

b   Yāt tou béi-gìn-nèih haih géi-dō gihn a?

Grammar

7   In what way?

You first met **dím-yéung** *in what way? how?* in Unit 5. In the dialogue you see that it appears with the verb ending -**faat** *way of*. . . . You do not have to use this new form, but it is quite good racy-sounding Cantonese to do so. Here are two example sentences each using both forms:

1   Kéuih dím-yéung heui fèi-gèi-chèuhng a?
     Fèi-gèi-chèuhng kéuih dím-yéung heui-faat a?
2   Kéuih dím-yéung hàan chín a?
     Chín kéuih dím-yéung hàan-faat a?

Sentence 1 means *How is he going to the airport?* and Sentence 2 means *How does she save money?* When the **-faat** form is used, note how in each case the object of the verb moves to the front of the sentence and the **-faat** tacks onto the verb. There is a useful principle to be learned: Cantonese verbs are sensitive creatures (remember how some of them feel lonely?) and they don't feel happy with too many ideas hanging on them. Verb endings *must* add directly onto the verb and so if there is an object as well and it makes the verb feel overburdened, it often feels more comfortable to shift that object to the front of the sentence.

8 *Sìh-hauh* time

Haih sìh-hauh is a colloquial way to say *it is the right time to.* . . . Here are two ways of using it, both of which mean *it's time to go to the office now*:

Yìh-gā haih sìh-hauh fàan sé-jih-làuh la.
Yìh-gā fàan sé-jih-làuh haih sìh-hauh la.

Perhaps more common is the expression . . . **ge sìh-hauh**, which means *when . . .* or *while.* . . . Study these two sentences carefully:

Ngóh jyu-sung ge sìh-hauh m̀h séung màh-mā bòng ngóh sáu.	*I don't want mummy to help me while I'm cooking.*
Kéuih hái Yìng-gwok ge sìh-hauh sìh-sìh dōu làih taam ngóh.	*She often comes to see me when she's in Britain.*

Now look back to Unit 4 and see how . . . **ge sìh-hauh** is really just like other **ge** phrases:

hóu gwai ge ga-fē	*coffee which is very expensive*
máaih-gán bāt ge yàhn	*the person who is buying a pen*
kéuih hái Yìng-gwok ge sìh-hauh	*the time when she is in Britain*

9 Making adverbs from adjectives

If you bracket an adjective with **hóu** . . . **gám** you turn it into an adverb:

hòi-sām	*happy*	→ **hóu hòi-sām gám**	*happily*
haak-hei	*polite*	→ **hóu haak-hei gám**	*politely*
Kéuih hóu nàu.			*He's very angry.*
Kéuih hóu nàu gám wah ngóh jì.			*He told me angrily.*

10 -dóu to succeed in

It is not easy to put a specific meaning on the verb ending -dóu. Sometimes you might want to translate it as *to succeed in*, sometimes as *successfully*, sometimes as *actually* and quite often it seems to add nothing much at all to the meaning of the verb to which it is attached. Here are four examples of it with different verbs:

Ngóh tái-dóu Wòhng Síu-jé hái gó-syu.	*I caught sight of Miss Wong there.*
Ngóh gú-dóu néih hái chyùh-fóng.	*I guessed rightly that you were in the kitchen.*
Kéuih daap-dóu bā-sí.	*He actually caught the bus.*
Ngóh gin-dóu néih taai-táai.	*I met your wife.*

11 -sèhng to become

As a verb ending -sèhng means *to become* or *to make into*. You will find an example in the dialogue where Mrs Cheung claims to make a tie into a bikini. Here is another one:

Ngóh yuhng ngàuh-yuhk jýu-sèhng yāt go tòng.	*I'm making the beef into a soup.*

Exercise 1
Match the correct part B with its part A to make meaningful sentences.

A Tìn-hei jihm-jím yiht . . .
   Láahng-hei-gèi m̀h syun hóu gwai . . .
   Yùh-gwó máaih m̀h saht-yuhng ge yéh . . .
   Ngóh yíh-gìng yuh-beih-jó . . .

B . . . jīk-haih sàai chín.
   . . . máaih láahng-hei-gèi haih sìh-hauh la.
   . . . ngóh-deih dī láahng-tīn sāam la.
   . . . daahn-haih hóu yáuh-yuhng.

Exercise 2
How can you turn these two sentences into one?

Gó-syu yáuh chē.   Chē hóu gwai.

Answer: Gó-syu yáuh hóu gwai ge chē.

Try to do the same with the following sentences.

a Jèung Síu-jé haih Yaht-bún-yàhn. Kéuih hóu leng.
b Ngóh m̀h séung máaih bāt. Chàhn Sìn-sàang ge pou-táu maaih Méih-gwok bāt.
c Ngóh hóu séung sihk lùhng-hā. Hòh Táai jíng lùhng-hā.

Exercise 3

From the list of words and phrases 1–9 you need to select the right ones to complete sentences a–d. Obviously, that means you will have to reject five of them as unsuitable or less suitable.

1 sàn-sìn   2 Méih-gwok ge   3 Yìng-gwok ge
4 sáu-tàih   5 míhn-fai   6 yāt tou leng ge
7 gaai-siuh   8 hùhng-sīk   9 yùh-góng

a __ miht-fó-túng hóu yáuh-yuhng.
b Hái nī-syu yám séui haih __ ge: néih m̀h sái béi chín.
c __ béi-gìn-nèih m̀h pèhng.
d Yùh-gwó dī ngàuh-yuhk m̀h __, ngóh jauh m̀h séung sihk.

A creative test

Can you supply the cartoon caption in Cantonese? Mr Wong is saying: *Don't be angry. I told you the fire extinguisher was a practical object!*

09

娛樂同運動
yuh-lohk tùhng
wahn-duhng

fun and games

In this unit you will learn
- some words for leisure activities
- some words to do with going on holiday

▶ Dialogue 1

Mr Chan finds out how his colleague Miss Cheung spends her time off.

張小姐，昨日同前日都放假。你有冇去打波呀？
我唔中意打波嘅。
有冇去其他地方玩呢？
我都唔中意離開香港嘅，我只係中意睇電影啫。
我知道昨日喺大會堂有一齣好有名嘅電影。你有冇去睇呀？
有呀！真係好好睇呀。而且重好刺激添。
刺激！我唔覺得噃。你記唔記得嗰齣電影嘅內容呀？
對唔住，我一啲都唔記得嘞，因為我同男朋友一齊去睇嘅。

Mr Chan	Jèung Síu-jé, johk-yaht tùhng chìhn-yaht dōu fong-ga. Néih yáuh móuh heui dá-bō a?
Miss Cheung	Ngóh m̀h jùng-yi dá-bō ge.
Mr Chan	Yáuh móuh heui kèih-tà deih-fòng wáan nē?
Miss Cheung	Ngóh dōu m̀h jùng-yi lèih-hòi Hèung-góng ge, ngóh jí-haih jùng-yi tái-dihn-yíng jē.
Mr Chan	Ngóh jì-dou johk-yaht hái Daaih-wuih-tòhng yáuh yāt chēut hóu yáuh-méng ge dihn-yíng. Néih yáuh móuh heui tái a?
Miss Cheung	Yáuh a! Jàn-haih hóu hóu-tái a. Yìh-ché juhng hóu chi-gīk tìm.
Mr Chan	Chi-gīk! Ngóh m̀h gok-dāk bo. Néih gei m̀h gei-dāk gó chēut dihn-yíng ge noih-yùhng a?
Miss Cheung	Deui-m̀h-jyuh, ngóh yāt-dī dōu m̀h gei-dāk lak, yàn-waih ngóh tùhng nàahm-pàhng-yáuh yāt-chàih heui tái ge.

前日	**chìhn-yaht**	*the day before yesterday*
放假	**fong-ga**	*to be on holiday, take days off*
打波	**dá-bō**	*to play a ball game*
電影	**dihn-yíng**	*cinema film, movie*
齣	**chēut**	*classifier for films and stage plays*
離開	**lèih-hòi**	*to leave, depart from*
而且	**yìh-ché**	*moreover*
刺激	**chi-gīk**	*exciting*
覺得	**gok-dāk**	*to feel*
記得	**gei-dāk**	*to remember*
內容	**noih-yùhng**	*contents*
一啲	**yāt-dī**	*a little bit*
男	**nàahm**	*male*

Give the cartoon a caption

Supply the caption for the market researcher's question. He is asking: *Did you feel that this was an exciting film?*

Grammar

1 Plurality with *dōu* again

In Unit 8 you learned about the use of **dōu** to back up plurals. Did you spot the new example in the first speech of the dialogue?

2 *Fong-ga* to have a holiday

Fong-ga literally means *to release a day off*. It is one of quite a large group of expressions which are made up of a verb and an object and these expressions can all be split up if the sense allows. Here are a couple of examples:

Ngóh nī go sìng-kèih *fong* sàam yaht *ga*.	I have three days' holiday this week.
Kéuih *jouh* jáu-làuh ge sàang-yi.	He is in the restaurant business.

3 Playing ball

The word **bō** originally came from the English word *ball*. **Dá** means *to hit* and **dá-bō** is the regular way to say *to play a ball game*. The problem is: Which ball game? For a majority of people it means *soccer*, but if you happen to be a snooker fan then it means *snooker*, or for a basketball fan it means *basketball*, and then of course there is table tennis, rugby. . . . For the moment, **dá-bō** is all you need, but you might note the very logical difference between the following:

Ngóh heui dá-bō.	*I'm going off to play ball.*
Ngóh heui tái dá-bō.	*I'm going off to watch the game.*

4 Going to the movies

Tái-dihn-yíng means *to see a film* and **heui tái-dihn-yíng** is *to go to the movies.* You will notice that **tái-dihn-yíng** is also a verb plus object expression, so another example for 2 might be:

Wòhng Táai séung heui tái Méih-gwok dihn-yíng.	*Mrs Wong wants to go to see an American film.*

There is another expression **tái-hei**, which means *to see a play*, but far more people go to the cinema than go to the live theatre and it is now very common to hear someone say **ngóh heui tái-hei** when they mean *I'm going to the pictures.*

5 Overkill

You may or may not have realized that in Miss Cheung's third speech in the dialogue, she uses three different ways of saying *moreover* (**yìh-ché/juhng/tìm**). This may feel like overkill in English, but it is perfectly all right, indeed common, in Cantonese.

6 Taking shortcuts again

In Unit 3 you met the sentence **Néih fàan m̀h fàan-heui a?** and it was explained that this was a common shortened form of **Néih fàan-heui m̀h fàan-heui a?** You can do the same thing with any two-syllable verb and in the dialogue you will have noticed **néih gei m̀h gei-dāk** where Mr Chan might equally well correctly have said **néih gei-dāk m̀h gei-dāk**. Here is another example:

Néih jùng m̀h jùng-yi Lèuhn-dēun a?	Do you like London?

7 Not even a little bit!

Yāt-dī means *a little bit* and combined with **dōu** and the negatives **m̀h** or **móuh** it means *not even a little bit.* In a later unit you will find that this fits in with a regular grammar pattern, but for the time being you should just accept it as an idiomatic expression. Along the same lines you can also say **Ngóh-deih yāt-dī chín dōu móuh**. If you are like us you probably need to say it quite often!

ℹ️ It's electric!

In this unit we have met the word **dihn-yíng** for *movie film*. It literally means *electric shadows* and was an ingenious way of coping with the new concept when it first burst onto the Chinese scene. The word **dihn** *electric* was itself originally borrowed from the word meaning *lightning* and it has been put to very good use ever since. You met *electric heater* **dihn-nyúhn-lòuh** in Unit 8. Nowadays everyone is familiar with **dihn-chē** (*electric vehicle*) for *tram*, **dihn-wá** (*electric speech*) for *telephone*, **dihn-sih** (*electric vision*) for *television*, **dihn-nóuh** (*electric brain*) for *computer* and many more.

▶ Dialogue 2

Mr Wong and Mr Cheung discuss keeping fit, but Mr Wong is not sure that the theories apply to his wife!

張先生，你話時時運動可以減少身體裡便多餘嘅脂肪，對健康好好，係唔係呀？

係呀！我時時都行路，爬山，同打波。你睇我已經五十幾歲嘞，重係好健康，好似四十歲咁上下。

但係我覺得運動對我太太一啲用都冇。

一定有用嘅。只要你太太時時運動，身體裡便一定冇多餘脂肪嘅。

我太太成日講嘢，口部嘅肌肉有好多運動喇。點解佢重有一個好多脂肪嘅雙下巴呢？

Mr Wong	Jèung Sìn-sàang, néih wah sìh-sìh wahn-duhng hó-yíh gáam-síu sàn-tái léuih-bihn dò-yùh ge jì-fōng, deui gihn-hòng hóu hóu, haih m̀h haih a?
Mr Cheung	Haih a! Ngóh sìh-sìh dōu hàahng-louh, pàh-sàan, tùhng dá-bō. Néih tái ngóh yíh-gìng ńgh-sahp-géi seui lak, juhng haih hóu gihn-hòng, hóu-chíh sei-sahp seui gam-seuhng-há.
Mr Wong	Daahn-haih ngóh gok-dāk wahn-duhng deui ngóh taai-táai yāt-dī yuhng dōu móuh.
Mr Cheung	Yāt-dihng yáuh yuhng ge. Jí-yiu néih taai-táai sìh-sìh wahn-duhng, sàn-tái léuih-bihn yāt-dihng móuh dò-yùh jì-fōng ge.
Mr Wong	Ngóh taai-táai sèhng-yaht góng-yéh, háu-bouh ge gèi-yuhk yáuh hóu dò wahn-duhng lā. Dím-gáai kéuih juhng yáuh yāt go hóu dò jì-fōng ge sēung hah-pàh nē?

運動 **wahn-duhng**	physical exercise; to exercise
減少 **gáam-síu**	to reduce, cut down
身體 **sàn-tái**	the body
裡便 **léuih-bihn**	inside
多餘 **dò-yùh**	surplus
脂肪 **jì-fōng**	(body)fat
對 **deui**	with regard to, towards
健康 **gihn-hòng**	health
行路 **hàahng-louh**	to walk
爬山 **pàh-sàan**	to climb mountains, walk the hills
山 **sàan**	mountain, hill
幾 **géi**	several
歲 **seui**	year of age
咁上下 **gam-seuhng-há**	approximately, thereabouts
只要 **jí-yiu**	so long as, provided that
成日 **sèhng-yaht**	the whole day
講 **góng**	to speak, talk, say
口部 **háu-bouh**	the mouth
肌肉 **gèi-yuhk**	muscle
雙 **sēung**	double
下巴 **hah-pàh**	chin

Grammar

8 *Géi* several

You met **géi** in the expression **gei-dō?** *how many?* in Unit 5 and **géi-sí?** *when?* in Unit 8. On its own **géi** can also mean *how many?*, but it has the meaning *several* as well, and that could be quite confusing. Supposing someone were to say to you **géi go yàhn**, you couldn't be sure whether they were saying *how many people?* or *several people*. Obviously the context in which they said it would help a lot, but in practice if it were a question most people would add **a?** on the end and that would of course make it clear.

In its *several* meaning, **géi** gets involved with numbers quite a lot and you will see one example in Mr Cheung's first speech in the dialogue. Here are a few other examples:

| **yih-sahp-géi go yàhn** | *more than 20 people* (i.e. more than 20 but fewer than 30) |
| **sahp-géi seui ge Jùng-gwok-yàhn** | *a Chinese in his teens* |

géi-sahp go yàhn   *dozens of people* (several tens of people)
géi-sahp nìhn   *several decades*

9 *Seui* years of age

There are two points to be noted about **seui**. First, it is one of those few words which (like **yaht** and **nìhn**) do not need a classifier. Second, it is often used without a verb. Look again at the dialogue where Mr Cheung says **ngóh yíh-gìng ńgh-sahp-géi seui lak**: there is no verb in this expression at all, yet it is perfectly acceptable Cantonese. If you want to or feel the need to put in a verb, the most commonly used one is **haih** *to be*. Mr Cheung could have said: **ngóh yíh-gìng haih ńgh-sahp-géi seui lak** and it would have meant the same.

10 Approximately

Gam-seuhng-há literally means *thus up and down* and from that comes to mean *approximately*. It usually follows whatever it refers to, as it does where you met it in the dialogue: **sei-sahp seui gam-seuhng-há** *about 40 years old*.

11 *Sèhng* the whole

Sèhng- combines with classifiers to make *the whole*.... So **sèhng-go láih-baai** is *the whole week*, **sèhng-yaht** is *the whole day* or *all day long* and **sèhng-nìhn** is *the whole year long*. (Remember that **yaht** and **nìhn** are nouns which act like classifiers – see Unit 8.)

12 Another 'lonely verb'

In Mr Wong's last speech, he says **Ngóh taai-táai sèhng-yaht góng-yéh**. **Yéh** means *things*, as you learned in Unit 8, but here it is merely doing duty as the supplied object for the verb **góng** which is one of those which gets lonely on its own. **Yéh** is quite handy for this purpose: here are a few more examples of it with lonely verbs:

Néih séung ṁh séung sihk-yéh?   *Do you want to eat?*
Ngóh taai-táai heui-jó máaih-yéh.   *My wife's gone shopping.*
Kéuih sèhng-yaht dōu yám-yéh.   *He drinks all day long.*

ℹ️ A problem of age

When someone gives his age he (or of course she) will give it in **seui** not in **nìhn** – it would be wrong to use **nìhn** in this way. Well, that's easy enough. What is sometimes a problem is sorting out what **seui** means, because traditionally Chinese people were born one **seui** old and then added another **seui** to their age at each lunar new year. So a Chinese born on the last day of the lunar year would already be **léuhng seui** old the next day, while a western baby born on the same day would not even have got to 'one' yet! Worse than that, if the Chinese baby were born just before a short lunar year (the lunar years vary in length and can be much longer or much shorter than the solar year), he has time to become **sàam seui** before the poor little western baby has opened his score! If it is ever important to be certain, you can always ask whether the Chinese or the westerner (**sài-yàhn**) **seui** is meant.

Exercise 1

Here are some jumbled elements from which to make meaningful sentences.

a gam-seuhng-há/Hòh Sìn-sàang/ńgh-sahp seui/hóu-chíh
b hóu hóu/sìh-sìh/deui/wahn-duhng/gihn-hòng
c ngóh/dá-bō/jùng-yi/jē/pàh-sàan/jí-haih/tùhng yàuh-séui

Exercise 2

There is a relationship between each of the words in A and one of the words in B. Make the connections.

A	B
sung	yàuh-séui
fó-gei	sàn-sìn
daaih-gáam-ga	jáu-làuh
laahn	laahp-saap-túng
hói-tāan	dihn-nýuhn-lòuh
lohk-syut	baak-fo-gūng-sī

Exercise 3

You've made it to the big time: you are a professional interpreter. The fate of nations hangs in the balance, so make sure you translate the following remarks by the British Foreign Secretary accurately or there may be a diplomatic incident with the state of Cantonia!

FS	Good morning, Mr Wong.
You	_____a_____
Wong	**Jóu-sàhn**
FS	Would you like to have a beer?
You	_____b_____
Wong	**Ngóh m̀h jùng-yi yám bē-jáu**
FS	Oh, well how about coffee? Or tea?
You	_____c_____
Wong	**Ga-fē tùhng chàh dōu deui sàn-tái m̀h hóu. Ngóh jí-haih yám séui jē**
FS	I'm sorry, we have no water. The waiter told me that the water here is not good to drink. Why don't you have some beer?
You	_____d_____
Wong	**Néih sèhng-yaht wah ngóh yiu yám bē-jáu. Ngóh yíh-gìng wah néih jì ngóh m̀h jùng-yi yám. Néih jàn-haih hóu m̀h haak-hei**
FS	The beer is very good, it's British beer. Please drink a little.
You	_____e_____
Wong	**Nī go yàhn jeui m̀h haak-hei lak! Ngóh jáu lak!**
FS	Oh, he's gone!
You	_____f_____

Oh dear, it doesn't look as though that went too well, and you wasted your breath translating the last remark, didn't you? Still it wasn't your fault, was it? Or was it?

Exercise 4
Pair off the most likely objects in **B** with their verbs in **A**. Some of **B** of course won't do at all, but sometimes there may be more than one possible pairing.

A	tái	B	yéh
	jýu		dihn-yíng
	góng		tìhm-bán
	chàam-gwùn		chỳuh-fóng
	sihk		yī-sāng
			chi-fo
			chèuhng-gok
			Gim-kìuh Daaih-hohk

Exercise 5

Answer these questions in Cantonese so that all the answers have one word in common.

a Wòhng Sàang jouh māt-yéh a?
b Wòhng Táai jouh mī-yéh a?
c Wòhng Síu-jé jouh mī-yéh a?
d Jèung Sìn-sàang jouh mī-yéh a?
e Nī sàam go yàhn jouh māt-yéh a?

10

健康 gihn-hòng

health care for beginners

In this unit you will learn
- how to say how you are feeling
- how to consult a doctor

▶ Dialogue 1

Mr Wong phones his family doctor to make an appointment. The nurse answers:

喂！呢處係唔係張醫生嘅診所呀？
係呀！
我想睇醫生，唔該你幫我掛號喇。
你貴姓呀？有乜嘢唔舒服呀？
我係王一港先生，我覺得有啲頭痛，間中有啲頭暈，重有啲作嘔添。
你嘅病唔算好嚴重。我話你知，張醫生好忙......
噉，我幾時可以睇醫生呀？
我估你要等三四日先至可以見到張醫生嘴！
乜嘢話？三四日之後！我估嗰陣時我已經死咗啦？
唔緊要，嗰陣時請你太太打電話嚟話我知取消掛號就得喇！
唔得，唔得！我唔想等嘞，我而家就要去醫院嘞！

Mr Wong	Wái! Nī-syu haih m̀h haih Jèung Yī-sāng ge chán-só a?
Nurse	Haih a!
Mr Wong	Ngóh séung tái-yī-sāng, m̀h-gòi néih bòng ngóh gwa-houh lā.
Nurse	Néih gwai-sing a? Yáuh māt-yéh m̀h sỳu-fuhk a?
Mr Wong	Ngóh haih Wòhng Yāt Góng Sìn-sàang, ngóh gok-dāk yáuh-dī tàuh-tung, gaan-jūng yáuh-dī tàuh-wàhn, juhng yáuh-dī jok-áu tìm.
Nurse	Néih ge behng m̀h syun hóu yìhm-juhng. Ngóh wah néih jì, Jèung Yī-sāng hóu mòhng . . .
Mr Wong	Gám, ngóh géi-sí hó-yíh tái-yī-sāng a?
Nurse	Ngóh gú néih yiu dáng sàam-sei yaht sìn-ji hó-yíh gin-dóu Jèung Yī-sāng bo!
Mr Wong	Māt-yéh wá? Sàam-sei yaht jì-hauh! Ngóh gú gó-jahn-sìh ngóh yíh-gìng séi-jó la!
Nurse	M̀h gán-yiu. Gó-jahn-sìh chéng néih taai-táai dá go dihn-wá làih, wah ngóh jì chéui-sìu gwa-houh jauh dāk lā!
Mr Wong	M̀h dāk, m̀h dāk! Ngóh m̀h séung dáng lak, ngóh yìh-gā jauh yiu heui yì-yún lak!

喂！	**wái!**	hello! (especially on the phone)
診所	**chán-só**	clinic
幫	**bòng**	on behalf of, for the benefit of
掛號	**gwa-houh**	to register
舒服	**sỳu-fuhk**	comfortable
唔舒服	**m̀h sỳu-fuhk**	unwell, uncomfortable
有啲、有一啲		some, a little bit
yáuh-dī or **yáuh-yāt-dī**		
頭痛	**tàuh-tung**	headache
頭	**tàuh**	the head
痛	**tung**	pain, ache
間中	**gaan-jūng**	occasionally, periodically
頭暈	**tàuh-wàhn**	dizzy
作嘔	**jok-áu**	to retch, be about to vomit
嘔	**áu**	to vomit
病	**behng**	illness
嚴重	**yìhm-juhng**	serious, desperate
忙	**mòhng**	busy
先至	**sìn-ji**	only then
嗰陣時	**gó-jahn-sìh**	at that time
打電話	**dá-dihn-wá**	make a phone call
取消	**chéui-sìu**	to cancel
醫院	**yì-yún**	hospital

ℹ Chinese and western medicine

Chinese medicine (**Jùng-yì**) and western medicine (**sài-yì**) have very different traditions and practices. Each has begun to acknowledge and learn from the other in recent years and some practitioners now combine elements of both schools in their treatments. The contrast between Chinese (**Jùng**) and western (**sài**) is echoed in a number of expressions, perhaps most basically in **Jùng-gwok-yàhn** a Chinese and **sài-yàhn** a westerner. Another pair of terms which are more earthy and less formal are **Tòhng-yàhn** a Chinese and **gwái-lóu** a ghost fellow. This last term for a westerner is in very common use and is not really to be considered offensive, although the strictly politically correct would probably avoid it.

Grammar

1 *Bòng* on behalf of

You met the verb **bòng** *to help* in Unit 4. It can be used with other verbs to mean *on behalf of, for the benefit of, for*, but note that it always comes *in front of* the other verbs:

Ngóh bòng néih jíng sà-léut. *I'll make the salad for you.*
Kéuih bòng ngóh heui *She does the shopping for me.*
  máaih-yéh.

2 *Sỳu-fuhk* comfortable

Sỳu-fuhk nicely translates the English word *comfortable* and it follows naturally enough that **m̀h sỳu-fuhk** should mean *uncomfortable*. Indeed it does, but it is also very commonly used to mean *unwell, poorly, off colour* and, rather as in English, someone may tell you that they are *a bit off colour*, even if they are quite seriously ill.

3 *Yáuh-dī* a certain amount of

Yáuh-dī can be put in front of many other words to indicate *a certain quantity of, some*. Here are some useful examples:

yáuh-dī yàhn   *some people*
yáuh-dī m̀h sỳu-fuhk   *a bit off colour*
yáuh-dī m̀h séung heui   *a bit reluctant to go*

4 Approximate numbers

In the dialogue the nurse tells Mr Wong he will have to wait *three or four days* (**sàam-sei yaht**). You can make up approximate numbers like that whenever you want to. Here are a few chosen at random:

chāt-baat go yàhn   *seven or eight people*
Kéuih sahp-yih-sàam seui. *She's 12 or 13.*
sei-ńgh-sahp jek ngàuh   *40 or 50 head of cattle*

But beware! There is one combination you *cannot* use in this way: if you think about it **gáu-sahp** cannot mean *nine or ten* because it already means *ninety*. So some other way of saying it had to be found and Cantonese has come up with a real humdinger – **sahp-go-baat-go** (*ten or eight classifiers*). So *nine or ten days* is **sahp-yaht-baat-yaht** and *nine or ten pens* is **sahp-jì-baat-jì bāt**.

5 *Sìn-ji* only then

Sìn-ji is an adverb and obeys the usual rule for adverbs: it must come directly in front of a verb. It is best remembered as meaning *only then*, but you will find it very useful in coping with the English expression *not until*:

Kéuih tìng-yaht sìn-ji heui Yaht-bún.	*She's not going to Japan until tomorrow.* (lit: *She tomorrow only then is going to Japan.*)

6 *Dá* to hit

Although **dá** does literally mean *to hit* (**kéuih dá ngóh** *he hits me*), you will meet it used in many idiomatic ways as a general purpose verb. Here are a few:

dá-bō	*to play ball*
dá-léhng-tàai	*to tie a necktie*
dá-dihn-wá	*to make a phone call*
dá-syun	*to reckon on, to intend to*

A word of warning: don't try to invent idiomatic usages for yourself (by definition you cannot *invent* idioms).

▶ Dialogue 2

Mr Wong talks with his sick son, William.

威廉，你做乜嘢左搖右擺，跳高踎低呀？你唔舒服吖？

係呀！爸爸，我起身嗰陣時覺得個肚唔舒服。去完廁所之後，都重有啲痛，所以我就飲咗上個禮拜媽媽買返嚟嗰樽藥水嘞。

而家點呀？個肚重痛唔痛呀？

我啱啱飲咗藥水十分鐘啫，重未知。

噉，做乜嘢你要左搖右擺呢？

次次飲藥水之前，媽媽都要我搖勻啲藥水先然後至飲，但係頭先飲藥水嗰陣時，我唔記得搖勻，所以而家左搖右擺，希望可以補返數啦。

Mr Wong Wài-lìhm, néih jouh-māt-yéh jó-yìuh-yauh-báai, tiu-gòu-màu-dài a? Néih m̀h sỳu-fuhk àh?

William Haih a! Bàh-bā, ngóh héi-sàn gó-jahn-sìh gok-dāk go tóuh m̀h sỳu-fuhk. Heui-yùhn chi-só jì-hauh, dōu juhng yáuh-dī tung, só-yíh ngóh jauh yám-jó seuhng-go-láih-baai màh-mā máaih-fàan-làih gó jèun yeuhk-séui lak.

Mr Wong Yìh-gā dím a? Go tóuh juhng tung m̀h tung a?

William Ngóh ngāam-ngāam yám-jó yeuhk-séui sahp fàn jūng jē, juhng meih jì.

Mr Wong Gám, jouh māt-yéh néih yiu jó-yìuh-yauh-báai nē?

William Chi-chi yám yeuhk-séui jì-chìhn, màh-mā dōu yiu ngóh yìuh-wàhn dī yeuhk-séui sìn yìhn-hauh ji yám. Daahn-haih tàuh-sīn yám yeuhk-séui gó-jahn-sìh, ngóh m̀h gei-dāk yìuh-wàhn, só-yíh yìh-gā jó-yìuh-yauh-báai, hèi-mohng hó-yíh bóu-fàan-sou lā.

威廉 **Wài-lìhm**	a Cantonese version of *William*
左搖右擺 **jó-yìuh-yauh-báai**	*shaking from side to side*
跳高踎低 **tiu-gòu-mau-dài**	*jumping up and down*
起身 **héi-sàn**	*to get up in the morning*
肚 **tóuh**	*stomach*, abdomen
廁所 **chi-só**	*toilet*, lavatory
上個禮拜 **seuhng-go-láih-baai**	*last week*
樽 **jèun**	(classifier) *a bottle of* (**jēun** is *a bottle*, classified by **go**)
藥 **yeuhk**	*medicine*
藥水 **yeuhk-séui**	(liquid) *medicine*
點呀 = 點樣呀？ **dím a? = dím-yéung a?**	*how is it? how's things?*
啱啱 **ngāam-ngāam**	*a moment ago, a moment before*
一分鐘 **yāt fàn jūng**	*a minute*
未 **meih**	*not yet*
之前 **jì-chìhn**	*before*
搖勻 **yìuh-wàhn**	*to shake up*
然後 **yìhn-hauh**	*afterwards*, after that
頭先 **tàuh-sīn**	*just now*
希望 **hèi-mohng**	*hope*
補返數 **bóu-fàan-sou**	*to make up for*

True or false?

Answer **haih** or **m̀h haih** to the following questions. Now spell out a longer answer in Cantonese. So for the first question, you could reply **M̀h haih. Dī yeuhk-séui haih màh-mā seuhng-go-láih-baai máaih-fàan-làih ge.**

a Gó jèun yeuhk-séui haih màh-mā johk-yaht máaih-fàan-làih ge.

b Chi-chi yám yeuhk-séui jì-chìhn, màh-mā dōu yiu Wàih-lìhm yìuh-wàhn dī yeuhk-séui sìn.

c Wàih-lìhm gok-dāk go tàuh m̀h sỳu-fuhk.

d Wàih-lìhm yám-jó yeuhk-séui léuhng go jūng-tàuh lak.

Grammar

7 Four-character phrases

All the Chinese languages seem to thrive on using combinations of four characters as set phrases. Mr Wong uses two of them in his first speech in the dialogue. It can often be misleading to translate these phrases literally, so we generally will not do so, but in this case the second four-character phrase is made up of two common useful words which you might as well learn now:

tiu-gòu means *to jump high* (**gòu** = *high, tall*) and in athletics is *high jump*

màu-dài means *to squat down, to crouch down*

8 *Last week, this week* and *next week*

Seuhng-go-láih-baai means *last week*. **Seuhng** means *above*, so it literally means *the week above*. Logically enough, the word for *next week* is *the week below* **hah-go-láih-baai**. You now have the full set:

seuhng-go-láih-baai/sìng-kèih	*last week*
nī-go-láih-baai/sìng-kèih	*this week*
hah-go-láih-baai/sìng-kèih	*next week*

And you can go further:

seuhng-go-Láih-baai-sei	*Thursday of last week*
nī-go-Sìng-kèih-luhk	*Saturday of this week*
hah-go-Sìng-kèih-sàam	*Wednesday of next week*

As a matter of fact you have met **seuhng** and **hah** as a pair meaning *up and down, above and below* before (see Unit 9: the word **hah** in that case had changed its tone) and you will meet them again later.

9 'Time how long' again

In Unit 6 you met the idea of *time how long* and you will remember that such time expressions are placed *after* the verb. *An hour* was **yāt go jūng-tàuh** and now you can deal in minutes too: *a minute* is **yāt fàn jūng**. In the dialogue, William says **Ngóh ngāam-ngāam yám-jó yeuhk-séui sahp fàn jūng jē** – *I've only had the medicine down me for ten minutes.*

10 *Before* and *after*

In Unit 6 you met **jì-hau** meaning *after*. Its opposite is **jì-chìhn** *before*. Both words follow the phrases they refer to, although in English they come in front of them:

Ngóh sihk-faahn jì-chìhn, hóu séung heui máaih bē-jáu.	*Before I eat, I would very much like to go and buy some beer.*
Kéuih fàan ūk-kéi jì-hauh, néih yiu wah kéuih jì!	*After he returns home, you must tell him!*

Like **seuhng** and **hah** (see Point 8), **chìhn** and **hauh** are a regular pair. You learned **chìhn-yaht** *the day before yesterday* in Unit 9, so you can now make a good guess at what *the day after tomorrow* must be ... Of course, it is **hauh-yaht**!

chìhn-yaht	*the day before yesterday*
hauh-yaht	*the day after tomorrow*
chìhn-nìn	*the year before last*
hauh-nìn	*the year after next*

11 *Sìn-ji* again

You met **sìn-ji** earlier in this unit. It is actually made up of two separate words **sìn** *first* and **ji** *only then* and sometimes they can be separated, although the meaning remains the same. In William's last speech in the dialogue you will see a good example:

Màh-mā dōu yiu ngóh yìuh-wàhn dī yeuhk-séui sìn yìhn-hauh ji yám.

Translated literally this means *mummy requires me to shake the medicine first* (and) *afterwards only then to drink it*. It is a little more long-winded than **màh-mā dōu yiu ngóh yìuh-wàhn dī yeuhk-séui sìn-ji yám** and for that reason sounds slightly more emphatic, as though William is relaying the lesson his mother carefully taught him.

Exercise 1

Read these questions aloud in Cantonese, then give the answer clearly and as quickly as you can. Remember that most of the answer will be the same as the question, but there will of course be no **a**?!

a Yī-sāng hái bīn-douh tái behng-yàhn a?
b Wòhng Sìn-sàang haih bīn-gwok-yàhn a?
c Màh-mā hái bīn-syu máaih-yéh a?
d Hèung-góng-yàhn hái bīn-douh jyuh a?
e Wòhng Wài-lìhm ge bàh-bā sing māt-yéh a?

Exercise 2

Wòhng Sàang, Wòhng Táai dōu yáuh-behng. Dím-gáai yáuh-behng nē? Yàn-waih Wòhng Taai-táai yám ga-fē yám-jó taai dò lak, Wòhng Sìn-sàang yám bē-jáu yám-jó taai dò lak. Léuhng go yàhn dōu heui tái Léih Yī-sāng. Néih gú yī-sāng deui kéuih-deih dím-yéung góng nē?

Make up some lines for a very severe Dr Li, who tells them that they are both ruining their health and then tells each of them separately not to indulge their favourite vice any more.

Exercise 3

You are advanced enough now to translate a suitably modified nursery rhyme into Cantonese. A *pig* is **jȳu** and the word for *a son* (**jái**) can be tacked onto any noun to show that it is a little one, so **jȳu-jái** is a *piglet*, a *piggy*, or just a *small pig*; and **jȳu-yuhk** is *pork*. OK, off you go . . . and forgive us for the last line!

This little piggy went to market (went shopping).
This little piggy stayed at home.
This little piggy had roast beef (well, you can forget the 'roast' bit).
And this little piggy had none.
And this little piggy went 'Oh! Oh! Oh!' to see the doctor.

Exercise 4 The five stages of Chan

Describe in Cantonese what Mr Chan is doing in each of the five pictures. Begin the first answer with **Chàhn Sáang . . .** , and the others with **Kéuih. . . .**

時裝 sìh-jōng

the world of fashion

In this unit you will learn
- some more ways of passing judgements
- how to express likes and dislikes

▶ Dialogue 1

Miss Wong shops for a new hat and finally thinks she has found the very thing, but . . .

呢頂帽嘅設計唔錯，顏色又好可惜太貴嘞！
小姐，試吓呢頂喇：係最新運到㗎。
我唔中意佢嘅質地，我覺得太硬嘞，戴起嚟好唔舒服。
小姐，再試吓呢兩頂啦。佢哋都唔錯㗎。
係，佢哋都唔錯，但係呢兩頂帽都係舊年嘅款式，你哋重有冇啲新款嘅呀？……咦！呢頂唔錯嘞，又新款又大方。等我試吓！
真係好靚！
你都話靚吖！唔知要幾多錢呢？
九百五十蚊。
佢都冇價錢牌，你點知呀？
小姐，你戴住嘅帽正係我嘅！

Miss Wong	Nī déng móu ge chit-gai m̀h-cho, ngàahn-sīk yauh hóu – hó-sīk taai gwai lak!
Assistant	Síu-jé, si-háh nī déng lā: haih jeui sàn wahn-dou ga.
Miss Wong	Ngóh m̀h jùng-yi kéuih ge jāt-déi, ngóh gok-dāk taai ngaahng lak, daai-héi-làih hóu m̀h sỳu-fuhk.
Assistant	Síu-jé, joi si-háh nī léuhng déng lā. Kéuih-deih dōu m̀h-cho ga.
Miss Wong	Haih, kéuih-deih dōu m̀h-cho, daahn-haih nī léuhng déng móu dōu haih gauh-nín ge fún-sīk. Néih-deih juhng yáuh móuh dī sàn-fún ge a?.... Yí! Nī déng m̀h-cho bo, yauh sàn-fún yauh daaih-fōng. Dáng ngóh si-háh!
Customer	Jàn-haih hóu leng!
Miss Wong	Néih dōu wah leng àh! M̀h-jì yiu géi-dō chín nē?
Customer	Gáu-baak-ńgh-sahp mān.
Miss Wong	Kéuih dōu móuh ga-chìhn-páai, néih dím jì a?
Customer	Síu-jé, néih daai-jyuh ge móu jing-haih ngóh ge!

頂 **déng**	classifier for hats
帽 **móu**	*hat, cap*
設計 **chit-gai**	*design, to design*
唔錯 **m̀h-cho**	*not bad, pretty good*
可惜 **hó-sīk**	*it is a pity that, unfortunately*
試 **si**	*to try, to test*
運、運輸	*to transport*
wahn or **wahn-sỳu**	
運到、運輸到	*to arrive by transport*
wahn-dou or **wahn-sỳu-dou**	
硬 **ngaahng**	*hard, unyielding*
帶 **daai**	*to wear, put on* (accessories)
......起嚟 **-héi-làih**	verb ending, *when it comes to, once you start*
新款 **sàn-fún**	*new style*
大方 **daaih-fōng**	*tasteful, sophisticated*
唔知 **m̀h-jì**	*I wonder*
百 **baak**	*hundred*
價錢牌 **ga-chìhn-páai**	*price tag*
價錢 **ga-chìhn**	*price*
住 **-jyuh**	verb ending, *ongoing state of*
正係 **jing-haih**	*just happens to be*

Grammar

1 *-héi-làih* when it comes to it

-héi-làih is a verb ending which will mean *once you start . . .* or
when it comes to . . . depending on context. Here are two
examples which should give you the feel of its use:

| Góng-héi-làih, ngóh dōu sīk Hòh Sìn-sàang. | *Now you come to mention it, I know Mr Ho as well.* |
| Yuhng-héi-làih, néih jauh gok-dāk hóu sỳu-fuhk. | *When you start using it, you will find it very comfortable.* |

2 Higher numbers

Up to now you have been able to count as far as 99 only.
One hundred is **yāt-baak**, 200 is **yih-baak**, 999 is **gáu-baak-
gáu-sahp-gáu** and 1,000 is **yāt-chìn**; 2,000 is **yih-chìn**, 9,999
is **gáu-chìn-gáu-baak-gáu-sahp-gáu** . . . and then there is a
difference from English. The Chinese have a special word for

10,000, which is **maahn**, so 10,000 is **yāt-maahn**, 20,000 is **yih-maahn**, 90,000 is **gáu-maahn**, 100,000 is **sahp-maahn** and 1,000,000 is **yāt-baak-maahn**. In short, Cantonese goes up to 10,000 and then starts counting in units of 10,000, while English goes up to 1,000 and starts counting in units of 1,000 until it gets to units of a million. Here it is in table form:

1	**yāt**
10	**(yāt-)sahp**
100	**(yāt-)baak**
1,000	**(yāt-)chìn**
10,000	**(yāt-)maahn**
100,000	**(yāt-)sahp-maahn**
1,000,000	**(yāt-)baak-maahn**

Be warned that some overseas Chinese (notably those in Singapore and Britain) seem to be slipping into western ways, so that you might hear them saying **sahp-chìn** instead of **yāt-maahn** for 10,000. The natural progression in Cantonese, then, is from **sahp** to **baak** to **chìn** to **maahn**. If one or more of these categories is missed out, as for instance with the number 103 where there is no number in the **sahp** column, Cantonese indicates this by throwing in the word **lìhng** *zero*. So 103 is **yāt-baak-lìhng-sàam**. If more than one category is missed out it is still only necessary to put in one **lìhng**, so 10,003 is **yāt-maahn-lìhng-sàam**.

ℹ Round numbers

Chinese loves round numbers. *May you have a hundred sons and a thousand grandsons* was a very common good wish to someone at New Year or on other happy occasions. *The Old Hundred Surnames* is a regular way of talking of *The Chinese People*. *Thousand Mile Eyes* was the name of a protective god who acted as lookout for trouble. *The Ten Thousand Mile Long Wall* is what is known in English as the *Great Wall* of China. None of these numbers is meant to be taken literally: they all mean something like *lots of*.

3 The verb endings *-jyuh* and *-gán* compared

In Unit 4 **-gán** was introduced as a verb ending which showed continuing action. At first sight **-jyuh** does not seem so different, but they are not interchangeable. **-gán** tells us that activity is still going on, but **-jyuh** says that the activity has come to a halt and that we are left with a steady ongoing state. The following examples should make it clear:

Wòhng Táai daai-gán yāt déng hóu leng ge móu.	*Mrs Wong is putting on a beautiful hat.*
Wòhng Táai daai-jyuh yāt déng hóu leng ge móu.	*Mrs Wong is wearing a beautiful hat.*
Ngóh tái-gán kéuih.	*I'm taking a glance at her.*
Ngóh tái-jyuh kéuih.	*I'm keeping an eye on her.*

▶ Dialogue 2

Mrs Wong explains to her husband why she talked so much at a party.

太太，今晚我哋參加嘅時裝展覽酒會你一定覺得好開心嘞。

唔係嘛！啱啱相反，我覺得好唔開心。

唔係吖：我睇見你坐喺梳化椅處，唔停咁同張太太，何太太，王小姐佢哋傾偈。你重大聲讚王小姐件衫裙好靚，又讚張太太件外套嘅款式好新。

我係被迫要唔停噉大聲傾偈啫，實在我唔想㗎。

點解呢？

因為我著嗰套衫裙嘅顏色同花樣，同啲梳化椅嘅布料一樣。我坐喺梳化椅處，如果唔講嘢，有人經過以為有一張空椅，想坐落嚟添。

Mr Wong	Taai-táai, gàm-máahn ngóh-deih chàam-gà ge sìh-jōng jín-láahm jáu-wúi néih yāt-dihng gok-dāk hóu hòi-sām lak.
Mrs Wong	M̀h haih bo! Ngāam-ngāam sèung-fáan. Ngóh gok-dāk hóu m̀h hòi-sām.
Mr Wong	M̀h haih a: ngóh tái-gin néih chóh hái sō-fá-yí syu, m̀h tìhng gám tùhng Jèung Taai-táai, Hòh Taai-táai, Wòhng Síu-jé kéuih-deih kìng-gái. Néih juhng daaih-sèng jaan Wòhng Síu-jé gihn sāam-kwàhn hóu leng, yauh jaan Jèung Taai-táai gihn ngoih-tou ge fún-sīk hóu sàn.
Mrs Wong	Ngóh haih beih-bīk yiu m̀h tìhng gám daaih-sèng kìng-gái jē, saht-joih ngóh m̀h séung ga.
Mr Wong	Dím-gáai nē?
Mrs Wong	Yàn-waih ngóh jeuk gó tou sāam-kwàhn ge ngàahn-sīk tùhng fā-yéung, tùhng dī sō-fá-yí ge bou-líu yāt-yeuhng. Ngóh chóh hái sō-fá-yí syu, yùh-gwó m̀h góng-yéh, yáuh-yàhn gìng-gwo yíh-wàih yáuh yāt jèung hùng yí, séung chóh-lohk-làih tìm.

今晚 **gàm-máahn**	*tonight, this evening*	
參加 **chàam-gà**	*to take part in*	
時裝 **sìh-jōng**	*fashion*	
展覽 **jín-láahm**	*show, exhibition*	
酒會 **jáu-wúi**	*reception, cocktail party*	
相反 **sèung-fáan**	*on the contrary*	
梳化椅 **sō-fá-yí**	*sofa, easy chair*	
椅 **yí**	*chair*	
停 **tìhng**	*to stop*	
傾偈 **kìng-gái**	*to chat*	
大聲 **daaih-sèng**	*loud, in a loud voice*	
讚 **jaan**	*to praise*	
外套 **ngoih-tou**	*jacket*	
被迫 **beih-bīk**	*to be forced to, compelled to*	
實在 **saht-joih**	*in fact, really*	
著 **jeuk**	*to wear (clothes)*	
花樣 **fā-yéung**	*pattern*	
布料 **bou-líu**	*material, fabric*	
一樣 **yāt-yeuhng**	*the same*	
有人 **yáuh-yàhn**	*somebody*	
經過 **gìng-gwo**	*to pass by*	
以為 **yíh-wàih**	*to think, to assume, to regard as*	
張 **jèung**	*classifier for flat things (paper, chairs, tables, sheets etc.)*	
空 **hùng**	*empty*	
...... 落嚟 **-lohk-làih**	*verb ending: downwards*	

The Chinese character for **tìhng** *to stop*.

Questions

1 Have you understood? What does the cartoon caption mean?

Johk-yaht ngóh yíh-wàih nī jèung yí hóu sỳu-fuhk, daahn-haih yìh-gā.....!

2 Quickly decide which of the alternatives in brackets to strike out, so that you leave a correct statement.

a Wòhng Sìn-sàang tùhng Wòhng Taai-táai chàam-gà ge haih (jouh-sàang-yi/dihn-yíng/sìh-jōng) jáu-wúi.

b Wòhng Táai wah, kéuih (m̀h hòi-sàm/hòu hòi-sàm).

c Wòhng Táai jaan Jèung Táai (sàn-tái hóu hóu/hóu sīk jýu-sung/hóu sīk yàuh-séui/gihn ngoih-tou hóu leng).

d Wòhng Taai-táai tou sàam-kwàhn ge ngàahn-sīk, fā-yéung tùhng (sō-fá-yí/laahp-saap-túng/dihn-nýuhn-lòuh) yāt-yeuhng.

Grammar

4 Late in the day

Máahn means *evening*, *late in the day* (not *late for an appointment*). *This evening* or *tonight* is **gàm-máahn** and from there you can build another little set of terms:

gàm-máahn	*this evening, tonight*
johk-máahn	*yesterday evening, last night*
tìng-máahn	*tomorrow evening, tomorrow night*
chìhn-máahn	*the evening of the day before yesterday*
hauh-máahn	*the evening of the day after tomorrow*

5 *Ngāam-ngāam* again

In Unit 10 we met **ngāam-ngāam** meaning *a moment ago*. It has a second meaning of *exactly*, *precisely*. In the dialogue Mrs Wong says **ngāam-ngāam sèung-fáan** – *its exactly to the contrary* – and you might note these other examples:

ngāam-ngāam yāt go jūng-tàuh	*exactly one hour*
ngāam-ngāam hóu	*exactly right*

6 *Hái-syu/hái-douh* at the indicated place

You met **nī-syu/nī-douh** *here*, **gó-syu/gó-douh** *there* and **bīn-syu/bīn-douh** *where?* in Units 3 and 5. **Hái-syu** and **hái-douh** (lit: *at the place*) are used rather loosely to mean either *here* or *there* and really seem to mean *at the place we both know about.* So you might say **Néih hái-syu jouh māt-yéh a?** to someone on the phone and it would mean *What are you doing there?* or you might say it to someone who is in the same room as you and it would mean *What are you doing here?*

Hái-syu or **hái-douh** can be split to surround a noun and then they indicate a rather vague relationship with the noun, like *in/on/at/in the general vicinity of.* In the dialogue Mr Wong says **ngóh tái-gin néih chóh hái sō-fá-yí syu** *I saw you sitting there on the sofa* and *on* seems the most likely place for Mrs Wong to be; but if you were to ask someone where they had thoughtlessly left their keys, they might reply **hái chē syu** and you would not be sure whether the keys were in, on top of, under or just somewhere on the ground near the car. It can be quite useful to be able to be so vague, so **hái-syu** and **hái-douh** are worth remembering.

7 Three verbs for *to wear*

You have now met three verbs which can all be translated as *to wear* in English:

jeuk is *to wear clothing*, that is shirts, jackets, trousers, underclothes, shoes and socks

daai is *to wear accessories*, that is hats, spectacles, watches, rings, jewellery, gloves, etc.

dá is the least common and means *to wear something which has to be tied on* like a necktie or headscarf

8 *Yíh-wàih* to think wrongly

Yíh-wàih means *to assume* or *to think, to consider*, but it is probably most often used when the speaker already knows that what he/she thought was actually wrong. In the dialogue Mrs Wong says that she was was talking so much so that no one would fail to know she was there and *think (wrongly) that there was a vacant chair*. Here are some more examples:

Ngóh yíh-wàih kéuih haih
   Yaht-bún-yàhn.

I thought she was Japanese (but now I know that she is actually Korean).

Kéuih yíh-wàih gàm-yaht
   haih Láih-baai-yaht

He thought that today was Sunday (but of course it's actually Saturday).

And you might like to learn a very slangy expression: **Néih yíh-wàih lā!**, which corresponds to the English *You reckon!*, *That's what you think!*, *Think again, pal!*

9 Verb ending *-lohk-làih*

You met **lohk** in **lohk síu-bā** *to alight from the mini-bus* and in **lohk-syut** *to snow*. The basic meaning of **lohk** is *to come down, to fall down, to go down*. As a verb ending *-lohk-làih* shows that the action of the verb is happening in a downward direction:

chóh-lohk-làih
yàuh fèi-gèi gó-syu tái-lohk-làih

come sitting down
looking down from the aircraft

Exercise 1

Try your number skills by putting these figures into Cantonese. You probably know that one of the hardest things to do is to count naturally in a second language, so the more practice you do the better.

a *16 young ladies*
b *200 sheets of paper*
c *$5,600*
d *1,000,000 Chinese people*
e *12,750*
f *8,034*
g *11 hours*
h *2 lobsters*

Exercise 2

Warning: only do this if you are not driving! When you are in a car or a bus, watch the vehicles that come towards you and try to read off their number plates in Cantonese before they have gone by. Until you get better at it, you can do it by saying **sàam-baat-chāt** rather than the full version **sàam-baak-baat-sahp-chāt**. It's quite an addictive little game, you'll find, but *very* good for making you slick with numbers.

Exercise 3

Give the opposites of the words on the left by filling in the blanks on the right.

a sàn-fún   __ fún
b taai gwai   taai __
c máaih ūk   __ ūk
d jì-hauh   jì __
e láahng   __
f dùng-bāk   __

Exercise 4

Here's a brain-teaser for you. Miss Ho's cryptic answer to my question does contain enough information to reveal all the facts, but you will have to work hard to find them out!

Hah-go-sìng-kèih Hòh Sìn-sàang, Hòh Taai-táai, Hòh Síu-jé dōu wúih fong yāt yaht ga. Hó-sīk kéuih-deih m̀h haih yāt-chàih fong: yāt go fong Láih-baai-yāt, yāt go fong Láih-baai-yih, yāt go fong Láih-baai-sàam. Kéuih-deih fong-ga séung jouh māt-yéh nē? Yāt go séung heui tái-hei, yāt go séung heui pàh-sàan, yāt go séung heui jáu-làuh sihk lùhng-hā. Ngóh mahn Hòh Síu-jé bīn-go séung hái bīn yāt yaht heui bīn-douh a? Kéuih wah:

'Bàh-bā séung heui pàh-sàan. Ngóh Láih-baai-yih fong-ga. Yáuh yàhn séung Láih-baai-yāt heui sihk lùhng-hā.'

Nàh! Néih hó m̀h hó-yíh wah ngóh jì nī sàam go yàhn léuih-bihn bīn-go séung heui tái-hei? Bīn-go séung heui sihk lùhng-hā? Sìng-kèih-sàam fong-ga haih bīn-go a?

教育
gaau-yuhk
education for life

In this unit you will learn
- some of the terms you will need to carry on a conversation on education
- colours
- how to make comparisons
- how to describe the position of one thing relative to another

▶ Dialogue 1

Parents chat about the hardships of education.

我覺得香港學生讀書真係辛苦嘞。

係呀！我都同意。佢哋每日都要讀中文、英文、數學、地理、歷史同
科學。而且平均每個禮拜都有兩三科要測驗。

重有呀！佢哋嘅課本又重又多，每日要帶返學校嘅課本同練習簿就唔
會少過十磅重。

我個仔今年只係十歲之嘛，喺小學讀書，但係佢晚晚都要溫習差唔多
四個鐘頭先至可以做完啲功課。我唔明白啲先生上堂嘅時候點樣
教書嘅。

我話喺中學教書重麻煩呀！又要教佢哋又要管佢哋，尤其是管佢哋，
因為而家啲後生仔個個都唔中意被人管嘅喇。

好彩我哋個個都唔係教書生先啫。如果唔係，我哋都冇時間一齊喺呢
處傾偈啦。

Mr Wong	Ngóh gok-dāk Hèung-góng hohk-sāang duhk-sýu jàn-haih sàn-fú lak.
Mr Cheung	Haih a! Ngóh dōu tùhng-yi. Kéuih-deih múih yaht dōu yiu duhk Jùng-màhn, Yìng-màhn, Sou-hohk, Deih-léih, Lihk-sí tùhng Fō-hohk. Yìh-ché pìhng-gwàn múih go láih-baai dōu yáuh léuhng-sàam fō yiu chāak-yihm.
Mr Wong	Juhng yáuh a! Kéuih-deih ge fo-bún yauh chúhng yauh dò, múih yaht yiu daai-fàan hohk-haauh ge fo-bún tùhng lihn-jaahp-bóu jauh m̀h wúih síu-gwo sahp bohng chúhng.
Mrs Lee	Ngóh go jái gàm-nín jí-haih sahp seui jī-ma, hái síu-hohk duhk-sỳu, daahn-haih kéuih máahn-máahn dōu yiu wàn-jaahp chà-m̀h-dō sei go jūng-tàuh sìn-ji hó-yíh jouh-yùhn dī gùng-fo. Ngóh m̀h mìhng-baahk dī sìn-sàang séuhng-tòhng ge sìh-hauh dím-yéung gaau-sỳu ge.
Mr Wong	Ngóh wah hái jùng-hohk gaau-sỳu juhng màah-fàahn a! Yauh yiu gaau kéuih-deih yauh yiu gwún kéuih-deih, yàuh-kèih-sih gwún kéuih-deih, yàn-waih yìh-gā dī hauh-sāang-jái go-go dōu m̀h jùng-yi beih yàhn gwún ge la.
Mr Cheung	Hóu-chói ngóh-deih go-go dōu m̀h haih gaau-sỳu sìn-sàang jē. Yùh-gwó-m̀h-haih, ngóh-deih dōu móuh sìh-gaan yāt-chàih hái nī-syu kìng-gái la.

學生 **hohk-sāang**	*student, pupil*
讀 **duhk**	*to read*
書 **sỳu**	*a book*
讀書 **duhk-sỳu**	*to study*
辛苦 **sàn-fú**	*hard, distressing*
每 **múih**	*each, every*
中文 **Jùng-màhn**	*Chinese language*
英文 **Yìng-màhn**	*English language*
數學 **sou-hohk**	*mathematics*
地理 **deih-léih**	*geography*
歷史 **lihk-sí**	*history*
科學 **fō-hohk**	*science*
平均 **pìhng-gwàn**	*average, on average*
科 **fō**	*a subject, a discipline*
測驗 **chāak-yihm**	*to test; evaluation*
課本 **fo-bún**	*textbook*
重 **chúhng**	*heavy*
學校 **hohk-haauh**	*school*
練習簿 **lihn-jaahp-bóu**	*exercise book*
過 **gwo**	*than*
磅 **bohng**	*pound* (weight)
之嘛 **jī-ma**	*particle* (only)
小學 **síu-hohk**	*primary school*
溫習 **wan-jaahp**	*to revise lessons*
差唔多 **chà-m̀h-dō**	*almost*
功課 **gùng-fo**	*homework*
明白 **mìhng-baahk**	*to understand, be clear about*
先生 **sìn-sàang**	*teacher*
上堂 **séuhng-tòhng**	*to attend class*
中學 **jùng-hohk**	*secondary school*
教書 **gaau-sỳu**	*to teach*
麻煩 **màah-fàahn**	trouble, troublesome
管 **gwún**	to control, be in charge of
尤其是 **yàuh-kèih-sih**	especially
後生仔 **hauh-sāang-jái**	youngsters
後生 **hauh-sāang**	young
被 **beih**	by; to endure, suffer
好彩 **hóu-chói**	lucky, fortunately
如果唔係（呢） **yùh-gwó-m̀h-haih(-nē)**	otherwise

Whoops! Something is wrong!

Each of the following sentences contains an error either in the sense or in the grammar. Can you spot the deliberate mistakes?

a Gó dī hohk-sāang jek-jek dōu sīk góng Yìng-màhn.
b Ngóh m̀h sīk góng Jùng-màhn.
c Wòhng Táai go jái m̀h yáuh lihk-sí fo-bún.
d Gó léuhng Méih-gwok síu-jé m̀h jùng-yi jeuk hùhng-sīk ge sāam-kwàhn.
e Wòhng Sìn-sàang ge bàh-bā gàm-nín jí-haih baat seui jī-ma.

Grammar

1 *Múih* each, every

There are two things to remember about using **múih**. First, it requires the use of a classifier:

múih go yàhn	*each person, everybody*
múih jì bāt	*each pen*
múih yaht	*every day* (refer back to Unit 8 if this one puzzles you)

Second, because **múih** involves *wholeness* and *inclusiveness* it is almost always backed up by **dōu** placed before the verb:

Múih gihn sāam-kwàhn dōu yáuh síu-síu laahn-jó. *Each one of the dresses is slightly damaged.*

2 Simple comparisons with *gwo*

The same word **gwo** which you met in Unit 6 (meaning *to go past, to go by*) is used to make simple comparisons (*X is —er than* Y):

Ngóh ge chē daaih-gwo néih ge chē. *My car is bigger than yours.*

Yìng-gwok chē gwai m̀h gwai-gwo Yaht-bún chē a? *Are British cars more expensive than Japanese cars?*

The pattern, then, is **X adjective gwo Y** and you can probably see how logically it works – *X is adjective surpassing* Y:

Ngóh gòu-gwo kéuih. (*I am tall surpassing him*) *I am taller than he is.*

In the dialogue Mr Wong talks about the heavy load of books and exercise books carried by students and he says **m̀h wúih síu-gwo sahp bohng chúhng** *they cannot be less than ten pounds in weight.*

3 Classifiers as possessives

You learned in Unit 2 that that useful word **ge** shows possession, so that *my pen* is **ngóh ge bāt**. There is a minor snag with this: as you know, nouns can be either singular or plural without changing their form and so **ngóh ge bāt** can mean either *my pen* or *my pens*. In many cases it doesn't matter that this is unclear or else the context makes it obvious whether you mean *pen* or *pens*. If you wish to be more precise, however, you can be and it is the classifier which gives you the power:

ngóh ge bāt	*my pen* or *my pens*
ngóh jì bāt	*my pen* (singular only)
ngóh dī bāt	*my pens* (plural only)

In the dialogue Mrs Lee talks about **ngóh go jái** and that tells you that she only has one son or at least that she is only talking about one son in this instance.

4 *Beih* the passive construction

Beih literally means *to suffer*, *to endure*, but you will seldom need to worry about that. You will usually only meet it used like the English word *by* in the passive construction. The following two examples should suffice to show how it works:

Hòh Sìn-sàang chéng Wòhng Sìn-sàang heui sihk-faahn.
Wòhng Sìn-sàang beih Hòh Sìn-sàang chéng heui sihk-faahn.

The first sentence is active (*Mr Ho invites Mr Wong out for a meal*) and the second is passive (*Mr Wong is invited out for a meal by Mr Ho*). Cantonese does not use this passive construction very often, but you need to be aware that it exists so that you will not be taken by surprise when you meet it.

5 Recap on classifiers

You have now met all the major uses of classifiers, so perhaps this little checklist will be helpful to you:

1 When you specify a noun with **nī, gó, bīn, múih, géi, sèhng-** (*this, that, which?, each, how many?/several, the whole*) you should use the correct classifer between the specifier and the noun:

nī go yàhn	gó tìuh léhng-tàai
bīn jek lùhng-hā?	múih gihn sāam-kwàhn
géi jì bāt	sèhng-go láih-baai

2   When you count nouns you should use the correct classifier between the specifier and the noun:

yāt go Yaht-bún-yàhn   **léuhng chàan faahn**
sàam gàan ūk   **yih-sahp-sei jì bāt**

3   The classifier for uncountable things (like *water*) is **dī**. **Dī** also is the plural classifier, that is the classifier used when a noun is plural but uncounted:

gó dī séui   **nī dī sung**
nī dī Yìng-gwok-yàhn   **bīn dī Jùng-màhn sỳu?**

4   The classifier can be used at the beginning of a sentence where English uses the definite article:

Dī sung hóu hóu-sihk   **Gihn sāam leng m̀h leng a?**

5   Doubling the classifier and adding **dōu** before the verb gives the meaning *every one of*, *each one of*:

Gihn-gihn sāam-kwàhn dōu hóu leng.
Gàan-gàan ūk léuih-bihn dōu móuh yàhn.

6   The correct classifier or the plural classifier **di** can be used to indicate possession:

kéuih gàan ūk
Wòhng Sìn-sàang dī chē

7   A very few words seem to act as noun and classifier combined. Of these you have already met the most common – **nìhn, yaht** and **seui**:

sàam nìhn   **léuhng yaht**   **sahp seui**

8   Finally, here are three new classifiers which you will find useful:

bouh   classifier for books (interchangeable with **bún**)
bún   classifier for books (interchangeable with **bouh**)
ga   classifier for vehicles, aircraft and machinery

ℹ️ Large, medium and small

Have you noticed how neatly Cantonese copes with the different levels of the school education system? Primary or junior school is **síu-hohk** *small learning*; middle or secondary school is **jùng-hohk** *middle learning*; and university is **daaih-hohk** *large learning*. You will find the same set (**daaih, jùng, síu**) on Chinese restaurant menus, showing that you can have different size dishes of the same order and, of course, the menu will also show different prices for the three sizes. Quite often off-the-peg clothes are marked in the same way.

▶ Dialogue 2

An encounter with a traffic policeman shows that education does not always succeed in getting the main point across.

香港政府教育香港市民真係失敗嘞。
你講邊方面嘅教育呢？
好多方面喇，尤其是一般嘅公共秩序方面。
咦！前便有個警察好似要檢控個汽車司機嘅！我哋去睇吓喇。
先生，你睇唔睇到嗰盞交通燈呀？
睇到丫！
你睇唔睇到係紅燈呀？
睇到丫！
噉，點解你重要衝紅燈呢？
因為我睇唔到你！
張先生，你睇吓，呢啲就係香港人對一般公共秩序嘅教育嘞！
每個社會都有一啲壞份子，唔好話個個人都一樣，香港嘅教育都有好嘅方面嘅。

Mr Wong	Hèung-góng jing-fú gaau-yuhk Hèung-góng síh-màhn jàn-haih sāt-baaih lak.
Mr Cheung	Néih góng bīn fòng-mihn ge gaau-yuhk nē?
Mr Wong	Hóu dò fòng-mihn lā, yàuh-kèih-sih yāt-bùn ge gùng-guhng diht-jeuih fòng-mihn.
Mr Cheung	Yí! Chìhn-bihn yáuh go gíng-chaat hóu-chíh yiu gím-hung go hei-chè sī-gēi bo! Ngóh-deih heui tái-háh lā.
Policeman	Sìn-sàang, néih tái m̀h tái-dóu gó jáan gàau-tùng-dāng a?
Driver	Tái-dóu ā!
Policeman	Néih tái m̀h tái-dóu haih hùhng-dāng a?
Driver	Tái-dóu ā!
Policeman	Gám, dím-gáai néih juhng yiu chùng hùhng-dāng nē?
Driver	Yàn-waih ngóh tái-m̀h-dóu néih!
Mr Wong	Jèung Sìn-sàang, néih tái-háh, nī dī jauh haih Hèung-góng-yàhn deui yāt-bùn gung-guhng diht-jeuih ge gaau-yuhk lak!
Mr Cheung	Múih go séh-wúi dōu yáuh-yāt-dī waaih-fahn-jí, m̀h-hóu wah go-go yàhn dōu yāt-yeuhng. Hèung-góng ge gaau-yuhk dōu yáuh hóu ge fòng-mihn ge.

政府 **jing-fú**	government
教育 **gaau-yuhk**	to educate; education
市民 **síh-màhn**	citizen
失敗 **sāt-baaih**	a loss, a failure
方面 **fòng-mihn**	aspect
一般 **yāt-bùn**	general, common, the general run of
公共 **gùng-guhng**	public
秩序 **diht-jeuih**	order
前便 **chìhn-bihn**	in front; the front side
警察 **gíng-chaat**	policeman
檢控 **gím-hung**	accuse
汽車 **hei-chè**	vehicle, car
司機 **sī-gēi**	driver
盞 **jáan**	classifier for lamps and lights
交通燈 **gàau-tùng-dāng**	traffic light
交通 **gàau-tùng**	traffic, communications
燈 **dāng**	a light
衝 **chùng**	to rush, dash against, jump
社會 **séh-wúi**	society
壞 **waaih**	bad
份子 **fahn-jí**	element, member

Grammar

6 Colours

Hùhng-dāng is *a red light*. The other important traffic light colour is **luhk** *green* and **luhk-dāng** is *a green light*. It would be useful now to introduce all the major colours. You should note that they work with **-sīk ge** in the same way as does **hùhng** (see Unit 5).

baahk-sīk	*white*	**hùhng-sīk**	*red*
cháang-sīk	*orange*	**jí-sīk**	*purple*
fūi-sīk	*grey*	**làahm-sīk**	*blue*
ga-fē-sīk	*brown*	**luhk-sīk**	*green*
gām-sīk	*gold*	**ngàhn-sīk**	*silver*
hāak-sīk or **hāk-sīk**	*black*	**wòhng-sīk**	*yellow*

ℹ Colour symbolism in Chinese culture

The most dominant colour in Chinese culture is red. It stands for happiness and good luck. Brides traditionally have dressed in red and wept into red handkerchiefs, their grooms wear red sashes, and the house where they set up home is decorated with auspicious sayings written on red paper. White is the colour for funerals (although most people wear a flash of something red about them in order to offset the ill luck which surrounds death and burial). Yellow was the Imperial colour, and the roofs of the Forbidden City in Beijing are still covered with yellow tiles: yellow also stands for China, probably because it is the colour of the loess soil which covers the northern homeland of the Chinese, the same soil which is carried along by the Yellow River and deposited in the Yellow Sea. You will have noticed that the word for brown is *coffee colour*, clearly a comparatively recent import. In the traditional colour scheme, red ran into yellow uninterrupted by brown and browns were classified either as **hùhng** or **wòhng**. What English calls a brown cow, Cantonese calls a **wòhng-ngàuh** and dark tan shoes are deemed to be **hùhng-sīk**.

7 Telling your whereabouts

In the dialogue you met the word **chìhn-bihn** *in front, in front of, the front side*. You had better now meet its friends:

chìhn-bihn	*in front, in front of, the front side*
hauh-bihn	*the back, behind, the rear side*
seuhng-bihn	*the top, on top of, above, the top side*
hah-bihn	*the underneath, under, beneath, the underside*
jó-(sáu-)bihn	*on the left, the left(-hand) side*
yauh-(sáu-)bihn	*on the right, the right(-hand) side*
léuih-bihn or yahp-bihn	*inside, in, the inside*
ngoih-bihn or chēut-bihn	*outside, out, the outside*
dùng-bihn	*the east side*
nàahm-bihn	*the south side*
sài-bihn	*the west side*
bāk-bihn	*the north side*
deui-mihn	*opposite, the opposite side*

Note that **deui-mihn** is exceptional in that -**bihn** gives place to -**mihn**. All these whereabouts words combine happily with **hái** (*at, in, on, to be at, to be in, to be on*):

Kéuih *hái* léuih-bihn.	*She is inside.*
Gàan ūk *hái* fèi-gèi-chèuhng nàahm-bihn.	*The house is on the south side of the airport.*
Bouh sỳu *hái* sō-fá-yíh seuhng-bihn.	*The book is on the sofa.*
Wòhng Síu-jé *hái* néih hauh-bihn.	*Miss Wong is behind you.*
Hái ūk jó-bihn yáuh chē-fòhng.	*There is a garage on the left of the house.*
Chóh *hái* gó gàan jáu-làuh *chēut*-bihn yáuh léuhng go waaih-fahn-jí.	*There are two bad lots sitting outside that restaurant.*

Notice that in the last two examples the verb **yáuh** *to have* is used to mean *there is* or *there are*. If you have learned French, you will find a similarity with the expression **il y a** (*there is, there are*) which also uses the verb *to have*.

Another whereabouts word is **jùng-gāan** *in the middle of, in between*. When it means *in the middle of* it acts just like the other words:

Kéuih chóh *hái* fà-yún jùng-gāan.	*She is sitting in the middle of the garden.*

But when it means *in between* it has a pattern all to itself (**hái X Y jùng-gāan** or **hái X tùhng Y jùng-gāan**):

Kéuih chóh *hái* Wòhng Sàang (tùhng) Chàhn Táai jùng-gāan.	*She is sitting between Mr Wong and Mrs Chan.*

Exercise 1

Go back and read the first dialogue of this unit once more. Then without looking at it again try to choose from the brackets the words which will complete the following sentences correctly.

a Wòhng Sìn-sàang wah dī hohk-sāang ge fo-bún (yauh gwai yauh leng/yauh pèhng yauh sàn/yauh chúhng yauh dò).

b Léih Taai-táai go jái máahn-máahn dōu yiu wàn-jaahp (sei go jūng-tàuh/sàam go jūng-tàuh/yāt go jūng-tàuh).

c Wòhng Sìn-sàang wah gaau (síu-hohk/jùng-hohk/daaih-hohk) juhng màah-fàahn.

d Jèung Sàang wah hóu-chói kéuih-deih m̀h haih (gíng-chaat/sī-gēi/gaau-sỳu sìn-sàang/jáu-làuh fó-gei).

Exercise 2

Imagine you are a worried parent trying to place your son in a Hong Kong school. You have an interview with the headmaster tomorrow and are preparing some questions to ask him, but you are nervous that your newly acquired language will let you down, so you had better write out the questions in Cantonese on a slip of paper in case you get stuck. Go ahead and translate them now:

a Does my son need to study Chinese?
b How many hours of homework must he do each evening?
c My son has studied at junior school in London for five years. British pupils do not go to secondary school until they are 11 years old. Is it the same in Hong Kong?
d How much a year does it cost to study in your school?
e Does the pupil need to buy textbooks and exercise books?

Exercise 3

Here are the answers which we happen to know the headmaster will give to your questions, but he is so bored with hearing the same thing from every parent who sees him that he deliberately gives the answers in the wrong order. You will have to try to match the lettered answers with the numbered questions before you know what is what, but our advice is to try another school for your son!

i Yiu. Hóu gwai tìm!
ii Yiu. Kéuih yāt go sìng-kèih yiu hohk sàam-sahp go jūng-tàuh.
iii Hèung-góng ge gaau-yuhk tùhng Yìng-gwok ge chà-m̀h-dō lak.
iv M̀h-sái hóu dò jē. Ǹgh-luhk go jūng-tàuh jē.
v M̀h-sái hóu dò jē. Yāt nìhn sei-baak-maahn māan jē.

Exercise 4

Describe the scene you see here by answering the questions in Cantonese.

a Hái ūk ngoih-bihn yáuh māt-yéh a?
b Wòhng Sàang hái Wòhng Táai bīn-bihn a?
c Bouh sỳu hái bīn-douh a?
d Néih gú Wòhng Sàang Wòhng Táai jouh-yùhn māt-yéh fàan-làih a?
e Hái Wòhng Táai chìhn-bihn yáuh māt-yéh a?
f Néih gei m̀h gei-dāk gó go miht-fó-túng haih bīn-go máaih ga?
g Wòhng Sàang Wòhng Táai go jái hái bīn-douh a?
h Néih wah Wòhng Táai hòi m̀h hòi-sām a?

13

投機
tàuh-gēi
speculation

In this unit you will learn
- how to speculate in Cantonese!

▶ Dialogue 1

Mr Cheung lets slip that he is not entirely immune from Hong Kong's passion for gambling.

昨日電台嘅新聞廣播話，舊年香港市民投注喺賽馬嘅錢有一百三十二
　億元，入馬場嘅人數係三百二十萬人！

嘩！香港人真係有錢嘞。張先生，你中唔中意賭馬㗎。

唔中意。賭馬、賭狗、賭啤牌、賭股票……樣樣我都唔中意。

你真係乖嘞！喺香港好似你一樣嘅人而家真係好少嘞。

有人話，香港咁繁榮係同香港人中意賭錢有關係嘅嘛！你話啱唔啱
　呀？

我話冇關係，但係賭錢同罪案嘅增加就有關係嘞。

對唔住，王先生，我而家夠鐘要去參加一個慈善籌款抽獎會。

抽獎會吖！獎品豐唔豐富㗎？

頭獎係一間屋，二獎係一架車。

咦！噉算唔算係賭錢呢？

Mr Cheung	Johk-yaht dihn-tòih ge sàn-màhn gwóng-bo wah, gauh-nín Hèung-góng síh-màhn tàuh-jyu hái choi-máh ge chín yáuh yāt-baak-sàam-sahp-yih-yīk yùhn, yahp máh-chèuhng ge yàhn-sou haih sàam-baak-yih-sahp-maahn yàhn!
Mr Wong	Wàh! Hèung-góng-yàhn jàn-haih yáuh-chín lak. Jèung Sìn-sàang, néih jùng m̀h jùng-yi dóu-máh ga?
Mr Cheung	M̀h jùng-yi. Dóu-máh, dóu-gáu, dóu-pē-páai, dóu-gú-piu . . . yeuhng-yeuhng ngóh dōu m̀h jùng-yi.
Mr Wong	Néih jàn-haih gwàai lak! Hái Hèung-góng hóu-chíh néih yāt-yeuhng ge yàhn yìh-gā jàn-haih hóu síu lak.
Mr Cheung	Yáuh-yàhn wah, Hèung-góng gam fàahn-wìhng haih tùhng Hèung-góng-yàhn jùng-yi dóu-chín yáuh gwàan-haih ge bo! Néih wah ngāam m̀h ngāam a?
Mr Wong	Ngóh wah móuh gwàan-haih, daahn-haih dóu-chín tùhng jeuih-on ge jàng-gà jauh yáuh gwàan-haih lak.
Mr Cheung	Deui-m̀h-jyuh, Wòhng Sìn-sàang, ngóh yìh-gā gau-jūng yiu heui chàam-gà yāt go chìh-sihn chàuh-fún chàu-jéung-wúi.
Mr Wong	Chàu-jéung-wúi àh! Jéung-bán fùng m̀h fùng-fu ga?
Mr Cheung	Tàuh-jéung haih yāt gàan ūk, yih-jéung haih yāt ga chē.
Mr Wong	Yí! Gám, syun m̀h syun haih dóu-chín nē?

電台 **dihn-tòih**	radio station
新聞 **sàn-màhn**	news
廣播 **gwóng-bo**	broadcast
投注 **tàuh-jyu**	to stake, to bet
賽馬 **choi-máh**	to race horses, horse racing
馬 **máh**	a horse
億 **yīk**	a hundred million, a billion
元 **yùhn**	dollar
馬場 **máh-chèuhng**	racetrack
人數 **yàhn-sou**	number of people
有錢 **yáuh-chín**	rich
賭馬 **dóu-máh**	to bet on horses
賭 **dóu**	to gamble on, to bet on
賭狗 **dóu-gáu**	to bet on dogs
狗 **gáu**	a dog
賭啤牌 **dóu-pē-páai**	to gamble at cards
啤牌 **pē-páai**	playing cards
賭股票 **dóu-gú-piu**	to gamble on shares
股票 **gú-piu**	stocks and shares
樣樣 **yeuhng-yeuhng**	all kinds of, all sorts of
乖 **gwàai**	well behaved, obedient, a 'good boy'
繁榮 **fàahn-wìhng**	prosperous
賭錢 **dóu-chín**	to gamble with money
關係 **gwàan-haih**	relationship, connection, relevance
啱 **ngāam**	correct
罪案 **jeuih-on**	criminal case
增加 **jàng-gà**	increase, to increase
夠鐘 **gau-jūng**	time's up, it's time to
慈善 **chìh-sihn**	charity
籌款 **chàuh-fún**	to raise money, fund raising
抽獎 **chàu-jéung**	lucky draw
會 **wúi**	meeting; club, association
獎品 **jéung-bán**	prize
豐富 **fùng-fu**	rich, abundant
頭獎 **tàuh-jéung**	first prize

ℹ The Cantonese as gamblers

The Cantonese have been renowned for their love of gambling for a long while and they pursue their love with dedication and not infrequently with recklessness. A 19th-century missionary reported that in the city of Canton (**Gwóng-jàu**) the orange sellers would take bets with their customers on the number of pips which the oranges they bought might contain, offering different odds on various numbers. It would hardly be an exaggeration to say that next to eating, the favourite pastimes of Hong Kong have for many years been mahjong and horse racing and since the 1960s the stock exchange has become a fourth passion. At weekends high-speed ferries, jet-driven hydrofoils and helicopters carry thousands of Hong Kong people the 40 miles to Macau where other forms of gambling are legally available; and many Cantonese high rollers are to be found in casinos all over the world.

Grammar

1 Different dollars

In Unit 5 you learned the word **mān** for *dollar*. Now you have a different word **yùhn** which has the same meaning. There are in fact two different systems for talking about money, a colloquial system (**mān**) and a more formal written system (**yùhn**). When people write they always use the formal system and when they speak they usually (but not always) use the colloquial system. It is perhaps closest to the American *dollars* and *bucks* system, where no banknote carries the word *bucks* but where, in speech, either *bucks* or *dollars* is acceptable. In the dialogue Mr Cheung uses **yùhn** because a figure as large and important as *130 billion* seems to command more formality and the radio newscaster he is quoting would certainly not descend into the colloquial **mān** for such an important item. The money system will be explained further in Unit 20.

2 Dropping classifiers

In Mr Cheung's first speech you will notice that he talks of **sàam-baak-yih-sahp-maahn yàhn** (*3,200,000 people*), but he does not use the classifier **go** which you would expect between the number and the noun. The larger numbers get, the less likely it is that a classifier will be used: as a rule of thumb you can assume that the classifier will be used up to 100 and will seldom be used for numbers greater than 100, but if you are in doubt put it in; it is never wrong to do so.

3 Striking it rich

The reason why **yáuh-chín** means *rich* is clear enough – it comes from *having money*. But notice that although **yáuh-chín** is made up of a verb plus a noun (**yáuh** + **chín**) it acts as if it were any other adjective:

Hòh Sìn-sàang hóu yáuh-chín.	*Mr Ho is very rich.*
Yáuh-chín yàhn chóh hái chē hauh-bihn.	*The rich ride in the back.*

4 *The same, almost the same* and *related to*

In the dialogue Mr Cheung says **tùhng Hèung-góng-yàhn jùng-yi dóu-chín yáuh gwàan-haih** – *is related to Hong Kong people's loving to gamble.* Notice how **tùhng** introduces the construction. You have met similar constructions before, and you might like to consolidate your understanding of them here:

hóu-chíh jáu-làuh ge yāt-yeuhng (Unit 4)	*seems like restaurant food*
tùhng dī sō-fá-yí ge bou-líu yāt-yeuhng (Unit 11)	*the same as the material of the sofa*
hóu-chíh sei-sahp seui gam-seuhng-há (Unit 9)	*seem like about 40*
tùhng Yìng-gwok ge chà-m̀h-dō (Unit 12)	*almost like the British*

▶ Dialogue 2

Why Mr Chan is welcomed at the mahjong table.

老陳，你咁中意去澳門賭錢，老實話俾我聽，你贏錢嘅時候多定係輸錢嘅時候多呢？

當然係贏錢嘅時候多喇。但係每次都係贏少少啫。

你中意賭輪盤定係廿一點呀？

兩樣都唔中意；我中意賭番攤。

你去賭場定係喺屋企賭錢呀？

我有時去賭場，有時喺屋企，但係我一定唔去大檔賭錢，因為係非法嘅。

噉，賭波同賭外匯呢？

我估你話‘賭波’就係賭英國足球嘅。呢樣嘢我冇興趣。賭外匯就一定要有好多本錢。所以兩樣都唔適合我。

香港人最中意打麻雀嘅嘞；噉你呢？

我覺得打麻雀最好玩，最吸引我，但係我好少贏錢嘅。

真好嘞！下個禮拜如果你得閒請嚟我屋企，我哋一齊打場麻雀喇！

Mr Lee	Lóuh Chán, néih gam jùng-yi heui Ou-mún dóu-chín, lóuh-saht wah béi ngóh tèng, néih yèhng chín ge sìh-hauh dò dihng-haih sỳu chín ge sìh-hauh dò nē?
Mr Chan	Dòng-yín haih yèhng chín ge sìh-hauh dò lā. Daahn-haih múih chi dōu haih yèhng síu-síu jē.
Mr Lee	Néih jùng-yi dóu Lèuhn-pún dihng-haih Yah-yāt-dím a?
Mr Chan	Léuhng yeuhng dōu m̀h jùng-yi; ngóh jùng-yi dóu Fāan-tāan.
Mr Lee	Néih heui dóu-chèuhng dihng-haih hái ūk-kéi dóu-chín a?
Mr Chan	Ngóh yáuh-sìh heui dóu-chèuhng, yáuh-sìh hái ūk-kéi, daahn-haih ngóh yāt-dihng m̀h heui daaih-dong dóu-chín, yàn-waih haih fèi-faat ge.
Mr Lee	Gám, dóu-bō tùhng dóu-ngoih-wuih nē?
Mr Chan	Ngóh gú néih wah 'dóu-bō' jauh haih dóu Yìng-gwok jūk-kàuh lak. Nī yeuhng yéh ngóh móuh hing-cheui. Dóu-ngoih-wuih jauh yāt-dihng yiu yáuh hóu dò bún-chìhn. Só-yíh léuhng yeuhng dōu m̀h sīk-hahp ngóh.
Mr Lee	Hèung-góng-yàhn jeui jùng-yi dá-Màh-jeuk ge lak: gám néih nē?
Mr Chan	Ngóh gok-dāk dá-Màh-jeuk jeui hóu-wáan, jeui kāp-yáhn ngóh, daahn-haih ngóh hóu síu yèhng chín ge.
Mr Lee	Jàn hóu lak! Hah-go-láih-baai yùh-gwó néih dāk-hàahn chéng làih ngóh ūk-kéi, ngóh-deih yāt-chàih dá chèuhng Màh-jeuk lā!

澳門	**Ou-mún**	*Macau*
老實	**lóuh-saht**	*honest, honestly*
贏	**yèhng**	*to win*
定係	**dihng-haih**	*or, or rather*
輸	**sỳu**	*to lose*
當然	**dòng-yín**	*of course*
輪盤	**Lèuhn-pún**	*roulette*
廿一點	**Yah-yāt-dím**	*blackjack, pontoon*
樣	**yeuhng**	*kind, sort, type*
番攤	**Fāan-tāan**	*fantan*
賭場	**dóu-chèuhng**	*casino*
有時	**yáuh-sìh**	*sometimes*
大檔	**daaih-dong**	*gambling den*
非法	**fèi-faat**	*illegal*
賭波	**dóu-bō**	*to bet on football*
賭外匯	**dóu-ngoih-wuih**	*to gamble on foreign exchange*
外匯	**ngoih-wuih**	*foreign exchange*
足球	**jūk-kàuh**	*soccer*

興趣 **hing-cheui**	*interest*
本錢 **bún-chìhn**	*capital*
適合 **sīk-hahp**	*suitable to, fitting*
打麻雀 **dá Màh-jeuk**	*to play mahjong*
好玩 **hóu-wáan**	*good fun, amusing, enjoyable*
吸引 **kāp-yáhn**	*to attract*
得閒 **dāk-hàahn**	*to be free, at leisure*
場 **chèuhng**	*classifier for performances, bouts, games*

Grammar

5 Telling options

In Unit 6 you met **wah . . . tèng** meaning *to inform someone, to tell someone about something* and in Unit 8 you were told that **wah . . . jì** meant the same. Now you can add other variants, because **góng** *to speak*, which you met in Unit 9, can be substituted for **wah** in either of the phrases and you can add in **béi** *to* to any of them. So all the following forms mean the same – *she tells me . . .*:

Kéuih wah ngóh tèng . . .   Kéuih wah béi ngóh tèng . . .
Kéuih wah ngóh jì . . .   Kéuih wah béi ngóh jì . . .
Kéuih góng ngóh tèng . . .   Kéuih góng béi ngóh tèng . . .
Kéuih góng ngóh jì . . .   Kéuih góng béi ngóh jì . . .

6 *Dihng-haih* or rather

Dihng-haih nicely translates *or* when a question is being asked, and the final particle **nē?** is usually there to back it up:

Kéuih haih Jùng-gwok-yàhn dihng-haih Yaht-bún-yàhn nē?	*Is she Chinese or Japanese?*
Néih Láih-baai-yāt dihng-haih Láih-baai-yih heui Ou-mún nē?	*Is it Monday or Tuesday that you are going to Macau?*
Néih séung sihk ngàuh-yuhk dihng-haih jỳu-yuhk nē?	*Which do you want to have, beef or pork?*

But remember that it is *only in questions* that **dihng-haih** will translate *or*. If you think back to Unit 10 you will remember that *seven or eight people* was translated by **chāt-baat go yàhn**. The difference can be shown by comparing the following two examples:

| Gó-douh yáuh chāt-baat go yàhn. | *There are (approximately) seven or eight people over there.* |
| Gó-douh yáuh chāt dihng-haih baat go yàhn nē? | *Are there seven or eight people over there, which is it?* |

7 Blackjack teaches you numbers!

The card game Blackjack, sometimes known as Pontoon or *Vingt et un*, is popular among the Cantonese, who call it **yah-yāt-dím** (*21 spots*). **Dím** means *a dot*, *a spot* and **yah-yāt** is an alternative way of saying **yih-sahp-yāt** 21. Here is a list of the alternative forms of numbers, all of which really consist of nothing more than slurring over the word **sahp** in numbers above 20:

yih-sahp-yāt = yih-ah-yāt = yah-yāt = yeh-yāt
sàam-sahp-yāt = sàam-ah-yāt = sà-ah-yāt
sei-sahp-yāt = sei-ah-yāt
ńgh-sahp-yāt = ńgh-ah-yāt
luhk-sahp-yāt = luhk-ah-yāt
chāt-sahp-yāt = chāt-ah-yāt
baat-sahp-yāt = baat-ah-yāt
gáu-sahp-yāt = gáu-ah-yāt

We have only shown 21, 31, 41 etc., but the same shortcuts work for 22, 32, 42 . . . and any other such number up to 99. You can use these alternatives quite freely provided you observe one rule – *you should not use the shortcuts for the round numbers 20, 30, 40, . . . 90*, which are always said in their full **yih-sahp, sàam-sahp, sei-sahp . . . gáu-sahp** form.

8 Making adjectives with *hóu*

In the dialogue you met the word **hóu-wáan** *good fun, enjoyable*. You may have realized that this was a new word made up of two that you already knew: **hóu** *good* and **wáan** *to play, enjoy, amuse oneself* and hence *good to enjoy, good to play*. If you are brave enough, you can make up such words for yourself, but here are a few common ones which you can hardly avoid:

hóu-sihk	'good to eat'	*delicious*
hóu-yám	'good to drink'	*delicious*
hóu-tái	'good to look at'	*good looking, attractive*
hóu-tèng	'good to listen to'	*harmonious, melodic*

9 At leisure

Dāk-hàahn literally means *attaining leisure* and so *not busy*. In Unit 10 you learned the word mòhng *busy*. Cantonese usually seem to like to take shortcuts with their language, but many people prefer to say m̀h dāk-hàahn and hóu m̀h dāk-hàahn rather than mòhng and hóu mòhng despite the extra syllables involved.

10 Another shortcut: dropping *yāt*

In the dialogue Mr Lee delightedly invites Mr Chan to dá chèuhng màh-jeuk lā! (have a round of mahjong). You might have expected the Cantonese to read dá yāt chèuhng màh-jeuk lā! and, of course, that would be grammatically correct, but quite often yāt is missed out when it comes between a verb and a classifier with its noun:

sihk chàan faahn	*have a meal*
máaih ga chē	*buy a car*

ℹ️ Mahjong and fantan

Fantan is a Chinese gambling game which consists of guessing how many stones will be left when a random pile is diminished by taking away four stones at a time – that is, the gamblers bet on whether there will be one, two, three or four stones left at the end. There is no skill involved at all, it is just a pure gamble. Mahjong is played by four players with heavy plastic or bone tiles which are crashed down onto a deliberately resonant table to enhance the noise and excitement. It can be equally well played with paper cards, but that would be quiet and far less fun! Luck plays its part, but skilled players have an advantage over unskilled. While to play fantan is called dóu-Fāan-tāan, the far more active process of playing mahjong is called dá-Màh-jeuk.

Exercise 1

In the following sentences interchange mòhng and dāk-hàahn without altering the sense.

a Chàhn Táai gàm-máahn hóu mòhng.
b Ngóh bàh-bā sèhng-nìhn dōu mòhng.
c M̀h-gòi néih wah béi ngóh tèng néih go jái tìng-yaht dāk m̀h dāk-hàahn a?
d Kéuih Láih-baai-yih hóu m̀h dāk-hàahn.
e Ngóh jeui mòhng ge sìh-hauh haih jìu-jóu.

Exercise 2

Insert the correct classifiers in the gaps.

a   __ Jùng-màhn sỳu dōu haih Hòh Sàang ge.
b   Hái gó __ ūk chìhn-bihn yáuh ńgh __ jýu-jái.
c   Johk-yaht gó __ jūk-kàuh hóu hóu-tái àh.
d   Bīn léuhng __ chē haih Chàhn Sàang máaih ga?

Exercise 3

Find the words in **A** which are the opposites of the words in **B**.

A gwàai, síu-síu, tàuh-jyu, dāk-hàahn, sỳu, sàn-fú, sìn-sàang, jàng-gà, síh-màhn, gwóng-bo, sìh-sìh, fèi-gèi, dihn-wá.

B mòhng, sỳu-fuhk, gaan-jūng, yèhng, hohk-sāang, jing-fú, fùng-fu, gáam-síu.

Exercise 4

'Gáu houh! Gáu houh!'

a Néih gú haih Wòhng Sàang yèhng chín dihng-haih Wòhng Táai yèhng chín nē?
b Wòhng Sìn-sàang hóu hòi-sām, haih m̀h haih a?
c Daih-luhk jek máh haih géi-dō houh a?
d Bīn jek máh yèhng a?
e Néih wah haih Wòhng Taai-táai hóu sīk dóu-máh dihng-haih Wòhng Sìn-sàang hóu sīk dóu-máh né?
f Sei houh máh hóu-gwo gáu houh máh, ngāam m̀h ngāam a?
g Sàam houh máh nē? Hóu m̀h hóu-gwo gáu houh a?
h Jeui hóu gó jek máh haih m̀h haih luhk houh máh a?
i Nī yāt chèuhng choi-máh yáuh géi-dō jek máh a?
j Wòhng Sìn-sàang dóu-máh múih chèuhng dōu jùng-yi dóu hóu daaih, yùh-gwó yèhng jauh yèhng hóu dò, sỳu jauh sỳu hóu dò. Wòhng Táai m̀h haih gám ge, kéuih chèuhng-chèuhng dōu dóu hóu sai jē. Gám, néih gú, nī chèuhng kéuih-deih haih sỳu dò-gwo yèhng dihng-haih yèhng dò-gwo sỳu nē?

14

溫習 (二)
wan-jaahp (yih)
revision (2)

Another six units under your belt. It all gets more interesting now; you can say so many more things and begin to have some flexibility in your language. Remember that what you are learning is a living colourful language spoken by a very dynamic people, not a bookish sober exercise in style and complex grammar. Try to speak what you learn so that you can hear the cadences and become familiar with the zest of it. Cantonese people enjoy life, they talk loudly and laugh a lot – a Cantonese whisper is almost a contradiction in terms. Start by reading this first passage through, then read it out loud several times until it begins to feel part of you. Even better, learn it off by heart so that you can recite it.

Passage 1

Wòhng Sìn-sàang chāt seui ge jái johk-yaht fàan hohk-haauh gó-jahn-sìh hóu hòi-sām gám wah ngóh jì, kéuih bàh-bā seuhng-go-láih-baai máaih-jó yāt gàan sàn ūk. Gó gàan ūk yauh daaih yauh leng, yáuh sàam gàan fan-fóng,* gàan ūk chìhn-bihn juhng yáuh go fà-yún tùhng-màaih yāt gàan chē-fòhng tìm. Kéuih wah: 'Yìh-gā ngóh yāt-go-yàhn yuhng yāt gàan fan-fóng, jàn-haih sỳu-fuhk lak. Daahn-haih màh-mā jauh yiu tùhng bàh-bā yāt-chàih yuhng yāt gàan. Ngóh gú màh-mā yāt-dihng m̀h hòi-sām lak. Ngóh m̀h jì dím-gáai bàh-bā m̀h béi màh-mā yuhng daih-sàam gàan fan-fóng nē? Gó gàan fan-fóng yìh-gā móuh yàhn yuhng, jí-haih bàh-bā jài-jó hóu dò sỳu hái gó-syu jē.'

(*fan-fóng = *bedroom*)

Exercise 1
Try to answer these questions now without referring back to the passage.

a Wòhng Sìn-sàang ge jái géi-dō seui a?
b Wòhng Sàang seuhng-go-sìng-kèih máaih-jó māt-yéh a?
c Ūk chìhn-bihn yáuh dī māt-yéh a?
d Bīn-go yàhn yiu tùhng bàh-bā yāt-chàih yuhng yāt gàan fan-fóng a?
e Daih-sàam gàan fan-fóng léuih-bihn yáuh dī māt-yéh a?
f Yáuh móuh yàhn yuhng daih-sàam gàan fan-fóng a?

Exercise 2
It is time to remind you that you should be paying attention to your tones: if you don't you will never sound like a Cantonese! Put the correct tone marks on the following words. You will

have to look up those you have forgotten, but that at least will help to cement them in your mind.

a	hei-mohng	b	tin-hei	c	laahng-tin
d	da-syun	e	dihn-ying	f	wahn-duhng
g	gei-yuhk	h	do-yuh	i	gihn-hong
j	noih-yuhng	k	siu-leuhn	l	pihng-gwan

Exercise 3

Hunt the **yaht**. All the words here use **yaht** *sun* or *day*. What are they?

a	*tomorrow*	b	*Sunday*	c	*the day before yesterday*
d	*the whole day*	e	*yesterday*	f	*Japan*
g	*today*	h	*every day*	i	*the day after tomorrow*

Exercise 4

The following sentence pairs differ by only one word, but the sense changes a great deal. Try to put them into English which will bring out the meanings clearly.

a i Daih-yāt jek máh jīk-haih gáu houh máh.
   ii Daih-yāt jek máh m̀h haih gáu houh máh.

b i Jùng-sàan Síu-jé jing-haih Yaht-bún-yàhn.
   ii Jùng-sàan Síu-jé jàn-haih Yaht-bún-yàhn.

c i Kéuih tìng-yaht jauh heui Gwóng-jàu.
   ii Kéuih tìng-yaht sìn-ji heui Gwóng-jàu.

d i Chàhn Taai-táai heui-gwo Méih-gwok sahp-géi chi lak.
   ii Chàhn Taai-táai heui-gwo Méih-gwok géi-sahp chi lak.

Exercise 5

Choose the right element from the brackets to complete the sense of the sentences.

a Yāt go yàhn yuhng yāt gàan fan-fóng hóu (sàn-fú, yáuh-méng, yáuh-yuhng, sỳu-fuhk).
b Chē-fòhng yuhng làih (jài sỳu ge, jýu-faahn ge, wahn-duhng ge, tìhng-chē ge).
c Hái gó gàan gūng-sī jouh-yéh hóu hóu yàn-waih wúih yáuh (hóu dò chín, m̀h sīk jýu-sung, hóu síu chín, hóu màh-fàahn).

Exercise 6

Make one sentence out of each of the following pairs using the words in brackets to make the link and making whatever other slight adjustments are necessary. For instance, the first pair would give the sentence: **Kéuih séuhng-tòhng jì-chìhn, sìh-sìh dōu heui taam kéuih nàahm pàhng-yáuh.**

a Kéuih séuhng-tòhng. Kéuih sìh-sìh dōu heui taam kéuih nàahm-pàhng-yáuh. (jì-chìhn)
b Wòhng Táai séung máaih gó ga chē. Ga chē hóu leng. (yàn-waih)
c Ngóh m̀h mìhng-baahk. Gó go yàhn láahng-tīn séung máaih láahng-hei-gèi. (jouh-māt-yéh?)
d Gó dī hā m̀h sàn-sìn. Chàhn Táai m̀h séung máaih. (só-yíh)
e Kéuih sihk-gán yéh. Kéuih m̀h góng-wah. (ge sìh-hauh)

Exercise 7
Here are the answers. What were the questions?

a Máaih gó ga chē yiu *sahp-ńgh-maahn mān jē*.
b Wòhng Sàang *Sìng-kèih-luhk* lèih-hòi Yaht-bún.
c Hái Léih Táai jó-sáu-bihn gó jek gáu-jái haih *Léih Sìn-sàang* sung béi kéuih ge.
d Gó dī yàhn *jí-haih Hòh Síu-jé* haih gaau-syu jē.

Passage 2

This little anecdote finishes with a pun, but you may as well get used to it – Cantonese people love punning. The particular pun involved is one that all gamblers know about and it is safe to say that no one other than the naive Mr Ho would have taken the bad advice which his wife gives him here!

Hòh Sìn-sàang Máaih-Máh

Yùh-gwó yāt go yáuh-chín yàhn séung máaih máh, kéuih jauh heui máaih máh, daahn-haih gám-yéung máaih máh hóu gwai bo! Hái Hèung-góng néih sìh-sìh dōu wúih tèng-dóu móuh chín ge yàhn dōu wah 'Gàm-yaht ngóh séung máaih-máh.' Dím-gáai nē? Néih gú-háh, móuh chín ge yàhn wah 'máaih-máh' haih māt-yéh nē? Ngāam lak, 'máaih-máh' jīk-haih 'dóu-máh', só-yíh móuh chín ge yàhn wah kéuih séung heui máaih-máh jīk-haih wah kéuih séung heui dóu-máh.

Hòh Sìn-sàang m̀h haih hóu yáuh-chín. Yáuh yāt yaht kéuih ge hóu pàhng-yáuh Jèung Sìn-sàang dá-dihn-wá làih mahn kéuih: 'Gàm-máahn choi-máh. Ngóh séung chéng néih tùhng ngóh yāt-chàih heui máh-chèuhng wáan-háh, néih wah hóu m̀h hóu nē?' Hòh Sàang hóu hòi-sàm gám wah: 'Hóu! Hóu! Hóu jyú-yi!'

Tèng-yùhn dihn-wá jì-hauh kéuih wah béi Hòh Táai tèng. Hòh
Táai wah: 'Néih móuh heui-gwo tái choi-máh, nī chi haih néih
daih-yāt chi jē. M̀h jì-dou néih wúih m̀h wúih jùng-yi tái nē?'
Hòh Sàang wah: 'Òu! Haih bo! Haih ngóh daih-yāt chi heui tái
choi-máh bo! Yùh-gwó m̀h hóu tái, gám ngóh yiu chóh hái-
douh, móuh yéh jouh bo! Dím-syun-hóu-nē?'* Hòh Táai wah:
'Néih jeui hóu máaih bún sỳu sìn-ji heui máh-chèuhng lak. Néih
yùh-gwó gok-dāk tái choi-máh hóu-wáan, jauh hó-yíh m̀h-sái
tái-sỳu. Yùh-gwó-m̀h-haih-nē, gám néih jauh hó-yíh chóh hái-
douh tái-sỳu lā. Néih wah hóu m̀h hóu nē?' Hòh Sàang hóu
gwàai: taai-táai wah māt-yéh, kéuih jauh jouh māt-yéh. Dòng-
yín kéuih gó máahn heui máh-chèuhng jì-chìhn máaih-jó bún
sỳu sìn.

Hóu-chói Hòh Sìn-sàang gok-dāk choi-máh dōu géi hóu-wáan,
m̀h-sái tái-sỳu. Daahn-haih kéuih yāt-dī chín dōu móuh yèhng,
sèung-fáan juhng sỳu-jó hó dò chín tìm! Kéuih fàan ūk-kéi, hóu
nàu gám wah béi taai-táai tèng: 'Ngóh daih-yih chi heui dóu-
máh m̀h wúih tèng néih góng lak! Máaih-máh yiu máaih yèhng,
m̀h-hóu máaih sỳu ā-ma!'

(*Dím-syun-hóu-nē? = *What's to be done about it? What can
I do?*)

Exercise 8

That second passage was just to get you used to the idea of puns
and wordplay. When you are sure that you understand how
the pun worked, try this one. This time the only clue you have
is 'a hyphen'!

Jèung Sìn-sàang yàuh gáu-chèuhng dóu-yùhn gáu fàan ūk-kéi.
Kéuih go jái mahn kéuih:

'Bàh-bā, néih gàm-yaht dóu-gáu dím a? Yèhng m̀h yèhng chín a?'

'Sahp chèuhng gáu chèuhng yèhng!'

'Wàh! Bàh-bā, néih jàn-haih hóu sīk dóu-gáu bo! Dóu sahp
chèuhng jí-haih sỳu yāt chèuhng.'

'Lóuh-saht góng, ngóh yāt-dī chín dōu móuh yèhng. Ngóh dóu
sahp chèuhng dōu haih gáu-chèuhng yèhng bo!'

15
旅遊
léuih-yàuh
travelling

In this unit you will learn
- useful vocabulary for the traveller
- an important grammar pattern which helps to describe the way in which actions are performed

▶ Dialogue 1

Mrs Lee talks of an inclusive hotel deal.

李太，你行得咁快，趕住去邊處呀？

我趕住去買旅遊飛啫。旅遊公司而家舉辦一個‘澳門兩日遊’節目，
　喺澳門玩兩日一晚，費用只係一千蚊之嘛。

咁平，我唔信。呢個旅遊節目有啲乜嘢服務同享受呢？

日頭有啲乜嘢服務同享受我唔知，但係夜晚喺五星級酒店住一晚就已
　經好抵嘞。呢啲酒店房間當然唔少得有電視機喇、雪櫃喇、雙人床
　喇、洗身房喇，酒店重有暖水泳池等等。

李太，你對澳門嘅酒店服務同設備都好熟識嘛！

當然喇，我係澳門一間大酒店嘅公關經理嘛。

你係內行人都話呢個旅遊節目抵玩，噉我都去買飛參加囉。

Mr Chan	Léih Táai, néih hàahng-dāk gam faai, gón-jyuh heui bīn-syu a?
Mrs Lee	Ngóh gón-jyuh heui máaih léuih-yàuh fēi jē. Léuih-yàuh gūng-sī yìh-gā géui-baahn yāt go 'Ou-mún léuhng yaht yàuh' jit-muhk, hái Ou-mún wáan léuhng yaht yāt máahn, fai-yuhng jí-haih yāt-chìn māan jì-máh.
Mr Chan	Gam pèhng, ngóh m̀h seun. Nī go léuih-yàuh jit-muhk yáuh dī māt-yéh fuhk-mouh tùhng héung-sauh nē?
Mrs Lee	Yaht-táu yáuh dī māt-yéh fuhk-mouh tùhng héung-sauh ngóh m̀h jì, daahn-haih yeh-máan hái ńgh-sīng-kāp jáu-dim jyuh yāt máahn jauh yíh-gìng hóu dái lak. Nī dī jáu-dim fòhng-gàan dòng-yín m̀h-síu-dāk yáuh dihn-sih-gèi lā, syut-gwaih lā, sèung-yàhn-chòhng lā, sái-sàn-fóng lā; jáu-dim juhng yáuh nýuhn-séui wihng-chìh, dáng-dáng.
Mr Chan	Léih Táai, néih deui Ou-mún ge jáu-dim fuhk-mouh tùhng chit-beih dōu hóu suhk-sīk bo!
Mrs Lee	Dòng-yín lā, ngóh haih Ou-mún yāt gàan daaih jáu-dim ge gùng-gwàan gìng-léih bo.
Mr Chan	Néih haih noih-hóng-yàhn dōu wah nī go léuih-yàuh jit-muhk dái wáan, gám ngóh dōu heui máaih fēi chàam-gà lo.

行（路） hàahng(-louh)	to walk
...... 得 -dāk	verb ending, *in such a way that*
快 faai	quick, quickly, fast
趕住 gón-jyuh	hurrying to
旅遊 léuih-yàuh	to travel; tourism
飛 fēi	a ticket, a fare
舉辦 géui-baahn	to run, hold, conduct
遊 yàuh	a tour, to tour
節目 jit-muhk	programme
費用 fai-yuhng	cost, fee
服務 fuhk-mouh	service, to give service
享受 héung-sauh	to enjoy; enjoyment, entertainment, treat
日頭 yaht-táu	daytime, by day
夜晚 yeh-máan	nighttime, at night
五星級 ńgh-sīng-kāp	five-star grade, top class
酒店 jáu-dim	hotel
抵 dái	to be worth it, a bargain, a good buy
房間 fòhng-gàan	a room
唔少得 m̀h-síu-dāk	not less than, must be at least
電視機 dihn-sih-gèi	television set
雪櫃 syut-gwaih	refrigerator
雙人床 sèung-yàhn-chòhng	double bed
床 chòhng	bed
洗身房 sái-sàn-fóng	bathroom
洗身 sái-sàn	to wash the body, to bathe
洗 sái	to wash
暖 nýuhn	warm
泳池 wihng-chìh	swimming pool
等等 dáng-dáng	etcetera, etc., and so on
設備 chit-beih	facilities, appointments, equipment
熟識 suhk-sīk	familiar with, well acquainted with
公關 gùng-gwàan	public relations
經理 gìng-léih	manager
內行人、行內人 noih-hóng-yàhn or hòhng-noih-yàhn	insider, expert
囉 lo	final particle: agreement with previous speaker; strong emotion

Answer the questions

a Jáu-dim fòhng-gàan léuih-bihn yáuh móuh láahng-hei-gèi a?
   Miht-fó-túng nē?
b Māt-yéh haih 'ńgh-sīng-kāp' jáu-dim a?
c Ńgh-sīng-kāp jáu-dim léuih-bihn yáuh móuh chán-só a?
   Wahn-duhng-fóng nē?

Grammar

1 To walk

Hàahng means *to walk* but it is a lonely verb and the normal object supplied for it is louh *road*, so hàahng-louh also means *to walk*. Louh is used for any grade of road or path, while máh-louh literally means *horse road* and generally is used for a main road, often with daaih *big* in front. You might note two other common uses of hàahng:

hàahng-sàan   'walk hills' to go for a country walk
hàahng-gāai   'walk street' to go out into the streets

2 Making adverbs with the verb ending *-dāk*

Adding -dāk to a verb enables you to describe in what way that verb is performed, that is it gives you a way of forming adverbs. It might be helpful to think of -dāk as meaning something like *in such a way that, to the extent that*:

Kéuih hàahng-dāk faai.   He walks quickly. (He walks in
                              such a way that it is quick.)

Néih góng-dāk ngāam.   You spoke correctly.
Wòhng Síu-jé jeuk-dāk leng. Miss Wong is dressed beautifully.

Each of these three examples converts a simple adjective into an adverb, but what comes after -dāk does not have to be so simple. In fact this is a very flexible pattern, as the following show:

Kéuih hàahng-dāk hóu faai.   He walks very quickly.
Kéuih hàahng-dāk   He walks not very quickly.
  m̀h-haih-géi-faai.
Kéuih hàahng-dāk taai faai la. He walks too quickly.
Kéuih hàahng-dāk   He walks faster than I do.
  faai-gwo ngóh.

Remember that -dāk *must be added direct to a verb*, nothing can come between them. If the verb has an object that you want to put in, you should give the verb and its object first and then give the verb again so that **-dāk** can be added to it. Compare these two sentences:

Kéuih góng-dāk hóu faai.	*He speaks very fast.*
Kéuih góng Jùng-màhn góng-dāk hóu faai.	*He speaks Chinese very fast.*

3 Questions expecting a plural answer

In the dialogue Mr Chan says **nī go léuih-yàuh jit-muhk yáuh dī māt-yéh fuhk-mouh tùhng héung-sauh nē?** (*what services and entertainments does this tour programme offer?*). Note how the use of the plural classifier **dī** presupposes that the answer is going to list more than one item. You can do this whenever you ask a question if you are expecting a plural answer and, of course, you can show that you expect a singular answer by using the appropriate classifer for whatever you are talking about:

Néih séung máaih māt-yéh sỳu a?	*What kind of book/books do you want to buy?*
Néih séung máaih bún māt-yéh sỳu a?	*What kind of book do you want to buy?*
Néih séung máaih dī māt-yéh sỳu a?	*What kind of books do you want to buy?*

4 *Double* and *single*

In **sèung-yàhn-chòhng** *double (person) bed*, **sèung** means *double* and it can also mean *a pair of*. The opposite word *single* is **dāan** and *a single bed* is **dāan-yàhn-chòhng**.

ℹ️ A bargain may not be cheap

You now know two similar words, **pèhng** *cheap* and **dái** *a bargain*, but be careful not to confuse them. A Rolls Royce bought at a bargain price might still be several years' salary for most of us, so it would not really be appropriate to say that it was *cheap* and Cantonese would be unlikely to use **pèhng** to describe it either. If you are treated to a meal in a restaurant by a friend and you see the bill and think it small, it would give offence to say it was **hóu pèhng** – that would sound as though your friend should have spent more money on you. You could happily comment **hóu dái**, though, because that sounds as if it was a very good meal and your friend was clever to choose it and not to get cheated into paying over the top. Interestingly, your friend could say **hóu pèhng jē**, because it is quite good manners to belittle one's own efforts as a host.

▶ Dialogue 2

A tourist checks in at the airport.

小姐，我要搭一五零號班機去倫敦。請問我喺呢處報到，啱唔啱呀？

一五零號班機喺下晝四點半鐘起飛去倫敦。你喺呢處報到就啱嘞。
　請你交你嘅護照，簽証同飛機票俾我嘞。

呢兩件係我嘅行李，請你幫我過磅喇。

先生，你嘅行李過重嘞！重有冇其他行李呀？

重有兩件手提行李都係好輕嘅。我嘅行李過重咗幾多磅呀？

唔算好多，只係兩磅啫。

對唔住，請你通融一吓喇，得嗎？

問題唔大，但係下次你就要多啲注意行李嘅重量啦。好嘞，你攞返你
　嘅護照同機票喇。

唔該你話我知旅遊保險嘅櫃枱喺邊處呀？免稅洋酒又喺邊處買呢？

嗰兩個櫃枱都喺四號閘口附近，你唔會搵唔到嘅。

唔該晒。

Yàuh-haak	Síu-jé, ngóh yiu daap yāt-ńgh-lìhng houh bāan-gèi heui Lèuhn-dēun. Chéng-mahn ngóh hái nī-syu bou-dou, ngāam m̀h ngāam a?
Fuhk-mouh-yùhn	Yāt-ńgh-lìhng houh bāan-gèi hái hah-jau sei-dím-bun-jūng héi-fèi heui Lèuhn-dēun. Néih hái nī-syu bou-dou jauh ngāam lak. Chéng néih gàau néih ge wuh-jiu, chìm-jing tùhng fèi-gèi-piu béi ngóh lā.
Yàuh-haak	Nī léuhng gihn haih ngóh ge hàhng-léih, chéng néih bòng ngóh gwo-bóng lā.
Fuhk-mouh-yùhn	Sìn-sàang, néih ge hàhng-léih gwo-chúhng bo! Juhng yáuh móuh kèih-tà hàhng-léih a?
Yàuh-haak	Juhng yáuh léuhng gihn sáu-tàih hàhng-léih dōu haih hóu hèng ge. Ngóh ge hàhng-léih gwo-chúhng-jó géi-dō bohng a?
Fuhk-mouh-yùhn	M̀h syun hóu dò, jí-haih léuhng bohng jē.
Yàuh-haak	Deui-m̀h-jyuh, chéng néih tùhng-yùhng yāt-háh lā, dāk ma?
Fuhk-mouh-yùhn	Mahn-tàih m̀h daaih, daahn-haih hah chi néih jauh yiu dò-dī jyu-yi hàhng-léih ge chúhng-leuhng la. Hóu lak, néih ló-fàan néih ge wuh-jiu tùhng gèi-piu lā.
Yàuh-haak	M̀h-gòi néih wah ngóh jì léuih-yàuh bóu-hím ge gwaih-tói hái bīn-syu a? Míhn-seui yèuhng-jáu yauh hái bīn-syu máaih nē?
Fuhk-mouh-yùhn	Gó léuhng go gwaih-tói dōu hái sei houh jaahp-háu fuh-gahn, néih m̀h wúih wán-m̀h-dóu ge.
Yàuh-haak	M̀h-gòi-saai.

遊客 **yàuh-haak**	*tourist*	
班機 **bāan-gèi**	*scheduled flight*	
報到 **bou-dou**	*check in, register, report for duty*	
服務員 **fuhk-mouh-yùhn**	*attendant, clerk, steward, one who serves*	
下晝 **hah-jau**	*afternoon, p.m.*	
四點半鐘 **sei-dím-bun-jūng**	*half past four o'clock*	
起飛 **héi-fèi**	*to take off* (of aircraft)	
交 **gàau**	*to hand over*	
護照 **wuh-jiu**	*passport*	
簽証 **chìm-jing**	*visa*	
（飛）機票 **(fèi-)gèi-piu**	*air ticket*	
行李 **hàhng-léih**	*luggage*	
過磅 **gwo-bóng**	*to weigh*	
過重 **gwo-chúhng**	*overweight*	
輕 **hèng**	*light (in weight)*	
通融 **tùng-yùhng**	*stretch a point, get round the rules, make an accommodation*	
一吓 **yāt-háh**	*a little bit, one time*	
問題 **mahn-tàih**	*problem, question*	
多啲 **dò-dī**	*a little more*	
注意 **jyu-yi**	*pay attention to*	
重量 **chúhng-leuhng**	*weight*	
攞 **ló**	*to collect, to take*	
保險 **bóu-hím**	*insurance*	
櫃枱 **gwaih-tói**	*counter*	
免稅 **míhn-seui**	*tax free, duty-free*	
洋酒 **yèuhng-jáu**	*liquor, (non-Chinese) alcoholic drinks*	
閘口 **jaahp-háu**	*gate, gateway*	
......晒 **-saai**	*verb ending, completely*	

Grammar

5 *Seuhng* and *hah* again

In Unit 10 you met **seuhng-go-láih-baai** *last week* and **hah-go-láih-baai** *next week*. In the dialogue there are two more cases where **hah** appears. Hah-jau means *afternoon, p.m.*, and you will not be surprised to learn that *a.m.* is **seuhng-jau**. Hah chi or **hah yāt chi** means *next time, on the next occasion* and as expected **seuhng chi** or **seuhng yāt chi** means *last time, on the previous occasion.*

6 Clock time

Telling the hours by the clock is very simple; they are called **dím** *dots* (you met that in Unit 13) and, of course, there are 12 of them on the clock (**jūng**). *One o'clock* is *one dot of the clock*, that is **yāt-dím-jūng**, *two o'clock* is **léuhng-dím-jūng** and so on up to *12 o'clock* **sahp-yih-dím-jūng**. *What time is it?* is *How many dots of the clock?* **Géi-dō dím jūng a?**

Half past uses the word **bun** *half*, which you met in Unit 4. So *half past one* is **yāt-dím-bun(-jūng)**, *half past two* is **léuhng-dím-bun(-jūng)** and *half past 12* is **sahp-yih-dím-bun(-jūng)**. The brackets around **jūng** are to show that people do not usually bother to say it unless for some reason they want to speak particularly clearly.

You met the word for *minutes* (**fān**) in Unit 10 and you can give precise times to the minute as follows:

1.01	**yāt-dím-lìhng-yāt-fān-jūng** (for **lìhng** see Unit 11)
1.09	**yāt-dím-lìhng-gáu-fān-jūng**
1.10	**yāt-dím-sahp-fān-jūng**
1.59	**yāt-dím-ńgh-sahp-gáu-fān-jūng**

In practice, rather than bothering to give such precise times, people normally deal in five minute periods only, just as you might say *Oh, it's 20 past 2* even if your watch showed that it was 2.19 or 2.22. The five-minute periods are called *characters* (**jih**) after the figures which appear on clock faces:

1.05 is **yāt-dím-yāt-go-jih**   *1.10* is **yāt-dím-léuhng-go-jih**
1.25 is **yāt-dím-ńgh-go-jih**   *1.50* is **yāt-dím-sahp-go-jih**

Some people like to use the word **gwāt** (from the English word *quarter*) in the following way:

yāt-dím-yāt-go-gwāt   *quarter past one*
yāt-dím-sàam-go-gwāt   *quarter to two*

But if you prefer, you can always say:

yāt-dím-sàam-go-jih   *quarter past one*
yāt-dím-gáu-go-jih   *quarter to two*

Finally, remember that Cantonese likes to put the large before the small and that applies to time as well, so: *4.35 p.m. on Tuesday* is **Sìng-kèih-yih hah-jau sei-dím-chāt-go-jih.**

7 *Fēi* and *piu* tickets

The formal word for *ticket* is **piu**, but generally Cantonese people prefer to use the colloquial word **fēi**. (**Fēi** is probably a corruption of the English word *fare*.) In the case of the word for *air ticket* most people now simply say **gèi-piu** or if there could be any doubt what that means they would use its fuller form **fèi-gèi-piu**. **Fèi-gèi-fēi** sounds rather odd and is not common.

8 *Sáu-tàih* portable

In Unit 8 you met **sáu-tàih miht-fó-túng** *portable fire extinguisher* and in the dialogue you met **sáu-tàih hàhng-léih** *hand baggage*. **Sáu-tàih** can be used freely with many other nouns, but probably the most common nowadays is the **sáu-tàih dihn-wá**, the *portable phone, mobile*.

9 *Mahn-tàih* a problem

Mahn-tàih m̀h daaih means *the problem is not a big one, no great problem*. You will frequently hear people respond to a request by saying **mòuh mahn-tàih**, a phrase echoed almost precisely in the English *no problem!*

10 Verb ending *-saai* completely

The verb ending **-saai** is a very useful one. In the dialogue it has attached itself to **m̀h-gòi** *thank you*. **M̀h-gòi-saai** really means *thank you totally*, but has been devalued so that many people say it rather than just **m̀h-gòi**, much as many English speakers say *thank you very much* rather than just *thank you* without meaning to show any great degree of gratitude. In the same way **dò-jeh-saai** is very common. Otherwise, **-saai** means what it says, as the following illustrate:

Dī yàhn dōu jáu-saai.	*All the people left.*
Ngóh móuh-saai chín.	*I've got no money at all.*
Kéuih ge sáu hāak-saai.	*His hands were completely black.*

Exercise 1

Change the following pairs of sentences into single sentence questions using **dihng-haih . . . nē?** The first one would become **Néih haih Yìng-gwok-yàhn dihng-haih Méih-gwok-yàhn nē?**

a Néih haih Yìng-gwok-yàhn. Néih haih Méih-gwok-yàhn.
b Fó-chē faai. Fèi-gèi faai.
c Kéuih Láih-baai-sàam làih. Kéuih Láih-baai-sei làih.

d   Hòh Sìn-sàang séung heui Hèung-góng. Hòh Sìn-sàang séung heui Gwóng-jàu.
e   Léih Táai móuh chín. Chàhn Táai móuh chín.

Exercise 2
Give the opposites of the following words.

a   yeh-máan
b   m̀h-síu-dāk
c   nýuhn-séui
d   chúhng
e   gìng-léih

Exercise 3
Make adverbial sentences from the following using -dāk and your translations of the phrases in brackets. The answer to the first one is **Kéuih góng-dāk faai**. Careful now!

a   Kéuih góng. (*quickly*)
b   Wòhng Sàang máaih hā. (*very cheaply*)
c   Néih hàahng-louh. (*faster than Miss Cheung*)
d   Néih yám yèuhng-jáu. (*more than I do*)
e   Léih Sìn-sàang jà-chē. (*not very well*)

Exercise 4
What are the correct classifiers for the following? Some of them you have not been specifically told, but by now you should be able to make a guess with a very good chance of being right.

a   dāan-yàhn-chòhng   b   gáu-jái   c   dihn-sih-gèi
d   wahn-duhng-fóng   e   máh-louh   f   fèi-gèi
g   jáu-dim   h   fèi-gèi-piu   i   hàhng-léih

Exercise 5
These questions are quite difficult. Answer them in Cantonese.

a   Yāt gàn tùhng yāt bohng bīn yeuhng chúhng a?
b   Hái Yìng-gwok máaih gihn-hòhng bóu-hím gwai m̀h gwai a?
c   Hái fèi-gèi-chèuhng léuih-bihn tùhng-màaih hái bīn-syu yáuh míhn-seui yèuhng-jáu maaih a?
d   Daap fèi-gèi ge sìh-hauh, sáu-tàih hàhng-léih yiu m̀h yiu gwo-bóng a?
e   Hái Lèuhn-dēun yáuh géi-dō go fèi-gèi-chèuhng a?

Exercise 6
Here are some clock times. How do you say them in Cantonese? See if you can come up with *three* different ways of saying the last one!

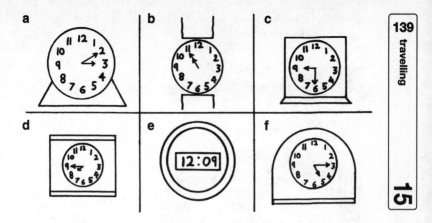

Exercise 7

A question of time. Can you give the answer (in Cantonese) to this puzzle?

Gàm-yaht haih Sìng-kèih-yih.

Ngóh sàam yaht jì-chìhn heui-jó máh-chèuhng.

Ngóh hái máh-chèuhng wáan-jó sàam go bun jūng-tàuh.

Ngóh luhk-dím-jūng lèih-hòi-jó máh-chèuhng.

Gám, ngóh séung mahn néih: Ngóh Láih-baai-géi géi-dō-dím-jūng dou-jó máh-chèuhng nē?

16

駕駛中
ga-sái
driving

In this unit you will learn
- how to make comparisons

▶ Dialogue 1

Mr Lee has just come back from his driving test.

你咁開心，我估你今朝早參加嘅汽車駕駛考試成績一定好好嘞。

我都估我嘅成績幾好。

考試官考咗你啲乜嘢呀？

佢考咗我好多野，譬如泊位喇，斜路開車喇，慢駛喇，停車喇，窄路
掉頭喇，手掣同腳掣用得好唔好喇，對路面嘅情況反應夠唔夠快喇
等等。

結果係點樣，你知唔知呀？

佢有講野㗎！我揸車返駕駛考試局嘅寫字樓嗰陣時，佢可能覺得好舒
服，瞓咗喺車裡便重未醒，要我同佢嘅同事兩個人一齊抬佢落車。

Mrs Lee	Néih gam hòi-sām, ngóh gú néih gàm-jìu-jóu chàam-gà ge hei-chè ga-sái háau-síh sìhng-jīk yāt-dihng hóu hóu lak.
Mr Lee	Ngóh dōu gú ngóh ge sìhng-jīk géi hóu.
Mrs Lee	Háau-síh-gwùn háau-jó néih dī māt-yéh a?
Mr Lee	Kéuih háau-jó ngóh hóu dò yéh, pei-yùh paak-wái lā, che-lóu hòi-chē lā, maahn sái lā, tìhng-chē lā, jaak-louh diuh-tàuh lā, sáu-jai tùhng geuk-jai yuhng-dāk hóu m̀h hóu lā, deui louh-mín ge chìhng-fong fáan-ying gau m̀h gau faai lā, dáng-dáng.
Mrs Lee	Git-gwó haih dím-yéung, néih jì m̀h jì a?
Mr Lee	Kéuih móuh góng-yéh bo! Ngóh jà-chē fàan Ga-sái Háau-síh-guhk ge sé-jih-làuh gó-jahn-sìh, kéuih hó-nàhng gok-dāk hóu sỳu-fuhk, fan-jó hái chē léuih-bihn juhng-meih séng, yiu ngóh tùhng kéuih ge tùhng-sih léuhng go yàhn yāt-chàih tòih kéuih lohk chē.

駕駛 **ga-sái**	to drive, driving	
考試 **háau-síh**	examination, test; to sit an examination	
成績 **sìhng-jīk**	result, score, report	
官 **gwùn**	an official, an officer	
考 **háau**	to examine, to test	
譬如 **pei-yùh**	for example, for instance	
泊位 **paak-wái**	to park a car	
斜路 **che-lóu**	steep road	
斜 **che**	steep	
開車 **hòi-chē**	to start a car; to drive a car	
慢 **maahn**	slow, slowly	
駛 **sái**	to drive	

窄 **jaak**	narrow
掉頭 **diuh-tàuh**	to turn to face the other way
手掣 **sáu-jai**	hand brake
腳掣 **geuk-jai**	foot brake
腳 **geuk**	foot, leg
路面 **louh-mín**	road surface
情況 **chìhng-fong**	situation, circumstances
反應 **fáan-ying**	reaction, response; to respond, react
夠 **gau**	enough
結果 **git-gwó**	the end result
局 **guhk**	a bureau, department, office
可能 **hó-nàhng**	it is possible that, possibly; possibility
瞓、瞓覺 **fan** or **fan-gaau**	to sleep; to lie down; to go to bed
重未 **juhng-meih**	still not yet
醒 **séng**	to wake up, recover consciousness
同事 **tùhng-sih**	colleague
抬 **tòih**	to carry, to lift

Háau-síh

Ngóh-deih séung mahn néih: néih gú gó go háau-síh-gwùn jàn-haih fan-jó gaau dihng-haih yàn-waih Léih Sàang jà-chē jà-dāk m̀h hóu só-yíh kéuih pa-dou tàuh-wàhn fan-jó hái chē léuih-bihn nē?

Grammar

1 Reactions to . . .

You first met **deui** (*with regard to, towards*) in Unit 9 and further examples of its use are to be found in Units 10, 12 and 15. In the dialogue here it teams up with **fáan-ying** to mean *reactions to road conditions*: when you have understood that, you will find it easier to make sense of the long section **deui louh-mín ge chìhng-fong fáan-ying gau m̀h gau faai lā** – *whether reactions to road conditions are fast enough*.

2 *Gau* enough

Gau means *enough*. It works very consistently because it always goes in front of the word it refers to, whether that word is a noun or an adjective, but as you will see from the translations of the examples, English is not so consistent:

Néih gau m̀h gau chín máaih fēi a?	*Do you have **enough money** to buy the tickets?*
Gó déng móu gau m̀h gau daaih a?	*Is that hat **big enough**?*

🛈 Carrying things

Cantonese uses a number of different verbs meaning *to carry*. To carry slung over the shoulder is one, to carry in the arms is another, to carry on the back is another, to carry on a pole over one shoulder is another and so on. **Tòih** is used for *to carry* between two people either holding the load or having it suspended from a pole between them.

▶ Dialogue 2

A lucky escape?

對唔住，先生，我一時唔小心用架單車撞到你，你有冇事呀？
大問題就冇，但係我隻腳而家好痛，有啲傷。你睇，重流緊血添。
你真好彩嘞，只係被架單車撞到啫。
豈有此理，你黐線㗎，你唔小心撞到我，重話我好彩？！
係呀，先生！我係認真㗎，唔係講笑㗎，千祈唔好誤會呀！
我點樣誤會呀，你講喇！
我係的士司機，又係電單車賽車手，今日喺的士公司輪到我放假，
　所以唔駛揸的士，啱啱我架電單車又壞咗，擰咗去修理，所以我
　先至用我個仔嘅單車咋。如果係我嘅的士或者電單車撞到你，
　嗽你就冇咁好彩啦。

Mr Chan　Deui-m̀h-jyuh, sìn-sàang, ngóh yāt-sìh m̀h síu-sàm yuhng ga dāan-chē johng-dóu néih. Néih yáuh móuh sih a?

Victim	Daaih mahn-tàih jauh móuh, daahn-haih ngóh jek geuk yìh-gā hóu tung, yáuh-dī sèung. Néih tái, juhng làuh-gán hyut tìm.
Mr Chan	Néih jàn hóu-chói lak, jí-haih beih ga dāan-chē johng-dóu jē.
Victim	Héi-yáuh-chí-léih, néih chì-sin gàh. Néih m̀h síu-sàm johng-dóu ngóh, juhng wah ngóh hóu-chói?!
Mr Chan	Haih a, sìn-sàang! Ngóh haih yihng-jàn ga, m̀h haih góng-siu ga. Chìn-kèih m̀h-hóu ngh-wuih a!
Victim	Ngóh dím-yéung ngh-wuih a? Néih góng lā!
Mr Chan	Ngóh haih dīk-sí sī-gēi, yauh haih dihn-dāan-chē choi-chē-sáu. Gàm-yaht hái dīk-sí gūng-sī lèuhn-dou ngóh fong-ga, só-yíh m̀h-sái jà dīk-sí, ngāam-ngāam ngóh ga dihn-dāan-chē yauh waaih-jó, nìng-jó heui sàu-léih, só-yíh ngóh sìn-ji yuhng ngóh go jái ge dāan-chē ja. Yùh-gwó haih ngóh ge dīk-sí waahk-jé dihn-dāan-chē johng-dóu néih, gám néih jauh móuh gam hóu-chói la.

一時 **yāt-sìh**	*momentarily, briefly*
小心 **síu-sàm**	*careful*
單車 **dāan-chē**	*bicycle*
撞 **johng**	*run into, knock into*
有事 **yáuh sih**	*to have something wrong with you*
傷 **sèung**	*a wound; to wound*
流 **làuh**	*to flow*
血 **hyut**	*blood*
豈有此理 **héi-yáuh-chí-léih**	*that's ridiculous; how could that be?*
黐線 **chì-sin**	*crazy; mixed up; off the rails*
認真 **yihng-jàn**	*serious, sincere*
講笑 **góng-siu**	*to joke*
笑 **siu**	*to smile, to laugh, to laugh at*
千祈 **chìn-kèih**	*whatever you do don't, don't ever*
誤會 **ngh-wuih**	*misunderstand, get it wrong*
電單車 **dihn-dāan-chē**	*motorbike*
賽車手 **choi-chē-sáu**	*racing driver*
賽車 **choi-chē**	*motor racing*
輪到 **lèuhn-dou**	*the turn of, it has come to the turn of*
壞 **waaih**	*to go wrong, break down*
擰 **nìng**	*to bring, to take*
修理 **sàu-léih**	*to repair, mend*
或者 **waahk-jé**	*or, perhaps*

Grammar

3 *Jek* one of a pair

Things that come in pairs are classified with **sèung** or with **deui**:

yāt deui sáu	*a pair of hands, pair of arms*
yāt sèung faai-jí	*a pair of chopsticks*
	(**faai-ji** = *chopsticks*)

One of a pair is usually **jek** regardless of the shape:

yāt jek sáu	*a hand, an arm*
yāt jek faai-jí	*a chopstick*

An exception is the case of human beings (such as *husband and wife*), where as a couple they are **sèung** but where one of the pair is still referred to as **go**. Other exceptions are *trousers*, *spectacles* and *scissors* which the Cantonese do not consider to be *pairs* at all – logically enough, since each is a single object – and so do not use **deui** or **sèung** for them.

4 Accentuating the negative

Chìn-kèih is a useful word when you want to make a negative command particularly strong:

Chìn-kèih m̀h-hóu góng-siu lā!	*Whatever you do don't joke!*
Chìn-kèih m̀h-hóu m̀h gei-dāk lā!	*You really must not forget!*

5 When *electric* is not electric

In Unit 9 you met a number of useful words which were made up using **dihn** (*electricity, electric*). Cantonese seems to have got rather carried away with the idea, though, and has applied **dihn** to things which have very little to do with electricity. So when motorbikes came along they dubbed them *electric bikes* **dihn-dāan-chē**. Here is another example:

dihn-yàuh	*petrol, gasoline*
yahp dihn-yàuh	*to refuel, put petrol in*

6 *Broken* and *broken down*

You met **waaih** meaning *bad* in Unit 12. **Waaih-jó** means *gone bad* or *broken down* and can be applied to fruit, meat, machinery, watches, radios and so on. But if the object is clearly physically damaged, then the word to use is **laahn-jó** which you met in Unit 5:

| Ngóh ge dihn-dāan-chē waaih-jó. | *Something's gone wrong with my motorbike.* |
| Ngóh ge dihn-dāan-chē laahn-jó. | *My motorbike is smashed.* |

7 More on *or*

Remember **dihng-haih**? Now you have also met **waahk-jé** and they both mean *or*. The difference is that **dihng-haih** means *or is it the case that?* and always appears in questions, while **waahk-jé** means *or maybe it is, or perhaps* and appears in statements:

Kéuih géi-sí làih a? Haih gàm-yaht dihng-haih tìng-yaht làih nē?	*When is she coming? Is it today or tomorrow that she is coming? (Which is it? It must be one or the other)*
Kéuih (waahk-jé) gàm-yaht waahk-jé tìng-yaht làih.	*She's coming today or maybe tomorrow. (It could be either)*
Kéuih yiu ga-fē dihng-haih chàh nē?	*Does he want coffee or tea?*
Kéuih waahk-jé yiu ga-fē waahk-jé yiu chàh.	*He may want coffee or he may want tea. (I'm not sure)*

8 Negative comparisons

In the last line of the dialogue Mr Chan says **néih jauh móuh gam hóu-chói la** (*you wouldn't be as lucky then*) and this gives you the clue to how to make negative comparisons. The pattern is:

X móuh Y gam . . .	*X isn't as . . . as Y*
Kéuih móuh ngóh gam gòu.	*He's not as tall as I am.*
Hei-chè móuh fèi-gèi gam faai.	*Cars aren't as fast as planes.*
Ngóh hàahng-dāk móuh néih gam maahn.	*I don't walk as slowly as you do.*

9 A recap on comparisons

Now we can set out the full range of comparisons so that you can bring real subtlety into your speech:

Ngóh hóu gòu.	I am tall.
Kéuih gòu dī.	He's taller.
Kéuih gòu hóu-dò.	He's a lot taller.
Néih juhng gòu.	You are even taller.
Kéuih móuh gam gòu.	He's not so tall.
Kéuih gòu gwo ngóh.	He is taller than I am.
Kéuih gòu gwo ngóh síu-síu. or	He is a bit taller than I am.
Kéuih gòu gwo ngóh yāt-dī.	
Kéuih gòu gwo ngóh hóu-dò.	He is a lot taller than I am.
Kéuih móuh ngóh gam gòu.	He is not as tall as I am.

And, of course, there is also the equivalent and the superlative:

Kéuih tùhng ngóh yāt-yeuhng gam gòu.	He is just as tall as I am.
Kéuih móuh ngóh yāt-yeuhng gam gòu.	He is not just as tall as I am.
Kéuih jeui gòu lak.	He is tallest.

ℹ Laughing and smiling

The word **siu** is heavily used in Cantonese, and Chinese culture in general stresses the need to smile. You will notice that Chinese people smile a great deal and sometimes in circumstances where westerners would think it inappropriate, in the face of tragedy or horror, for example. Chinese novels are full of *I smiled*, *she smiled coldly*, *he smiled sadly* and so on, where English novels use another set of words such as *he said*, *she exclaimed*, *they expostulated*, *I sighed*. One of the reasons why Chinese faces are said to be *inscrutable* may well be because westerners do not know how to read the various subtleties of smiling. Chinese people often find western faces disconcerting too – *Why doesn't he smile? Have I said something wrong?*

Exercise 1

Here are five English sentences. Which of the two possibilities given you is the correct translation?

a *I think he is also Japanese.*
   i Ngóh gú kéuih dōu haih Yaht-bún-yàhn.
   ii Ngóh dōu gú kéuih haih Yaht-bún-yàhn.

b *I give him ten dollars.*
   i Ngóh béi sahp mān gwo kéuih.
   ii Ngóh béi kéuih sahp mān.

c *Mrs Lee is going to Japan by air.*
   i   Léih Taai-táai daap fèi-gèi heui Yaht-bún.
   ii Léih Taai-táai heui Yaht-bún daap fèi-gèi.

d *Mr Wong and I are going to dine at City Hall.*
   i   Ngóh tùhng Wòhng Sìn-sàang heui Daaih-wuih-tòhng sihk-faahn.
   ii Wòhng Sìn-sàang tùhng ngóh heui Daaih-wuih-tòhng sihk-faahn.

e *Which lady is ill?*
   i   Bīn-go taai-táai yáuh behng a?
   ii Bīn-go ge taai-táai yáuh behng a?

Exercise 2
Now write out the translation of the above sentences which you think are incorrect.

Exercise 3

A really tough one. Can you say who is sitting in each of the six seats?

Gàm-máahn Lùhng Sàang, Lùhng Táai chéng Léih Sàang, Léih Táai tùhng-màaih Chàhn Sàang, Chàhn Táai sihk-faahn. Léih Sàang chóh hái bāk-bihn; Chàhn Sàang hái Lùhng Táai yauh-bihn; Chàhn Táai hái Lùhng Sàang deui-mihn; Léih Táai hái Lùhng Sàang jó-sáu-bihn.

Exercise 4

Can you match each of the six verbs **a–f** with a suitable noun from the list **i–xii**?

a dá   **b** dóu   **c** chàu
d tèng   **e** chùng   **f** tái

i jéung-bán   **ii** tìn-hei   **iii** gwóng-bo
iv pē-páai   **v** dihn-yíng   **vi** màh-jeuk
vii hói-tāan   **viii** noih-yùhng   **ix** hùhng-dāng
x sou-hohk   **xi** yàuh-haak   **xii** jit-muhk

Exercise 5

Mr Wong   Mr Chan   Mr Lee   Mrs Chan   Mrs Lee   Mrs Wong

Use Cantonese to describe Mr Wong's height in comparison with each of the other five people. How would you describe Mr Lee in comparison with Mrs Wong? How would you describe Mr Lee without reference to anyone else?

Exercise 6

Here are definitions of four words which you have learned in this unit. Can you work out what they are?

a Jīk-haih yāt go yàhn góng ge yéh, jouh ge yéh, séung ge yéh yāt-dī dōu m̀h ngāam.

b Jīk-haih néih góng nī yeuhng yéh, kéuih m̀h mìhng-baahk, yíh-waih néih góng gó yeuhng yéh.

c Jīk-haih dī yéh laahn-jó, waaih-jó jì-hauh, joi yāt chi jíng-fàan hóu.

d Jīk-haih 'sìh-sìh' ge sèung-fáan.

7

紀律部隊
géi-leuht
bouh-déui

the uniformed services

In this unit you will learn
- complicated descriptive phrases

▶ Dialogue 1

Problems with a photograph on an immigration application.

小姐，你呢張用嚟申請移民嘅相片唔合規格喎！

點樣唔合規格呀？

移民局規定申請人嘅相片唔准著軍服。

好彩我唔係軍人，我已經離開咗軍隊兩年嘞。

噉，你而家做緊乜野呀？

我而家係女警，不過下個月尾我會加入消防局做女消防員……嚇！
　警察同消防員都要著制服嘅喎！我點算好呢？

小姐，移民局規定申請移民嘅人唔准著任何制服影相，你可以
　唔著㗎。

乜野話？！你叫我唔著衫裸體影相吖？

唔……唔……係……你……你唔好誤會。我嘅意思係叫你唔著制服
　著便服啫！

Official	Síu-jé, néih nī jèung yuhng làih sàn-chíng yìh-màhn ge seung-pín m̀h hahp-kwài-gaak bo!
Applicant	Dím-yéung m̀h hahp-kwài-gaak a?
Official	Yìh-màhn-guhk kwài-dihng sàn-chíng yàhn ge seung-pín m̀h jéun jeuk gwàn-fuhk.
Applicant	Hóu-chói ngóh m̀h haih gwàn-yàhn, ngóh yíh-gìng lèih-hòi-jó gwàn-déui léuhng nìhn lak.
Official	Gám, néih yìh-gā jouh-gán māt-yéh a?
Applicant	Ngóh yìh-gā haih néuih-gíng, bāt-gwo hah-go-yuht-méih ngóh wúih gà-yahp Sìu-fòhng-guhk jouh néuih-sìu-fòhng-yùhn . . . Baih! Gíng-chaat tùhng sìu-fòhng-yùhn dōu yiu jeuk jai-fuhk ge bo! Ngóh dím-syun-hóu-nē?
Official	Síu-jé, Yìh-màhn-guhk kwài-dihng sàn-chíng yìh-màhn ge yàhn m̀h jéun jeuk yahm-hòh jai-fuhk yíng-séung. Néih hó-yíh m̀h jeuk ga.
Applicant	Māt-yéh wá?! Néih giu ngóh m̀h jeuk sāam ló-tái yíng-séung àh?
Official	M̀h . . . m̀h . . . haih . . . Néih . . . néih m̀h-hóu ngh-wuih. Ngóh ge yi-sì haih giu néih m̀h jeuk jai-fuhk, jeuk bihn-fuhk jē!

申請 **sàn-chíng**	to apply
移民 **yìh-màhn**	to migrate; immigration, emigration
相片 **seung-pín**	photograph
合規格 **hahp-kwài-gaak**	to qualify, meet requirements
規定 **kwài-dihng**	to regulate, lay down a rule
准 **jéun**	to allow, permit
軍服 **gwàn-fuhk**	military uniform
軍人 **gwàn-yàhn**	soldier, military personnel
軍隊 **gwàn-déui**	army
女 **néuih**	female
女警 **néuih-gíng**	policewoman
不過 **bāt-gwo**	but, however
月 **yuht**	moon, month
尾 **méih**	tail, end
加入 **gà-yahp**	to join, recruit into
消防局 **sìu-fòhng-guhk**	fire brigade
消防員 **sìu-fòhng-yùhn**	fireman
弊！ **baih!**	oh dear! oh, heck! alas!
制服 **jai-fuhk**	uniform
任何 **yahm-hòh**	any
影相 **yíng-séung**	to take a photograph, have a photo taken
裸體 **ló-tái**	naked, nude
意思 **yi-sì**	meaning, intention
叫 **giu**	to tell someone to, to order someone to
便服 **bihn-fuhk**	plain clothes

Grammar

1 Adjectives

In Unit 4 you first met **ge** used to link descriptive phrases or clauses to a noun (**hóu gwai ge ga-fē** – *very expensive coffee*; **máaih-gán bāt ge yàhn** – *the person who is buying a pen*). The first line of the dialogue in this unit has a more complicated version of that **ge** pattern (**nī jèung yuhng làih sàn-chíng yìh-màhn ge seung-pín**). At first sight this is rather frightening, but keep cool; you can quite easily break it down to see how it works. The basic unit is **nī jèung seung-pín** – *this photograph* (remember **jèung** is the classifier for sheet-like things). Splitting **nī jèung** and the noun **seung-pín** is the adjective **yuhng làih sàn-chíng yìh-màhn** *used for applying for immigration* and ge does the same job that it was doing when you met it in Unit 4, that is, it is linking the complex adjective to the noun. So the whole thing means *this photograph which is being used for applying for immigration*. In fact, although it looks complicated, when you break it down it is really only the same basic pattern as **nī go Méih-gwok-yàhn** – specifier–classifier–adjective–noun. Here are some more examples:

gó ga Wòhng Sàang séung máaih ge Yaht-bún chē	*that Japanese car which Mr Wong wants to buy*
nī chēut nàahm-yán hóu jùng-yi tái ge dihn-yíng	*this movie that men love watching*

2 Possessives with adjectives

Look again at the same speech by the immigration official and you will see that **néih** *you* is positioned in front of that complex adjectival pattern and it all means *this photograph of yours which is being used for applying for immigration*. This is the regular position for the possessive in such cases and the normal possessive indicator (**ge**) is not necessary:

néih gó ga Wòhng Sàang séung máaih ge Yaht-bún chē	*that Japanese car of yours which Mr Wong wants to buy*

3 *Jéun*: a two-way verb

Jéun can mean either *to allow* or *to be allowed*, so it can work two ways, both actively and passively:

Kéuih m̀h jéun yám-jáu.	*He's not allowed to drink alcohol.*
Kéuih m̀h jéun (ngóh) yám-jáu.	*He doesn't let me drink alcohol.*

As you become more familiar with Cantonese you will find other two-way verbs like **jéun**; and already in this unit you will find **yíng-séung**, which can mean *to photograph* or *to be photographed*.

4 Vive la différence!

You met **nàahm** *male* in Unit 9 and now you have met his mate **néuih** *female*. As you can see from the dialogue, **néuih** can be attached fairly freely to nouns – **néuih-gíng** *policewoman*, **néuih-sìu-fòhng-yùhn** *firewoman*. In these cases the nouns are assumed to be males, so that you would only meet the terms **nàahm-gíng** and **nàahm-sìu-fòhng-yuhn** if someone were specifically making a contrast between the two sexes. In other cases there is no assumption that a noun is male – **yàhn** *person*, for example, is completely non-commital and so you will meet **nàahm-yán** *man* just as often as you will meet **néuih-yán** *woman* (note the tone changes from **yàhn** to **yán**). Here are some more:

nàahm-pàhng-yáuh/ **néuih-pàhng-yáuh**	*boyfriend/girlfriend*
nàahm-chi(-só)/ **néuih-chi(-só)**	*gentlemen's/ladies' toilet*
nàahm-hohk-sāang/ **néuih-hohk-sāang**	*boy/girl pupils*

While on the subject, you might note that **néuih** changes its tone to become **néui** *daughter*, the pair to **jái** *son*.

5 *Yuht* month

Yuht means *the moon* and by extension has also come to mean *a month*. The classifier for it is **go**, so *one month* is **yāt go yuht**, *two months* is **léuhng go yuht** and so on. As with **láih-baai** and **sìng-kèih**, *last*, *this* and *next* are **seuhng**, **nī** and **hah**, so *last month* is **seuhng-go-yuht**, *this month* is **nī go yuht** and *next month* is **hah-go-yuht**.

The months of the year do not have fancy names as in English, they are just numbered without classifiers. The two sets that follow should make the system clear to you:

Yāt-yuht	*January*	**yāt go yuht**	*one month*
Yih-yuht	*February*	**léuhng go yuht**	*two months*
Sàam-yuht	*March*	**sàam go yuht**	*three months*
Chāt-yuht	*July*	**chāt go yuht**	*seven months*
Sahp-yih-yuht	*December*	**sahp-yih go yuht**	*twelve months*

6 To tell

To tell has different meanings in English and different words are used for them in Cantonese. When *to tell* means *to inform*, *to tell a fact*, you have learned that it is translated by **wah/góng . . . jì/tèng** (see Unit 13). When *to tell* means *to tell someone to do something*, *to order someone to do something*, then **giu** is used:

Sìn-sàang giu hohk-sāang **tái Yìng-màhn syù.**	*The teacher told the children to* *read their English books.*
Ngóh giu kéuih m̀h-hóu làih.	*I told him not to come.*

Sometimes English uses *to tell* when it would be more fitting to use *ask* or *invite* (**chéng** in Cantonese). Note the following sentence carefully:

**Gìng-léih giu fó-gei chéng
Wòhng Yī-sāng yahp-làih.**

*The manager told the waiter to
tell Dr Wong to come in.*

A waiter is unlikely to feel able to *order* a doctor around, although the manager feels quite happy with *ordering* the waiter around, so in this example *told* and *tell* become **giu** and **chéng** respectively.

▶ Dialogue 2

Plain-clothes police have a tough time with some suspects.

喂！你哋幾個，唔好郁呀！快啲跪低，擰你哋嘅身份証出嚟。
你哋係乜野人呀？你哋冇權睇我哋嘅身份証喎！
我係王沙展，呢位係我上司陳幫辦。我哋懷疑你哋販毒，你哋企埋
　路邊，俾我搜身。
你哋都冇著制服，又唔係坐警察巡邏車。你哋話係警察，要拉人，
　要搜身，邊個信你呀？
我哋冇著警察制服，係因為方便我哋做野。我哋兩個都係便衣警察。
　你哋瞪大對眼睇吓我哋嘅警員証喇！
你哋連手槍都冇，警員証都可能係假嘅，要我哋信你哋係警察就難
　啦。喂，手足！我哋散水囉！
咪走呀！你班死仔，等我拉晒你哋上警察局先！

Sergeant	Wai, néih-deih géi go, m̀h-hóu yūk a! Faai-dī màu-dài, nìng néih-deih ge sàn-fán-jing chēut-làih.
Youth	Néih-deih haih māt-yéh yàhn a? Néih-deih móuh kỳuhn tái ngóh-deih ge sàn-fán-jing bo!
Sergeant	Ngóh haih Wòhng Sà-jín, nī wái haih ngóh seuhng-sī Chàhn Bòng-báan. Ngóh-deih wàaih-yìh néih-deih fáahn-duhk. Néih-deih kéih-màaih louh-bīn, béi ngóh sáu-sàn.
Youth	Néih-deih dōu móuh jeuk jai-fuhk, yauh m̀h haih chóh gíng-chaat chèuhn-lòh-chē. Néih-deih wah haih gíng-chaat, yiu làai-yàhn, yiu sáu-sàn, bīn-go seun néih a?
Sergeant	Ngóh-deih móuh jeuk gíng-chaat jai-fuhk, haih yàn-waih fòng-bihn ngóh-deih jouh-yéh. Ngóh-deih léuhng go dōu haih bihn-yì gíng-chaat. Néih-deih dàng-daaih-deui-ngáahn tái-háh ngóh-deih ge gíng-yùhn-jing lā!

Youth		Néih-deih lìhn sáu-chēung dōu móuh, gíng-yùhn-jing dōu hó-nàhng haih gá ge, yiu ngóh-deih seun néih-deih haih gíng-chaat jauh nàahn la. Wai, sáu-jūk! Ngóh-deih saan-séui lo!
Sergeant		Máih jáu a! Néih bàan séi-jái, dáng ngóh làai-saai néih-deih séuhng gíng-chaat-guhk sìn!

喂！ **wai!**	hoy! hey!
郁 **yūk**	to move, make a movement
身份証 **sàn-fán-jing**	identity card
証 **jing**	a certificate, a pass
出 **chēut**	out
權 **kỳuhn**	right, authority, powers
沙展 **sà-jín**	sergeant
位 **wái**	polite classifier for people
上司 **seuhng-sī**	superior officer, direct boss
幫辦 **bòng-báan**	inspector
懷疑 **wàaih-yìh**	to suspect
販毒 **fáahn-duhk**	to peddle drugs
企 **kéih**	to stand
......埋 **-màaih**	verb ending, close up to
路邊 **louh-bīn**	the roadside
搜身 **sáu-sàn**	to conduct a body search
巡邏車 **chèuhn-lòh-chē**	patrol car
拉 **làai**	to arrest; to pull
方便 **fòng-bihn**	convenient
便衣 **bihn-yì**	plain clothes, civilian clothes
瞪大對眼	take a good look
dàng-daaih-deui-ngáahn	
瞪 **dàng**	to stare, open the eyes
眼 **ngáahn**	eye
警員証 **gíng-yùhn-jing**	warrant card
連......都...... **lìhn . . . dōu . . .**	even . . .
手槍 **sáu-chēung**	handgun, pistol
假 **gá**	false
難 **nàahn**	difficult, hard
手足 **sáu-jūk**	brothers (secret society slang)
散水 **saan-séui**	to scatter away
班 **bàan**	classifier for a group of, gang of
死仔 **séi-jái**	deadbeats, bastards, rats (strong abuse)

You are a Hong Kong immigration official

A foreign national in army uniform, wearing a handgun, comes up to your desk. Ask him for his passport and visa, ask him when he will be leaving Hong Kong and tell him that he is not allowed to bring a handgun into the territory and will he please hand it to that police sergeant at Counter No. 41.

Grammar

7 Hurry up!

Faai-dī means *quicker*, *faster*, as you will remember from your work on comparatives in Unit 16, but it has become the most common way of saying *get a move on!*, *hurry up!* Harassed mothers say it to their children constantly.

8 *Wái*: the polite classifier

The normal classifier for people is of course **go**, but if you wish to be polite to someone or about someone, you should use **wái** instead. So you might say **nī go yàhn** (*this person*), but you would almost certainly say **nī wái sìn-sàang** *this gentleman* and **gó wái síu-jé** *that young lady*. In the dialogue the sergeant uses **wái** when he refers to his superior officer, Inspector Chan. If you are introducing someone, you say **Nī wái haih Wòhng Taai-táai, gó wái haih Léih Síu-jé** . . . etc.

9 *-màaih* close up to

The verb ending **-màaih** can be used to indicate movement towards something or location close up to something. Its opposite, showing movement away from something, or location away from something is **-hòi**. You can use these two words quite freely where you feel them to be appropriate.

Kéuih hàahng-hòi-jó	*He's walked away* (= He is not here. Often said by secretaries over the telephone when you want to talk to their boss)
Chóh-màaih-dī	*Sit a bit closer* (Cuddle up to me!)
Chóh-hòi-dī	*Sit further away* (Stop crowding me!)

10 *Làai* to pull

Làai is the normal verb *to pull* and it is the character which you see marked on doors: the opposite is **tèui** *push*. **Làai** is also used, meaning *to pull someone in, to arrest*.

11 *lìhn . . . dōu . . .* even . . .

Lìhn is a very useful word provided you remember how to position it. The golden rules are that **lìhn** is placed before the word which it refers to and that they both *must* come before **dōu**. You will also remember from as far back as Unit 1 that **dōu** must itself always come before a verb, so there is a certain rigidity about this pattern. A few examples will show you how to use it:

Lìhn Wòhng Sìn-sàang dōu m̀h jùng-yi Wòhng Síu-jé.	*Even Mr Wong doesn't like Miss Wong.*
Ngóh lìhn yāt mān dōu móuh.	*I haven't got even one dollar.*
Kéuih lìhn faahn dōu m̀h séung sihk.	*She doesn't fancy even rice.*

12 *séuhng* to go up

The real meaning of **séuhng** is *to go up, to ascend*. **Séuhng-sàan** means *to go up the hill* and **séuhng-chē** is *to get (up) onto the vehicle*. In some cases, though, **séuhng** is used meaning *to go to*. In Unit 12 you met **séuhng-tòhng** *to go to class* and in the dialogue there is another example, **séuhng gíng-chaat-guhk** *to go to the police station*. You are advised not to make up your own phrases using **séuhng** in the sense of *to go to*, only use the ones you meet in this book.

i Secret society slang

One of the biggest influences on contemporary Cantonese language has been the great popularity of gangster films and programmes on television and in the cinema. The racy slang which gives authenticity to the shows passes rapidly into ordinary people's speech, but equally quickly is discarded again. At the end of the dialogue we have included just a couple of terms which seem to be likely to stay around, but there is little point in your learning any more – by the time that you are able to use it it may well not be current any longer!

Exercise 1

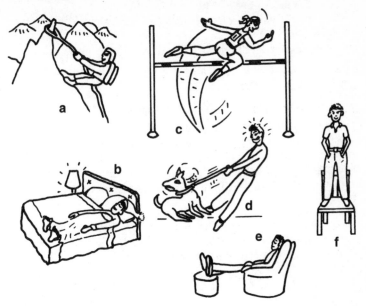

Try to describe in Cantonese what Mr Wong is doing in each of these pictures.

Exercise 2
Fill in the blanks to show the occupations of each of the following people.

a   Chàhn Sìn-sàang làai fáahn-duhk ge yàhn: kéuih haih __.
b   Wòhng Síu-jé hái jùng-hohk gaau-syu: kéuih haih __.
c   Léih Sàang sèhng-yaht jà dīk-sí: kéuih haih __.
d   Jèung Sàang hái jáu-làuh nìng yéh béi yàhn sihk: kéuih haih __.
e   Ngóh bàh-bā hái chán-só jouh-yéh: kéuih haih __.

Exercise 3
Into each of the following sentences put one of the randomly listed inserts i–v (overleaf), then translate the sentence into English.

a   Kéuih wah kéuih Sìng-kèih-yāt wúih fàan-làih, daahn-haih kéuih Sìng-kèih-sàam __ fàan.
b   Néih jáu-jó __, ngóh jauh dá dihn-wá béi néih taai-táai lak.

c Séuhng-go-yuht Wòhng Táai __ yāt ga chē dōu maaih-m̀h-dóu: kéuih ge gìng-léih hóu m̀h hòi-sām.
d Kéuih yaht-yaht __ dá-màh-jeuk, só-yíh m̀h dāk-hàahn tùhng ngóh heui máaih-sung.
e Yàuh-séui ge sìh-hauh __ m̀h haih géi fòng-bihn.

Inserts: i dōu ii lìhn iii jeuk sāam-kwàhn iv sìn-ji v jì-hauh

Exercise 4
Answer the following briefly in Cantonese.

a Yāt nìhn yauh géi-dò yaht a?
b Chìhn-yaht haih Láih-baai-sei: tìng-yaht nē?
c Sei-yuht yáuh géi-dò yaht a?
d Sàam go sìng-kèih dò m̀h dò yaht gwo yāt go yuht a?
e Yāt-chìn yaht noih dihng-haih sàam nìhn noih nē?

Exercise 5
Three complicated sentences laden with adjectives for you to put into Cantonese. Remember, keep cool – they aren't so bad if you work out what the basic patterns must be.

a *That young lady who is standing on the left of Mrs Chan is Mr Wong's 17-year-old daughter.*
b *Which is the Japanese car you bought when you were touring in the States?*
c *This old fire extinguisher of yours is not big enough. How about buying a bigger one?*

18

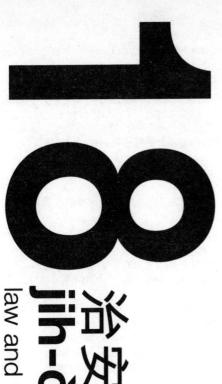

jih-ōn 治安
law and order

In this unit you will learn
- how to report a crime
- vocabulary dealing with law and crimes

▶ Dialogue 1

Three friends discuss the crime rate.

我每日睇報紙都一定睇到啲令我好唔開心嘅新聞嘅，譬如係謀殺喇，
　強姦喇，吸毒喇，打交喇，打劫喇，打荷包喇等等。

李太，呢啲嘅嘅情況唔只喺香港好普遍，喺外國好多大城市都一樣
　普遍㗎。

前幾年我住喺紐約，喺我住嘅附近，幾乎每日都有罪案發生，而且都
　係我親眼睇見嘅，但係都唔見本地報紙有報導，你可以想像罪案多
　到幾咁嚴重嘞！

張太，聽你咁樣講，香港嘅治安雖然唔係十分好，但係都唔算太壞
　嘴！

係呀，真係唔算太壞，最少到而家為止，我哋普通人重敢一個人喺
　夜晚出街買野。

Mrs Lee	Ngóh múih yaht tái bou-jí dōu yāt-dihng tái-dóu dī lihng ngóh hóu m̀h hòi-sām ge sàn-mán ge, pei-yùh haih màuh-saat lā, kèuhng-gàan lā, kāp-duhk lā, dá-gāau lā, dá-gip lā, dá-hòh-bāau lā, dáng-dáng.
Mrs Wong	Léih Táai, nī dī gám ge chìhng-fong m̀h-jí hái Hèung-góng hóu póu-pin, hái ngoih-gwok hóu dò daaih sìhng-síh dōu yāt-yeuhng póu-pin ga.
Mrs Jeung	Chìhn-géi-nìhn ngóh jyuh hái Náu-yeuk, hái ngóh jyuh ge fuh-gahn, gèi-fùh múih yaht dōu yáuh jeuih-on faat-sàng, yìh-ché dōu haih ngóh chàn-ngáahn tái-gin ge, daahn-haih dōu m̀h gin bún-deih bou-jí yáuh bou-douh. Néih hó-yíh séung-jeuhng jeuih-on dò dou géi-gam yìhm-juhng laak!
Mrs Wong	Jèung Táai, tèng néih gám-yéung góng, Hèung-góng ge jih-òn sèui-yìhn m̀h haih sahp-fàn hóu daahn-haih dōu m̀h syun taai waaih bo!
Mrs Jeung	Haih a, jàn-haih m̀h syun taai waaih. Jeui-síu dou-yìh-gā-wàih-jí ngóh-deih póu-tùng-yàhn juhng gám yāt-go-yàhn hái yeh-máan chēut-gāai máaih-yéh.

報紙 **bou-jí**	newspaper
令 **lihng**	to cause, to make
謀殺 **màuh-saat**	murder, to murder
強姦 **kèuhng-gàan**	rape, to rape
吸毒 **kāp-duhk**	to take drugs
打交 **dá-gāau**	brawling, to fight
打劫 **dá-gip**	robbery, to rob
打荷包 **dá-hòh-bāau**	purse snatching, to pick pockets
唔只 **m̀h-jí**	not only
普遍 **póu-pin**	common (widespread)
外國 **ngoih-gwok**	foreign, foreign country
城市 **sìhng-síh**	city, town
前幾年 **chìhn-géi-nìhn**	a few years ago
紐約 **Náu-yeuk**	New York
幾乎 **gèi-fùh**	almost but not quite
發生 **faat-sàng**	to occur, happen, transpire
親眼 **chàn-ngáahn**	with one's own eyes
本地 **bún-deih**	local, indigenous
報導 **bou-douh**	report, to report
想像 **séung-jeuhng**	to imagine
幾咁......嘞！ **géi-gam- . . . laak!**	how very . . . !
治安 **jih-òn**	law and order, public order
雖然...... 但係	although . . . yet . . .
sèui-yìhn . . . daahn-haih	
十分 **sahp-fàn**	totally, 100 per cent
最少 **jeui-síu**	at least
到而家為止 **dou-yìh-gā-wàih-jí**	up to now
普通 **póu-tùng**	common (ordinary)
敢 **gám**	to dare, to dare to
一個人 **yāt-go yàhn**	alone
出街 **chēut-gāai**	to go out into the street

ℹ Things foreign

Ngoih means outside, as you will remember from **ngoih-bihn**. **Ngoih-gwok** *outside country* is the standard word for *foreign country* and as you might expect, **ngoih-gwok-yàhn** means *a foreigner* and **ngoih-gwok-wá** means *a foreign language*. **Ngoih-gwok** is contrasted with **jùng-gwok** *central country*, the country around which all others revolve, China. The Chinese have always considered themselves to be at the centre of the world, just as the Romans did with their tellingly named 'Medi-terranean' sea and this means that it is something of a contradiction in terms for Chinese in another country to describe themselves as **ngoih-gwok-yàhn** – wherever they go they remain Chinese and so the indigenous peoples tend to be called *foreigners* in their own lands.

Grammar

1 *Póu-tùng* and *póu-pin*: 'common'

Both **póu-pin** and **póu-tùng** mean *common*, but there is a difference between them. **Póu-pin** means *common* in the sense of *widespread, universal, two-a-penny*: and **póu-tùng** means *common* in the sense of *ordinary, normal*. A **póu-tùng-yàhn** is *an ordinary chap, the man on the Clapham/Shanghai omnibus*.

ℹ Póu-tùng-wá

Póu-tùng-wá is *common language*, that is, the language which is to be used throughout China, what in English is usually called Mandarin and in China is known officially as *Putonghua*. One use of **póu-tùng** is as a way of responding to a compliment: *How beautiful your handwriting is, Mr Wong!* – **Póu-tùng jē**. (*It's just run of the mill*.) But sometimes this very modest response is said with a cock of the head which belies its apparent humility and Mr Wong can be understood in a boastful way to be saying something like *I'm just an ordinary genius, you know!*

2 *Póu-tùng-wá* and other languages

Wah means *to say*, as you learned in Unit 6, but when its tone is changed to **wá** it means *speech, language* and often appears as the object of the lonely verb **góng** *to speak*. *To speak Mandarin* is **góng Póu-tùng-wá** and *to speak a foreign language* is **góng ngoih-gwok-wá**. You can add **wá** to the name of any country to give the language spoken in that country:

Yìng-gwok-wá	*English language*
Yaht-bún-wá	*Japanese language*
Jùng-gwok-wá	*Chinese language*

You already know the words **Yìng-màhn** and **Jùng-màhn** for English and Chinese languages and the addition of -**màhn** can be made to the roots of other country names too, but it is a risky thing to do if you have not met the word before – could you have predicted that the -**màhn** word for **Yaht-bún** is **Yaht-màhn**, for instance? So you are safer to stick to the -**wá** words.

The **màhn** and **wá** forms are not quite the same in meaning. **Màhn** refers to the whole notion of spoken and written language together, while **wá** really refers only to the spoken language, but in practice they are mostly used interchangeably.

3 Up to now

Dou-yìh-gā-wàih-jí seems an awful mouthful to represent *up to now*: it may help you to remember it if you analyse it. **Dou** means *to arrive at*, **yìh-gā** means *now*, **wàih-jí** means *as a stop*, so *arriving at now as a stop – up to now*. You can adapt the expression to some extent, for instance, **dou gàm-nín wàih-jí** *up until this year* and **dou johk-yaht wàih-jí** *up until yesterday*.

▶ Dialogue 2

A thoughtful prisoner makes a special pleading.

你犯咗偷嘢罪，而且罪名成立。我判你坐兩年監。你如果唔同意可以 上訴。你明白未？

法官大人，我明白，不過如果我坐完兩年監之後出嚟，一定搵唔到 嘢做，因為我坐過監，冇人會請我做嘢。所以我搵唔到錢，冇辦法 生活，會再次偷嘢……噉，又會再次坐監嘅嘛！

噉，你想點樣呢？係唔係唔想坐監，想罰錢呢？

唔係呀，大人，我實在冇錢俾你罰，啱啱相反，我希望你而家就判我 坐二十五年監啫。

點解你自願要坐二十五年監咁耐呢？

因為坐完二十五年監之後，嗰陣時我會成為一個六十歲嘅老人， 可以去攞老人救濟金，唔駛再做嘢嘞。

Judge	Néih faahn-jó tàu-yéh jeuih, yìh-ché jeuih-mìhng sìhng-lraap. Ngóh pun néih chóh léuhng nìhn gāam. Néih yùh-gwó m̀h tùhng-yi hó-yíh seuhng-sou. Néih mìhng-baahk meih?
Prisoner	Faat-gwùn Daaih-yàhn, ngóh mìhng-baahk, bāt-gwo yùh-gwó ngóh chóh-yùhn léuhng nìhn gāam jì-hauh chēut-làih, yāt-dihng wán-m̀h-dóu yéh jouh, yàn-waih ngóh chóh-gwo gāam, móuh yàhn wúih chéng ngóh jouh-yéh. Só-yíh ngóh wán-m̀h-dóu chín, móuh baahn-faat sàng-wuht, wúih joi-chi tàu-yéh . . . gám, yauh wúih joi-chi chóh-gāam ge bo!
Judge	Gám, néih séung dím-yéung nē? Haih m̀h haih m̀h séung chóh-gāam, séung faht-chín nē?
Prisoner	M̀h haih a, Daaih-yàhn. Ngóh saht-joih móuh chín béi néih faht. Ngāam-ngāam sèung-fáan, ngóh hèi-mohng néih yìh-gā jauh pun ngóh chóh yih-sahp-ńgh nìhn gāam jē.
Judge	Dím-gáai néih jih-yuhn yiu chóh yih-sahp-ńgh nìhn gāam gam noih nē?
Prisoner	Yàn-waih chóh-yùhn yih-sahp-ńgh nìhn gāam jì-hauh, gó-jahn-sìh ngóh wúih sìhng-wàih yāt go luhk-sahp seui ge lóuh-yàhn, hó-yíh heui ló lóuh-yàhn gau-jai-gām, m̀h sái joi jouh-yéh laak.

犯	**faahn**	to offend, commit a crime
偷野	**tàu-yéh**	to steal things, theft
罪	**jeuih**	a crime
罪名	**jeuih-mìhng**	charge, accusation
成立	**sìhng-Iraap**	established, to establish
判	**pun**	to sentence
坐監	**chóh-gāam**	to be in prison
上訴	**seuhng-sou**	to appeal to a higher court
法官	**faat-gwùn**	a judge
大人	**Daaih-yàhn**	Your Honour, Your Excellency, Your Worship
辦法	**baahn-faat**	method, way, means
生活	**sàng-wuht**	to live, livelihood
再次	**joi-chi**	another time, a second time
罰錢	**faht-chín**	to fine, to be fined
自願	**jih-yuhn**	voluntarily, willing
成為	**sìhng-wàih**	to become
老人	**lóuh-yàhn**	the elderly, the aged
救濟金	**gau-jai-gām**	relief money

Grammar

4 More on 'lonely verbs'

You have met plenty of verbs which normally require objects and you will recognize more as your Cantonese improves. **Tàu** *to steal* is another one and you will notice that **yéh** *things* is the supplied object. But you should not feel that because a verb has a fall-back object assigned to it you cannot embellish it – you could, for instance, say **kéuih tàu-jó hóu dò yéh** (*he stole a lot of things*). The same applies to other verb–object pairings: **chóh-gāam** (*to sit in prison*) means *to be imprisoned*, but you can see from the dialogue that the verb and its object can be split (**kéuih chóh léuhng nìhn gāam** – *he's doing two years*).

5 *Meih* and *móuh*

Both **meih** *not yet* and **móuh** *have not* are used to form questions with the verb ending -**gwo**:

Néih yáuh móuh sihk-gwo lùhng-hā a?
Néih sihk-gwo lùhng-hā meih a?

These two examples can both be translated by *Have you ever had lobster?*, but note that the second one implies that at some time you probably will try it, so that you might prefer to translate the first one as *Have you ever had lobster?* and the second as *Have you had lobster yet?*

Meih (but not **móuh**) can happily be used also with the verb ending **-jó** when you want to know whether something has taken place yet. It is very common to greet someone with:

Néih sihk-jó faahn meih a?   *Have you eaten yet?*

6 Can do/no can do?

In Unit 12 you met **tái-m̀h-dóu** *could not see* and in Unit 15 came **wán-m̀h-dóu** *cannot find*. In both cases you were left to guess what they meant, but you were owed an explanation and it is time you had one. In the dialogue the prisoner says **yāt-dihng wán-m̀h-dóu yéh jouh** *I'll certainly not be able to find work to do*. **Wán**, of course, means *to look for* and **dóu** you met in Unit 8 meaning *to succeed in*, so **wán-m̀h-dóu** means *to look for but not succeed in it – to be unable to find*. Here are a few more examples:

tái-m̀h-dóu	*unable to see*
daap-m̀h-dóu bā-sí	*unable to catch the bus*
gú-m̀h-dóu kéuih haih bīn-go	*can't guess who she is*

The positive form of this pattern uses **dāk** instead of **m̀h**, so **tái-dāk-dóu** means *able to see*, **daap-dāk-dóu** means *able to catch* and **gú-dāk-dóu** means *able to guess*. To ask a question you can, of course, as always, put positive and negative together:

Néih *daap-dāk-dóu*   *Can you catch the bus?*
**   *daap-m̀h-dóu* bā-sí a?**

But it would save breath to say:

Néih *daap-m̀h-daap-dāk-dóu* bā-sí a?

7 As much as that

To stress the size of numbers it is quite common to add a **gam** (*so*) expression, just as in the dialogue the judge says **chóh yih-sahp-ńgh nìhn gāam gam noih**. **Gam noih** means *so long a time* and the effect is to say *as long as 25 years in prison*. Here are some other examples:

Kéuih yáuh sàam-maahn mān gam dò.	He's got as much as $30,000.
Néih yáuh yih-baak bohng gam chúhng.	You weigh as much as 200 lbs.
Ngóh gáu-sahp-yat seui gam lóuh.	I'm all of 91 years old.

8 *Older* and *younger*

You will need to be careful with *old*. **Lóuh** means *really old*, *elderly*, *aged* and is therefore the appropriate word in the term for *old age relief*. But when you are comparing ages (*Jack is older than Jill*) it would be absurd to use **lóuh** if both of them are young. Cantonese prefers to use **daaih** *big* for *old* in such a case:

| Wòhng Síu-jé daaih-gwo Jèung Síu-jé. | Miss Wong is older than Miss Cheung. |
| Ngóh móuh néih gam daaih. | I am not as old as you. |

It is not impossible to say **Kéuih lóuh-gwo ngóh**, but only if I am already very elderly and he is even more so.

Exercise 1
Mr Wong is insatiably curious. Unfortunately, although he writes down the answers, his memory is so bad he can't remember what his questions were afterwards. Can you help him by supplying them (in Cantonese of course)? Here is his list of answers:

a Gàm-yaht haih Sìng-kèih-yih.
b Lèuhn-dēun Fèi-gèi-chèuhng hái sìhng-síh sài-bihn.
c Ngóh sing Jèung.
d Dī hā sei-sahp-luhk mān yāt gàn.
e Yauh m̀h haih chāt-dím-jūng heui, yauh m̀h haih baat-dím-jūng heui, yàn-waih kéuih saht-joih móuh chéng ngóh heui.

Exercise 2
A quick and simple test. What are the opposites of the following?

a nàahm-bihn	b nàahm-yán	c nī-syu
d chēut-bihn	e chēut-nín	f chìhn-yaht
g jàn	h jái	i jìu-jóu

Exercise 3

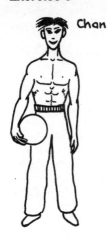

Chan

Cheung

Wong

Nī sàam go yàhn léuih-bihn, bīn-go jeui daaih a?

Exercise 4

Tone practice time again. Put in the tone marks on the following where necessary.

a   faai-di! (*hurry up!*)
b   fong-ga (*be on holiday*)
c   seuhng-bihn (*on top of*)
d   suhk-sik (*familiar with*)
e   yihng-jan (*sincere*)
f   yi-sang (*doctor*)
g   ngoih-tou (*jacket*)
h   ngaam-ngaam (*a moment ago*)

Exercise 5

Positive word power: dig into your vocabulary memory and find a word you know which is similar in meaning for each of the following.

a   bihn-yì
b   gíng-chaat-chē
c   m̀h haih jàn ge
d   bāt-gwo
e   m̀h hó-yíh

Exercise 6

Complete the unfinished words, remembering to get the tones right.

a   ____-wìhng (*prosperous*)
b   fòng-____ (*aspect*)
c   ____-léih (*to repair*)
d   yahm-____ (*any*)
e   ____-seui (*duty-free*)
f   ____-bihn (*convenient*)

19

經濟 gìng-jai

banking and finance

In this unit you will learn

- some vocabulary for your own banking transactions
- how to discuss higher financial matters
- grammar patterns for making your speech more lively, such as *the more . . . the more . . .*
- how to show reluctant agreement with someone

A customer has problems with his bank account.

小姐，呢張現金支票唔該你幫我兑咗佢，然後用嗰啲錢買五千蚊美金旅遊支票。

好呃。先生，重有乜嘢事呢？

嗱，呢張係我嘅銀行月結單，係今朝早收到嘅。張單上便寫明我個來往戶口上個月有赤字，而且重向銀行透支咗一萬三千蚊添。我實在冇向銀行透支過任何錢。我相信我嘅戶口一定唔會有赤字。唔該你幫我查一查，睇吓喺邊處錯咗。

好，請你交張月結單俾我喇，我會交俾有關嘅部門，有結果之後，銀行就會寫信俾你嘅嘞。

唔該晒。我希望你儘量快話我聽個結果係點樣。

好呃。我知道嘞。

唔該晒。我重想我幫我開一個外匯儲蓄戶口，好嗎？

好，冇問題。

呀，重有。今日馬克兑英鎊同埋港紙兑人民幣嘅兑換率係幾多呀？

我唔知嗎！請你去第三號櫃檯問嗰處嘅小姐喇！

Customer	Síu-jé, nī jèung yihn-gām jì-piu m̀h-gòi néih bòng ngóh deui-jó kéuih, yìhn-hauh yuhng gó dī chín máaih ńgh-chìn māan Méih-gām léuih-yàuh jì-piu.
Teller	Hóu ak. Sìn-sàang, juhng yáuh māt-yéh sih nē?
Customer	Nàh, nī jèung haih ngóh ge ngàhn-hòhng yuht-git-dāan, haih gàm-jìu-jóu sàu-dóu ge. Jèung dāan seuhng-bihn sé-mìhng ngóh go lòih-wóhng wuh-háu seuhng-go-yuht yáuh chek-jih, yìh-ché juhng heung ngàhn-hòhng tau-jì-jó yāt-maahn-sàam-chìn māan tìm. Ngóh saht-joih móuh heung ngáhn-hòhng tau-jì-gwo yahm-hòh chín. Ngóh sèung-seun ngóh ge wuh-háu yāt-dihng m̀h wúih yáuh chek-jih. M̀h-gòi néih bòng ngóh chàh-yāt-chàh, tái-háh hái bīn-syu cho-jó.
Teller	Hóu, chéng néih gàau jèung yuht-git-dāan béi ngóh lā, ngóh wúih gàau béi yáuh-gwàan ge bouh-mùhn. Yáuh git-gwó jì-hauh, ngàhn-hòhng jauh wúih sé-seun béi néih ge lak.
Customer	M̀h-gòi-saai. Ngóh hèi-mohng néih jeuhn-leuhng faai-dī wah ngóh tèng go git-gwó haih dím-yéung.
Teller	Hóu ak. Ngóh jì-dou lak.
Customer	M̀h-gòi-saai. Ngóh juhng séung néih bòng ngóh hòi yāt go ngoih-wuih chýuh-chūk wuh-háu, hóu ma?

Teller	Hóu, móuh mahn-tàih.
Customer	A, juhng yáuh. Gàm-yaht Máh-hāak deui Yìng-bóng tùhng-màaih Góng-jí deui Yàhn-màhn-baih ge deui-wuhn-léut haih géi-dō a?
Teller	Ngóh m̀h jì bo! Chéng néih heui daih-sàam-houh gwaih-tói mahn gó-syu ge síu-jé lā!

現金 yihn-gām	cash, ready money
支票 jì-piu	cheque
兌 deui	to cash a cheque, to exchange currency
美金 Méih-gām	American dollars
銀行 ngàhn-hòhng	bank
月結單 yuht-git-dāan	monthly statement
收到 sàu-dóu	to receive
寫 sé	to write
寫明 sé-mìhng	written clearly
來往 lòih-wóhng	coming and going; current (account)
戶口 wuh-háu	bank account
赤字 chek-jih	(red characters) in the red, deficit
透支 tau-jì	overdraft, to overdraw
相信 sèung-seun	to believe, to trust
查 chàh	to check, investigate
錯 cho	error, wrong, incorrect
有關 yáuh-gwàan	relevant, concerned
部門 bouh-mùhn	department
信 seun	a letter
儘量 jeuhn-leuhng	to the best of one's ability, so far as possible
開 hòi	to open
儲蓄 chýuh-chūk	savings, to save
馬克 máh-hāk or máh-hāak	Deutschmark
英鎊 yìng-bóng	pound sterling
港紙 Góng-jí	Hong Kong dollars
人民幣 yàhn-màhn-baih	renminbi, RMB
兌換率 deui-wuhn-léut	exchange rate

ℹ️ When *red* is not auspicious

It is hard to find red-coloured things which are not considered lucky by the Chinese, but to be *in the red* at the bank is no more desirable in a Chinese context than in a western one. It is perhaps significant that the usual word for *red* (**hùhng**) is not used, but instead the word **chek** (which also means *red*) appears in the expression **chek-jih**. **Chek** has another meaning (*naked*) and appears in the term **chek-geuk-yī-sāng** *barefoot doctors*, the practitioners who were trained to an elementary level in an effort to bring medical benefits down to the most deprived areas of China as it strove to develop after the Communist Revolution of 1949. There is a link of poverty between these two uses of **chek**, it seems.

Grammar

1 Positive commands with *-jó*

You first met the verb ending -jó in Unit 4. It indicates that an action has been completed. The same verb ending also gives the idea *go ahead and do it!*, a polite and gentle exhortation. You will see an example in the dialogue where the customer says **m̀h-gòi néih bòng ngóh deui-jó kéuih** – *please cash it for me*. Often the final particle **lā** gives additional force to the exhortation:

Sihk-jó kéuih lā!   *Eat it up!*

You should note that this use of -jó is always accompanied by an object, either **kéuih** or a more specific noun:

Dá-jó dihn-wá lā!   *Make the phone call!*

2 *Lòih-wóhng*

Lòih-wóhng means *coming and going*, so *a current account* is literally *a coming and going account*. You will sometimes hear people saying **lòih-lòih-wóhng-wóhng**, meaning *great to-ings and fro-ings*.

3 Look one look!

As you will remember from Unit 15, **yāt-háh** conveys the idea of doing something for a little while. You can also show this same idea by doubling a verb with **yāt** in the middle:

chàh-yāt-chàh   *run a little check*
tái-yāt-tái   *have a peep*

4 *Cho* mistake

Cho is a very useful little word. Its basic meaning is *incorrect, mistaken* and this is the meaning which you will find in the dialogue (**tái-háh hái bīn-syu cho-jó** – *and see where the error has occurred*). It can also be attached to other verbs as a verb ending:

Ngóh tèng-cho lak.	*I misheard.*
Nī go jih néih sé-cho lak.	*You've written this character wrongly.*

In Unit 11 you met the same word **cho** in **m̀h-cho** *not bad, pretty good*; and it appears yet again in another useful expression **móuh-cho** *there's no mistake, quite right*.

▶ Dialogue 2

Two puzzled friends discuss world finance.

上個禮拜五有幾間大銀行都公佈要增加利息。香港人做生意就會越嚟越難嘞。我估下個禮拜香港股票市場又會有大災難嘞。

我估香港今年嘅通貨膨脹一定會超過百分之十。

我都估會嘞。如果係噉樣，今年會係香港連續第三年通脹超過百分之十嘅嘞，不過通貨膨脹實在係乜野嚟嘅，我唔知。

老實講，我都唔知道係乜野嚟嘅。我只係知道我嘅錢越嚟越唔夠。歐洲嘅法國，德國，意大利同埋英國，佢哋嘅通脹重高過香港嘅喇！但係我覺得美國嘅通脹比較歐洲國家嘅重嚴重的添。

講起嚟，我唔明白點解最近幾年美國嘅經濟變得咁壞，美金貶值得咁多？

係呀！我都唔明白。最近幾年美國都冇參加大規模戰爭喇，點解經濟反而衰退呢？

對呢個問題，我哋兩個都係外行。我哋唔好再講啦！不如講啲比較容易明白嘅野喇。喂，你幾時同我去睇跑馬呀？你成日都話想去，但係好耐都冇去過。老實講，你想唔想去呀？

想係想，但係最近我冇乜錢，唔敢買馬嘞。

唔緊要喫！你可以睇，唔駛買。嚟喇！嚟喇！星期六你一定要同我一齊去玩。

Mr Wong Seuhng-go-Láih-baai-ńgh yáuh géi gàan daaih ngàhn-hòhng dōu gùng-bou yiu jàng-gà leih-sīk. Hèung-góng-yàhn jouh sàang-yi jauh wúih yuht-làih-yuht-nàahn lak. Ngóh gú hah-go-láih-baai Hèung-góng gú-piu síh-chèuhng yauh wúih yáuh daaih jòi-naahn lak.

Mr Lee	Ngóh gú Hèung-góng gàm-nín ge tùng-fo-pàahng-jeung yāt-dihng wúih chìu-gwo baak-fahn-jì-sahp.
Mr Wong	Ngóh dōu gú wúih lak. Yùh-gwó haih gám-yéung, gàm-nín wúih haih Hèung-góng lìhn-juhk daih-sàam nìhn tùng-jeung chìu-gwo baak-fahn-jì-sahp ge lak. Bāt-gwo tùng-fo-pàahng-jeung saht-joih haih māt-yéh làih-ga, ngóh m̀h jì.
Mr Lee	Lóuh-saht góng, ngóh dōu m̀h jì-dou haih māt-yéh làih-ge. Ngóh jí-haih jì-dou ngóh ge chín yuht-làih-yuht-m̀h-gau. Aù-jàu ge Faat-gwok, Dāk-gwok, Yi-daaih-leih tùhng-màaih Yìng-gwok, kéuih-deih ge tùng-jeung juhng gòu-gwo Hèung-góng ge lā! Daahn-haih ngóh gok-dāk Méih-gwok ge tùng-jeung béi-gaau Aù-jàu gwok-gà ge juhng yìhm-juhng-dī tìm.
Mr Wong	Góng-héi-làih, ngóh m̀h mìhng-baahk dím-gáai jeui-gahn-géi-nìhn Méih-gwok ge gìng-jai bin-dāk gam waaih, Méih-gam bín-jihk-dāk gam dò nē?
Mr Lee	Haih a! Ngóh dōu m̀h mìhng-baahk. Jeui-gahn-géi-nìhn Méih-gwok dōu móuh chàam-gà daaih-kwài-mòuh jin-jàng lā. Dím-gáai gìng-jai fáan-yìh sèui-teui nē?
Mr Wong	Deui nī go mahn-tàih, ngóh-deih léuhng go dōu haih ngoih-hóng. Ngóh-deih m̀h-hóu joi góng lā! Bāt-yùh góng dī béi-gaau yùhng-yìh mìhng-baahk ge yéh lā. Nàh, néih géi-sí tùhng ngóh heui tái páau-máh a? Néih sèhng-yaht dōu wah séung heui, daahn-haih hóu noih dōu móuh heui-gwo. Lóuh-saht góng, néih séung m̀h séung heui a?
Mr Lee	Séung-haih-séung, daahn-haih jeui-gahn ngóh móuh māt chín, m̀h gám máaih-máh lak.
Mr Wong	M̀h gán-yiu ga! Néih hó-yíh tái, m̀h-sái máaih. Làih lā! Làih lā! Sìng-kèih-luhk néih yāt-dihng yiu tùhng ngóh yāt-chaih heui wáan.

	公佈 **gùng-bou**	*to announce*
	利息 **leih-sīk**	*interest*
越......越......	**yuht . . . yuht . . .**	*the more . . . the more . . .*
	市場 **síh-chèuhng**	*market*
	災難 **jòi-naahn**	*disaster*
	通(貨膨)脹	*inflation*
	tùng(-fo-pàahng)-jeung	
	超過 **chìu-gwo**	*to exceed*
百分之十	**baak-fahn-jì-sahp**	*10 per cent*

連續 **lìhn-juhk**	in succession, consecutively
嗓嘅／嚟？ **làih-ge/ga?**	final particle: for identification
歐洲 **Aù-jàu**	Europe
法國 **Faat-gwok**	France
德國 **Dāk-gwok**	Germany
意大利 **Yi-daaih-leih**	Italy
比較 **béi-gaau**	comparatively, to compare
國家 **gwok-gà**	country, state
最近 **jeui-gahn**	recent, recently
經濟 **gìng-jai**	economy, economic
變 **bin**	to change
貶值 **bín-jihk**	to devalue
大規模 **daaih-kwài-mòuh**	large scale
戰爭 **jin-jàng**	war
反而 **fáan-yìh**	on the contrary, despite this
衰退 **sèui-teui**	to go into decline
外行 **ngoih-hóng**	layman, outsider
不如 **bāt-yùh**	it would be better if
跑馬 **páau-máh**	to race horses, horse racing

Grammar

5 The more . . . the more . . .

There are two similar patterns using **yuht . . . yuht. . . .** There is an example of the first one in the dialogue: **yuht-làih-yuht-nàahn** (literally, *the more comes the more difficult*) it gets *more and more difficult*. You can add any adjective to the **yuht-làih-yuht-** phrase:

Chóh fó-chē	It gets more and more expensive
yuht-làih-yuht-gwai.	to travel by train.
Kéuih go jái	Her son gets taller and taller.
yuht-làih-yuht-gòu.	

The second pattern does not use **làih** but instead uses two different adjectives or verbs to give the sense *the more it is this then the more it is that*:

Tái-bō, yàhn yuht dò	*When watching football, the*
yuht hóu-wáan.	*more people there are the more fun it is.*
Wòhng Táai yuht góng	*The more Mrs Wong talks the*
yuht hòi-sām.	*happier she is.*

6 Making fractions

Baak-fahn-jì-sahp literally means *ten of 100 parts* and therefore *ten parts in 100* or more normally *10 per cent*. All percentages are done the same way, so *12 per cent* is baak-fahn-jì-sahp-yih, and *75 per cent* is baak-fahn-jì-chāt-sahp-ńgh. In fact, all fractions are made in this way too:

sàam-fahn-jì-yāt	*one third*
sei-fahn-jì-sàam	*three quarters*
sahp-ńgh-fahn-jì-sahp-sei	*fourteen fifteenths*

7 Final particle for identification

When something is defined or described for recognition by the listener, the speaker uses the final particle làih-ge *that's what it is*. The question form is làih-ga? *what is it?* and is most often heard in haih māt-yéh làih-ga? *what is it?*

8 Reluctant agreement

In the dialogue, Mr Lee is pressed to join Mr Wong at the races and he has to admit that he would like to go but has a money problem. Note the neat little pattern which allows reluctant agreement to be shown: it is verb-**haih**-verb, **daahn-haih** . . . :

Ngóh jùng-yi-haih-jùng-yi kéuih, daahn-haih ngóh dōu m̀h séung tùhng kéuih heui tái-hei.	*Yes, I like him all right, but I still don't want to go to the pictures with him.*
Wòhng Síu-jé leng-haih-leng, daahn-haih móuh Jèung Síu-jé gam leng.	*Miss Wong is pretty all right, but she's not as pretty as Miss Cheung.*

9 *Móuh māt* not much

Ngóh móuh māt(-yéh) chín means *I haven't got much money*. Māt-yéh in this case changes its spots and instead of being a question word, comes to mean *whatever* (*I haven't got any money whatever*). All the question words can perform the same trick – bīn-go *whoever*, bīn-syu *wherever*, géi-dō *however much*, géi-sí *whenever*, dím-yéung *however*:

Néih heui bīn-douh a?	*Where are you going?*
Ngóh bīn-douh dōu m̀h heui.	*I'm not going anywhere. (I'm not going to any wherevers)*
Néih géi-sí heui Yìng-gwok a?	*When are you going to Britain?*
Ngóh géi-sí dōu m̀h heui.	*I'm not going anytime.*

Exercise 1

Mr Wong is on the phone to his stockbroker, and you can hear his end of the conversation. Can you supply what the stockbroker is saying (in Cantonese of course)?

Mr Wong	Chéng-mahn, gàm-yaht Yìng-bóng deui Góng-jí haih m̀h haih gòu-gwo johk-yaht a?
Broker	**a** *No, it's not as high as yesterday.*
Mr Wong	Dím-gáai Yìng-bóng bín-jihk-jó gam dò nē?
Broker	**b** *The British government recently said they wouldn't raise interest rates.*
Mr Wong	Néih gú hah-go-láih-baai Yìng-bóng wúih m̀h wúih hóu-fàan-dī nē?
Broker	**c** *I think the pound is sure to go a lot higher then.*
Mr Wong	Néih góng-dāk dōu-géi ngāam. Hóu, ngóh jauh hah-go-láih-baai sìn-ji máaih Yìng-bóng lā.
Broker	**d** *No problem. Phone me again at that time.*
Mr Wong	M̀h-gòi-saai. Joi-gin.

Exercise 2

Give simple answers to these simple alternative questions. You have a 50–50 chance of being right even if you do not understand the question!

a Daaih-wuih-tòhng haih hái hèung-há dihng-haih hái sìhng-síh nē?

b Néih yáuh-behng ge sìh-hauh gok-dāk sỳu-fuhk dihng-haih sàn-fú nē?

c Geuk-jai yuhng-làih tìhng-chē dihng-haih hòi-chē nē?

d Néih gú jóu-chāan haih māt-yéh a? Haih yeh-máahn sihk ge dihng-haih yaht-táu sihk ge nē?

Exercise 3

Which of **i** and **ii** is the correct translation of the English sentence?

a *I can't go there with you.*
   i Ngóh m̀h hó-yíh tùhng néih heui gó-syu.
   ii Ngóh tùhng néih m̀h hó-yíh heui gó-syu.

b *I can't drive to the outlying islands.*
   i Ngóh m̀h hó-yíh hái lèih-dóu jà-chē.
   ii Ngóh m̀h hó-yíh jà-chē heui lèih-dóu.

c *I won't be able to come until this afternoon.*
   i Ngóh hah-jau jauh làih-dāk lak.
   ii Ngóh hah-jau sìn-ji làih-dāk.

d *I like eating fruit salad.*
  i Ngóh jùng-yi sihk sàang-gwó tùhng sà-léut.
  ii Ngóh jùng-yi sihk sàang-gwó sà-léut.

e *What do you intend to do when you go to Japan?*
  i Néih géi-sí heui Yaht-bún, séung jouh māt-yéh a?
  ii Néih heui Yaht-bún ge sìh-hauh, séung jouh māt-yéh a?

Exercise 4
Write out the English translations of the five sentences which you decided were incorrect.

Exercise 5

a Chàhn Sàang ūk-kéi, bīn-go jeui daaih a?
b Nī dī yàhn léuih-bihn néuih-ge haih baak-fahn-jì-géi a?
c Nàahm-ge nē?
d Haih Chàhn Sàang gòu nē dihng-haih Chàhn Táai gòu nē?
e Chàhn Sàang, Chàhn Táai yáuh géi-dō go jái a?

20

郵政
yàuh-jing
using the postal system

In this unit you will learn
- words relating to money
- how to give the date

▶ Dialogue 1

A post office clerk patiently explains something to an anxious customer.

唔該俾十個郵柬，廿五個一蚊嘅郵票，同廿五個個八嘅郵票我。請問
　　幾時有新紀念郵票賣呀？

十月十八號。

好呃！噉，下個月幾時有新首日信封買呀？

下個月十二號。

呢封信我寄空郵去英國，請你幫我磅吓，要幾多郵費？

十二個六喇。

如果係平郵要幾多錢呀？要寄幾耐呀？

要三個二銀錢。差唔多要三個禮拜。

呢封信如果寄掛號要幾多錢呀？

掛號信嘅手續費係三蚊。

噉，呢封信我一共要俾幾多錢呀？

呀嘩吟要十四個六。

呢度係十五蚊。

找返四毫子俾你，多謝。

你哋有冇特快郵遞服務呀？

我哋呢間郵局太細嘞，暫時未有，請你去郵政總局喇。

Customer	M̀h-gòi béi sahp go yàuh-gáan, yah-ńgh go yāt mān ge yàuh-piu, tùhng yah-ńgh go go-baat ge yàuh-piu ngóh. Chéng-mahn géi-sìh yáuh sàn géi-nihm yàuh-piu maaih a?
Clerk	Sahp-yuht sahp-baat-houh.
Customer	Hóu ak! Gám, hah-go-yuht géi-sìh yáuh sàn sáu-yaht seun-fūng maaih a?
Clerk	Hah-go-yuht sahp-yih-houh.
Customer	Nī fùng seun ngóh gei hùng-yàuh heui Yìng-gwok, chéng néih bòng ngóh bohng-háh, yiu géi-dō yàuh-fai?
Clerk	Sahp-yih-go-luhk lā.
Customer	Yùh-gwó haih pìhng-yàuh yiu géi-dō chín a? Yiu gei géi-noih a?
Clerk	Yiu sàam-go-yih ngàhn-chín. Yiu sàam go géi láih-baai.
Customer	Nī fùng seun yùh-gwó gei gwa-houh yiu géi-dō chín a?
Clerk	Gwa-houh-seun ge sáu-juhk-fai haih sàam mān.
Customer	Gám, nī fùng seun ngóh yāt-guhng yiu béi géi-dō chín a?
Clerk	Hahm-baahng-laahng yiu sahp-sei go luhk.
Customer	Nī-douh haih sahp-ńgh mān.
Clerk	Jáau-fàan sei houh-jí béi néih, dò-jeh.
Customer	Néih-deih yáuh móuh dahk-faai yàuh-daih fuhk-mouh a?
Clerk	Ngóh-deih nī gàan yàuh-gúk taai sai lak, jaahm-sìh meih yáuh, chéng néih heui yàuh-jing-júng-gúk lā.

郵束	**yàuh-gáan**	*an airletter form*
郵票	**yàuh-piu**	*postage stamp*
個八	**go-sei**	*one dollar 40 cents*
紀念	**géi-nihm**	*memorial, to commemorate*
......號	**-houh**	*day of the month* (in dates)
首日	**sáu-yaht**	*first day*
信封	**seun-fūng**	*envelope*
封	**fùng**	*classifier for letters*
空郵	**hùng-yàuh**	*airmail*
郵費	**yàuh-fai**	*postage*
平郵	**pìhng-yàuh**	*surface mail*
寄	**gei**	*to post*
幾耐？	**géi-noih?** or **géi-nói?**	*how long?*
銀錢	**ngàhn-chín**	*dollar*
手續費	**sáu-juhk-fai**	*procedure fee, handling charge*
一共	**yāt-guhng**	*altogether*
呫嘩吟	**hahm-baah(ng)-laahng**	*all told, altogether, all*
找（返）錢	**jáau(-fàan)-chín**	*to give change*
特快郵遞	**dahk-faai yàuh-daih**	*express mail*
特快	**dahk-faai**	*express*
郵局	**yàuh-gúk**	*a post office*
暫時	**jaahm-sìh**	*temporary, temporarily*
郵政總局	**yàuh-jing-júng-gúk**	*general post office*

Grammar

1 Subtleties of classifiers

You are now happily at home with the idea of classifiers and the way in which they help to describe or categorize the nouns which follow them. Sometimes their ability to categorize makes them of use in conveying shades of meaning. In the first line of the dialogue the customer asks for **yah-ńgh go go-sei ge yàu-piu** (25 one dollar 40 cent stamps). Now if you think about it, the 'correct' classifier for stamps should be **jèung** because of their flat sheet-like nature, but in this case the customer is not thinking of them as physical shapes but rather as items, so he uses **go** instead of **jèung**. Don't be alarmed if you occasionally hear people doing such things – mostly it is clear enough what is meant.

2 More on money

When whole dollars are involved, the word for dollar is **mān** as you know; but when there is a sum of dollars plus cents, the word for dollar becomes the classifier **go** with or without the noun **ngàhn-chín**. So:

léuhng mān = *$2* and **sahp-sei mān** = *$14*

But:

léuhng-go-sei (ngàhn-chín) = *$2.40c*
sahp-sei-go-gáu (ngàhn-chín) = *$14.90c*

Fifty cents is more conveniently expressed as *a half* (**bun**) in such sums, so it is usual to say **sàam-go-bun (ngàhn-chín)** for *$3.50c*, **sahp-ńgh-go-bun (ngàhn-chín)** for *$15.50c* and so on.

Ten cents as a sum is **yāt hòuh-jí** or **yāt hòuh**, so:

Kéuih yáuh luhk hòuh-jí	*He's got 60 cents*
Ngóh yáuh ńgh hòuh-jí jē	*I've only got 50 cents*

The smallest coin now in circulation in Hong Kong is the 10 cent piece, so that there is no need to deal in single cents. The 10 cent piece is called **yāt go hòuh-jí** and the one dollar coin is **yāt go ngàhn-chín**.

3 Dates

The months are simply expressed with numbers (see Unit 17). Days of the month use the same number word (**-houh**) that you met for addresses (**Fà-yùhn Douh yih-sahp-baat-houh**) and bus numbers (**sahp-ńgh-houh bā-sí**), so *1 January* is **Yāt-yuht yāt-houh**, *23 May* is **Ńgh-yuht yah-sàam-houh**, etc. The years are given in 'spelled out' number form followed by **nìhn**, as for example with **yāt-gáu-gáu-chāt-nìhn** (*1997*). Remember that the general always comes before the particular, so *30 June 1997* is:

Yāt-gáu-gáu-chāt-nìhn Luhk-yuht sàam-sahp-houh

And don't forget to add **nìhn** on the end when giving the year!

ℹ 1997

The date 30 June 1997 was an important one for Hong Kong. At midnight, Britain's rule of more than 150 years came to end, and under the **yāt-gwok léuhng-jai** (one country, two systems) policy Hong Kong became a Special Administrative Region (**Dahk-biht hàhng-jing kèui** or **Dahk-kèui** for short) of the People's Republic of China. The government of the SAR is headed by the Chief Executive (**Hàhng-jing jéung-gwùn**) or **Dahk-sáu** (*Special Head* as he is more informally known). An impressive midnight handover ceremony was televised all over the world, and **Wùih-gwài** (*Reversion, Handover*) has become a date marker for Hong Kong people, who now talk of **Wùih-gwài-chìhn** (*before the Handover*) and **Wùih-gwài-hauh** (*after the Handover*).

4 How long a time?

In Unit 6 you met **géi-sí?** *when?*, the question word asking for a *time when* answer. The question word asking for a *time how long* answer is **géi-noih?**:

Néih géi-sí heui Yaht-bún a?	*When are you going to Japan?*
Ngóh Sahp-yuht sei-houh heui.	*I'm going on 4 October.*
Néih hái Yaht-bún séung jyuh géi-noih a?	*How long do you intend to stay in Japan?*
Ngóh hái gó-douh séung jyuh léuhng go yuht.	*For two months.*

5 A word you cannot forget

Hahm-baah(ng)-laahng just has to be the strangest word in the Cantonese language. It is peculiar because each of the three syllables is completely meaningless on its own and because it doesn't even sound much like a Cantonese word. Once heard it is very hard to forget, so we don't think you will have any difficulty with it. One of its meanings is *altogether*, as you will have seen from the dialogue:

Lùhng-hā, gáu-sahp-sei mān; hā, sàam-sahp-yih-go-bun; hahm-baah-laahng yāt-baak-yih-sahp-luhk-go-bun ngàhn-chín.	*$94 for the lobster; $32.50 for the prawns: $126.50 altogether.*

Its other meaning is *the whole lot* or *all* and in this it is usually accompanied by **dōu** (the adverb meaning *all* with which you are now very familiar):

Kéuih-deih sèhng-gà yàhn hahm-baahng-laahng dōu jáu-saai lak.	*The whole family went away, every last one of them.*

6 Not for the time being

The last line of the dialogue contains the expression **jaahm-sìh meih yáuh** (lit: *temporarily not yet got*) *for the time being it hasn't got it*. The expression is much used as a polite way of saying *not in stock* or *nothing yet* and it appears to offer hope that soon everything will be alright, but it would be best not to put too much faith in that hope; sometimes it seems to be merely a kindly way of saying *no*.

▶ Dialogue 2

A tourist plagues his hotel clerk with questions about mail.

我間房嘅信紙用晒嘞，你哋重有冇呀？咦！呢啲明信片設計得幾靚
　嗻！我想買五張要幾多錢呀？

多謝十二個半啦，先生。

喺酒店附近有冇郵局呀？

寄明信片唔駛去郵局，喺呢處或者喺酒店大門口右便都有郵筒。

我唔係寄明信片，我想寄一個包裹返英國，點樣寄法呀？

哦，原來你想寄包裹。嗽，好容易啫。你首先用白紙包好嗰個包裹，
　然後寫上地址……

最近酒店嘅郵局喺邊處呀？

喺酒店門口向左便行大約十分鐘就到嘞。到咗郵局之後，你要填寫一
　張寄包裹嘅表格，不過嗰張表格好簡單啫。包裹過磅之後，睇吓要
　幾多錢，然後買郵票，貼上郵票，嗽就得嘞！

我嘅包裹唔係好大，但係好容易爛嘅嗻！

嗽就麻煩嘞，因為郵局唔保證包裹裡便嘅嘢冇爛嘅。

嗽吖？等我諗一吓先。唔該晒。

Tourist	Ngóh gàan fóng ge seun-jí yuhng-saai lak, néih-deih juhng yáuh móuh a? Yí! Nī dī mìhng-seun-pín chit-gai-dāk géi leng bo! Ngóh séung máaih ńgh jèung yiu géi-dō chín a?
Clerk	Dò-jeh sahp-yih-go-bun la, sìn-sàang.
Tourist	Hái jáu-dim fuh-gahn yáuh móuh yàuh-gúk a?

Clerk	Gei mìhng-seun-pín m̀h-sái heui yàuh-gúk, hái nī-syu waahk-jé hái jáu-dim daaih-mùhn-háu yauh-bihn dōu yáuh yàuh-túng.
Tourist	Ngóh m̀h haih gei mìhng-seun-pín, ngóh séung gei yāt go bàau-gwó fàan Yìng-gwok, dím-yéung gei-faat a?
Clerk	Oh, yùhn-lòih néih séung gei bàau-gwó. Gám, hóu yùhng-yih jē. Néih sáu-sìn yuhng baahk-jí bàau-hóu gó go bàau-gwó, yìhn-hauh sé-seuhng deih-jí . . .
Tourist	Jeui káhn jáu-dim ge yàuh-gúk hái bīn-syu a?
Clerk	Hái jáu-dim mùhn-háu heung jó-bihn hàahng daaih-yeuk sahp fàn-jūng jauh dou lak. Dou-jó yàuh-gúk jì-hauh, néih yiu tìhn-sé yāt jèung gei bàau-gwó ge bíu-gaak, bāt-gwo gó jèung bíu-gaak hóu gáan-dàan jē. Bàau-gwó gwo-bóng jì-hauh, tái-háh yiu géi-dō chín, yìhn-hauh máaih yàuh-piu, tip-séuhng yàuh-piu, gám jauh dāk lak!
Tourist	Ngóh ge bàau-gwó m̀h-haih-hóu-daaih, daahn-haih hóu yùhng-yih laahn ge bo!
Clerk	Gám jauh màh-fàahn lak, yàn-waih yàuh-gúk m̀h bóu-jing bàau-gwó léuih-bihn ge yéh móuh laahn ge.
Tourist	Gám àh? Dáng ngóh nám yāt-háh sìn. M̀h-gòi-saai.

信紙	**seun-jí**	*letter paper*
明信片	**mìhng-seun-pín**	*postcard*
大門口	**daaih-mùhn-háu**	*main doorway*
門口	**mùhn-háu**	*doorway*
門	**mùhn**	*door, gate*
郵筒	**yàuh-túng**	*pillar box*
包裹	**bàau-gwó**	*parcel*
原來	**yùhn-lòih**	*originally, actually, in fact*
容易	**yùhng-yih**	*easy*
首先	**sáu-sìn**	*first of all*
白紙	**baahk-jí**	*blank paper*
紙	**jí**	*paper*
包	**bàau**	*to wrap up*
地址	**deih-jí**	*address*
近	**káhn**	*near, close*
大約	**daaih-yeuk**	*approximately*
填寫	**tìhn-sé**	*to fill in a form*
表格	**bíu-gaak**	*a form*
簡單	**gáan-dàan**	*simple*
貼上	**tip-séuhng**	*to stick on*
保證	**bóu-jing**	*to guarantee*
諗	**nám**	*to think, to think about, to think over*

Grammar

7 *Yùhn-lòih*

The basic meaning of **yùhn-lòih** is *originally*, but you will probably most often meet it meaning *in fact, so now I understand how it is*. When people use the phrase they usually are acknowledging that they had been under a misapprehension about something, so it is a natural partner of the verb **yíh-wàih** *to assume* which you met in Unit 11:

Ngóh yíh-wàih kéuih haih Yaht-bún-yàhn, daahn-haih yùhn-lòih kéuih haih Jùng-gwok-yàhn.	*I thought she was Japanese but actually she is Chinese.*

8 The verb ending *-hóu*

Hóu of course means *good* and *very*, but as a verb ending it gives the idea that the action of the verb has been completed satisfactorily:

Néih dī mìhng-seun-pín sé-hóu meih a?	*Have you written your postcards yet?*
Dī seun ngóh dá-hóu lak.	*I've typed the letters.*

There is only a slight difference between **-hóu** and **-yùhn** as verb endings: they both show that an action has come to an end, but **-hóu** indicates that the result of the action is a satisfactory one.

9 *Séuhng* as a verb ending

Séuhng means *onto, to go up*. As a verb ending it also means *on* or *onto* and you will find that it often matches English usage quite closely:

sé-séuhng deih-jí	*to write the address on*
tip-séuhng yàuh-piu	*to stick on stamps*
Mh-gòi néih daai-séuhng gó déng móu.	*Please put on that hat.*

Exercise 1

Some of the words in this exercise you have not met for quite a while. Try writing out your translations of the sentences and if you have to look up some of the words make a list of them for special study later.

a Wòhng Sàang jeui m̀h jùng-yi yám yeuhk-séui.
b M̀h-hóu dàng-daaih-deui-ngáahn tái-jyuh ngóh.
c M̀h hahp-kwài-gaak ge bou-líu dōu dong haih chi-fo.
d Hái daaih-dong dóu-chín dòng-yín haih fèi-faat lā.
e Ngóh-deih yiu dò-dī jyu-yi ngóh-deih dī jái tùhng néui ge duhk-sỳu chìhng-fong.

Exercise 2

Give the Cantonese for the following dates and times.

a *4 June*   b *1 July 1997*   c *15 May 2004*
d *6.15 p.m. Sunday 11 December*   e *31 August next year*

Exercise 3

Choose which of the items in brackets best fits the sentence.

a Jeui sìn yáuh yàuh-piu ge gwok-gà haih (Jùng-gwok/Yìng-gwok/Yaht-bún).
b Sai-gaai daih-yāt gàan yàuh-gúk haih hái (Lèuhn-dēun/Náu-yeuk/Gwóng-jàu).
c Yìh-gā sai-gaai seuhng jeui gwai ge yāt go yàuh-piu haih (chìu-gwo yāt-maahn Yìng-bóng/yāt-maahn Yìng-bóng/m̀h gau yāt-maahn Yìng-bóng).
d Yáuh-dī deih-fòng, yàuh-piu dong haih (yihn-gām/sàn-fán-jing/fo-bún).

Exercise 4

Find suitable two-syllable Cantonese expressions using the clues supplied. The answer to the first one would be **chēut-gāai** or perhaps **hàahng-gāai**.

a Lèih-hòi ūk-kéi.   (__ __)
b Yāt go gwok-gà tùhng daih-yih go gwok-gà
  dá-gāau.   (__ __)
c Chà-m̀h-dō, jīk-haih . . .   (__ __)
d Yuhng fèi-gèi wahn ge seun.   (__ __)
e Hái sé-jih-làuh gwún-jyuh néih ge yàhn.   (__ __)
f Yāt go yàhn m̀h jeuk sāam.   (__ __)

Exercise 5

Dóu-chèuhng ge gìng-léih hóu m̀h hòi-sām lak! Nī ńgh go pàhng-yáuh dóu Lèuhn-pún, hahm-baahng-laahng dōu yèhng-gán chín. Dou-yìh-gā-wàih-jí kéuih-deih yāt-guhng yèhng-jó ńgh-maahn-sei-chìn-luhk-baak mān Méih-gām. Yèhng jeui dò ge haih Jèung Taai-táai, kéuih yèhng-jó ńgh-maahn-sei-chìn-luhk-baak mān ge sàam-fahn-jì-yāt. Daih-yih haih Hòh Sìn-sàang, kéuih yèhng-jó sei-fahn-jì-yāt. Daih-sàam haih Wòhng Sìn-sàang, yèhng-jó ńgh-fahn-jì-yāt. Daih-sei haih Léih Taai-táai, yèhng-jó luhk-fahn-jì-yāt. Yèhng jeui síu ge haih Chàhn Sìn-sàang, kéuih bāt-gwo* yèhng-jó yih-sahp-fahn-jì-yāt jē. (Chàhn Sàang wah m̀h-gán-yiu, yèhng ge chín m̀h dò daahn-haih dōu haih hóu-gwo sỳu!)

a M̀h-gòi néih nám-yāt-nám, tái-háh múih yāt go pàhng-yáuh yèhng-jó géi-dō chín nē?

b Juhng yáuh nē . . . Jèung Táai yèhng-jó gam dò chín séung chéng dī pàhng-yáuh yám-jáu. Dī jáu m̀h pèhng, máaih ńgh go yàhn ge jáu yāt-guhng yiu béi sei-ah-chāt-go-bun gam dò. Jèung Táai gàau-jó yāt jèung yāt-baak mān jí béi fó-gei, yìh-gā dáng kéuih jáau-fàan géi-dō a?

(*bāt-gwo means *but, however*, but it also can mean *only* and is most often used in this way with numbers.)

21

溫習（三）
wàn-jaahp (sàam)
revision (3)

Two short anecdotes about horses. The first is an old story about faith and unflappability. The second is a typical Chinese joke about someone who gets things wrong through being literal-minded.

Passage 1

Géi baak nìhn jì-chìhn, hái Jùng-gwok bak-bouh deih-fòng, yáuh yāt go sing Wòhng ge yáuh-chín-yàhn. Kéuih yáuh hóu dò yauh gòu yauh daaih yauh leng ge máh, kéuih dōu hóu jùng-yi nī dī máh tìm. Yáuh yāt yaht, yāt jek hóu leng daahn-haih géi lóuh ge máh m̀h-gin-jó.* Wòhng Sìn-sàang dī pàhng-yáuh go-go dōu gok-dāk hóu hó-sīk, kéuih-deih dōu gú Wòhng Sàang wúih hóu nàu, hóu m̀h hòi-sām, daahn-haih ngāam-ngāam sèung-fáan, kéuih m̀h-jí m̀h nàu, yìh-ché juhng sèung-seun jek máh hóu faai jauh wúih fàan-làih tìm. Géi yaht jì-hauh, jek lóuh máh jàn-haih fàan-jó-làih lak. Dī pàhng-yáuh dōu wah Wòhng Sàang hóu-chói, kéuih jí-haih siu-háh-gám wah: 'Gó jek lóuh máh sīk louh, kéuih wúih wán louh fàan-làih jē.'

(*m̀h-gin-jó (no longer could be seen) lost, go missing)

Passage 2

Hóu noih jì-chìhn hái Gwóng-jàu yáuh yāt go yī-sāng. Yáuh yāt yaht kéuih sé-jó yāt fùng hóu gán-yiu* ge seun béi jyuh hái daih-yih go sìhng-síh ge yī-sāng. Gó-jahn-sìh Jùng-gwok juhng-meih yáuh yàuh-gúk, yìh-ché kéuih hóu mòhng m̀h dāk-hàahn nìng seun heui gó-douh, só-yíh kéuih giu kéuih go jái bòng kéuih nìng-heui. Kéuih deui go jái wah 'Nī fùng seun hóu gán-yiu, yiu jeuhn-leuhng faai sung-dou bo! Nàh, geuk yuht dò yuht faai: néih jí-yáuh léuhng jek geuk m̀h gau sei jek geuk faai ge. Néih bāt-yùh yuhng ngóh jek máh heui lā! Faai-dī a!'

Go hauh-sāang-jái jáu-jó laak, bàh-bā dáng kéuih fàan-làih. Kéuih jì-dou yāt jek máh lòih-wóhng gó go deih-fòng dōu yiu baat go jūng-tàuh gam-seuhng-há. Gú-m̀h-dóu kéuih go jái gwo-jó léuhng yaht sìn-ji fàan-làih, deui bàh-bā hóu hòi-sām gám wah: 'Bàh-bā, ngóh fàan-làih lak. Néih wah faai m̀h faai nē? Ngóh séung-làih-séung-heui git-gwó séung-dóu yāt go hóu faai ge baahn-faat. Néih wah geuk yuht dò yuht faai, léuhng jek geuk m̀h gau sei jek geuk faai a . . . gám, ngóh làai-jyuh jek máh tùhng kéuih yāt-chàih hàahng . . . léuhng jek geuk m̀h gau sei jek geuk faai, luhk jek geuk yāt-dihng faai-gwo sei jek geuk, haih m̀h haih a?'

(*gán-yiu means important. You met it in Unit 2 in m̀h gán-yiu never mind, it doesn't matter or literally it is not important.)

Exercise 1

Did you manage to work out what **séung-làih-séung-heui** means? If you skipped over it, go back and try again. And then make an intelligent guess at the English equivalents of the following.

a hàahng-làih-hàahng-heui
b jáu-làih-jáu-heui
c Ngóh-deih góng-ga góng-làih-góng-heui dōu góng-m̀h-màaih lak

Exercise 2

Perhaps you know something about horses? Can you say which of the alternatives offered are correct?

a Yāt jek póu-tùng ge máh daaih-yeuk yáuh (ńgh-baak bohng/chāt-baak bohng/yāt-chìn bohng) chúhng.
b Yāt jek máh daaih-yeuk dou (sahp-ńgh seui/yih-sahp seui/yih-sahp-ńgh seui) jauh wúih séi ge lak.
c Yāt jek máh múih yaht jeui-síu yiu wahn-duhng (bun go jūng-tàuh/yāt go jūng-tàuh/sei go jūng-tàuh) sìn-ji wúih gihn-hòng ge.
d Yāt jek máh múih yaht jeui-síu yiu sihk (sahp bohng/yih-sahp bohng/sàam-sahp bohng) yéh.

Exercise 3

MAY 23
Thursday

MAY 24
Friday

10 am
10.30 am
12.15 pm
3.30 pm
6.45 pm
7.30 pm

Oh dear, it's my memory again! I have to keep a diary or I will forget what I have to do, but it seems that when I was filling it in for 23 May I forgot to write down what it was I had to remember! I think this scrap of paper I found in my pocket has the information on it, but it's hard to understand. Can you fill in the diary entries for me in English, please?

Hái Daaih-wuih-tòhng tùhng Jèung Síu-jé sihk an-jau.

Tùhng Hòh Síu-jé hái Hèung-góng Jáu-dim yám-jó baat go jih jáu, yìhn-hauh jauh yāt-chàih hàahng ńgh fān jūng louh heui tái-hei.

Dou léuih-yàuh gūng-sī ló gèi-piu.

Heui Wòhng gìng-léih sé-jih-làuh bun go jūng-tàuh jì-chìhn jauh yiu dá-dihn-wá giu dīk-sí làih lak.

Exercise 4
You have learned a lot of vocabulary now, so much that you know more than one way of saying some things. Try finding another word with the same or almost the same meaning as the following.

a daaih-yeuk **b** yāt-guhng **c** bāt-gwo
d tàuh-sīn **e** gaan-jūng **f** dím-gáai

Exercise 5
A few more Chinese children's puzzles to make you groan. What are the (fiendishly difficult) answers – in Cantonese please?

a Johk-yaht tìn-hei hóu yiht. Jèung Sìn-sàang hái ūk ngoih-bihn jouh wahn-duhng, jouh-jó yāt go jūng-tàuh gam noih. Kéuih dōu wah m̀h-haih-hóu-sàn-fú, m̀h taai yiht. Dím-gáai nē?

b Jèung Sìn-sàang haih yāt go laahp-saap-chē sī-gēi, múih yaht kéuih jà laahp-saap-chē chēut-gāai ge sìh-hauh dōu yáuh hóu dò yàhn nìng dī laahp-saap làih kéuih ga chē syu. Jí-haih gàm-yaht kéuih jà-chē chēut-gāai, móuh yàhn nìng laahp-saap làih. Dím-gáai nē?

c Wòhng Sìn-sàang m̀h jouh-yéh. Kéuih yaht-yaht dōu yuhng hóu dò chín, nìhn-nìhn dōu heui léuih-yàuh, sìh-sìh dōu máaih jeui gwai ge sàn chē. Yih-sahp nìhn jì-hauh kéuih sìhng-wàih yāt go yáuh yāt-baak-maahn mān ge yáuh-chín yàhn lak. Dím-gáai nē?

Exercise 6
No two people seem to agree exactly on anything. Here are some comments by different people about Mr Wong's new car. Can you put their different views accurately into Cantonese?

a *It's a very handsome car.*
b *It's handsome, it's true, but not as handsome as Mr Cheung's new car.*
c *It's not very handsome.*
d *It's not big enough.*
e *It's too expensive.*
f *It's the most handsome car in the world.*
g *It's much more handsome than my car is.*
h *It's just as large and just as expensive as Mr Cheung's new car.*

Exercise 7

Supply the missing words in the following sentences. Be careful: there may be more than one possibility and you should try to get the best.

a Nī _____ sìn-sàang haih Wòhng gìng-léih.
b Kéuih _____ yāt mān dōu m̀h háng béi gó go móuh chín ge yàhn.
c Ngóh màh-mā haih baat-sahp-ńgh seui gam _____.
d Kéuih làih-jó ____-noih a? Ngóh m̀h jì, daaih-yeuk léuhng-sàam go sìng-kèih, waahk-jé yáuh sei go sìng-kèih gam ____ lak.
e Ngóh ńgh-sahp-chāt seui, néih bāt-gwo haih sei-sahp-gáu seui jē. Ngóh ____-gwo néih baat seui.

Exercise 8

Usually one person picks up the bill when Cantonese people dine out, and 'going Dutch' is rare. Still, sometimes it is felt that for one person to pay for everyone would be too much, so different shares are agreed. Someone *draws a ghost's leg* **waahk-gwái-geuk** (**gwái** is *a ghost*), a ladder diagram with one vertical line for each person and a share written at the bottom of each. With the shares covered up, each person can add a horizontal line anywhere in the diagram or indeed can choose not to add a line at all. Then one by one they trace out their fate, going down their vertical until the first horizontal, which they must follow to the next vertical, down that to the next horizontal, follow that . . . and so on down to the bottom. Six friends have recently had two meals each costing $2,000. On each occasion they agreed to make one share of $800, one of $500, one of $400, one of $300 and two zero-sum shares. Diagram **A** shows the ghost's leg as drawn at the first meal and Diagram **B** shows four additional lines, which four of the participants decided to put in at the second meal. You should have no difficulty in working out who had to pay how much each time and how the situation was changed by the extra lines.

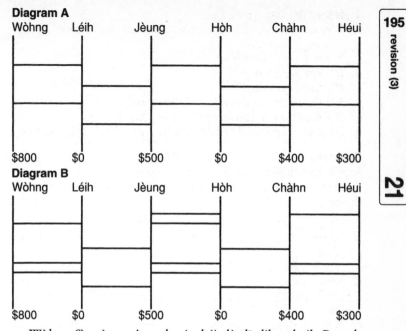

Diagram A

Wòhng   Léih   Jèung   Hòh   Chàhn   Héui

$800 $0 $500 $0 $400 $300

Diagram B

Wòhng   Léih   Jèung   Hòh   Chàhn   Héui

$800 $0 $500 $0 $400 $300

a Wòhng Sìn-sàang A-geuk yiu béi dò-dī dihng-haih B-geuk yiu béi dò-dī nē?

b B-geuk haih bīn wái yiu béi baat-baak mān a?

c Jèung Sìn-sàang A-geuk yiu béi, B-geuk dōu yiu béi. B-geuk kéuih yiu béi dò géi-dō chín a?

d Kéuih-deih yāt-chàih wáan A-geuk tùhng B-geuk, gám, bīn wái yiu béi jeui síu chín nē? bīn wái yiu béi jeui dò chín nē?

Exercise 9

Each of the sentences in this exercise uses one of the new grammar patterns from the last six units. If you can put them all into good Cantonese you can congratulate yourself on having really mastered some difficult material.

a When my mother speaks on the telephone she speaks quite slowly.

b Waiter, this coffee is not hot enough.

c Would you like beer or water?

d That pen of yours which you bought last month is not as expensive as this one of mine.

e She told me to tell you what time you should come.

f Mr Wong doesn't even like eating lobster.

g Two-thirds of these books are in Chinese.

h He gets richer and richer.

Exercise 10

Translate into English.

Hèung-góng ge tìn-hei Chāt-yuht, Baat-yuht, Gáu-yuht hóu
yiht. Tìn-hei yiht ge sìh-hauh dī yàhn hóu jùng-yi chóh dīk-sí,
yàn-waih dīk-sí yauh dò yauh sỳu-fuhk. Dím-gáai sỳu-fuhk nē?
Yàn-waih ga-ga dōu yauh láahng-hei. Yāt ga dīk-sí hó-yíh
chóh-dāk sei waahk-jé ńgh go yàhn, m̀h-sái hóu dò chín, hóu
pèhng jē. Póu-tùng hei-chē yáuh làahm-sīk ge, yáuh luhk-sīk ge,
baahk-sīk, hùhng-sīk, hāk-sīk, wòhng-sīk, māt-yéh sīk dōu
yáuh, daahn-haih dīk-sí m̀h tùhng, ga-ga dōu haih hùhng-sīk
tùhng-màaih ngàhn-sīk ge.

22

寫字樓
sé-jih-làuh
the office

In this unit you will learn
- some useful terms for the work environment
- two or three really colloquial speech patterns to add liveliness to your conversation

▶ Dialogue 1

Two friends discuss office working conditions.

呀陳，而家差唔多九點囉嗎，點解你重喺呢處食早餐呢？唔駛返工咩？

唔係，我要返工，我返九點半呀。

你哋公司有彈性上班制度咩？

係呀。有九點同九點半兩班。

噉，幾點放工呀？

六點放工。喺下晝有九個字食晏晝。

工作時間都幾長嗎！食晏晝嘅時間就太短嘞。過時工作有冇錢補㗎？

有。每個鐘頭補返三百五十蚊。

重有啲乜野福利呀？

每年有二十日係有薪水嘅假期。年尾有雙薪，有醫療津貼，有仔女教育津貼，女職員重有十個禮拜分娩假期。退休嘅時候重可以得到退休金添。王先生歡迎你加入我哋公司服務。

你講笑咩！？我太老，冇用啦！

Mr Wong	A-Chán, yìh-gā chà-m̀h-dō gáu-dím lo bo, dím-gáai néih juhng hái nī-syu sihk jóu-chàan nē? M̀h-sái fàan-gùng mē?
Mr Chan	M̀h haih, ngóh yiu fàan-gùng, ngóh fàan gáu-dím-bun a.
Mr Wong	Néih-deih gūng-sī yáuh daahn-sing séuhng-bāan jai-douh mē?
Mr Chan	Haih a. Yáuh gáu-dím tùhng gáu-dím-bun léuhng bāan.
Mr Wong	Gám, géi-dím fong-gùng a?
Mr Chan	Luhk-dím fong-gùng. Hái hah-jau yáuh gáu go jih sihk an-jau.
Mr Wong	Gùng-jok sìh-gaan dōu-géi chèuhng bo! Sihk an-jau ge sìh-gaan jauh taai dýun lak. Gwo-sìh gùng-jok yáuh móuh chín bóu ga?
Mr Chan	Yáuh. Múih go jūng-tàuh bóu-fàan sàam-baak-ńgh-sahp mān.
Mr Wong	Juhng yáuh dī māt-yéh fūk-leih a?
Mr Chan	Múih nìhn yáuh yih-sahp yaht haih yáuh sàn-séui ge ga-kèih. Nìhn-méih yáuh sèung-sàn, yáuh yì-lìuh jèun-tip, yáuh jái-néui gaau-yuhk jèun-tip, néuih-jīk-yùhn juhng yáuh sahp go láih-baai fàn-míhn ga-kèih. Teui-yàu ge sìh-hauh juhng hó-yíh dāk-dóu teui-yàu-gām tìm. Wòhng Sìn-sàang fùn-yìhng néih gà-yahp ngóh-deih gūng-sī fuhk-mouh.
Mr Wong	Néih góng-siu mè!? Ngóh taai lóuh, móuh yuhng la!

呀...... A-	familiar prefix for names and relationships
早餐 **jóu-chàan**	breakfast
返工 **fàan-gùng**	to go to work
彈性 **daahn-sing**	flexible
上班 **séuhng-bāan**	to go to work, go on shift
制度 **jai-douh**	system
放工 **fong-gùng**	to finish work
晏晝 **an-jau**	midday, early afternoon, lunchtime; lunch
工作 **gùng-jok**	work, job; to work
長 **chèuhng**	long
短 **dýun**	short
過時 **gwo-sìh**	overtime
補 **bóu**	to compensate
福利 **fūk-leih**	benefits, welfare
薪水 **sàn-séui**	salary
假期 **ga-kèih**	holiday
雙薪 **sèung-sàn** or **sèung-lèuhng**	double salary
醫療 **yì-lìuh**	medical
津貼 **jèun-tip**	allowance, grant
仔女 **jái-néui**	sons and daughters, children
職員 **jīk-yùhn**	staff, employee, clerk
分娩 **fàn-míhn**	to give birth
退休 **teui-yàu**	to retire
退休金 **teui-yàu-gām**	pension
歡迎 **fùn-yìhng**	welcome, to welcome

Grammar

1 Familiar terms of address

In Unit 6 you learned that **Lóuh** *old* is used with surnames as a familiar way of addressing someone. You can refer to a younger person or a child by putting **Síu-** (*little*) in front of their name. In both cases a surname which has a mid level, low level or low falling tone changes to a mid rising tone. Another way is to put **A-** in front of the surname (again with the same tone changes). In fact the sound **A-** seems to be intimately connected with referring to or addressing people. It can be used with personal names as well (someone with the name **Chàhn Jī Bāk**, for instance, might be addressed as **A-Bāk** by his family and friends) and it can be used with kinship terms (you could address your father as **A-bà** instead of **bàh-bā**). It is almost as though when you say **A-** you are warning your listener that you are about to talk to them or to talk about a person.

2 *Fàan-gùng* and *fong-gùng*

In Unit 3 you met **fàan** meaning *to return* or *to go where you usually go*: one of the examples was **fàan sé-jih-làuh** *to go to the office*. **Gùng** means *work* and **jouh-gùng** means *to do work, to work*. **Fàan-gùng** means *to go to work* in the same way that **fàan sé-jih-làuh** means *to go to the office*, but *to finish work* and *to leave the office at the end of the day* are both expressed the same way – **fong-gùng**.

It is worth noting for your own use the colloquial way in which in the dialogue Mr Chan says that he goes in to work at 9.30: **ngóh fàan gáu-dím-bun.**

i Fun with characters

咩 mē?

The Chinese character used for **mē?** is an interesting one: it shows a mouth and a sheep and so indicates the bleating of a sheep, which is rather what **mē?** sounds like. The character for **ma?** shows a mouth and a horse, but you may find that a less convincing sound guide – everyone English-speaking person knows that horses go 'neigh' not 'ma', don't they?

嗎 ma?

3 The *long* and the *short* of it

Another pair of opposites: **chèuhng** *long* and **dýun** *short*. Both of them can be used for periods of time, as they are in the dialogue, but they are equally good for distances (*a long piece of string, a short pencil*) and even for more abstract things like *a long novel* and *a shortcoming*.

4 The tail again

In Unit 17 you met **yuht-méih** *the end of the month* and in this unit there is **nìhn-méih** *the end of the year*. **Méih** literally means *the tail*, but since tails are found at the end, it is logical enough that it should also mean *the end* and you will probably meet it quite often. One common expression is **daih-mēi** *the last* (note the tone change), which of course contrasts with **daih-yāt** *the first*.

5 Sons and daughters

Jái-néui means *sons and daughters* and you need to bear that in mind when translating the word *children*. Only use **jái-néui** where *sons and daughters* would be appropriate. In English it would sound odd to say *Oh look, there are several hundred sons and daughters over there in the school playground* – you would say *children*. Similarly in Cantonese you would not use **jái-néui** in this case, you would use **sai-màn-jái** *children*.

🅸 Double salary

The Chinese have traditionally used two separate calendars, a lunar and a solar one. To keep them roughly in step it has been necessary to add an extra month into 7 years in every 19. So lunar years consist of either 12 or 13 months. Chinese monthly salaries are nowadays usually paid according to the western solar calendar in which, of course, the years always have only 12 months, but it has become a custom among some employers to pay an additional month's salary every solar year as if it were a 13-month lunar year: it is the equivalent perhaps of a western 'Christmas bonus'. That is what is referred to in the dialogue as **sèung-sàn** *double salary*.

▶ Dialogue 2

Interviewing a secretary for a job.

李小姐，你申請做我哋公司嘅秘書，我啱啱見過你打字嘑，表現都幾好。你識語識用電腦呀？

經理先生，對唔住，我唔識。

唔識咩？今日嘅世界唔識用電腦唔得㗎！噉，你識唔識用傳真機呀？

呢啲先進嘅設備我見都未見過，當然唔識用喇。不過如果經理肯俾機會我，我會好俾心機學嘅。

你喺上海做過幾多年秘書呀？

差唔多有十七年嘑。

喺上海嘅寫字樓有幾多位秘書呀？

只有我一個係秘書，我要獨立處理一切公司嘅文件，而且要直接向經理負責。

好喇！我就請你喇，不過第一個月係試用期，我想睇吓你嘅工作表現先。其他詳細嘅福利同工作條件，等過咗試用期再講喇。你聽日可以嚟開工嘑。

多謝經理。聽日見。

Manager   Léih Síu-jé, néih sàn-chíng jouh ngóh-deih gūng-sī ge bei-syù, ngóh ngāam-ngāam gin-gwo néih dá-jih lak, bíu-yihn dōu-géi hóu. Néih sīk m̀h sīk yuhng dihn-nóuh a?

Miss Lee	Gìng-léih sìn-sàang, deui-m̀h-jyuh, ngóh m̀h sīk.
Manager	M̀h sīk mē? Gàm-sìh-gàm-yaht m̀h sīk yuhng dihn-nóuh m̀h dāk bo! Gám, néih sīk m̀h sīk yuhng chỳuhn-jàn-gèi a?
Miss Lee	Nī-dī sìn-jeun ge chit-beih ngóh gin dōu meih gin-gwo, dòng-yín m̀h sīk yuhng lā. Bāt-gwo yùh-gwó gìng-léih háng béi gèi-wuih ngóh, ngóh wúih hóu béi sàm-gèi hohk ge.
Manager	Néih hái Seuhng-hói jouh-gwo géi-dō nìhn bei-sỳu a?
Miss Lee	Chà-m̀h-dō yáuh sahp-chāt nìhn lak.
Manager	Hái Seuhng-hói ge sé-jih-làuh yáuh géi-dō wái bei-sỳu a?
Miss Lee	Jí yáuh ngóh yāt go haih bei-sỳu, ngóh yiu duhk-laahp chýu-léih yāt-chai gūng-sī ge màhn-gín, yìh-ché yiu jihk-jip heung gìng-léih fuh-jaak.
Manager	Hóu lā! Ngóh jauh chéng néih lā! Bāt-gwo daih-yāt go yuht haih si-yuhng-kèih, ngóh séung tái-háh néih ge gùng-jok bíu-yihn sìn. Kèih-tà chèuhng-sai ge fūk-leih tùhng gùng-jok tìuh-gín, dáng gwo-jó si-yuhng-kèih joi góng lā. Néih tìng-yaht hó-yíh làih hòi-gùng lak.
Miss Lee	Dò-jeh gìng-léih. Tìng-yaht gin.

秘書	**bei-sỳu**	secretary
打字	**dá-jih**	to type (lit: to hit characters)
打字機	**dá-jih-gèi**	typewriter
打字員	**dá-jih-yùhn**	typist
表現	**bíu-yihn**	performance, to perform
電腦	**dihn-nóuh**	computer (lit: electric brain)
今時今日	**gàm-sìh-gàm-yaht**	nowadays
傳真機	**chỳuhn-jàn-gèi**	fax machine
傳真	**chỳuhn-jàn**	fax, to fax
先進	**sìn-jeun**	advanced
肯	**háng**	to be willing to
機會	**gèi-wuih**	chance, opportunity
心機	**sàm-gèi**	mind, thoughts
上海	**Seuhng-hói**	Shanghai
獨立	**duhk-laahp**	independent, independently
處理	**chýu-léih**	to handle, manage, deal with
一切	**yāt-chai**	every single one of, the whole run of, all
文件	**màhn-gín**	document
直接	**jihk-jip**	direct, directly
負責	**fuh-jaak**	to be responsible
試用期	**si-yuhng-kèih**	probationary period, trial period
詳細	**chèuhng-sai**	detailed, minute, fine
條件	**tìuh-gín**	a condition, terms
開工	**hòi-gùng**	to start work, to start a job

Grammar

6 Simply must

You probably found no difficulty with the sentence **Gàm-sìh-gàm-yaht m̀h sīk yuhng dihn-nóuh m̀h dāk bo!** (*In today's world you simply must know how to use a computer!*). Note how the pattern works: it is **m̀h** + verb + **m̀h dāk**, that is, *if you don't verb it won't do!* or *you simply must verb!* Here are some other examples:

Gó dī hā néih m̀h sihk m̀h dāk.	*You really must eat those prawns.*
Wòhng Táai wah néih m̀h heui taam kéuih m̀h dāk.	*Mrs Wong says you simply must go to visit her.*

7 Never even . . .

In the dialogue Miss Lee says **gam sìn-jeun ge chit-beih ngóh gin dōu meih gin-gwo** *I haven't even seen such newfangled equipment.* The pattern **gin dōu meih gin-gwo** may have struck a chord with you – do you remember the **lìhn . . . dōu . . .** pattern which you met in Unit 17? Here instead of **lìhn** + **dōu** the same verb appears twice + **dōu**, but the meaning is still *not even. . . .*

8 *Sàm-gèi*

Sàm-gèi is quite a difficult word to grasp. Its closest equivalent in English is *mind*, but perhaps the following examples of its most common usage will be the easiest way to come to terms with it:

Ngóh wúih hóu béi sàm-gèi hohk.	*I will do my best to give my mind to learning it.*
Ngóh móuh sàm-gèi heui.	*I have no enthusiasm for going.*
Kéuih hóu móuh sàm-gèi.	*She's very out of sorts/listless/without enthusiasm/non-committal.*

9 *Direct* and *indirect*

Jihk-jip literally means *directly in contact* and so *directly.* Its opposite is **gaan-jip** *touching at an interval,* that is, *indirectly.*

10 *Fuh-jaak* to be responsible to

Note the way in which this word **fuh-jaak** is used with **heung**. Miss Lee says in the dialogue that she **jihk-jip heung gìng-léih fuh-jaak** *was directly answerable to the manager*. You met **heung** first in Unit 6 where it meant *towards*, but here it may be better to think of it as meaning something like *vis-à-vis* or *as regards*. There was a similar example in the first dialogue of Unit 19: **heung ngàhn-hòhng tau-jì** *to be overdrawn at (vis-à-vis) the bank*.

Exercise 1

The following questions all use **mē?** The short answer (either **Haih** or **Mh haih**) has been supplied. In each case supply the long full answer after the short one. For instance, the first answer would be **Mh haih, ngóh mh haih Méih-gwok-yàhn.** Easy? Well, you may need to watch your step . . .

a Néih haih Méih-gwok-yàhn mē? Mh haih, . . .
b Wòhng Sìn-sàang dī jái-néui yuht-làih-yuht-waaih mē? Haih, . . .
c Néih meih sihk-gwo jóu-chāan mē? Haih, . . .
d Kéuih mh-haih-géi-jùng-yi fàan-gùng mē? Mh haih, . . .
e Yìng-gwok-yàhn tùhng Jùng-gwok-yàhn yāt-yeuhng gam jùng-yi tái-bō mē? Haih, . . .

Exercise 2
Fill in the blanks.

a Gáu go yàhn yāt-go-yāt-go-gám hàahng-louh, daih-yāt go hó-yíh wah haih 'tàuh-yāt go': daih-gáu go nē? Hó-yíh wah haih 'daih-____ go'.
b Wòhng Síu-jé sèhng-yaht dá-dihn-wá ____ ngóh, sàai ngóh hóu dò sìh-gaan!
c Chàhn Táai baat-dím-gáu-go-jih sìn-ji fàan sé-jih-làuh. Ngóh ____ baat-dím.
d 'Kéuih bàh-bā jí-haih jouh-gwo yih-sahp nìhn yī-sāng jauh teui-yàu lak.' 'Wàh, gam ____ sìh-gaan! Kéuih dī behng-yàhn tái yī-sāng yāt-dihng yiu béi hóu dò chín la!'

Exercise 3
Supply an appropriate verb ending in each of the blanks.

a Wài-lìhm yìh-gā sihk-____ faahn, chìh-dī hó-yíh chēut-gāai wáan.
b Láahng àh? Dòng-yín mh gok-dāk láahng. Ngóh jeuk-____ hóu nýuhn ge sāam a.

c Ngóh meih si-____ lùhng-hā. Hóu m̀h hóu sihk a?
d Dī hā sihk-_____ lak; yìh-gā lìhn yāt jek dōu móuh lak.
e Wai! Néih wán bīn wái a? Hòh Síu-jé nē? Òu, Hòh Síu-jé ngāam-ngāam hàahng-____-jó lak. Kéuih fàan-làih ngóh wúih wah kéuih jì néih dá-gwo dihn-wá làih lak.

Exercise 4

Some higher mathematical problems for you to solve (in Cantonese, of course).

a Wòhng Síu-jé ge sàn-séui m̀h gòu, bāt-gwo haih ńgh-chìn-sei-baak mān yāt go yuht. Hóu-chói kéuih nìhn-méih yáuh sèung-sàn. Gám, kéuih yāt nìhn yāt-guhng ló géi-dō chín a?
b Chàhn Sàang Sei-yuht ge sàn-séui haih yih-maahn-ńgh-chìn mān. Hòh Sàang Sei-yuht fàan-jó baat yaht gùng, múih yaht ló ge chín yáuh sàam-chìn mān gam dò. Gó go yuht Chàhn Sàang dihng-haih Hòh Sàang ló ge chín dò nē?
c Wòhng Táai hóu hàan. Yàn-waih chóh deih-tit gwai-gwo chóh bā-sí, kéuih juhng-meih chóh-gwo deih-tit. Chóh síu-bā dōu móuh chóh bā-sí gam pèhng, só-yíh kéuih hóu síu daap síu-bā. Gàm-yaht kéuih hàahng-louh heui síh-chèuhng, máaih-jó jeui pèhng jeui pèhng daahn-haih m̀h sàn-sìn ge hā tùhng-màaih bun-gàn ngàuh-yuhk, yauh máaih-jó yāt-dī kèih-tà sung. Ngàuh-yuhk maaih sahp-ńgh mān yāt gàn, dī hā bāt-gwo yiu chāt-go-bun, kèih-tà sung jí-haih sei-go-baat ngàhn-chín jē. Kéuih máaih-jó ge yéh hóu chuhng, m̀h chóh bā-sí fàan ūk-kéi m̀h dāk. Daap bā-sí yiu léuhng-go-luhk. Nàh, Wòhng Táai gàm-yaht yāt-guhng yuhng-jó géi-dō chín a?
d Ngóh bàh-bā sei-jó hóu noih lak, màh-mā juhng hái-syu; yáuh sei go hīng-daih, sàam go jí-muih; yáuh ngóh taai-táai tùhng-màaih ńgh go jái-néui. Ngóh-deih hahm-baahng-laahng dōu jyuh hái yāt chàhng m̀h daaih m̀h sai ge láu. Chéng-mahn yāt-guhng yáuh géi-dō go yàhn a?

Exercise 5

The idea of this silly game is to climb the Peak. But it is a game full of social significance: to live on the Peak (**sàan-déng**) is the height (so to speak) of ambition for many people in Hong Kong! You will need a die and at least one opponent (if he/she/they cannot read the instructions, so much the better for you!). Start at the airport where you arrive penniless. Just as in real life, it's very hard to win!

By the way, **héi-dím** *lift-off point* and **jùng-dím** *end point* mean *start* and *finish* in board games like this.

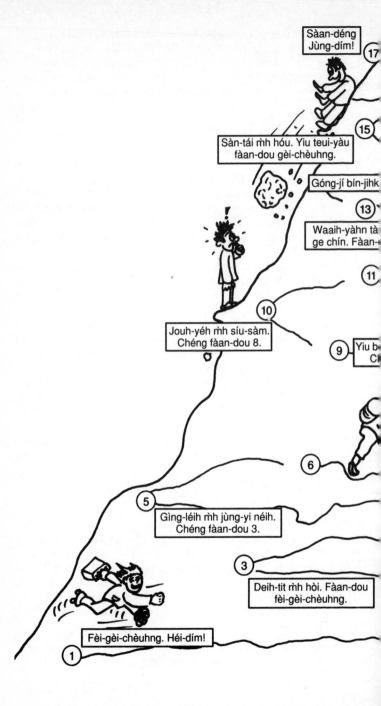

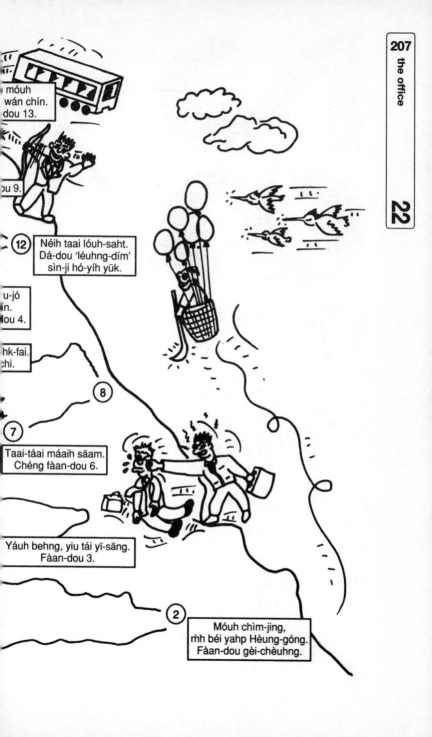

23

香港酒樓
hèung-góng
jáu-làuh
eating out in Hong Kong

In this unit you will learn
- more about food

▶ Dialogue 1

A food-loving visitor talks with a Hong Kong gourmet.

我嚟咗香港差唔多有兩個禮拜嘞，對香港嘅酒家同餐廳都有好感。我覺得一個嚟香港玩嘅遊客如果唔去酒家試吓中國菜，噉，真係一個大損失嘞。

你好中意食中國菜咩？

喺香港中國菜唔只種類多，款式齊全，價錢平，而且色香味都係一流嘅。

請問你喺貴國做乜野生意㗎？

我係法國人，我開餐廳嘅。

唔怪得你對食物咁有認識喇。你最中意食乜野呀？

廣東點心同海鮮。

可惜最近幾年香港嘅海鮮越嚟越貴。喺酒家食咗海鮮之後我有時唔敢叫'埋單'，唔知帶嚟嘅錢夠唔夠。'污染'我估就係直接影響海鮮價錢嘅原因嘞。

重有一點，我估香港嘅酒樓同餐廳係世界上最多，最集中嘅嘞。你睇香港有一條街不過兩公里咁長之嘛，酒樓同餐廳就超過五百間嘞。我唔知邊處有咁多顧客日日都嚟幫趁呢？

你喺香港住耐啲，你就知點解嘅嘞。

Visitor	Ngóh làih-jó Hèung-góng chà-m̀h-dō yáuh léuhng go láih-baai lak, deui Hèung-góng ge jáu-gā tùhng chāan-tēng dōu yáuh hóu-gám. Ngóh gok-dāk yāt go làih Hèung-góng wáan ge yàuh-haak yùh-gwó m̀h heui jáu-gā si-háh Jùng-gwok-choi, gám, jàn-haih yāt go daaih syún-sāt lak.
Local	Néih hóu jùng-yi sihk Jùng-gwok-choi mē?
Visitor	Hái Hèung-góng Jùng-gwok-choi m̀h-jí júng-leuih dò, fún-sīk chàih-chyùhn, ga-chìhn pèhng, yìh-ché sīk-hèung-meih dōu haih yāt-làuh ge.
Local	Chéng-mahn néih hái gwai-gwok jouh māt-yéh sàang-yi ga?
Visitor	Ngóh haih Faat-gwok-yàhn, ngóh hòi chāan-tēng ge.
Local	M̀h-gwaai-dāk néih deui sihk-maht gam yáuh yihng-sīk lā. Néih jeui jùng-yi sihk māt-yéh a?
Visitor	Gwóng-dùng dím-sām tùhng hói-sīn.
Local	Hó-sīk jeui-gahn-géi-nìhn Hèung-góng ge hói-sīn yuht-làih-yuht-gwai. Hái jáu-gā sihk-jó hói-sīn jì-hauh ngóh yáuh-sìh m̀h gám giu 'Màaih-dāan', m̀h jì daai-làih ge chín gau m̀h gau. 'Wù-yíhm' ngóh gú jauh haih jihk-jip yíng-héung hói-sīn ga-chìhn ge yùhn-yàn lak.

Visitor Juhng yáuh yāt dím, ngóh gú Hèung-góng ge jáu-làuh tùhng chāan-tēng haih sai-gaai seuhng jeui dò, jeui jaahp-jùng ge lak. Néih tái, Hèung-góng yáuh yāt tìuh gāai bāt-gwo léuhng gūng-léih gam chèuhng jī-máh, jáu-làuh tùhng chāan-tēng jauh chìu-gwo ńgh-baak gàan lak. Ngóh m̀h jì bīn-syu yáuh gam dò gu-haak yaht-yaht dōu làih bòng-chan nē?

Local Néih hái Hèung-góng jyuh noih-dī, néih jauh jì dím-gáai ge lak.

酒家 **jáu-gā**	*Chinese restaurant*	
餐廳 **chāan-tēng**	*restaurant serving non-Chinese food*	
好感 **hóu-gám**	*favourable impression, good opinion*	
菜 **choi**	*food, cuisine; vegetables*	
損失 **sýun-sāt**	*a loss*	
種類 **júng-leuih**	*type, kind, species, variety*	
齊全 **chàih-chyùhn**	*complete, all embracing*	
色香味 **sīk-hèung-meih**	*appearance, aroma and flavour*	
香 **hèung**	*fragrant, nice smelling*	
一流 **yāt-làuh**	*first rate*	
貴國 **gwai-gwok**	*your country*	
開 **hòi**	*to run a business, start a business*	
唔怪得 **m̀h-gwaai-dāk**	*no wonder*	
食物 **sihk-maht**	*food*	
認識 **yihng-sīk**	*to recognize, to be knowledgeable about, to understand*	
廣東 **Gwóng-dùng**	*Guangdong (province)*	
點心 **dím-sām**	*'dim sum', hot delicacies for breakfast or lunch*	
海鮮 **hói-sīn**	*seafood*	
埋單 **Màaih-dāan**	*May I have the bill? (in restaurants)*	
污染 **wù-yíhm**	*pollution, to pollute*	
影響 **yíng-héung**	*to affect, influence*	
原因 **yùhn-yàn**	*reason*	
點 **dím**	*a point, a spot, a dot*	
集中 **jaahp-jùng**	*concentrated, centralized*	
公里 **gūng-léih**	*a kilometre*	
顧客 **gu-haak**	*customer, client*	
幫趁 **bòng-chan**	*to patronize, give custom to*	

Grammar

1 *Sung* and *choi*

In Unit 4 you met the term **jýu-choi** for *main course* and it is the same word **choi** which appears in this unit meaning *food* or *cuisine*:

Jùng-gwok-choi	*Chinese food*
Gwóng-dùng-choi	*Cantonese food*
Bāk-gìng-choi	*Peking food* (**Bāk-gìng** = *Beijing/Peking*)
Sei-chyùn-choi	*Sichuan food*
	(**Sei-chyùn** = *Sichuan/Szechwan*)

The basic meaning of **choi** is *vegetables*:

Ngóh-deih yáuh yuhk, dím-gáai móuh choi a?	*We have meat, why don't we have any vegetables?*

Both meat and vegetables are included in the word **sung** (see Unit 4), but **máaih-choi** and **máaih-sung** mean the same thing – *shopping for food*. Confusing isn't it?

ℹ️ Where does *Cantonese* come from?

The word *Canton* probably comes from a Portuguese romanization of the Cantonese word **Gwóng-dùng**. **Gwóng-dùng** is the name of the province of which the capital city is **Gwóng-jàu**. It is somewhat confusing that Canton became the name by which the city rather than the province was known to the west. It is even more confusing that in the province there are a number of Chinese languages spoken, of which what we call Cantonese is only one. Casting the history aside, the situation now is clear: the province is called **Gwóng-dùng**, the capital city is called **Gwóng-jàu** and the language which you are learning, which is the language of **Gwóng-jàu**, is known as **Gwóng-jàu-wá**. By the way, the official name of the city is actually Guangzhou, which is the Putonghua (Mandarin) version of **Gwóng-jàu**.

2 Not only . . . but also

The pattern which translates *not only . . . but also . . .* is quite straightforward: **m̀h-jí . . . yìh-ché . . . (dōu)**. . . . **Dōu** is not essential to the pattern, but as so often when plural ideas are mentioned it is likely to be used:

Wòhng Sìn-sàang m̀h-jí sīk góng Yìng-màhn yìh-ché Yaht-màhn dōu góng-dāk hóu hóu.	*Mr Wong cannot only speak English, his Japanese is very good too.*

3 Sīk-hèung-meih

You met **meih** in Unit 4 in the term **hóu-meih** *delicious*. Its basic meaning is *flavour*. **Sīk** means *colour* or *appearance*, and **hèung** means *nice smelling, fragrant* (as in **Hèung-góng** *Fragrant Harbour = Hong Kong*). The three together make up the three qualities which ideally all Chinese food is supposed to have – good appearance, good aroma, good flavour. As with other set phrases, do not be tempted to use the individual words outside this phrase. Of the three, only **hèung** is a 'free' word which you can use in normal speech like any other adjective/verb:

Chàhn Táai, nī dī sung hóu hèung. Néih jàn-haih hóu sīk jýu-sung bo!	*Mrs Chan, this food smells wonderful. You really know how to cook!*

4 Honorific words

Way back in Unit 1 you met **gwai-sing a?** *what is your surname?* and it was explained that this actually meant *what is your distinguished name?* (Later you met the same word **gwai** meaning *expensive*.) Chinese politeness traditionally demanded that other people's attributes and belongings were always spoken of as *precious, honourable, distinguished* and so on, while one's own were always mentioned as *despicable, humble, miserable* etc. In the dialogue the Hong Kong man is properly polite when he asks the visitor what his occupation is in his *honourable country* (**gwai-gwok**). Much of the very fancy honorific terminology is no longer used, you will be relieved to hear, but it is still polite to 'cry up' other people and to 'play down' yourself. You will find that when you try out your halting Cantonese on someone, he or she will inevitably come back at you by saying what wonderful Cantonese you speak – that is the polite thing for them to say. Do not be fooled into believing them and, above all, even if you happen arrogantly to think them to be correct, do not reply *I know I do* or *Thank you very much, I am a genius at languages*. You should always respond by saying, for instance, how poorly you speak it, how ashamed you are at speaking so little or how you can only say a very few words.

ℹ The extremes of politeness

Arthur Smith in his famous book *Chinese Characteristics*, published in 1900, tells a Chinese story of a visitor who, while waiting in his best robes for his host to come in, is drenched in oil when a rat knocks a jar off the beam above his head. When his host enters, the guest explains what has happened: 'As I entered your honourable apartment and seated myself under your honourable beam, I inadvertently terrified your honourable rat, which fled and upset your honourable oil-jar upon my mean and insignificant clothing, which is the reason of my contemptible appearance in your honourable presence.' Now, that is politeness!

▶ Dialogue 2

William has his own way of beating inflation.

威廉，點解你咁客氣請我嚟呢間餐廳食飯呀？係唔係你今日生日呀？
　恭喜！恭喜！

我唔係今日生日。冇特別意義嘅，只係我聽到一個消息話呢間餐廳就
　快要拆啦，我又好中意喺呢間餐廳食嘢，所以我就邀請你嚟一齊
　食飯啫。

我唔知道你咁中意呢間舊餐廳嘅喎。

係呀，我重好中意懷舊添，咦！……點解今日餐牌啲餸貴過昨日嘅咁
　多嘅？我昨日啱啱先至喺呢處食過飯啫！

對唔住啦，先生，你哋真係唔好彩嘞。我哋間餐廳啱啱由今日開始加
　價。如果你哋昨日嚟食飯，我哋嘅餐廳重未加價。

你哋昨日嘅食物全部都係賣舊價吖？

係呀。

好呃。我要一條昨日你哋賣剩嘅游水魚，一斤昨日賣剩嘅游水蝦，
　同埋一啲昨日賣剩嘅生果添。

哈！原來你對食物都懷舊嘅。

Mr Ho	Wài-lìhm, dím-gáai néih gam haak-hei chéng ngóh làih nī gàan chāan-tēng sihk-faahn a? Haih m̀h haih néih gàm-yaht sàang-yaht a? Gùng-héi! Gùng-héi!
William	Ngóh m̀h haih gàm-yaht sàang-yaht. Móuh dahk-biht yi-yih ge, jí-haih ngóh tèng-dóu yāt go sìu-sīk wah nī gàan chāan-tēng jauh-faai yiu chaak la, ngóh yauh hóu jùng-yi hái nī gàan chāan-tēng sihk-yéh, só-yíh ngóh jauh yìu-chéng néih làih yāt-chàih sihk-faahn jē.
Mr Ho	Ngóh m̀h jì-dou néih gam jùng-yi nī gàan gauh chāan-tēng ge bo.

William	Haih a, ngóh juhng hóu jùng-yi wàaih-gauh tìm. Yí! . . . dím-gáai gàm-yaht chāan-páai dī sung gwai-gwo johk-yaht ge gam dò gé? Ngóh johk-yaht ngāam-ngāam sìn-ji hái nī-syu sihk-gwo faahn jē!
Waiter	Deui-m̀h-jyuh la, sìn-sàang, néih-deih jàn-haih m̀h hóu-chói lak. Ngóh-deih gàan chāan-tēng ngāam-ngāam yàuh gàm-yaht hòi-chí gà-ga. Yùh-gwó néih-deih johk-yaht làih sihk-faahn, ngóh-deih ge chāan-tēng juhng-meih gà-ga.
William	Néih-deih johk-yaht ge sihk-maht chyùhn-bouh dōu haih maaih gauh ga àh?
Waiter	Haih a.
William	Hóu ak. Ngóh yiu yāt tìuh jok-yaht néih-deih maaih-jihng ge yàuh-séui yú, yāt gàn johk-yaht maaih-jihng ge yàuh-séui hā, tùhng-màaih yāt dī johk-yaht maaih-jihng ge sàang-gwó tìm.
Mr Ho	Hà! Yùhn-lòih néih deui sihk-maht dōu wàaih-gauh ge.

生日 **sàang-yaht**	*birthday*
恭喜！ **gùng-héi!**	*congratulations!*
特別 **dahk-biht**	*special, especially*
意義 **yi-yih**	*meaning, significance*
消息 **sìu-sīk**	*news, item of news, information*
就快 **jauh-faai**	*soon*
拆 **chaak**	*to demolish, tear down*
邀請 **yìu-chéng**	*to invite*
懷舊 **wàaih-gauh**	*nostalgia, to be nostalgic*
餐牌 **chāan-páai**	*menu*
開始 **hòi-chí**	*to begin, to start*
加價 **gà-ga**	*to increase price*
全部 **chyùhn-bouh**	*all, the whole lot*
...... 剩 **-jihng**	*verb ending: left over, surplus*
魚 **yú**	*fish*
哈！ **hà!**	*'the sound of laughter', ha! ha!*

ℹ️ Different restaurants

You have now met three different words for *restaurant*: **jáu-làuh**, **jáu-gā** and **chāan-tēng**. The first two are used in the titles of restaurants serving Chinese food and both include **jáu** in the name, probably reflecting the fact that Chinese people generally only drink alcohol when they are eating on special occasions. Restaurants which call themselves **chāan-tēng** serve styles of cuisine other than Chinese.

There is a similar distinction in words for *eating*. **Sihk-faahn** would normally imply *eating a proper meal of Chinese food*, whereas **sihk-chāan** means to have a meal of western food or some other non-Chinese variety. English-style breakfast is quite popular with many Chinese and the word for *breakfast* used nowadays is usually **jóu-chāan**, but the evening meal is **máahn-faahn** or **máahn-chāan** depending on the style of food eaten.

Oddly, there is no distinction in the normal pair of words which contrast western and Chinese cuisines. *Western food* is **sài-chāan**, as you might expect, but *Chinese food* is **Tòhng-chāan**.

Grammar

5 Birthdays

Sàang means either *to be born* or *to give birth to*. **Sàang-yaht** is *the day of birth*, *birthday*. **Sàang-yaht** is unusual in that although it doesn't appear to be a verb it doesn't seem to need any other verb either. Note the first speech of Mr Ho in the dialogue: **Haih m̀h haih néih gàm-yaht sàang-yaht a?** – *Is it your birthday today?* What he actually seems to be saying is *Is it the case that you are birthdaying today?* Don't worry about it, just accept that this is how **sàang-yaht** is usually used.

6 Inviting people

Yìu-chíng means *to invite* and so does **chéng** (which is actually a colloquial version of the second element in **yìu-chíng**). There is no real difference in meaning, but **yìu-chíng** is slightly more formal than **chéng**.

7 Starting from . . .

Yàuh means *from* (see Unit 6) and it pairs with **hòi-chí** *to begin* to make a pattern for *starting from*. . . . In the dialogue the waiter says **yàuh gàm-yaht hòi-chí** meaning *starting from today*. You can use the pattern quite freely:

Yàuh luhk-dím-jūng hòi-chí yáuh hóu dò fó-chē.	*There are lots of trains from 6 o'clock onwards.*
Yàuh sahp-baat seui hòi-chí kéuih jauh meih sihk-gwo yuhk la.	*She hasn't had meat since she was 18.*

i Swimming seafood

Cantonese cuisine excels in its treatment of seafood, but the food is only considered properly fresh if it is alive until the last possible moment before cooking. The best seafood restaurants (**hói-sīn jáu-gā**) have large saltwater tanks in which the fish, prawns and shellfish are kept alive and customers can select what they wish to eat from this *swimming seafood* (**yàuh-séui hói-sīn**).

Exercise 1

Select the words which will make sense of the following sentences.

a Hèung-góng yáuh hóu dò (yāt-guhng/yāt-chai/yāt-làuh/yāt-sìh) ge jáu-dim.

b Jeui-gahn-géi-nìhn Hèung-góng ge (gìng-léih/gìng-gwo/gìng-jai) yuht-làih-yuht-hóu.

c Hái Hèung-góng, gíng-chaat (gwàn-yàhn/daaih-yàhn/làai-yàhn/lóuh-yàhn) yāt-dihng yiu yáuh léih-yàuh.

d Hèung-góng ge bā-sí sī-gēi hòi-gùng ge sìh-hauh yiu jeuk (gwàn-fuhk/bihn-fuhk/sỳu-fuhk/jai-fuhk).

e Ngóh-deih géi-sìh yáuh (sàn-séui/yàuh-séui/saan-séui/yeuhk-séui) ló a?

Exercise 2

When you have read the following passage carefully, answer the two questions in Cantonese.

Hái Hòh Sìn-sàang ūk-kéi bāk-bihn léuhng gūng-léih gó-syu yáuh yāt gàan hohk-haauh. Hái hohk-haauh dùng-bihn ńgh gūng-léih haih yāt gàan yì-yún. Hái yì-yún nàahm-bihn léuhng gūng-léih jauh haih gíng-chaat-guhk lak. Méih-gwok ngàhn-hòhng hái gíng-chaat-guhk sài-bihn sàam gūng-léih gó-syu. Chéng-mahn:

a Yàuh ngàhn-hòhng heui Hòh Sàang ūk-kéi yáuh géi-dō gūng-léih a?

b Ngàhn-hòhng hái Hòh Sàang ūk-kéi bīn-bihn a?

Exercise 3

Here are some Chinese brainteaser 'old chestnuts' for you to solve:

a Síu-Jeung wah: 'Ngóh sàn-tái chúhng-leuhng ge yāt bun joi gà yih-sahp bohng jauh haih ngóh sàn-tái ge chỳuhn-bouh chúhng-leuhng lak. Chéng-mahn ngóh haih géi-dō bohng a?'

b Yáuh yāt yeuhng yéh, néih jí hó-yíh yuhng jó-sáu nìng, m̀h hó-yíh yuhng yauh-sáu nìng. Néih gú haih māt-yéh nē?

c Síu-Wóng wah: 'Ngóh yìh-gā géi-dō seui ngóh m̀h wah néih jì, daahn-haih sàam nìhn jì-chìhn gó-jahn-sìh ngāam-ngāam jauh haih ngóh sàam nìhn jì-hauh ge baak-fahn-jì-sàam-sahp-sàam. Gám, néih jì m̀h jì ngóh yìh-gā géi-dō seui a?'

d Wòhng Sìn-sàang daai-jó yāt-baak mān chēut-gāai. Hái pou-táu máaih-jó sàam bún syù, múih bún dōu haih yih-sahp-ńgh mān. Daahn-haih pou-táu ge fó-gei jí-haih jáau-fàan ńgh mān kéuih. Dím-gáai nē?

Exercise 4

Can you remember your colours? Give the answers to the following in Cantonese.

a Néih jà-chē gin-dóu hùhng-dāng yiu jouh māt-yéh nē?
b Làahm-sīk gà māt-yéh sīk haih luhk-sīk a?
c Làahm-sīk ga hùhng-sīk haih māt-yéh sīk a?
d Hóu dò hóu dò nìhn jì-chìhn hóu gauh ge dihn-yíng haih māt-yéh sīk a?

Exercise 5

Can you interpret for your friend who is about to foot the bill for a meal in a restaurant? Unlike you he has not taken the trouble to learn Cantonese.

Friend	*Waiter, the seafood here is really delicious, very fresh and beautifully cooked. All three of the ideal qualities were superbly realized.*
You	_____a_____
Waiter	Ngóh-deih nī-douh dī yú dōu haih yàuh-séui ge, dòng-yín sàn-sìn lā!
You	_____b_____
Friend	*May I have the bill, please?*
You	_____c_____
Waiter	Dò-jeh. Yih-chìn-baat-baak-gáu-sahp mān.
You	_____d_____
Friend	*What?! So much? That's really not cheap!*
You	_____e_____
Waiter	Sìn-sàang néih yiu jì-dou, yìh-gā yàuh-séui yú dahk-biht nàahn-máaih. Juhng yáuh nē, ngóh-deih jáu-gā sung faai-jí, múih go gu-haak sung yāt deui.
You	_____f_____
Friend	*I have never bought such expensive chopsticks before. OK. It wasn't cheap but it was worth it. Here's $3,000.*
You	_____g_____
Waiter	Dò-jeh.
You	_____h_____

Exercise 6

Supply the bubble caption in Cantonese: *This is a beautiful fish, sure to be very tasty. Who will give $1,000?*

24

嗜好 sih-hou

leisure activities

In this unit you will learn
- about hobbies and the hidden dangers therein
- a final word on **dou**

▶ Dialogue 1

Mr Cheung has changed his habits and Mr Wong wonders why.

老張，我知道你嘅嗜好係揾郵票同捉棋，有時都見你影相同畫畫，
　　但係好少見你跳舞或者散步嘅嘛！

係呀！尤其是呢幾個月我畫咗好多幅畫。但係運動呢，連一次都冇
　　做過。我最憎運動。

點解最近我見你晚晚食完飯之後就一個人離開屋企去花園散步呢？
　　第一次見到你，我重以為你唔見咗嘢，出嚟揾，但係你唔會晚晚都
　　唔見咗嘢㗎。

唉！我去散步係有個目的嘅。

嗰個目的係唔係秘密嚟？可唔可以講俾我聽呀？

唔係秘密，我只係想離開屋企一陣啫。

真奇怪嘞！你一向都中意留喺屋企，好少出街嘅嘛！

老實講你聽喇，最近我個女參加咗初級鋼琴訓練班；我太太又參加咗
　　歌劇訓練班。晚飯之後就係佢哋練習時間嘞。你話我點可以留喺
　　屋企呢？

Mr Wong	Lóuh-Jēung, ngóh jì-dou néih ge sih-hou haih chóuh-yàuh-piu tùhng jūk-kéi, yáuh-sìh dōu gin néih yíng-séung tùhng waahk-wá, daahn-haih hóu síu gin néih tiu-móuh waahk-jé saan-bouh ge bo!
Mr Cheung	Haih a! Yàuh-kèih-sih nī-géi-go-yuht ngóh waahk-jó hóu dò fūk wá. Daahn-haih wahn-duhng nē, lìhn yāt chi dōu móuh jouh-gwo. Ngóh jeui jàng wahn-duhng.
Mr Wong	Dím-gáai jeui-gahn ngóh gin néih máahn-máahn sihk-yùhn faahn jì-hauh jauh yāt-go-yàhn lèih-hòi ūk-kéi heui fà-yún saan-bouh nē? Daih-yāt chi gin-dóu néih, ngóh juhng yíh-wàih néih m̀h-gin-jó yéh, chēut-làih wán, daahn-haih néih m̀h wúih máahn-máahn dōu m̀h-gin-jó yéh ga.
Mr Cheung	Ài! Ngóh heui saan-bouh haih yáuh go muhk-dīk ge.
Mr Wong	Gó go muhk-dīk haih m̀h haih bei-maht ga? Hó m̀h hó-yíh góng béi ngóh tèng a?
Mr Cheung	M̀h haih bei-maht, ngóh jí-haih séung lèih-hòi ūk-kéi yāt-jahn jē.
Mr Wong	Jàn kèih-gwaai lak! Néih yāt-heung dōu jùng-yi làuh hái ūk-kéi, hóu síu chēut-gāai ge bo!
Mr Cheung	Lóuh-saht góng néih tèng lā, jeui-gahn ngóh go néui chàam-gà-jó chò-kāp gong-kàhm fan-lihn-bāan; ngóh taai-táai yauh chàam-gà-jó gò-kehk fan-lihn-bāan. Máahn-faahn jì-hauh jauh haih kéuih-deih lihn-jaahp sìh-gaan lak. Néih wah ngóh dím hó-yíh làuh hái ūk-kéi nē?

嗜好 **sih-hou**	hobby
揸郵票 **chóuh-yàuh-piu**	to collect stamps
捉棋 **jūk-kéi**	to play chess
畫畫 **waahk-wá**	to paint, to draw
跳舞 **tiu-móuh**	to dance
散步 **saan-bouh**	to stroll, to go for a walk
幅 **fūk**	classifier for paintings, drawings and photographs
憎 **jàng**	to hate, detest
唔見咗 **m̀h-gin-jó**	lost, to lose, to mislay
唉！**ài!**	alas! (a sigh)
目的 **muhk-dīk**	purpose, aim, goal
秘密 **bei-maht**	secret
一陣（間）**yāt-jahn(-gāan)**	a moment, in a moment, for a moment
奇怪 **kèih-gwaai**	strange, weird, odd
一向 **yāt-heung**	all along, up to now
留 **làuh**	to stay, to remain; to leave behind
初級 **chò-kāp**	elementary, first grade
鋼琴 **gong-kàhm**	piano
訓練班 **fan-lihn-bāan**	training class
訓練 **fan-lihn**	training, to train
歌劇 **gò-kehk**	opera
練習 **lihn-jaahp**	to practise

Grammar

1 These last few . . .

In Unit 19 you met **jeui-gahn-géi-nìhn** meaning *in the last few years*. Another way of saying the same thing is **nī-géi-nìhn** and you can extend either of the patterns to days, weeks and months too:

jeui-gahn-géi-yaht = **nī-géi-yaht**	*these last few days*
jeui-gahn-géi-go-láih-baai = **nī-géi-go-láih-baai**	*these last few weeks*
jeui-gahn-géi-go-yuht = **nī-géi-go-yuht**	*these last few months*

And **géi** is not essential to these patterns: you can be more specific if you wish, although normally only small numbers are involved:

jeui-gahn léuhng-sàam yaht = **nī léuhng-sàam yaht**	*these last two or three days*
jeui-gahn sei-ńgh nìhn = **nī sei-ńgh nìhn**	*these last four or five years*

2 *Ṁh-gin-jó* lost

Ṁh-gin-jó literally means *became unseen, not seen any more* and it is a useful way of saying that you have lost or mislaid something:

Ngóh m̀h-gin-jó ngóh dī chín; m̀h-jì haih m̀h haih béi yàhn tàu-jó nē?	*I can't find my money; I wonder if it's been stolen?*
Kéuih m̀h-gin-jó yàhn lak.	*She went missing.*

3 For a moment

Yāt-jahn (or its longer form yāt-jahn-gāan) means *a moment of time*. It can be used as either a specific time or a duration of time and its position can therefore be either in front of or after the verb in a sentence:

Ngóh yāt-jahn lohk-làih lā!	*I'll be down in a moment!*
Hóu lā! daahn-haih ngóh jí hó-yíh lohk-làih yāt-jahn jē!	*OK, but I can only come down for a moment!*

4 In your opinion

Just in case you have not picked it up without being told, néih-wah or néih-tái (*you say* or *you see*) both are used in the sense *in your opinion*. Similarly, ngóh-wah or ngóh-tái can mean *in my opinion*.

ℹ️ It's the same the whole world over!

The hobbies mentioned in the dialogue are much as you might find anywhere in the world: Cantonese people like sport and games and collecting things. Mind you, the chess may well be Chinese Chess, which is played on a different board with different pieces and operates with different rules from western chess or it might be **Wàih-kéi** *Surrounding Chess*, which is played with black and white stones on the intersections of the lines on a multi-squared board: it tends to be known in the west under its Japanese name *Go*. One hobby which is much more common with the Chinese than with westerners is calligraphy (**sỳu-faat**). Writing Chinese characters with a brush is a very high art form in China and Japan and many people spend hours painstakingly cultivating their skill.

▶ Dialogue 2

Two mothers discuss the changing leisure pursuits of the young.

我覺得而家啲後生仔同我哋後生嘅時候好唔同。

你講邊方面唔同呢？

我講嘅係嗜好方面。我哋後生嘅時候好中意種花，養魚，養雀，
養狗，養貓等等。但係而家啲後生仔就中意去的士高，卡拉OK，
玩電腦遊戲，呢啲嘅樣嘅嘢。

係呀，我個仔可以一個人對住喫電腦遊戲機玩一晚都唔覺得瘖。
你話，佢對呢方面幾有興趣呢。

李太，你要勸你個仔唔好玩咁多電腦遊戲嘞。專家話如果一個人習慣
自己同自己玩遊戲就會缺乏同別人溝通，漸漸就會養成孤獨嘅性
格，嗽樣係好危險嘅嘣！

我都覺得科學越進步，我哋就越依賴科技。而家連我哋嘅嗜好都受到
科技嘅影響慢慢改變，而且越變越快，越改越多。將來係點樣冇人
可以預知。係嘞，我一返到屋企就叫我個仔唔好再玩電腦遊戲嘞。

Mrs Wong	Ngóh gok-dāk yìh-gā dī hauh-sāang-jái tùhng ngóh-deih hauh-sāang ge sìh-hauh hóu m̀h tùhng.
Mrs Lee	Néih góng bīn fòng-mihn m̀h tùhng nē?
Mrs Wong	Ngóh góng ge haih sih-hou fòng-mihn. Ngóh-deih hauh-sāang ge sìh-hauh hóu jùng-yi jung-fā, yéuhng-yú, yéuhng-jeuk, yéuhng-gáu, yéuhng-māau dáng-dáng. Daahn-haih yìh-gā dī hauh-sāang-jái jauh jùng-yi heui dīk-sih-gōu, kā-lāai-ōu-kēi, wáan dihn-nóuh yàuh-hei, nī dī gám-yéung ge yéh.
Mrs Lee	Haih a, ngóh go jái hó-yíh yāt-go-yàhn deui-jyuh ga dihn-nóuh yàuh-hei-gèi wáan yāt máahn dōu m̀h gok-dāk guih. Néih-wah, kéuih deui nī fòng-mihn géi yáuh hing-cheui nē.
Mrs Wong	Léih Táai, néih yiu hyun néih go jái m̀h-hóu wáan gam dò dihn-nóuh yàuh-hei lak. Jyūn-gā wah yùh-gwó yāt-go-yàhn jaahp-gwaan jih-géi tùhng jih-géi wáan yàuh-hei, jauh wúih kyut-faht tùhng biht-yàhn kàu-tùng jihm-jím jauh wúih yéuhng-sìhng gù-duhk ge sing-gaak, gám-yéung haih hóu ngàih-hím ge bo!
Mrs Lee	Ngóh dōu gok-dāk fō-hohk yuht jeun-bouh, ngóh-deih jauh yuht yí-laaih fō-geih. Yìh-gā lìhn ngóh-deih ge sih-hou dōu sauh-dou fō-geih ge yíng-héung, maahn-máan gói-bin, yìh-ché yuht bin yuht faai, yuht gói yuht dò, jèung-lòih haih dím-yéung móuh yàhn hó-yíh yuh-jì. Haih lak, ngóh yāt fàan-dou ūk-kéi jauh giu ngóh go jái m̀h-hóu joi wáan dihn-nóuh yàuh-hei lak.

同 **tùhng**	the same, alike
種花 **jung-fā**	to cultivate flowers
養 **yéuhng**	to rear, to keep (pets)
雀 **jeuk**	bird
貓 **māau**	cat
的士高 **dīk-sih-gōu**	discotheque
卡拉OK **kā-lāai-ōu-kēi**	karaoke
遊戲 **yàuh-hei**	games
瘡 **guih**	tired, weary
勸 **hyun**	to advise, to urge, to plead with
專家 **jȳun-gā**	expert, specialist
習慣 **jaahp-gwaan**	to be accustomed to, to get used to; habit
自已 **jih-géi**	self, oneself
缺乏 **kyut-faht**	to lack, be short of
別人 **biht-yàhn**	other people
溝通 **kàu-tùng**	to communicate
養成 **yéuhng-sìhng**	to inculcate, to form, breed
孤獨 **gù-duhk**	solitary, lone
性格 **sing-gaak**	temperament, disposition
危險 **ngàih-hím**	dangerous; danger
進步 **jeun-bouh**	progress
依賴 **yí-laaih**	to rely on
科技 **fo-geih**	science and technology
受 **sauh**	to suffer
改變 **gói-bin**	to change, alter
將來 **jèung-lòih**	future, in future
預知 **yuh-jì**	to predict
一...... 就...... **yāt . . . jauh . . .**	as soon as . . . then . . .

The large Chinese characters for **ngàih-hím** *danger* read from left to right.

Grammar

5 *Gèi* machine

The full word for *a machine* or *machinery* is **gèi-hei**, but there are plenty of instances where **gèi** on its own also means *machine*, usually when it is tacked onto other words:

yàuh-hei *games*	→ **yàuh-hei-gèi** *games machine*
dihn-sih *television*	→ **dihn-sih-gèi** *television set*
fèi *to fly*	→ **fèi-gèi** (*flying machine*) *aircraft*
dá-jih *to type*	→ **dá-jih-gèi** *typewriter*
dá-fó *to strike fire*	→ **dá-fó-gèi** *cigarette lighter*

6 *Dōu* does it again!

In Unit 22 you saw how **dōu** could still convey the idea of *even* without the assistance of **lìhn**. In the dialogue there is another rather trickier example: **ngóh go jái . . . wáan yāt máahn dōu mh gok-dāk guih** *my son can play the whole evening and still not feel tired*. You may find it easier to see how **dōu** achieves its effect if you twist the English slightly – *my son even though he plays the whole evening does not feel tired*.

7 Self

Jih-géi means *self* and is a very useful word for giving stress to individuality, usually coming after a person's name or a personal pronoun:

Wòhng Sìn-sàang jih-géi mh sīk góng Yìng-màhn.	*Mr Wong himself cannot speak English.*
Néih jih-géi séung mh séung heui a?	*Do you yourself want to go?*

Jih-géi yāt-go-yàhn means *all by oneself alone*:

Kéuih jih-géi yāt-go-yàhn chóh hái-douh.	*He sat there all alone.*

ℹ️ Helping yourself

When you are eating a Chinese meal with chopsticks from communal bowls in the middle of the table, you will find that the host or other people will often select tasty morsels and put them in your personal bowl. Don't find this odd; it is meant as a great politeness. Of course, it could be that they give you something which you do not want to eat, in which case you are at liberty to leave it lying there. However, whether you want it or not, it can be embarrassing to be constantly waited on in this way and it is polite to try to stop people doing it. Try saying **ṁh-sái gam haak-hei** *no need to be so polite* and following it with **ngóh jih-géi làih** *I'll come at it myself*. If you have a really persistent host nothing you say will deter him, but at least you will have made the right disclaiming noises.

8 As soon as

One of the beauties of Cantonese grammar is that patterns of some complexity are often made up from very simple words. **Yāt** means *one* and **jauh** means *then*: you met them both long ago, but put them together in a grammar pattern and they produce *as soon as . . . then . . . :*

Kéuih yāt chóh chē jauh tàuh-wàhn.	*He gets dizzy as soon as he gets in a car.*
Ngóh yāt gin-dóu kéuih, kéuih jauh jáu-jó lak.	*As soon as I saw him he ran away.*
Wòhng Taai-táai yāt chēut-jó gāai, jauh ṁh gei-dāk-jó yiu máaih māt-yéh sung.	*No sooner had Mrs Wong got outside than she forgot what food she had to buy.*

Note that in this pattern both **yāt** and **jauh** act as adverbs and each comes before a different verb.

▶ Exercise 1

Let's start with a couple of Chinese riddles.

a Can you guess (in English) what this represents?
Yáuh yāt yeuhng yéh móuh chúhng-leuhng ge, daahn-haih sahp go yàhn dōu ṁh hó-yíh tòih-héi kéuih. Yùh-gwó yeh-máahn yāt làih-dou, kéuih jauh ṁh-gin-jó. Néih gú haih māt-yéh nē?

b And what is the answer to this one (in Cantonese)?
Síu-Léih deui Síu-Wóng wah: 'Ngóh ge sàang-yaht hái johk-yaht ge johk-yaht ge tìng-yaht.' Síu-Wóng wah: 'Móuh cho, néih ge sàang-yaht haih tìng-yaht ge chìhn-yaht. Gùng-héi! Gùng-héi!' Síu-Léih haih géi-sí sàang-yaht a?

Exercise 2

Make the following pairs of sentences into one by incorporating the bracketed idea. The first answer would be: Wòhng Síu-jé sihk jóu-chāan jì-chìhn, jaahp-gwaan heui saan-bouh sìn.

a Wòhng Síu-jé sihk jóu-chāan. Kéuih jaahp-gwaan saan-bouh.
   (*before*)
b Ngóh hái ūk-kéi. Ngóh m̀h daai móu. (*when*)
c Nàahm-yán luhk-sahp-ńgh seui. Kéuih-deih hó-yíh ló teui-
   yàu-gām. (*not until*)
d Ngóh gàm-jìu-jóu tái bou-jí. Ngóh jì-dou ngóh-deih gūng-sī
   ge chìhng-fong hóu ngàih-hím. (*as soon as*)
e Chàhn Sìn-sàang yám bē-jáu. Kéuih jùng-yi yám. (*the more
   . . . the more*)

Exercise 3

Chéng néih yuhng Gwóng-dùng-wá góng nī sei fūk wá léuih-
bihn faat-sàng dī māt-yéh sih a.

Exercise 4
A quick test of your place words. Supply the missing words as
rapidly as you can.

a Ngóh hái néih hauh-bihn, gám néih hái ngóh _____.
b Seuhng-hói hái Bāk-gìng nàahm-bihn, gám Bāk-gìng hái
   Seuhng-hói _____.
c Néih hái gó-douh, gám ngóh hái _____.
d Wòhng Sàang hái Wòhng Táai jó-sáu-bihn, gám Wòhng
   Táai hái Wòhng Sàang _____.
e Bouh syù hái baahk-jí léuih-bihn, gám baahk-jí hái syù
   _____.

Exercise 5

You are on Hong Kong Island and you want to get to the airport. You have managed to get through on the phone to the airport enquiry office, but the person answering can only speak Cantonese. You have a plane to catch, so you had better produce your best accent and keenest understanding to ask the following.

a Is there a bus which goes to the airport?
b How much is the fare from City Hall?
c How long will it take to get to the airport?
d Is there a toilet on the bus?
e What time does flight 251 take off?
f When does flight 251 get in to London?

25

房屋
fóhng-ūk
household affairs

In this unit you will learn
- basic words for living
  accommodation
- a little more about food

▶ Dialogue 1

Mr Wong's friend Mr Cheung lives alone in a large flat.

老王，歡迎你嚟探我。請入嚟坐喇！
咦！點解唔見張太同你哋啲仔女喋？
哦！佢哋半年之前已經移咗民去英國啦！而家只有我一個人住喺香港
之嘛。
嘩，你間屋真係大嘞。我最中意你嘅露台。呢間屋有幾多間瞓房呀？
有三間瞓房，兩個廁所同洗身房，一間客廳一間飯廳，同埋一個
廚房。
你哋嘅廚房設備都好齊全喎……有洗衣機，洗碗機，煮食爐，碗櫃，
重有微波爐添。
呢啲嘢我同太太都打算運去英國嘅，但係後來知道運費太貴嘞，
而且，如果喺英國買新嘅，價錢都唔算太貴，所以我哋就決定唔運
嘞，留喺香港自己用。
啲窗簾布同地氈都重係好新喎！點解唔運去英國呢？
唉！唔好提起地氈同窗簾布嘞。我嗰陣時都同你一樣，話要運去英國，
但係我太太堅持要留返佢哋喺香港。佢嘅理由就係啲窗簾布嘅顏色
太深嘞，唔好睇，啲地氈嘅花樣佢又唔中意。
我嚟咗咁耐，你都冇斟茶俾我飲。我估喺呢半年來你一個人住一定好
孤獨嘞，老張，等我今日陪你一齊出街去飲茶逛公司喇。

Cheung	Lóuh-Wóng, fùn-yìhng néih làih taam ngóh. Chéng yahp-làih chóh lā!
Wong	Yí! Dím-gáai m̀h gin Jèung Táai tùhng néih-deih dī jái-néui ga?
Cheung	Óh, kéuih-deih bun nìhn jì-chìhn yíh-gìng yìh-jó màhn heui Yìng-gwok la! Yìh-gā jí-yáuh ngóh yāt-go-yàhn jyuh hái Hèung-góng jī-máh.
Wong	Wà, néih gàan ūk jàn-haih daaih lak. Ngóh jeui jùng-yi néih ge louh-tòih. Nī gàan ūk yáuh géi-dō gàan fan-fóng a?
Cheung	Yáuh sàam gàan fan-fóng, léuhng go chi-só tùhng sái-sàn-fóng, yāt gàan haak-tēng, yāt gàan faahn-tēng, tùhng-māaih yāt go chyùh-fóng.
Wong	Néih-deih ge chyùh-fóng chit-beih dōu hóu chàih-chyùhn bo . . . yáuh sái-yì-gèi, sái-wún-gèi, jyú-sihk-lòuh, wún-gwaih, juhng yáuh mèih-bō-lòuh tìm.
Cheung	Nī dī yéh ngóh tùhng taai-táai dōu dá-syun wahn-heui Yìng-gwok ge, daahn-haih hauh-lòih jì-dou wahn-fai taai gwai lak, yìh-ché, yùh-gwó hái Yìng-gwok máaih sàn ge, ga-chìhn dōu m̀h syun taai gwai, só-yíh ngóh-deih jauh kyut-dihng m̀h wahn lak, làuh hái Hèung-góng jih-géi yuhng.

Wong   Dī chēung-lím-bou tùhng deih-jīn dōu juhng haih hóu sàn bo! Dím-gáai m̀h wahn-heui Yìng-gwok nē?

Cheung Aài! M̀h-hóu tàih deih-jīn tùhng chēung-lím-bou lak. Ngóh gó-jahn-sìh dōu tùhng néih yāt-yeuhng, wah yiu wahn-heui Yìng-gwok, daahn-haih ngóh taai-táai gìn-chìh yiu làuh-fàan kéuih-deih hái Hèung-góng. Kéuih ge léih-yàuh jauh haih dī chēung-lím-bou ge ngàahn-sīk taai sàm lak, m̀h hóu-tái, dī deih-jīn ge fā-yéung kéuih yauh m̀h jùng-yi.

Wong   Ngóh làih-jó gam noih, néih dōu móuh jàm chàh béi ngóh yám. Ngóh gú hái nī bun nìhn néih yāt-go-yàhn jyuh yāt-dihng hóu gù-duhk lak. Lóuh-Jēung, dáng ngóh gàm-yaht pùih néih yāt-chàih chēut-gāai heui yám-chàh kwāang-gūng-sī lā.

露台 **louh-tòih**	*balcony*
客廳 **haak-tēng**	*living room, lounge*
飯廳 **faahn-tēng**	*dining room*
洗衣機 **sái-yì-gèi**	*washing machine*
洗碗機 **sái-wún-gèi**	*dishwasher*
碗 **wún**	*a bowl*
煮食爐 **jyu-sihk-lòuh**	*cooking stove*
碗櫃 **wún-gwaih**	*cupboard, dresser*
微波爐 **mèih-bō-lòuh**	*microwave oven*
後來 **hauh-lòih**	*later, afterwards*
運費 **wahn-fai**	*transportation costs*
決定 **kyut-dihng**	*to decide*
窗簾布 **chēung-lím-bou**	*curtains*
地氈 **deih-jīn**	*carpet*
提 **tàih**	*to mention, bring up*
堅持 **gìn-chìh**	*to insist, insist on*
留返 **làuh-fàan**	*to leave behind*
理由 **léih-yàuh**	*reason*
顏色 **ngàahn-sīk**	*colour*
深 **sàm**	*deep*
斟 **jàm**	*to pour into a cup, glass or bowl*
陪 **pùih**	*to accompany, keep company with*
飲茶 **yám-chàh**	*to drink tea = to have a* **dím-sām** *snack meal*
逛公司 **kwaang gūng-sī**	*to go window shopping*
逛 **kwaang**	*to cruise*

Grammar

1 Verb + object verbs

You may have found Mr Cheung's remark **yíh-gìng yìh-jó màhn heui Yìng-gwok la** grammatically strange because **-jó** has split **yìh** and **màhn**. The reason is quite simple: the verb **yìh-màhn** *to migrate* is composed of **yìh** *to move* and **màhn** *people*, so that it is actually a verb + object verb and, of course, **-jó** is an ending which must be attached to a verb, not to an object.

2 Another classifier oddity

Mr Cheung uses the classifier **gàan** for **fan-fóng** and for **haak-tēng** and for **faahn-tēng**, but uses **go** for **chi-só** and **chyuh-fóng**. Somehow toilets and kitchens do not seem to qualify as proper rooms (rooms in which people socialize, perhaps), so they are often not given **gàan** status.

3 *Bowls* and other containers

Wún *bowl* is a very handy word, because bowls are so much used at the Chinese table. There are **faahn-wún** *rice bowls*, **tòng-wún** *soup bowls* and **chàh-wún** *tea bowls*, not to mention **daaih-wún** *big bowls* and **sai-wún** *little bowls*. But **wún** is even more useful because it is also a classifier, as in **yāt wún tòng** *a bowl of soup* and **léuhng wún baahk-faahn** *two bowls of boiled rice* (**baahk-faahn** literally means *white rice*, hence *steamed* or *boiled rice* as opposed to **cháau-faahn** *fried rice*). You can see how the two functions of **wun** operate in the following comparison:

sàam wún faahn	*three bowls of rice*
sàam jek faahn-wún	*three rice bowls* (the classifier for a bowl can be either **jek** or **go**)

Other container words or measure words work the same way. Most common perhaps is **bùi** *a cup, a glass, a mug*:

léuhng jek chàh-būi	*two teacups* (note the tone change on **bui**)
léuhng bùi chàh	*two cups of tea*

4 Not any more

In Unit 3 you were given an example of the use of **lak** with **m̀h**. In the previous dialogue Mr Cheung says **ngóh-deih kyut-dihng m̀h wahn lak** *we decided not to transport them after all*, that is, they had at first decided otherwise but not any more. **M̀h + lak** is a very convenient way of conveying the notion *not any more*.

5 *Deep* and *shallow*: *dark* and *light*

Sàm literally means *deep* (**Néih yiu síu-sàm bo! Gó-syu di séui hóu sàm!** *You should be careful, the water is very deep there!*) and the opposite word *shallow* is **chín**. Both words are capable of being extended in use, so that you can describe someone's thought as **sàm**, for example. With colours, **sàm** means *dark* or *deep* and **chín** means *light*, so **sàm-hùhng-sīk** is *crimson* or *dark red* and **chín-làahm-sīk** is the colour sported by **Gim-kìuh Daaih-hohk** on boat race day.

ℹ More than a cup of tea

Cantonese people never say *let's go and have some dím-sām*, they always say *let's go and drink tea* (**yám-chàh**). **Yám-chàh** goes on in specialist teahouses and restaurants from early morning to about 2.30 p.m. You order your preferred tea from the waiter – Dragon Well Tea, Jasmine Tea, Iron Guan-Yin Tea, Chrysanthemum Pu-er, or whatever – and you then sit back and wait till someone comes by with a tray or trolley of steaming hot **dím-sām** from the kitchen. If you fancy what is there you ask for it, but otherwise you wait until another trolley comes round with something on it that you *do* want. There is great variety and you will find it hard to stop ordering. Until about 30 years ago the bill was calculated according to the number of little dishes left on your table when you had finished, but smart customers would slip dishes onto other people's tables and get up to other tricks to cut down the bill, so that nowadays a running tally is kept on a menu slip in a holder on your table. And of course the tea will be charged for as well. **Yám-chàh** is a Cantonese must: one of the great gastronomic treats in a land where food is king.

▶ Dialogue 2

Mr Wong looks at house purchase.

先生，你睇呢座樓嘅管理唔錯嘟！廿四小時都有保安服務，每日保安
人員會嚟兩次，有清潔工人打掃走廊同樓梯，每個月都有人檢查呢
三架較……好安全㗎！

係，都唔錯。有冇車位呀？

有一個車位包括喺樓價裡便。先生，到啦，請出較喇。你睇呢度大門
有法國電子鎖，壞人好難開㗎。

唔錯，唔錯。我哋入屋睇吓囉。

嚤，你睇，客廳同飯廳又大又光猛，個露台對住個海，真舒服嘞。

唔錯。可惜樓底太矮啫。

先生，唔算太矮啦，離地面都有九呎嘅啦。請過嚟呢處睇吓啲房間
喇。

咦，點解冇套房廁所同沖涼房嘅咩？

有呃，主人房就有喇，嚤，請睇吓呢間喇。

嘩，重係用煤氣熱水爐咁落後嘅。

先生，如果你唔中意，我可以換一個電子熱水爐俾你。你睇，主人房
咁舒服，地方咁靜，一啲都唔嘈，喺呢處瞓覺一定會發好夢嘅。

我話唔係嘞。屋價咁貴，如果我買咗，會瞓唔著覺就真。

Salesman	Sìn-sàang, néih tái nī joh láu ge gwún-léih m̀h cho bo! Yah-sei síu-sìh dōu yáuh bóu-ōn fuhk-mouh, múih-yaht bóu-ōn yàhn-yùhn wúih làih léuhng chi, yáuh chìhng-git gùng-yàhn dá-sou jáu-lóng tùhng làuh-tài, múih go yuht dōu yáuh yàhn gím-chàh nī sàam ga līp . . . hóu òn-chyùhn ga!
Mr Wong	Haih, dōu m̀h-cho. Yáuh móuh chē-wái a?
Salesman	Yáuh yāt go chē-wái bàau-kwut hái ūk-ga léuih-bihn. Sìn-sàang, dou la, chéng chēut līp lā. Néih tái nī douh daaih-mùhn yáuh Faat-gwok dihn-jí-só, waaih-yàhn hóu nàahn hòi ga.
Mr Wong	M̀h-cho, m̀h-cho. Ngóh-deih yahp ūk tái-háh lo.
Salesman	Nàh, néih tái, haak-tēng tùhng faahn-tēng yauh daaih yauh gwòng-máahng, go louh-tòih deui-jyuh go hói, jàn sỳu-fuhk lak.
Mr Wong	M̀h-cho. Hó-sīk làuh-dái taai ngái jēk.
Salesman	Sìn-sàang, m̀h syun taai ngái la, lèih deih-mín dōu yáuh gáu chek ge la. Chéng gwo-làih nī-syu tái-háh dī fòhng-gāan lā.
Mr Wong	Yí, dím-gáai móuh tou-fóng chi-só tùhng chùhng-lèuhng-fóng ge mē?
Salesman	Yáuh ak, jýu-yàhn-fóng jauh yáuh lā. Nàh, chéng tái-háh nī gàan lā.

Mr Wong   Wàh, juhng haih yuhng mùih-hei yiht-séui-lòuh gam lohk-hauh ge.

Salesman   Sìn-sàang, yùh-gwó néih m̀h jùng-yi, ngóh hó-yíh wuhn yāt go dihn-jí yiht-séui-lòuh béi néih. Néih tái, jýu-yàhn-fóng gam sýu-fuhk, deih-fòng gam jihng, yāt-dī dōu m̀h chòuh. Hái nī-syu fan-gaau yāt-dihng wúih faat hóu muhng ge.

Mr Wong   Ngóh wah m̀h haih lak. Ūk-ga gam gwai, yùh-gwó ngóh máaih-jó, wúih fan-m̀h-jeuhk-gaau jauh-jàn.

座	**joh**	classifier for massive things (large buildings, mountains etc.)
管理	**gwún-léih**	*management*, to manage
小時	**síu-sìh**	*an hour*
保安	**bóu-ōn**	*security*, keep secure
人員	**yàhn-yùhn**	*personnel*, staff
清潔	**chìng-git**	*cleanliness*, to clean
工人	**gùng-yàhn**	*worker*, servant
打掃	**dá-sou**	*to sweep*
樓梯	**làuh-tài**	*staircase*
檢查	**gím-chàh**	*check*, inspect
軩	**līp**	*lift*, elevator
安全	**òn-chỳuhn**	*safe*, safety
車位	**chē-wái**	*parking space*
包括	**bàau-kwut**	*to include*
屋價	**ūk-ga**	*house price*
度	**douh**	classifier for doors
電子	**dihn-jí**	*electronic*
鎖	**só**	a lock, to lock
光猛	**gwòng-máahng**	*bright*
海	**hói**	*the sea*
樓底	**làuh-dái**	*the ceiling*
矮	**ngái**	*low, short in height*
離	**lèih**	*distant from*
地面	**deih-mín**	*the floor*
呎	**chek**	*foot* (length)
套房	**tou-fóng**	*en suite*
沖涼房	**chùng-lèuhng-fóng**	*bathroom*
主人房	**jýu-yàhn-fóng**	*master bedroom*
煤氣	**mùih-hei**	*town gas*
熱水爐	**yiht-séui-lòuh**	*boiler, water heater*
落後	**lohk-hauh**	*backward, old fashioned*
換	**wuhn**	*to change, exchange*
靜	**jihng**	*quiet*
嘈	**chòuh**	*noisy*
發夢	**faat-muhng**	*to dream*
瞓唔著（覺）**fan-m̀h-jeuhk(-gaau)**		*unable to get to sleep*

Grammar

6 *Yah-sei síu-sìh*

Síu-sìh is an alternative word for **jūng-tàuh** *hour* which you have met and **yah-sei síu-sìh** is the regular way to say *24 hour* (as in *24-hour service*).

7 Workers

Gùng-yàhn means quite simply *work person*, but just like *worker* in English it implies that the person works for someone else, that he or she is not in charge. In Hong Kong it is the common word for *a house servant* and there is a general assumption that house servants are female, so that if you have a male house servant you would refer to him as a **nàahm-gùng-yàhn** (compare this with the police situation described in Unit 17).

ℹ The English invasion

Līp is the Cantonese attempt at the English word *lift*, the proper Cantonese word being tediously long (**sìng-gong-gèi** *rising and falling machine*). You have met **bō** *ball*, **bā-sí** *bus*, **dīk-sí** *taxi*, **sà-léut** *salad* and **fēi** *fare*. **Fēi-lám** is *film*, **sih-dō** is *a store*, **bō-sí** is *the boss*, **baht-lāan-déi** is *brandy* and there are many many more, but it is possible that the trend is away from using such words and towards a more pure Cantonese vocabulary. Incidentally, *to ride in a lift* is **chóh-līp**, though few lifts have seats in them.

8 Distant from

Lèih means *to be distant from*, *to be separated from* and it is very handy for showing distance relationships. In the dialogue the salesman says that the ceiling **lèih deih-mín dōu yáuh gáu chek ge la** *is nine feet from the floor*. Similarly, you might say:

Lèuhn-dēun lèih Hèung-góng (yáuh) yāt-maahn-yāt-chìn gūng-léih.	*London is 11,000 kilometres from Hong Kong.*

Yáuh *to have* is the verb which appears with numbers most often. Its use in this pattern is optional, although you are more likely to put it in if you are trying to stress the notion *is **all** of 11,000 kilometres*.

The word most often associated with **lèih** is **yúhn** *far, distant*:

Gwóng-jàu lèih Hèung-góng
m̀h-haih-géi-yúhn.

Canton is not very far from Hong Kong.

Néih ūk-kéi lèih Daaih-
wuih-tòhng yúhn m̀h
yúhn a?

Is your home far from the City Hall?

You will remember from Unit 20 that *to be close to* is a different pattern:

Bā-sí-jaahm hóu káhn
Daaih-wuih-tòhng.

The bus stop is very close to the City Hall.

9 A last look at *dōu*

In the dialogue the salesman is put in a difficult situation – he has to contradict Mr Wong who claims that the ceilings are too low when in fact they are the usual height. What he does is to slip in an otherwise unnecessary **dōu** and that somehow takes the confrontational edge off the contradiction. It is a standard politeness not to disagree too violently with someone else, but rather to show that while you cannot agree with them you do not wish to be offensive about it. In English you might say *that's not quite right* when what you mean is *that's wrong!*: in Cantonese you would add in a **dōu**. So **m̀h haih!** sounds abrupt and rude (*it's not!*), but **dōu m̀h haih** gives the same answer in an acceptably soft way (*I'm afraid that's not the case*).

10 Bathrooms

In Unit 15 you learned that the word for *bathroom* is **sái-sàn-fóng** and now you have met another and newer word **chùng-lèuhng-fóng**. It seems that this newer term is slowly driving out the older one, but you are bound to come across both of them. There is a difference in their origins: **sái-sàn** *to wash the body* is *to have an all over wash* or *to have a bath*, while **chùng-lèuhng** is really *to have a shower*, but the distinction is becoming blurred.

11 And that's for sure!

Jauh-jàn means *then that would be true* and it is used at the ends of statements to make them more emphatic. It coincides quite nicely with the English *and that's for sure!*, *and that's the truth!*

26

溫習 (四)
wàn-jaahp (sei)
revision (4)

This is the shortest unit in the book – just a few exercises and a couple of passages of Cantonese for you to understand and to help you realize how far you have come in the space of 25 units. As usual you will find translations of these passages in the key at the back, but probably you will not need them.

Of course you are not yet at native-speaker standard, but you should find that you have reached the stage where you know enough to be able to hold a conversation and, more importantly, to find out more for yourself by asking and by working out what some of the things you hear must mean on the basis of what you already know.

Persevere – having come this far you have shown that you are capable of learning Cantonese: it would be a great pity to stop just when you have reached 'critical velocity' for take off into the cheerful exciting world of Cantonese conversation.

Exercise 1
Name the buildings or rooms which you associate with the following. The first answer would be **gíng-chaat** → **gíng-chaat-guhk**.

a	gíng-chaat	b	sái-yì-gèi
c	yeuhk-séui	d	gong-kàhm
e	bei-sỳu	f	jì-piu
g	lèuhn-pún	h	yàuh-gáan

Exercise 2
Make the following sentences less aggressive by using **dōu**, other polite words such as **m̀h-gòi, chéng** and **deui-m̀h-jyuh** or perhaps by rephrasing in a softer way.

a Máih yūk!
b Néih góng-cho.
c Néih m̀h mìhng-baahk.
d Ngóh m̀h tùhng-yi.
e Gim-kìuh Daaih-hohk m̀h haih sai-gaai seuhng jeui yáuh-méng ge.

Exercise 3
Here are the estate agent's details and plan of a flat which you want to buy. Using Cantonese explain to your partner what it is like, giving the size of the rooms, the address and other details.

A TWO-BEDROOM FLAT
AT No. 27 CANTON ROAD, 8TH FLOOR
PARKING SPACE INCLUDED IN THE PRICE
ONLY HK$5,500,000!

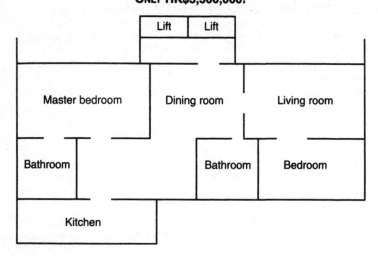

Exercise 4
Make meaningful sentences with these pairs of words. (We have given simple models in the key to the exercises at the back of the book.)

a gwún-léih   gìng-léih
b hòi-chí   hòi-chē
c hói-sīn   sàn-sìn
d yāt-làuh   jáu-làuh

Exercise 5

a Bīn yeuhng yéh tùhng kèih-tà ge yéh m̀h tùhng júng-leuih a?
    (yàuh-gáan/yàuh-séui/yàuh-piu/yàuh-guhk/yàuh-fai)
b Bīn yeuhng yéh hái sé-jih-làuh léuih-bihn móuh ge nē?
    (dihn-wá/dihn-nóuh/dihn-dāng/dihn-yíng/dihn-nyúhn-lòuh)
c Bīn yeuhng deui ngóh-deih ge sàn-tái hóu nē?
    (dá-bō/dá-gāau/dá-gip/dá-jih/dá-dihn-wá)
d Bīn yeuhng haih jeui gwai nē?
    (bou-jí/baahk-jí/seun-jí/Góng-jí/m̀h-jí)
e Yùh-gwó néih séung heui ngoih-gwok, néih yāt-dihng yiu yáuh bīn yeuhng 'jing' a?
    (bóu-jing/sàn-fán-jing/gíng-yùhn-jing/chìm-jing)

Exercise 6
Put suitable final particles in the blanks.

a Gàm-yaht ge tìn-hei m̀h hóu, ngóh-deih m̀h heui yàuh-séui __.

b Nī ga chē gam pèhng, néih dōu m̀h jùng-yi __? Dím-gáai __?

c Kéuih m̀h jùng-yi ngóh heui __? Gám, ngóh jauh m̀h heui __.

d Jà dihn-dāan-chē hóu ngàih-hím __. Dím-gáai néih juhng béi néih ge jái jà __?

Exercise 7
Hái bīn-douh.

a sihk-dāk-dóu hói-sīn a?

b máaih-máh a?

c daap-dóu bā-sí a?

d sihk-dāk-dóu ngóh taai-táai jýu ge sung a?

e gin-dāk-dóu Wòhng Bei-syù a?

Exercise 8
Insert the missing classifiers.

a yāt _____ deih-jīn   **b** yāt _____ wá

c yāt _____ yiht-séui-lòuh   **d** yāt _____ chāan-tói tùhng yí

e yāt _____ jai-fuhk   **f** yāt _____ daaih-mùhn

Exercise 9
There are deliberate mistakes in each of the following. Can you spot them?

a Léih Sàang hóu yáuh-chín, kéuih lìhn yāt mān dōu móuh.

b Ngóh daaih-gwo ngóh màh-mā.

c Gó chēut dihn-yíng ngóh m̀h tái-gwo.

d Kéuih hàahng sahp-fàn faai.

e Kéuih sèui-yìhn haih gìng-léih, yìh-ché sīk dá-jih.

Passage 1

Lùhng Dragons

Hóu noih hóu noih jì-chìhn hái Jùng-gwok yáuh yāt go hóu jùng-yi waahk-wá ge yàhn. Kéuih ge wá waahk-dāk hóu hóu, yàuh-kèih-sìh waahk Lùhng, jàn-haih hóu-chíh wúih yūk ge yāt-yeuhng. Yáuh yāt chi, yāt go daaih-gwùn jì-dou kéuih hóu sīk waahk Lùhng jauh hóu hòi-sām gám deui kéuih wah: 'Ngóh jih-géi dōu hóu jùng-yi Lùhng. Yùh-gwó néih háng bòng ngóh waahk yāt tìuh Lùhng, ngóh wúih béi hóu dò chín néih.'

Géi yaht jì-hauh, git-gwó tìuh Lùhng jauh waahk-hóu lak, yìh-
ché waahk-dāk hóu hóu, juhng kāp-yáhn-jó hóu dò yàhn làih
chàam-gwùn tìm. Daahn-haih jeui hó-sìk jauh haih tìuh Lùhng
móuh ngáahn ge. Daaih-gwùn m̀h mìhng-baahk jauh mahn
kéuih dím-gáai m̀h waahk ngáahn nē? Kéuih wah, yùh-gwó
waahk-jó ngáahn jì-hauh, tìuh Lùhng jauh wúih fèi-jáu ge la!

Dòng-yín kéuih góng ge yéh móuh yàhn wúih sèung-seun lā.
Daaih-gwùn hóu nàu, yāt-dihng yiu kéuih waahk-màaih deui
ngáahn. Jàn kèih-gwaai, kéuih yāt waahk-yùhn deui ngáahn,
tìuh Lùhng jauh yūk-jó géi háh, jàn-haih yàuh jèung jí syu
tiu-jó chēut-làih, fèi-jáu-jó lak.

Passage 2

Sei-ǹgh-sahp nìhn jì-chìhn, gó-jahn-sìh Seuhng-hói syun haih
yāt go hóu sìn-jeun ge daaih sìhng-síh, daahn-haih Jùng-gwok
kèih-tà hóu dò sìhng-síh tùhng-màaih hèung-há deih-fòng dōu
juhng haih hóu lohk-hauh ge. Yāt yaht, yáuh yāt go hèung-há-
yàhn, Léih Sìn-sàang, yáuh sih yiu heui Seuhng-hói taam kéuih
ge pàhng-yáuh Wòhng Daaih Gwok. Wòhng Sìn-sàang jyuh hái
yāt gàan yauh daaih yauh leng, chit-beih yauh chàaih-chyùhn ge
jáu-dim léuih-bihn.

Léih Sàang làih-dou jáu-dim, hái daaih-tòhng* dáng Wòhng
Sìn-sàang ge sìh-hauh, gin-dóu yāt go lóuh taai-táai maahn-
máan gám hàahng-yahp yāt gàan fóng-jái léuih-bihn. Léih Sìn-
sàang meih gin-gwo līp, só-yíh kéuih m̀h jì gó ga haih līp làih-ge.
Léuhng fàn jūng jì-hauh, fóng-jái ge mùhn hòi-jó lak, yāt go
yauh leng yauh hauh-sāang ge síu-jé hàahng-chēut-làih.

Léih Sàang hòi-chí ge sìh-hauh gok-dāk hóu kèih-gwaai, yìhn-
hauh kéuih jauh hóu hòi-sām gám wah: 'Sìhng-síh yàhn jàn-
haih sìn-jeun lak: hah chi ngóh yāt-dihng daai-màaih taai-táai
làih.'

(*daaih-tòhng = *lobby, great hall.*)

grammar summary

This Grammar summary gives some of the basic principles of Cantonese grammar, which you can use for quick reference. Where helpful it refers you back to earlier parts of the book where particular points are discussed in greater detail. These references are in the form 1.3, where the first number is the unit number and the second is the number of the heading in the grammar section of that particular unit.

1 Adjectives

a Adjectives go before the nouns they limit (**yāt jek daaih būi** *a large cup*). [1.3]
b Adjectives can also function as verbs. [1.3; 13.3]
c Adjectival clauses and phrases go before the nouns they limit and are linked to them with **ge**:

ngóh hóu séung máaih ge chē . . .   *the car I very much want to buy . . .* [4.6; 17.1]

2 Adverbs

a Fixed adverbs such as **dōu** *all*, *both*, *also*, **jauh** *then*, **joi** *again* come immediately before verbs (although the negative **m̀h** can be placed between a fixed adverb and a verb). [1.7; 4.9; 6.3; 8.3; 10.5; 24.8]
b Adverbs of degree such as **hóu** *very* and **taai** *too* go immediately in front of adjectival verbs and auxiliary verbs such as **séung** *want to* and **yiu** *need to* (but again the negative **m̀h** can intervene).
c Adverbs of time when something occurs must come before the verb, but not necessarily directly before the verb. [6.10; 8.2; 24.3]

d Adverbs of duration of time come after the verb, but not necessarily directly after the verb. [6.12; 10.9; 20.4; 24.3]

e Adverbs of location normally come before the verb, although not necessarily directly before the verb, but if the location is the result of the action of the verb then the adverb comes after the verb:

Hái Yìng-gwok Wòhng Sàang móuh ūk.	*Mr Wong has not got a house in Britain.*
Kéuih chóh hái sō-fá-yí seuhng-bihn.	*She seats herself on the sofa.* [4.3; 12.7]

f Adverbs of manner can be made by joining them to a verb with the verb ending -dāk:

Kéuih jáu-dāk hóu faai.	*He runs very quickly.* [15.2]

g Adverbs can be made from adjectives by the formula **hóu adjective gám**:

hóu leng gám	*very prettily* [8.9]

3 Alternatives

a When *or* occurs in a question it is translated by **dihng-haih**:

Néih tìng-yaht heui dihng-haih hauh-yaht heui nē?	*Are you going tomorrow or the day after?* [13.6; 16.7]

b When *or* occurs in a statement it is usually translated by **waahk-jé**:

Kéuih waahk-jé làih waahk-jé m̀h làih.	*He'll come or he won't.* [16.7]

c When *or* occurs with numbers, indicating an approximate figure, two numbers are given together without other device (although it is possible to separate them with **waahk-jé**):

luhk-chāt yaht	*six or seven days* [10.4; 13.6]

4 Classifiers

a Whenever nouns are counted or specified with *this*, *that*, *which?*, *each*, *the whole* the correct classifier must be placed between the number or specifier and the noun. [2.4; 2.6; 4.8; 12.1; 12.5; 13.2; 16.3; 17.8; 20.1; 25.2; 25.3]

b The plural classifier and the classifier for uncountable things is **dī**. [4.8; 12.5; 15.3]

c The classifier can be used to form possessives in place of **ge**. [12.3; 12.5]

d At the beginning of a sentence the classifier can be used with definite reference (like *the* in English). [12.5]

e The classifier can be doubled in conjunction with the adverb **dōu** to give the meaning *each one of*. [5.10; 12.5]

f A very small number of nouns do not need a classifier. [8.6; 9.9; 12.5]

5 Commands

a Negative commands (*don't!*) are made with **m̀h-hóu** or its more abrupt form **máih**. [4.11; 16.4]

b Positive commands (*do!*) use abruptly spoken verbs (**jáu!** *go!*), or (rather less forcefully) the final particle **lā!**, or the verb ending **-jó** with a following object, or some adjectival verbs and verb endings with the comparative **-dī** ending. [3.10; 17.7; 19.1]

6 Comparatives and superlatives

a Comparatives are formed with **-gwo** *surpassing*. The pattern is **X** adjective**-gwo Y**. *A bit more* is expressed with **síu-síu** and *a lot more* with **hóu-dò**:

Ngóh gòu-gwo néih.	*I am taller than you.*
Ngóh gòu-gwo néih síu-síu.	*I am a bit taller than you.*
Ngóh gòu-gwo néih hóu-dò.	*I am a lot taller than you.*
	[12.2; 16.9]

b Negative comparison uses the pattern **X móuh Y gam** adjective:

Néih móuh ngóh gam gòu.	*You are not as tall as I am.*
	[16.8; 16.9]

c If there is only an **X** and no **Y** the patterns are:

Ngóh gòu-dī.	*I'm taller.*
Ngóh gòu hóu-dò.	*I'm a lot taller.*
Néih móuh gam gòu.	*You're not so tall.* [16.9]

d Superlatives make use of **jeui** *most*, often adding **lak** after the adjective:

Kéuih jeui gòu lak.	*He is tallest.* [8.4; 16.9]

e Equivalence is expressed by X **tùhng/móuh** Y **yāt-yeuhng gam** adjective:

Ngóh tùhng néih yāt-   *I'm just as tall as you are.*
  yeuhng gam gòu.
Kéuih móuh ngóh yāt-   *He's not just as tall as I am.*
  yeuhng gam gòu.   [13.4; 16.9]

7 Nouns

Nouns only have one form and do not change according to case, number or gender. The exception is the noun **yàhn** *person* which has a plural form **yàhn-deih**, but this plural form is reserved for the meaning *other people* and as an oblique way of referring to oneself or to the person being addressed – it is *not* used in such expressions as *three people* which is **sàam go yàhn**. [1.9; 2.6]

8 Particles

Particles are words which for the most part have no meaning in themselves, but which add nuance or sentiment or some other gloss to a sentence or phrase. Some (such as **ma?, mē?, àh?, nē?, sìn, tìm, bo, jē**) are capable of clear definition, but usage of many others is not consistent among native speakers and so defies adequate definition. Unfortunately, all speakers of Cantonese use many particles, but they do not all use the same particles, neither do they all necessarily agree on which particle to use when. Often the ill-defined particles seem to add little or nothing to the meaning and may be treated as 'voiced pauses' ('spoken commas' if you like) and ignored. [1.11; 3.6; 3.8; 3.10; 5.2; 5.8; 25.4]

9 Passives

The passive construction is not common in Cantonese, but uses the pattern X **beih** Y verb and the verb usually carries a verb ending of some kind:

Tìuh yú beih māau   *The fish was eaten by the cat.*
  sihk-gwo lak.   [12.4]

10 Possessives

a Possessives are formed with **ge** which is positioned as if it were the English apostrophe *'s*:

Wòhng Síu-jé ge nàahm-pàhng-yáuh.	Miss Wong's boyfriend. [2.2; 17.2]

b They can also be formed with the appropriate classifier (single or plural) instead of **ge**:

ngóh go jái *my son*	ngóh dī néui *my daughters* [12.3]

11 Potentials

Potentials (*can, to be able*) are formed in three ways:

a with the verbs **hó-yíh** and **sīk**. **Hó-yíh** often implies *permission to* and so is rather like *may* in English, while **sīk** indicates *acquired ability to* and so is like *to know how to*:

Ngóh hó-yíh heui yàuh-séui.	*I may go swimming.*
Ngóh sīk yàuh-séui.	*I can swim.* [6.11]

b with the verb ending **-dāk**:

Ngóh yàuh-dāk séui.	*I can swim* (= *may* or = *know how to*). [6.11]

c with the positive ending **-dāk-dóu** and/or the negative ending **-m̀h-dóu**:

Néih tái-m̀h-tái-dāk-dóu kéuih a?	*Can you see her?* [18.6]

12 Questions

Questions do not change basic word orders. There are four main ways of forming them:

a Using a question word such as **bīn? māt-yéh? géi-sí?** The final particle **a?** is often used in association with these question words:

Néih séung máaih māt-yéh a?	*What do you want to buy?*

Answers to these questions echo the form of the question, the answer appearing in the same place in the sentence as the question word:

Ngóh séung máaih dī choi.	*I want to buy some vegetables.*

The question words **dím-gáai?** and **jouh-māt-yéh?** are exceptional in that they are usually answered by **yàn-waih** ... *because*.... [2.1; 3.1; 3.3; 8.7; 9.8] b Using the *choice-type* question form verb–negative–verb, again backed up often by **a?**:

Kéuih sīk m̀h sīk　　　　*Does he know how to speak*
　góng Jùng-màhn a?　　*Chinese?*

These questions can be simply answered *yes* or *no* by using the positive or negative form of the verb:

M̀h sīk.　　　　　　　*He doesn't (know how to speak Chinese).* [1.11]

c Using a question particle such as **ma? àh? mē? nē?** at the end of the sentence:

Néih haih Jùng-gwok-yàhn　*Do you mean to say you're*
　mē?　　　　　　　　　　*Chinese?*

Type **c** questions are often answered simply by **haih** *yes* or **m̀h haih** *no*:

M̀h haih, ngóh m̀h　　　*No, I'm not Chinese.*
　haih Jùng-gwok-yàhn.
Haih, ngóh haih Jùng-　　*Yes, I am Chinese.*
　gwok-yàhn.　　　　　　[1.4; 1.6; 3.5]

d Questions about past events can be asked using **meih** or **móuh** and the verb endings **-jó** and **-gwo**. [18.5]

13 Sentence word order

a The basic word order of Cantonese is subject–verb–object, just as in English:

Ngóh jùng-yi néih.　　　*I love you.*

b Other word orders generally have in common that they put the stressed part of the sentence first regardless of whether it is the grammatical object, a time word, a location or whatever:

Bē-jáu ngóh jùng-yi yám.　*I like drinking **beer** (but not those other drinks).*

Tìng-yaht kéuih m̀h làih.　*She's not coming **tomorrow** (although she is coming today and the day after tomorrow).*

14 Verb endings

a A number of suffixes can be attached directly to verbs to convey aspects of meaning (**-gán** indicates that the action of the verb is still going on, **-gwo** that it has been experienced at some time, **-saai** that it is wholly committed, **-jó** that the action has been completed, and so on.) [4.4; 5.4; 6.9; 6.13; 8.10; 8.11; 11.1; 11.3; 11.9; 15.10; 17.9; 19.1; 19.4; 20.8; 20.9]

b The suffix **-dāk** has two functions: **i** it enables adverbs of manner to be attached to verbs and may be thought of as meaning *in such a way that*; **ii** it adds the notion *able to* to the verb (**góng-dāk** *able to speak*). [6.11]

15 Verbs

a Verbs only have one form (they do not conjugate) and do not change according to tense or number or person. [1.8]

b Verbs are negated by **m̀h**, **móuh** or **meih** placed before them. There are two exceptions: **i** the verb **yáuh** *to have* does not have a negative form with **m̀h** or with **móuh**: normally the verb **móuh** *not to have* is used as the negative of **yáuh** and **ii** the negative of the verb **yiu** *to need* is usually **m̀h-sái** *not need*. [3.7; 3.9; 4.5; 18.5]

c Verbs normally have subjects, which may or may not be stated depending on whether they can be understood from the context. Exceptions are rare, although it is doubtful if there is really any subject to the weather sentences **lohk-syut** *it is snowing* or **lohk-yúh** *it is raining*.

d Verbs do not all take objects, although some verbs such as **sihk** *to eat* and **góng** *to speak* (called 'lonely verbs' in the units) usually require a generalized object if a specific one is not mentioned. [4.2; 9.2; 9.4; 9.12; 15.1; 18.4; 25.1]

e Where there is a series of verbs together it is the first of them which normally is the grammatically operative one, that is the one which takes the negative or is acted on by an adverb:

Néih gàm-yaht séung m̀h séung heui Bāk-gìng a?	*Do you want to go to Beijing today?*

f Adjectival verbs. All adjectives can be used with verbal function:

Kéuih ge chē hóu daaih.	*His car is very large.* [1.3]

Alphabetic systems attempt to show in writing the noises people make when they speak. By reconverting the symbols on the page into sounds, the reader can put himself in the position of a listener and so understand what the writer is 'saying'.

Ideographic systems, of which Chinese is the main example, do not make any consistent attempt to show the noises of speech, instead they try to show the ideas in a speaker's head when he speaks. The reader doesn't reconvert the written symbols into noises and then convert the noises into meanings, he goes straight for the throat, seeing the symbols as meanings without having to go through the medium of noises.

Each syllable of Cantonese is written with one character and that symbol carries meaning or in a small number of cases shows the function of the syllable. So the character 人 **yàhn** carries the meaning *person*, while the character for the syllable **nē?** 呢 is not actually meaningful but does have the function of asking a follow-up question.

There are over 50,000 different Chinese characters in existence. This body of characters is large because unlike the restricted number of sounds with which the language expresses itself, the number of different meanings is limitless and each meaningful or functional syllable needs its own unique symbol. A well-educated Chinese person will be able to write perhaps 4–5,000 characters and recognize maybe 5–6,000 without the aid of a dictionary. About 3,500 different characters are used in middle-brow newspapers.

The first characters (early second millennium BC) seem to have been pictures of the objects they represented and some of those pictures in stylized form remain standard today. 羊 **yèuhng** is *a* *goat* – it is not hard to see how it derives from a picture of a goat's head with horns: and 目 **muhk** is *an eye*, a squared-off vertical version of a picture of a wide open eye. William Tell fans with arrows through apples in mind will recognize the symbolism of 中 **jùng** *middle*.

Gradually, other ways of creating characters were devised, some of them making use of similarities of sound, so that it is not accidental that the characters 由 **yàuh** *from* and 油 **yàuh** *oil* have the same element in common. But such common elements are at best an unreliable guide to pronunciation and sometimes can be downright misleading. It is most sensible to think of characters as being unique symbols for meanings rather than for pronounced sounds.

Chinese writing speaks more directly and more colourfully to the reader than does an alphabetic system. The two simple sounds **Jùng-gwok** tell you that *China* is meant, but the characters for **Jùng-gwok** 中國 mean *Middle Kingdom* and carry with them additional messages (such as that *middle* means *central* and hence *most important*, thus reducing other countries (**ngoih-gwok** *outside kingdoms*) to periperal unimportant status.

Contrariwise, the sheer volume and clumsiness of the character base has made the computerization of Chinese a very tough nut to crack. A computer can easily cope with storing the symbols and reproducing them – the problem is how to access them. The traditional Chinese methods used in printing and in dictionaries were slow and sometimes haphazard, and faster methods, such as accessing through romanization, fall foul of homophones and of the many different dialects which each have their own ways of pronouncing words. At present Chinese computer software tends to offer the user a choice of several different access methods, but there are problems with all of them.

You may well have worked out for yourself by now that the use of unique symbols attached to meanings allows Chinese script to cope with the homophone problem very well. Two words may be pronounced the same and so be spelled the same in an alphabetic system, but their characters can be totally different and easily distinguishable one from the other. **Gáu**, as you know, can mean *nine* but it can also mean *dog*. The two characters, however, are not at all confusing: 九 = *nine* and 狗 = *dog*. Similarly 酒 *alcoholic drink* and 走 *to run, to leave* are both pronounced **jáu**, but there is no mistaking one character for the other.

Learning the thousands of characters necessary to be fully literate in Chinese is a time-consuming business (for Chinese people as well as for foreigners) and that is why you have learned through romanization. A Chinese, of course, learns to speak at his mother's knee and he does not need romanization with that language teaching method!

You may like to learn to recognize some common characters. You will find that knowing them gives an extra dimension to learning Chinese, a very satisfying depth of 'feel' for the language which you have to experience to appreciate. See if you can accommodate the few offered here. If you want more, you could look at the character versions of the dialogues.

See page 224 for the large Chinese characters for **ngàih-hím** *danger*, which read from left to right.

See page 97 for the character **tìhng** *to stop*.

See page 47 where the front door (left) of the bus reads in white **séuhng** *board* and the other door reads **lohk** *alight*.

Writing a character is subject to certain rules of stroke order – you cannot write the different strokes in random order or direction. If you do not observe the correct order it is difficult to get the character to balance properly and it will probably become illegible if written in any kind of a hurry. Here are some useful characters written stroke by stroke for you to practise:

丨 卜 上 **seuhng** *above*; **séuhng** *to go up*
丨 冂 口 中 **jùng** *middle*
一 丁 下 **hah** *below*
人 女 女 **néuih** *female*
丨 冂 冂 冃 田 甲 男 **nàahm** *male*
丶 宀 广 广 庀 庐 庐 庐 庽 廁 廁
厂 厂 斤 斤 斤 所 所 　　　　所 **chi-só** *toilet*
丨 凵 屮 屮 屮 出 出 丨 冂 口 **chēut-háu** *exit*
一 扌 扌 扌 扩 扩 拉 拉 **làai** *pull*

The general rule is that you start at the top left-hand corner of the character and work downwards to finish at the bottom right, but the exceptions to this are numerous and you will need to find a teacher or a specialist book to guide you.

Incidentally, you may write your character text from left to right across the page as English does (that's the modern way), from right to left down the page (that's the traditional way and, of course, means that you start at what would be the end of an English book) or indeed any way you like, because each character is a discrete entity – you can write round in a circle anti-clockwise if that's how the mood takes you. Chinese newspapers quite often print captions to photographs in a different direction from the rest of the text that they illustrate and this produces no confusion, although if an English newspaper were to try it it would be *deedni yrev gnisufnoc*.

taking it further

Where do you go from here? Very few textbooks go beyond elementary level and they use a variety of other romanization systems which are confusingly different from the Yale system which you have learned, so they would not be easy. Of course, if you have mastered everything in this book you should be able to carry on building up vocabulary and fluency through talking with Cantonese-speaking friends, but there are also some useful works to help you to study on your own.

Far and away the best reference book is *Cantonese: a Comprehensive Grammar* by Stephen Matthews and Virginia Yip, published in 1994 by Routledge. Don't be put off by the title or the size of the book – it is a goldmine of information and full of sparklingly colloquial examples to illustrate the wealth of points it makes. And as a bonus it uses a version of the Yale system almost identical with that with which you are now familiar.

If you want to expand your vocabulary, you could do worse than get hold of a copy of *The Right Word in Cantonese* by Kwan Choi Wah, published by the Commercial Press in 1989 and reissued many times since. It has a long list of everyday vocabulary and some supplementary lists designed specifically for convenience in getting by in Hong Kong. It too uses the Yale system and at the front it has a table of some of the most common romanization systems, so that you could use that to make sense of other books not written in Yale. To enable you to get help from Chinese people the Chinese characters are given for all terms.

The *Cantonese Dictionary* by Parker Po-fei Huang has a Cantonese–English and an English–Cantonese section and because it was published by Yale University Press it uses the Yale system, but it first appeared in 1970 and is hard to get hold of now. The *Chinese–English Dictionary* by Chik Hon Man and Ng Lam Sim Yuk was published in 1989 by the Chinese University of Hong Kong Press. It gives Mandarin pronunciations as well as the Cantonese ones (which again are in the Yale system). Sidney Lau's *A Practical Cantonese–English Dictionary* (Hong Kong Government Printer, 1977) is still easily available and contains lots of good colloquial material, but it can only be used to look up Cantonese words of which you know the pronunciation, and it uses Lau's own romanization which shows the tones by superscript numbers (Kwan's book tells you how to convert Lau to Yale and it is not too difficult).

Sidney Lau's textbooks published by the Hong Kong government are perhaps the most complete, with two volumes each of *Elementary Cantonese*, *Intermediate Cantonese* and *Advanced Cantonese*, all of them using his romanization system. They are somewhat unexciting in content, but they are generally reliable and would help to build vocabulary and understanding of grammar to a high level.

If you find you are making good progress with the spoken language and you are really serious about going on, your next step should probably be to start learning Chinese characters, so that you can get to grips with Chinese on its own terms. Because all Chinese nowadays is written using the grammar, vocabulary and character stock of Mandarin, this is quite a tall order and you will need to explore the availability of Mandarin textbooks when the time comes.

key to the exercises

Unit 1

Exercise 1

a Kéuih-deih hóu hóu.
b Wòhng Sìn-sàang hóu.
c Jèung Síu-jé dōu hóu.

Exercise 2

a Jóu-sàhn.
b Ngóh hóu hóu. Néih nē?
c Joi-gin.

Exercise 3

a m̀h b m̀h c haih d Méih-gwok chē

Exercise 4

a Yaht-bún chē m̀h gwai.
b Kéuih m̀h hóu.
c Néih hóu leng.
d Kéuih-deih yiu m̀h yiu chē a?
e Kéuih dōu (hóu) leng.
f Kéuih-deih haih Méih-gwok-yàhn.
g Wòhng Sìn-sàang maaih chē.
h Yìng-gwok-yàhn m̀h maaih Méih-gwok chē.

Unit 2

True or false?

a False b False c Maybe: they are colleagues d False

Exercise 1

a Ngóh sing . . . (add whatever your surname is).
b Haih, kéuih haih Jùng-gwok-yàhn.
c M̀h máaih, ngóh m̀h máaih chē.
d Yáuh, ngóh yáuh Yaht-bún pàhng-yáuh.

Exercise 2

a The watch and the pen are both Mr Ho's.
b That watch is very handsome.
c Mr Ho is going to ask Mrs Wong later.
d Which pen is Miss Cheung's?

Exercise 3

a go **b** -yàhn **c** bún **d** m̀h **e** māt **f** bīn **g** dōu **h** mahn

Exercise 4

A	Wòhng Sìn-sàang, ngóh séung heui Yìng-gwok máaih Yìng-gwok chē.
Wong	Yìng-gwok chē hóu gwai.
A	Néih yáuh māt-yéh chē a?
Wong	Ngóh dōu yáuh Yìng-gwok chē.

Exercise 5

Sei go Méih-gwok-yàhn.
Sàam go Jùng-gwok-yàhn.
Ńgh go Yaht-bún-yàhn.
Wòhng Sìn-sàang maaih léuhng go sáu-bīu.
Yāt go Méih-gwok-yàhn máaih bāt.

Unit 3

Picture quiz

C should address A as **Bàh-bā**.
D should address B as **Màh-mā**.
D should address A as **Bàh-bā**.
You should address D as **Wòhng Síu-jé**.
You should address B as **Wòhng Taai-táai**.
Probably C since he is responsible enough to take his mother to the doctor's.

Haih m̀h haih a?

a M̀h haih **b** M̀h haih **c** Haih **d** M̀h haih **e** Haih

Answer the questions

a Hòh Sìn-sàang jyuh hái Ga-fē Gāai.
b Jèung Sìn-sàang jyuh hái Fà-yùhn Douh.
c Hòh Sìn-sàang ge láu móuh chē-fòhng.
d Jèung Sìn-sàang séung taam kéuih.
e Yáuh, yáuh hóu-dò bā-sí heui Fà-yùhn Douh.

Exercise 1

a Hòh Sìn-sàang bàh-bā haih yī-sāng.
b Wòhng Taai-táai hái ūk-kéi jouh māt-yéh a?
c Ngóh m̀h séung heui tái yī-sāng.
d Ngóh-deih yāt-chàih fàan sé-jih-làuh.

Exercise 2

a yī-sāng b séung . . . ūk-kéi c yī-sāng d Yìng-gwok

Exercise 3

Wòhng Sìn-sàang, hóu-noih-móuh-gin. Néih hóu ma? Taai-táai
nē? Néih-deih yìh-gā hái bīn-syu jyuh a?
Deui-m̀h-jyuh, Wòhng Sìn-sàang, ngóh yiu daap bā-sí heui Fà-
yùhn Douh. Ngóh yiu heui taam ngóh bàh-bā, daai kéuih heui
tái yī-sāng.

Unit 4

True or false?

a False b False c False d False e True

Exercise 1

a Wòhng Sìn-sàang séung dáng Hòh Taai-táai yāt-chàih sihk-
  faahn.
b Hòh Taai-táai hái chyùh-fóng jýu-gán faahn.
c Hòh Taai-táai mahn Wòhng Sìn-sàang kéuih jyu ge sung
  hóu-meih ma?
d Hòh Sìn-sàang yáuh móuh bòng Hòh Taai-táai sáu a?
e Hòh Taai-táai jýu ge sung hóu-chíh jáu-làuh ge yāt-yeuhng.

Exercise 2

a Sīk, ngóh sīk jýu ngàuh-yuhk tòng.
b Móuh, ngóh ūk-kéi fuh-gahn móuh jáu-làuh.
c Móuh, ngóh móuh bòng kéuih sáu.
d Ngóh m̀h nàu.
e M̀h haih.

Exercise 3

a Hái chyùh-fóng yáuh lùhng-hā, dōu yáuh sàang-gwó, yáuh faahn, yáuh tòng, yáuh tìhm-bán. Dōu yáuh Jèung Sìn-sàang.

b Yáuh, yáuh Jèung Sìn-sàang: kéuih haih laahp-saap-túng!

Unit 5

Picture quiz

a Hóu pèhng. M̀h leng.

b Yáuh laahn. Jèung Síu-jé gó gihn dōu yáuh laahn.

Answer the questions

a Kéuih séung máaih hā.

b Dī hā baat-sahp-ńgh mān yāt gàn.

c Kèih-tà dong-háu ge hā chāt-sahp-yih mān yāt gàn jē.

d Yàn-waih yáuh séi hā!

Exercise 1

a Hùhng-sik ge Méih-gwok chē hóu gwai.

b Ngóh bàh-bā sīk yàuh-séui.

c Wòhng Taai-táai heui pou-táu máaih-yéh.

d Kéuih gàm-yaht m̀h séung sihk-faahn.

e Hòh Sàang m̀h sihk Hòh Taai-táai jyu ge sung.

Exercise 2

a gàan b No classifier needed c No classifier needed
d jì e jek f jek-jek

Exercise 3

a Wòhng Táai yiu béi yih-sahp-baat mān.

b Kéuih yiu béi luhk-sahp-sei mān.

Unit 6

True or false?

a True b False c False d False e False

Answer the questions

a M̀h haih Chàhn Sìn-sàang daih-yāt chi, haih Wòhng Sìn-sàang daih-yāt chi.

b Gim-kìuh Daaih-hohk m̀h haih hái Lèuhn-dēun fuh-gahn;
   yiu daap fó-chè heui.
c Haih.
d Hóu-chíh haih.

Exercise 1

1 c Gim-kìuh Daaih-hohk haih sai-gaai jeui yáuh-méng ge
      daaih-hohk jì-yāt.
2 a Yàuh Lèuhn-dēun heui Gim-kìuh Daaih-hohk chàam-
      gwùn yiu daap chē heung bak hàhng.
3 b Yàuh nī-syu daap sahp-ńgh-houh bā-sí heui fèi-gèi-
      chèuhng yiu géi-dō chín a?
4 d Nī-syu ge deih-hah-tit-louh m̀h heui fèi-gèi-chèuhng jí
      heui Daaih-wuih-tòhng.
5 e Néih yiu gwo sàam go gàai-háu dou Fà-yùhn Douh daap
      bā-sí heui fèi-gèi-chèuhng.

Exercise 2

Hái fèi-gèi-chèuhng daap deih-hah-tit-louh heung dùng hàhng
dou Daaih-wuih-tòhng lohk chē. Hái Daaih-wuih-tòhng heung
nàahm hàhng, gwo léuhng go gàai-háu, jýun heung dùng jauh
dou lak.

Unit 7

Passage 1

Yesterday mum asked us if we wanted to have salad. We all said
we would like that. Mum said: 'Fine, so I'll make a lobster salad
for you. Now, I'm going off to buy the lobster now, and you can
go and buy some fresh fruit.' We bought lots of fresh fruit and
prepared it all in the kitchen too. Mum came back half an hour
later. She said: 'Today the lobsters are small and not fresh, so I
didn't buy any, I only bought large prawns. You can pretend the
prawn salad is lobster salad!'

Exercise 1

a False b Unknown c True d False e False

Exercise 2

a Kéuih máaih-jó daaih hā fàan ūk-kéi.
b Ngóh-deih máaih-jó hóu dò sàn-sìn sà-léut fàan ūk-kéi.
c M̀h sàn-sìn.
d Sīk, go-go yàhn dōu sīk jíng sà-léut.
e Yáuh.

Exercise 3

a Néih sihk-gwo ngàuh-yuhk sà-léut ma?

b Nī jì Méih-gwok bāt haih ngóh jeui séung máaih ge bāt jì-yāt.

c Nī chi haih ngóh daih-yāt chi làih néih sé-jih-làuh.

Exercise 4

X Deui-m̀h-jyuh, yìh-gā hóu jóu.

X Ngóh hái ūk-kéi.

X Ngóh séung chéng néih sihk-faahn.

X Néih hóu ma?

X Ngóh dōu hóu. Néih taai-táai nē?

X Kéuih dōu-géi hóu. Néih tùhng m̀h tùhng ngóh fàan sé-jih-làuh a?

X Hóu. Néih jà-chē heui ma?

X Chóh géi-dō houh bā-sí a?

X Hóu, Láih-baai-sei ngóh tùhng néih yāt-chàih fàan sé-jih-làuh.

Exercise 5

a kéuih màh-mā   b yāt   c pèhng   d m̀h   e hó-yíh

Exercise 6

a Ngóh-deih sàam go yàhn nī go Sìng-kèih-luhk daap fèi-gèi heui Yìng-gwok wáan.

b Wòhng Taai-táai tùhng Wòhng Sìn-sàang yāt-chàih làih ngóh ge sé-jih-làuh.

c Néih ge jýu-yi yāt-dihng haih jeui hóu ge.

d Nī gàan daaih-hohk haih sai-gaai yáuh-méng ge daaih-hohk.

e Lèuhn-dēun haih Yìng-gwok jeui dò yàhn ge deih-fòng jì-yāt.

Passage 2

Today I went to the office. Mr Ho told me he will be flying back to England on Thursday and so would not be coming into the office after Wednesday. Mr Ho is one of my best friends and I guess that he will not be returning here after he goes back this time. So, what can I give him as a present? I thought about it for a long while without any ideas, and then went to ask Miss Wong and Mrs Cheung. Miss Wong said: 'How about if the three of us were to ask Mr Ho out for a meal?' Mrs Cheung said: 'It would be best if Mrs Ho could come with him too.'

I think that women have the best ideas. Do you agree?

Unit 8

Have you understood?

a dihn-nyuhn-lòuh   b m̀h saht-yuhng
c chèuhng-gok   d móuh yuhng-gwo

Picture quiz

a M̀h dāk.   b Haih léuhng gihn.

Exercise 1

Tìn-hei jihm-jím yiht, máaih láahng-hei-gèi haih sìh-hauh la.
Láahng-hei-gèi m̀h syun hóu gwai, daahn-haih hóu yáuh-yuhng.
Yùh-gwó máaih m̀h saht-yuhng ge yéh, jīk-haih sàai chín.
Ngóh yíh-gìng yuh-beih-jó ngóh-deih dī láahng-tīn sāam la.

Exercise 2

a Jèung Síu-jé haih hóu leng ge Yaht-bún-yàhn.
b Ngóh m̀h séung máaih Chàhn Sìn-sàang pou-táu maaih ge Méih-gwok bāt.
c Ngóh hóu séung sihk Hòh Táai jíng ge lùhng-hā.

Exercise 3

a sáu-tàih   b míhn-fai   c yāt tou leng ge   d sàn-sìn

A creative test

'M̀h-hóu nàu lā! Ngóh m̀h haih wah néih jì nī go miht-fó-túng haih saht-yuhng ge yéh mē?!'

Unit 9

Caption for the cartoon

Néih-deih gok-dāk nī chēut dihn-yíng chi m̀h chi-gīk a?

Exercise 1

a Hòh Sìn-sàang hóu-chíh ńgh-sahp seui gam seuhng-há.
b Sìh-sìh wahn-duhng deui gihn-hòng hóu hóu.
c Ngóh jí-haih jùng-yi dá-bō, pàh-sàan tùhng yàuh-séui jē.

Exercise 2

sung/sàn-sìn; fó-gei/jáu-làuh; daaih-gáam-ga/baak-fo-gūng-sī; laahn/laahp-saap-túng; hói-tāan/yàuh-séui; lohk-syut/dihn-nýuhn-lòuh.

Exercise 3

a Wòhng Sìn-sàang, jóu-sàhn.
b Néih séung m̀h séung yám bē-jáu a?
c Òu, gám ga-fē nē? chàh nē?
d Deui-m̀h-jyuh, ngóh-deih móuh séui. Fó-gei wah ngóh jì nī-syu dī séui m̀h hóu-yám. Dím-gáai m̀h yám bē-jáu a?
e Dī bē-jáu hóu hóu-yám, haih Yìng-gwok bē-jáu. Chéng yám síu-síu lā.
f Òu, kéuih jáu lak!

Exercise 4

tái . . . yī-sāng/dihn-yíng/yéh
jyú . . . tìhm-bán/yéh
góng . . . yéh
chàam-gwùn . . . Gim-kìuh Daaih-hohk/chyuh-fóng
sihk . . . yéh/tìhm-bán

Exercise 5

a Wòhng Sàang sihk-yéh.
b Wòhng Táai jyú-yéh.
c Wòhng Síu-jé máaih-yéh.
d Jèung Sàang góng-yéh.
e Nī sàam go yàhn yám-yéh.

Unit 10

True or false?

a M̀h haih. Dī yeuhk-séui haih màh-mā seuhng-go-láih-baai máaih-fàan-làih ge.
b Haih, màh-mā chi-chi dōu yiu kéuih yìuh-wàhn dī yeuhk-séui sìn.
c M̀h haih, kéuih gok-dāk (haih) go tóuh m̀h syù-fuhk.
d M̀h haih, kéuih ngāam-ngāam yám-jó sahp fàn jūng jē.

Exercise 1

a Yī-sāng hái chán-só tái behng-yàhn.
b Wòhng Sìn-sàang haih Jùng-gwok-yàhn.
c Màh-mā hái pou-táu máaih-yéh.
d Hèung-góng-yàhn hái Hèung-góng jyuh.
e Wòhng Wài-lìhm ge bàh-bā dōu haih sing Wòhng.

Exercise 2

Néih-deih léuhng-go yàhn yám-jó gam dò m̀h ngāam yám ge
yéh deui sàn-tái m̀h hóu ge! Néih-deih dōu séung séi àh?!
Wòhng Sìn-sàang, néih yám taai dò bē-jáu – m̀h-hóu yám lā!
Wòhng Taai-táai néih yám taai dò ga-fē – m̀h-hóu yám lā!

Exercise 3

Nī jek jỳu-jái heui-jó máaih-yéh.
Nī jek jỳu-jái móuh lèih-hòi ūk-kéi.
Nī jek jỳu-jái sihk-jó ngàuh-yuhk.
Nī jek jỳu-jái móuh sihk-yéh.
Nī jek jỳu-jái wah: 'Òu! òu! òu!' jauh heui tái yī-sāng.

Exercise 4

a Chàhn Sàang dá-gán bō
b Kéuih sihk-gán lùhng-hā.
c Kéuih yám-gán bē-jáu.
d Kéuih áu-gán.
e Kéuih séi-jó lak.

Unit 11

Questions

1 Yesterday I thought this chair was very comfortable, but
   now . . . !
2 You should have left: a sìh-jōng b m̀h hòi-sām c gihn
   ngoih-tou hóu leng d sō-fá-yí

Exercise 1

a sahp-luhk go síu-jé;
b yih-baak jèung jí;
c ńgh-chìn-luhk-baak mān;
d yāt-baak-maahn go Jùng-gwok yàhn;
e yāt-maahn-yih-chìn-chāt-baak-ńgh-sahp;
f baat-chìn-lìhng-sàam-sahp-sei;
g sahp-yāt go jūng-tàuh;
h léuhng jek lùhng-hā.

Exercise 3

a gauh-fún   b taai pèhng   c maaih ūk
d jì-chìhn   e yiht   f sài-nàahm

Exercise 4

Mrs Ho is going to eat lobster on Monday; Miss Ho is going to see a film on Tuesday; and Mr Ho is going climbing on Wednesday.

Unit 12

Whoops! Something is wrong!

a jek is not the correct classifier for *students*: it should be go-go.
b How can I say this sentence if it is true?
c *Never ever* say m̀h yáuh – it is always móuh.
d The classifier is missing. It should read Gó léuhng go Méih-gwok . . .
e Must be wrong. How could the father be only 8 years old?!

Exercise 1

a yauh chúhng yauh dò   b sei go jūng-tàuh
c jùng-hohk   d gaau-syu sìn-sàang

Exercise 2

a Ngóh go jái sái m̀h sái hohk Jùng-màhn a?
b Kéuih múih máahn dōu yiu jouh géi-dō go jūng-tàuh gùng-fo a?
c Ngóh go jái hái Lèuhn-dēun yíh-gìng duhk-gwo ńgh nìhn Síu-hohk. Yìng-gwok hohk-sāang sahp-yāt seui sìn-ji duhk Jùng-hohk. Hèung-góng haih m̀h haih yāt-yeuhng a?
d Hái néih ge hohk-haauh duhk-syu, duhk yāt nìhn yiu géi-dō chín a?
e Hohk-sāang sái m̀h sái máaih fo-bún tùhng lihn-jaahp-bóu a?

Exercise 3

i = e   ii = a   iii = c   iv = b   v = d

Exercise 4

a Ūk ngoih-bihn yáuh hei-chè.
b Wòhng Sàang hái Wòhng Táai jó-sáu-bihn.
c Bouh syu hái sō-fá-yí seuhng-bihn.
d Ngóh gú kéuih-deih máaih-yùhn yéh fàan-làih.
e Hái kéuih chìhn-bihn yáuh hóu dò séui.
f Go miht-fó-túng haih Wòhng Sìn-sàang máaih ge.
g Kéuih-deih go jái hái yí hah-bihn.
h Wòhng Táai yāt-dihng hóu m̀h hòi-sām.

Unit 13

Exercise 1

a Chàhn Táai gàm-máahn hóu m̀h dāk-hàahn.
b Ngóh bàh-bā sèhng-nìhn dōu m̀h dāk-hàahn.
c M̀h-gòi néih wah béi ngóh tèng néih go jái tìng-yaht mòhng m̀h mòhng a?
d Kéuih Láih-baai-yih hóu mòhng.
e Ngóh jeui m̀h dāk-hàahn ge sìh-hauh haih jìu-jóu.

Exercise 2

a dī b gāan . . . jek c chèuhng d ga

Exercise 3

mòhng/dāk-hàahn; sỳu-fuhk/sàn-fú; gaan-jūng/sìh-sìh; yèhng/sỳu; hohk-sāang/sìn-sàang; jing-fú/síh-màhn; fùng-fu/síu-síu; gáam-síu/jàng-gà

Exercise 4

a Ngóh gú haih Wòhng Táai yèhng chín.
b M̀h haih, kéuih hóu m̀h hòi-sām.
c Daih-luhk jek máh haih sei-houh (máh).
d Gáu-houh máh yèhng.
e Haih Wòhng Taai-táai hóu sīk dóu-máh.
f M̀h ngāam, gáu-houh máh hóu-gwo sei-houh máh.
g Gáu-houh máh dōu hóu-gwo sàam-houh máh.
h M̀h haih, jeui hóu go jek máh haih gáu-houh máh.
i Nī chèuhng choi-máh yáuh luhk jek máh.
j Ngóh gú kéuih-deih haih sỳu dò-gwo yèhng lak.

Unit 14

Passage 1

When Mr Wong's seven-year-old son came to school yesterday he cheerfully told me that his father had bought a new house last week. The house was large and looked nice, with three bedrooms and there was a front garden and a garage as well. He said: 'Now I have a room to myself, it's really comfortable. But mummy has to share a room with daddy, so I think she must be unhappy. I don't know why daddy won't let mummy use the third bedroom. No one is using that room now, daddy has only put a lot of books in there, that's all.'

Exercise 1

a Kéuih haih chāt seui.
b Kéuih máaih-jó yāt gàan sàn ūk.
c Ūk chìhn-bihn yáuh fà-yún tùhng-màaih yāt gàan chē-fòhng tìm.
d Haih màh-mā yiu tùhng kéuih yāt-chàih.
e Daih-sàam gàan fan-fóng léuih-bihn yáuh hóu dò sỳu.
f Móuh.

Exercise 2

a	hèi-mohng	b	tìn-hei	c	láahng-tīn
d	dá-syun	e	dihn-yíng	f	wahn-duhng
g	gèi-yuhk	h	dò-yùh	i	gihn-hòng
j	noih-yùhng	k	síu-lèuhn	l	pìhng-gwàn

Exercise 3

a	tìng-yaht	b	Láih-baai-yaht	c	chìhn-yaht
d	sèhng-yaht	e	johk-yaht	f	Yaht-bún
g	gàm-yaht	h	yaht-yaht	i	hauh-yaht

Exercise 4

a i The first horse is No. 9.
   ii The first horse is not No. 9.
b i Miss Jung-san happens to be Japanese.
   ii Miss Jung-san really is Japanese.
c i He is going to Canton tomorrow.
   ii He is not going to Canton until tomorrow.
d i Mrs Chan has been to the States more than ten times.
   ii Mrs Chan has been to the States dozens of times.

Exercise 5

a sỳu-fuhk   b tìhng-chē ge   c hóu dò chín

Exercise 6

a Kéuih séuhng-tòhng jì-chìhn, sìh-sìh dōu heui taam kéuih nàahm-pàhng-yáuh.
b Wòhng Táai séung máaih gó ga chē, yàn-waih ga chē hóu leng.
c Ngóh m̀h mìhng-baahk gó go yàhn láahng-tīn séung máaih láahng-hei-gèi jouh-māt-yéh a?
d Gó dī hā m̀h sàn-sìn, só-yíh Chàhn Táai m̀h séung máaih.
e Kéuih sihk-gán yéh ge sìh-hauh, m̀h góng-wá.

Exercise 7

a Máaih gó ga chē yiu géi-dō chín a?
b Wòhng Sàang Sìng-kèih-géi (*or* géi-sí) lèih-hòi Yaht-bún a?
c Hái Léih Táai jó-sáu-bihn gó jehk gáu-jái haih bīn-go sung béi kéuih ga?
d Gó dī yàhn yáuh géi-dō go haih gaau-syù sìn-sàang a?

Passage 2   Mr Ho bets on the horses

If a rich person wants to buy a horse then he goes and buys one, but that's a very expensive way to 'buy a horse'! In Hong Kong you will often hear poor people saying 'I think I'll buy a horse today.' What's the explanation? Have a guess, what could it mean if a poor person talks about 'buying a horse'? That's right, 'to buy a horse' means 'to bet on a horse', so when poor people say they want to buy a horse that means they want to bet on a horse.

Mr Ho is not very rich. One day his good friend Mr Cheung phoned him up and asked him: 'There's horse racing tonight. I'd like to invite you to go with me to the racecourse to enjoy ourselves. What do you say?' Mr Ho happily said 'Fine. Fine. Terrific idea!'

After finishing the phone call he told Mrs Ho. She said: 'You have never been horse racing before, this will only be your first time. I wonder if you'll like it?' Mr Ho said: 'Oh, you're right. This will be my first time horse racing. If I don't like it, I'll have to sit there with nothing to do! What can I do about it?' Mrs Ho said: 'You'd best buy a book before you go to the course. If you feel that it's fun watching the horses, then there's no need to read it. Otherwise, you can sit there and read. What do you think?' Mr Ho is a very docile man: he does whatever his wife says. So of course that evening before he went to the racecourse he bought a book.

Luckily, Mr Ho found the racing quite good fun and there was no need to read. But he didn't win a brass farthing, on the contrary he lost a great deal of money. When he went home he angrily said to his wife: 'Next time I go horse racing I won't listen to you! When you bet on a horse you want to bet to win, you shouldn't bet to lose!'

Do you get it? The pun is on **máaih-sỳu** which could be either 'buy a book' or 'bet and lose' and superstitious gamblers believe that doing the one results in the other.

Exercise 8

Mr Cheung came home from gambling at the dog track. His son asked him: 'Daddy, how did the gambling go today? Did you win?' 'Won nine races out of ten.' 'Wow! Daddy, you really know how to gamble. You bet on ten races and only lost on one.' 'To tell you the truth, I didn't win a cent. I bet on ten races and the dog track was the winner on each race!'

Here the pun is on **gáu-chèuhng** which sounds like either 'dog track' or 'nine races'. Mr Cheung's son naturally enough at first heard what he most wanted to hear, that his father had won handsomely.

Unit 15

Answer the questions

a Jáu-dim fòhng-gāan léuih-bihn láahng-hei-gèi miht-fó-túng dōu móuh.
b Ńgh-sīng-kāp jáu-dim haih jeui hóu jeui hóu ge jáu-dim.
c Yáuh-dī ńgh-sīng-kāp jáu-dim léuih-bihn yáuh chán-só tùhng-màaih wahn-duhng fóng.

Exercise 1

a Néih haih Yìng-gwok-yàhn dihng-haih Méih-gwok-yàhn nē?
b Fó-chē faai dihng-haih fèi-gèi faai nē?
c Kéuih Láih-baai-sàam dihng-haih Láih-baai-sei làih nē?
d Hòh Sìn-sàang séung heui Hèung-góng dihng-haih Gwóng-jàu nē?
e Haih Léih Táai móuh chín dihng-haih Chàhn Táai móuh chín nē?

Exercise 2

a yaht-táu b yāt-dihng (yáuh) c láahng-séui d hèng
e fó-gei

Exercise 3

a Kéuih góng-dāk faai.
b Wòhng Sàang máaih hā máaih-dāk hóu pèhng.
c Néih hàahng-louh hàahng-dāk faai-gwo Jèung Síu-jé.
d Néih yám yeuhng-jáu yám-dāk dò-gwo ngóh.
e Léih Sìn-sàang jà-chē jà-dāk m̀h-haih-géi-hóu.

Exercise 4

a jèung   b jek   c ga   d gàan   e tìuh
f ga   g gàan   h jèung   i gihn

Exercise 5

a Yāt gàn chúhng-gwo yāt bohng.
b Hái Yìng-gwok máaih gihn-hòng bóu-hím hóu gwai.
c Tùhng-màaih chóh-gán fèi-gèi ge sìh-hauh dōu yáuh míhn-
    seui yèuhng-jáu maaih.
d M̀h-sái. (remember the normal negative of **yiu** is m̀h-sái)
e Hái Lèuhn-dēun yáuh sei go fèi-gèi-chèuhng.

Exercise 6

a sàam-dím-léuhng-go-jih
b sahp-dím-sahp-yāt-go-jih
c gáu-dím-bun
d chāt-dím-sàam-go-gwāt
e sahp-yih-dím-lìhng-gáu-fàn(-jūng)
f ńgh-dím-sahp-ńgh-fàn(-jūng) ńgh-dím-sàam(-go-jih) ńgh-
    dím-yāt-go-gwāt

Exercise 7

Néih Láih-baai-luhk léuhng-dím-bun dou-jó máh-chèuhng.

Unit 16

Haau-sih

Ngóh gú yàn-waih gó go háau-síh-gwùn pa-dou tàuh-wàhn
fan-jó hái-douh jē.

Exercise 1

a i   b i   c i   d i Generally Chinese people mention themselves
first, in contrast to polite western practice which is to put self
last.   e i

Exercise 2

a **ii** I also think he is Japanese.
b **ii** I give away his ten dollars.
c **ii** Mrs Lee is going to Japan to get on a plane.
d **ii** (Closest might be) I and Mr Wong are going to the City
    Hall to eat.
e **ii** Whose wife is ill?

Exercise 3

a = Mr Lee   b = Mrs Chan   c = Mr Chan
d = Mrs Lung   e = Mr Lung   f = Mrs Lee

Exercise 4

a dá-Màh-jeuk
b dóu-pē-páai
c chàu jéung-bán
d tèng gwóng-bo
e chùng hùhng-dāng
f tái dihn-yíng

Exercise 5

Wòhng Sàang gòu-gwo Chàhn Táai tùhng Wòhng Táai, móuh
Léih Sàang Léih Táai gam gòu, daahn-haih tùhng Chàhn Sàang
yāt-yeuhng gam gòu. Léih Sàang gòu-gwo Wòhng Táai hóu-dò.
Léih Sàang jeui gòu.

Exercise 6

a Waaih-yàhn   b Ngh-wuih   c Sàu-léih   d yāt-sìh *or* yáuh-sìh

Unit 17

You are a Hong Kong immigration official:

Sìn-sàang, m̀h-gòi néih gàau bún wuh-jiu tùhng-màaih chìm-
jing béi ngóh lā. Néih géi-sí séung lèih-hòi Hèung-góng a? Nàh,
jing-fú kwài-dihng m̀h jéun daai sáu-chēung yahp-làih Hèung-
góng: m̀h-gòi néih gàau-béi daih-sei-sahp-yāt-houh gwaih-tói ge
gíng-chaat Sà-jín lā.

Exercise 1

a Wòhng Sàang pàh-gán sàan.
b Kéuih hái sēung-yàhn-chòhng seuhng-bihn fan-gaau.
c Kéuih tiu-gòu.
d Kéuih làai-jyuh jek gáu.
e Kéuih chóh hái sō-fá-yí seuhng-bihn.
f Kéuih kéih hái yāt jèung yí seuhng-bihn.

Exercise 2

a gíng-chaat   b sìn-sàang   c sī-gēi   d fó-gei   e yī-sāng

Exercise 3

a **sìn-ji** She said she would come back on Monday, but she
didn't return until Wednesday.

b **jì-hauh** After you had left I rang your wife.
c **lìhn** Last month Mrs Wong didn't even sell one car: her manager was very unhappy about it.
d **dōu** He plays Mahjong every day, so he has no time to go shopping with me.
e **jeuk sāam-kwàhn** It's not very convenient to wear a dress when swimming.

Exercise 4

a Yāt nìhn yáuh sàam-baak-luhk-sahp-ńgh yaht.
b Tìng-yaht haih Láih-baai-yaht.
c Sei-yuht yáuh sàam-sahp yaht.
d Sàam go sìng-kèih móuh yāt go yuht gam dò yaht.
e Sàam nìhn noih-dī.

Exercise 5

a Kéih hái Chàhn Táai jó-bihn gó go síu-jé haih Wòhng Sàang sahp-chāt seui ge néui.
b Néih hái Méih-gwok léuih-yàuh máaih ge Yaht-bún chē haih bīn yāt ga chē a?
c Néih nī go gauh ge miht-fó-túng m̀h gau daaih. Máaih yāt go daaih-dī ge, hóu m̀h hóu a?

Unit 18

Exercise 1

a Gàm-yaht haih Sìng-kèih-géi a?
b Lèuhn-dēun Fèi-gèi-chèuhng hái sìhng-síh bīn-bihn a?
c Gwai-sing-a?
d Dī hā géi-dō chín yāt gàn a?
e Néih chāt-dím-jūng dihng-haih baat-dím-jūng heui nē?

Exercise 2

a Bāk-bihn	b Néuih-yán	c Gó-syu
d Yahp-bihn	e Gauh-nín	f Hauh-yaht
g Gá	h Néui	i Yeh-máahn

Exercise 3

Wòhng Sàang jeui daaih. (remember that **daaih** is used for comparative age, not **lóuh**)

Exercise 4

a faai-dī!	b fong-ga	c seuhng-bihn	d suhk-sīk
e yihng-jàn	f yī-sāng	g ngoih-tou	h ngāam-ngāam

Exercise 5

a bihn-fuhk   b chèuhn-lòh-chē   c gá ge
d daahn-haih   e m̀h jéun

Exercise 6

a fàahn-wìhng   b fòng-mihn   c sàu-léih
d yahm-hòh   e míhn-seui   f fòng-bihn

Unit 19

Exercise 1

a M̀h haih, móuh johk-yaht gam gòu.
b Yìng-gwok jing-fú jeui-gahn gùng-bou m̀h wúih jàng-gà
   leih-sīk.
c Ngóh gú gó-jahn-sìh Yìng-bóng yāt-dihng wúih gòu hóu-dò.
d Móuh mahn-tàih. Gó-jahn-sìh m̀h-gòi néih joi dá-dihn-wá
   béi ngóh lā.

Exercise 2

a Hái sìhng-síh.
b Gok-dāk sàn-fú.
c Geuk-jai yuhng-làih tìhng-chē ā-ma.
d Jóu-chàan haih yāt yaht daih-yāt chi sihk yéh. Haih yaht-táu
   sihk ge.

Exercise 3

a i   b ii   c ii   d ii   e ii

Exercise 4

a ii You and I may not go there.
b i I cannot drive on the outlying islands.
c i I'll come in the afternoon.
d i I like eating fruit with salad.
e i When are you going to Japan and what do you intend to do
   there?

Exercise 5

a Chàhn Sàang jeui daaih.
b Néuih-ge haih baak-fahn-jī-luhk-sahp.
c Nàahm-ge dòng-yín haih baak-fahn-jī-sei-sahp lā.
d Haih Chàhn Táai gòu.
e Kéuih-deih yáuh sàam go jái.

Unit 20

Exercise 1

a Mr Wong hates taking medicine.
b Don't open your eyes wide and stare at me!
c Materials which are not up to standard are treated as seconds.
d It is, of course, illegal to gamble in a gambling den.
e We should pay more attention to the study conditions of our children.

Exercise 2

a Luhk-yuht sei-houh.
b Yāt-gáu-gáu-chāt-nìhn Chāt-yuht yāt-houh.
c Yih-lìhng-lìhng-sei-nìhn Ńgh-yuht sahp-ńgh-houh.
d Sahp-yih-yuht sahp-yāt-houh Láih-baai-yaht hah-jau luhk-dím-sàam-go-jih.
e Chēut-nín Baat-yuht sà-ah-yāt-houh.

Exercise 3

a Yìng-gwok
b Lèuhn-dēun
c chìu-gwo yāt-maahn Yìng-bóng
d yihn-gām

Exercise 4

a chēut-gāai/hàahng-gāai
b jin-jàng
c daaih-yeuk
d hùng-yàuh
e gìng-léih
f ló-tái

Exercise 5

a Jèung Táai yèhng-jó yāt-maahn-baat-chìn-yih-baak mān. Hòh Sàang yèhng-jó yāt-maahn-sàam-chìn-luhk-baak-ńgh-sahp mān. Wòhng Sàang yèhng-jó yāt-maahn-lìhng-gáu-baak-yih-sahp mān. Léih Táai yèhng-jó gáu-chìn-yāt-baak mān. Chàhn Sàang yèhng-jó yih-chìn-chāt-baak-sàam-sahp mān jē.
b Ńgh-sahp-yih-go-bun.

Unit 21

Passage 1

Several hundred years ago in a place in the north of China there lived a rich man called Wong. He had lots of horses, all of them tall, mighty and handsome and he loved them very much. One day a handsome but rather old horse went missing. Mr Wong's friends all felt it was a great pity and they thought that he would be angry and very unhappy, but quite on the contrary he was not only not angry but believed that the horse would come back very soon. After a few days the horse really did come back. His friends said Mr Wong was very fortunate, but he just smiled and said: 'That old horse knows what's what, [I knew] he could find the way home, that's all.'

Passage 2

Long ago there was a doctor in Canton. One day he wrote a letter of great importance to a doctor in another city. At that time China did not have a post office and he was very busy and had no time to take the letter there, so he told his son to take it for him. He said to his son: 'This letter is very important, it must get there quickly! Let's see, the more legs the quicker: your two legs won't be as quick as four legs. You had better use my horse to go. Hurry up!'

The young man set off and his father awaited his return. He knew that a horse would need about eight hours to get to that place and back. Who could have guessed that it was two days before his son returned. He said cheerfully to his father: 'I'm back, dad. Was I quick? I thought and thought and thought up a very fast method. You said the more legs the quicker and that two legs were not as fast as four . . . so I walked leading the horse along . . . if two legs aren't as fast as four, then six legs were bound to be faster than four legs, right?'

Exercise 1

Séung-làih-séung-heui *think coming think going* means *to rack your brains, to think and think.*

a walking up and down
b running to and fro
c We bargained and bargained but couldn't agree a price.

Exercise 2

a An average horse weighs about 1,000 lbs (yāt-chìn bohng).
b On average a horse dies at about 20 years of age (yih-sahp seui).
c A horse can only stay healthy if it exercises for at least half an hour a day (bun go jūng-tàuh).
d A horse must eat at least 20 lbs of food a day (yih-sahp bohng).

Exercise 3

10 a.m.	Call taxi
10.30 a.m.	To Manager Wong's office
12.15 p.m.	Lunch in City Hall with Miss Cheung
3.30 p.m.	Get air ticket from travel company
6.45 p.m.	Drinks with Miss Ho at Hong Kong Hotel
7.30 p.m.	Cinema with Miss Ho

Exercise 4

a chà-m̀h-dō b hahm-baahng-laahng c daahn-haih
d ngāam-ngāam e yáuh-sìh f jouh-māt-yéh

Exercise 5

a Kéuih yàuh-séui, só-yíh m̀h yiht m̀h sàn-fú.
b Kéuih gàm-yaht m̀h jà laahp-saap-chē, kéuih jà kèih-tà chē a.
c Kéuih yih-sahp nìhn jì-chìhn haih yāt go yáuh yāt-chìn-maahn mān ge yáuh-chín yàhn.

Exercise 6

Wòhng Sìn-sàang ge sàn chē:

a hóu leng.
b leng-haih-leng, daahn-haih móuh Jèung Sàang ge sàn chē gam leng.
c m̀h-haih-géi-leng.
d m̀h gau daaih.
e taai gwai la.
f haih sai-gaai seuhng jeui leng ge chē.
g leng-gwo ngóh ga chē hóu-dò.
h tùhng Jèung Sàang ge sàn chē yāt-yeuhng gam daaih yāt-yeuhng gam gwai.

Exercise 7

a wái (or go, *but that is not really polite enough*)
b lìhn c lóuh d géi . . . noih e daaih

Exercise 8

a Wòhng Sàang A-geuk yiu béi dò-dī (B-geuk kéuih m̀h sái béi).

b B-geuk haih Léih Sàang yiu béi baat-baak mān.

c Jèung Sàang A-geuk yiu béi sàam-baak mān, B-geuk yiu béi ńgh-baak mān, jīk-haih wah kéuih B-geuk yiu béi dò yih-baak mān.

d Béi jeui síu ge haih Chàhn Sàang: béi jeui dò ge haih Léih Sàang.

Exercise 9

a Ngóh màh-mā dá-dihn-wá (ge sìh-hauh) góng-dāk dōu-géi maahn.

b Fó-gei, nī dī ga-fē m̀h gau yiht.

c Néih séung yám bē-jáu dihng-haih séui nē?

d Néih gó jì seuhng-go-yuht máaih ge bāt móuh ngóh nī jì gam gwai. or Néih seuhng-go-yuht máaih ge gó jì bāt . . .

e Kéuih giu ngóh wah béi néih jì néih yiu géi-dò dím jūng làih.

f Wòhng Sìn-sàang lìhn lùhng-hā dōu m̀h jùng-yi sihk.

g Nī dī sỳu yáuh sàam-fahn-jì-yih haih Jùng-màhn sỳu.

h Kéuih yuht-làih-yuht-yáuh-chín.

Exercise 10

In July, August and September the weather in Hong Kong is very hot. When it's hot people like to travel by taxi, because cabs are plentiful and comfortable. Why comfortable? Because they all have air-conditioning. Four or five people can get in a taxi and it's not very expensive, in fact, very cheap. Ordinary cars are blue or green, white, red, black or yellow, every colour under the sun, but taxis are different, they are all painted red and silver.

Unit 22

Exercise 1

a M̀h haih, ngóh m̀h haih Méih-gwok-yàhn.

b Haih, kéuih-deih yuht-làih-yuht-waaih.

c Haih, ngóh meih sihk-gwo jóu-chāan.

d M̀h haih, kéuih hóu jùng-yi fàan-gùng.

e Haih, yāt-yeuhng gam jùng-yi.

Exercise 2

a mēi b béi c fàan d dýun

Exercise 3

a -gán **b** -jyuh **c** -gwo **d** -saai **e** -hòi

Exercise 4

a Chāt-maahn-lìhng-yih-baak-mān.

b Haih Chàhn Sàang ló ge chín dò. (Hòh Sàang yāt-guhng jí-haih ló yih-maahn-sei jē.)

c Wòhng Táai gàm-yaht bāt-gwo yuhng-jó yah-yih-go-sei jē.

d Ngóh ūk-kéi yāt-guhng yáuh sahp-ńgh go yàhn. (M̀h-hóu m̀h gei-dāk ngóh lā!)

Unit 23

Exercise 1

a yāt-làuh **b** gìng-jai **c** làai-yàhn **d** jai-fuhk **e** sàn-séui

Exercise 2

a Yàuh ngàhn-hòhng heui Hòh Sàang ūk-kéi jí yáuh léuhng gūng-léih jē.

b Ngàhn-hòhng hái Hòh Sàang ūk-kéi dùng-bihn.

Exercise 3

a Kéuih haih sei-sahp bohng.

b Haih yauh-sáu.

c Kéuih yìh-gā luhk seui.

d Kéuih jí-haih gàau-jó baat-sahp mān béi fó-gei jē!

Exercise 4

a Yiu tìhng-chē bo!

b Làahm-sīk gà wòhng-sīk haih luhk-sīk.

c Làahm-sīk gà hùhng-sīk haih jí-sīk.

d Hóu gauh ge dihn-yíng haih hāk-baahk-sīk ge.

Exercise 5

a Fó-gei, nī-syu dī hói-sīn jàn haih hóu-meih, yauh sàn-sìn yauh jíng-dāk leng. Sīk-hèung-meih dōu haih yāt-làuh ge.

b *All our fish are live here, of course they're fresh.*

c M̀h-gòi màaih-dāan lā.

d *Thank you. $2890.*

e Māt-yéh wá?! Gam dò gé! Jàn-haih m̀h pèhng a!

f *You should know, sir, that it's very hard to buy live fish now. Added to that, our restaurant presents you with chopsticks, one pair for each customer.*

g Ngóh meih máaih-gwo gam gwai ge faai-jí a. Hóu lā. M̀h
  pèhng, daahn-haih dōu dái. Nī-douh haih sàam-chìn mān.
h *Thank you.*

Exercise 6

'Nī tìuh yú jàn-haih leng, yāt-dihng hóu hóu-meih. Bīn-wái
háng béi yāt-chìn mān a?'

Unit 24

Exercise 1

a a shadow b johk-yaht

Exercise 2

a Wòhng Síu-jé sihk jóu-chāan jì-chìhn, jaahp-gwan heui saan-
  bouh sìn.
b Ngóh hái ūk-kéi ge sìh-hauh, m̀h daai móu.
c Nàahm-yán luhk-sahp-ńgh seui sìn-ji hó-yíh ló teui-yàu-gām.
d Ngóh gàm-jìu-jóu yāt tái bou-jí jauh jì-dou ngóh-deih gūng-
  sī ge chìhng-fong hóu ngàih-hím.
e Chàhn Sìn-sàang yuht yám bē-jáu yuht jùng-yi yám. *or*
  Chàhn Sìn-sàang yuht-làih-yuht-jùng-yi yám bē-jáu.

Exercise 3

a Yāt go sai-mān-jái séung làai gáu, daahn-haih jek gáu m̀h
  séung hàahng.
b Yāt go nàahm-yán tèui-jyuh yāt ga waaih-jó ge chē. Kéuih
  taai-táai jà-jyuh gó ga waaih chē.
c Yáuh yàhn hòi faai chē chùng-gwo hùhng-dāng.
d Gíng-chaat yuhng sáu-chēung dá-séi-jó yāt go yáuh chēung
  ge waaih yàhn.

Exercise 4

a chìhn-bihn   b bāk-bihn   c nī-douh
d yauh-sáu-bihn e chēut-bihn

Exercise 5

a Chéng-mahn, yáuh móuh bā-sí heui gèi-chèuhng a?
b Yàuh Daaih-wuih-tòhng heui gèi-chèuhng yiu géi-dō chín a?
c Yiu chóh géi-noih (bā-sí) a?
d Bā-sí yáuh móuh chi-só a?
e Yih-ńgh-yāt-houh bàan-gèi géi-dō-dím-jūng héi-fèi a?
f Yih-ńgh-yāt-houh bàan-gèi géi-sí dou Lèuhn-dēun a?

Unit 26

Exercise 1

a gíng-chaat → gíng-chaat-guhk
b sái-yì-gèi → chỳuh-fóng
c yeuhk-séui → chán-só *or* yì-yún
d gong-kàhm → haak-tēng
e bei-sỳu → sé-jih-làuh
f jì-piu → ngàhn-hòhng
g lèuhn-pún → dóu-chèuhng
h yàuh-gáan → yàuh-gúk

Exercise 2

a M̀h-gòi néih m̀h-hóu yūk a.
b Néih góng-dāk dōu m̀h-haih-géi-ngāam bo.
c Néih yáuh-dī m̀h-haih-géi-mìhng-baahk ah.
d Ngóh dōu m̀h hó-yíh (*or* m̀h-wúih) tùhng-yi.
e Deui-m̀h-jyuh, Ghim-krìu Daaih-hohk dōu m̀h haih sai-gaai seuhng jeui yáuh-méng ge.

Exercise 3

Taai-táai, gó chàhng láu yauh daaih yauh leng. Jýu-yàhn-fóng hóu daaih, yáuh tou-fóng chi-só tùhng chùng-lèuhng-fóng; juhng yáuh daih-yih gàan fan-fóng tùhng-màaih daih-yih go chùng-lèuhng-fóng tìm. Haak-tēng tùhng chỳuh-fóng dōu-géi daaih. Yáuh léuhng ga līp, juhng yáuh chē-wái bàau-kwut hái ūk-ga léuih-bihn. Deih-jí hóu hóu, jīk-haih Gwóng-jàu Douh yah-chāt-houh baat láu. Ga-chìhn hóu pèhng: bāt-gwo yiu ńgh-baak-ńgh-sahp-maahn mān Góng-jí jē. Ngóh hóu séung máaih!

Exercise 4

a Gìng-léih ge gùng-jok jauh haih yiu gwún-léih-hóu kéuih ge gūng-sī.
b Hòi-chí hòi-chē jì-chìhn néih yiu jyu-yi māt-yéh a?
c Sàn-sìn ge hói-sìn hóu hóu-sihk.
d Hèung-góng yáuh hóu dò yāt-làuh ge jáu-làuh.

Exercise 5

a = yàuh-séui b = dihn-yíng c = dá-bō
d = Góng-jí e = chìm-jing

Exercise 6

a la b àh . . . a c mē/àh . . . lā d bo . . . nē

Exercise 7

a hái hói-sīn jáu-gā b hái máh-chèuhng
c hái bā-sí-jaahm   d hái ngóh ūk-kéi   e hái sé-jih-làuh

Exercise 8

a jèung b fūk c ga d tou e tou f douh

Exercise 9

a It doesn't make sense: how can he be rich if he hasn't got even $1?
b How can you be older than your mother?
c **Mh** does not go with **-gwo**: it should be **meih tái-gwo**.
d It should be **hàahng-*dāk* sahp-fan faai**.
e **Yìh-ché** does not go with **sèui-yìhn**: change **yìh-ché** to **daahn-haih**.

Passage 1

A very long time ago in China there was a man who loved painting. His pictures were superb, especially when he was painting dragons, they looked just as though they could move. Once a high official, getting to know that he was good at painting dragons, said to him with great delight: 'I myself love dragons too. If you were willing to paint a dragon for me I would pay you very well.'

A few days later sure enough the dragon was done and very well painted at that. It attracted a lot of people who came to look at it. But alas the dragon had no eyes. The official was mystified and asked why he did not paint the eyes. The painter replied that if he did so the dragon would fly away.

Of course no one could believe what he said. The official was very angry and insisted on him putting the eyes in. Strange as it may seem, as soon as he had painted them the dragon gave a few shakes and really did jump out from the paper and fly away.

Passage 2

Forty or 50 years ago Shanghai was considered a very advanced city, but many other cities and rural areas of China were still very backward.

One day a certain Mr Lee came up from the country with matters about which he needed to see his friend Wong Tai Kwok in Shanghai. Mr Wong lived in a large and beautiful hotel with all possible facilities.

When Mr Lee got to the hotel and was waiting in the lobby for Mr Wong, he saw an elderly lady slowly walk into a tiny room. He had never seen a lift, so he didn't know that that was what it was. A couple of minutes later the doors of the little room opened and out walked a beautiful young lady.

Mr Lee at first thought it very strange, but afterwards he said gleefully: 'The city folks really are advanced: next time I'll be sure to bring my wife with me.'

Numbers in brackets indicate the unit in which the entry is introduced. Abbreviations:

    ap = appendix
    cl = classifier
    fp = final particle

a-	prefix for names/relationships	(22)
a?	fp: finishes a question	(1)
a?	fp: triumphantly scoring	(8)
àai!	*alas!*	(24)
aan-jau	*midday; lunch*	(22)
àh?	fp: that's right, isn't it?	(3)
ā-ma!	fp: you should realize	(5)
áu	*to vomit*	(10)
Aù-jàu	*Europe*	(19)
baahk-faahn	*boiled/steamed rice*	(25)
baahk-jí	*blank paper*	(20)
baahk-sīk	*white*	(12)
baahn-faat	*method, way, means*	(18)
baak	*hundred*	(11)
baak-fahn-jì-sahp	*10 per cent*	(19)
baak-fo-gūng-sī	*department store*	(8)
bàan	cl: group of, gang of	(17)
bāan-gèi	*scheduled flight*	(15)
baat	*eight*	(2)
bàau	*wrap up*	(20)
bàau-gwó	*parcel*	(20)
bàau-kwut	*to include*	(25)
bàh-bā	*father*	(3)
baht-lāan-déi	*brandy*	(25)

baih!	*oh dear! oh heck! alas!*	(17)
bāk	*north*	(6)
bāk-bihn	*the north side*	(12)
Bāk-gìng	*Beijing (Peking)*	(23)
Bāk-gìng-choi	*Peking food*	(23)
bā-sí	*bus*	(3)
bā-sí-jaahm	*bus stop*	(6)
bāt	*pen*	(2)
bāt-gwo	*but, however*	(17)
bāt-gwo	*only*	(20)
bāt-yùh	*it would be better if*	(19)
behng	*illness*	(10)
behng-yàhn	*a patient*	(10)
béi	*give*	(4)
béi-gaau	*compare*	(19)
béi-gìn-néih	*bikini*	(8)
beih	*by (passive)*	(12)
beih-bīk	*be forced to*	(11)
bei-maht	*secret*	(24)
bei-sỳu	*secretary*	(22)
bē-jáu	*beer*	(8)
bihn-faahn	*pot luck*	(4)
bihn-fuhk	*plain clothes*	(17)
bihn-yì	*plain clothes*	(17)
biht-yàhn	*other people*	(24)
bin	*to change*	(19)
bīn?	*which?*	(2)
bīn-douh?	*where?*	(3)
bīn-go?	*who? which one?*	(2)
bín-jihk	*to devalue*	(19)
bīn-syu?	*where?*	(3)
bíu-gaak	*a form*	(20)
bō	*ball*	(9)
bo!	*fp: let me tell you*	(5)
bohng	*pound (weight)*	(12)
bòng	*on behalf of, for the benefit of*	(10)
bòng . . . sáu	*help*	(4)
bòng-báan	*inspector*	(17)
bòng-chan	*patronize, give custom*	(23)
bō-sí	*boss*	(25)
bóu	*to compensate*	(22)
bou-dou	*check in, register*	(15)
bou-douh	*to report, a report*	(18)
bóu-fāan-sou	*to make up for*	(10)

bouh	*area, part, portion*	(6)
bouh	cl: for books	(12)
bóu-hím	*insurance*	(15)
bouh-mùhn	*department*	(19)
bou-jí	*newspaper*	(18)
bóu-jing	*to guarantee*	(20)
bou-líu	*material, fabric*	(11)
bóu-òn	*security, keep secure*	(25)
bui, bùi	*cup, glass*	(25)
bun	*half*	(4)
bún	cl: for books	(12)
bún-chìhn	*capital*	(13)
bún-deih	*local, indigenous*	(18)
chaak	*to demolish, tear down*	(23)
chāak-yihm	*to test; evaluation*	(12)
chàam-gà	*take part in*	(11)
chàam-gwùn	*visit a place*	(6)
chāan	*meal*	(4)
chāan-páai	*menu*	(23)
chāan-tēng	*restaurant*	(23)
cháang-sīk	*orange*	(12)
cháau-faahn	*fried rice*	(25)
chàh	*tea*	(4)
chàh	*to investigate, check*	(19)
Chàhn	a surname: *Chan*	(1)
chàhng	cl: for a flat, apartment; storey, deck	(3)
chàh-wún	*tea bowl*	(25)
chàih-chyuhn	*complete, all embracing*	(23)
chà-m̀h-dō	*almost*	(12)
chàn-ngáahn	*with one's own eyes*	(18)
chán-só	*clinic*	(10)
chāt	*seven*	(2)
chàuh-fún	*fund raising*	(13)
chàu-jéung	*lucky draw*	(13)
che	*steep*	(16)
chē	*car*	(1)
chē-fòhng	*garage*	(3)
chek	*foot* (length)	(19)
chek	*red; naked*	(19)
chek-geuk-yī-sāng	*barefoot doctor*	(19)
chek-jih	*in the red, deficit*	(19)
Chek-laahp-gok	*Chek Lap Kok* (airport)	(6)

che-lóu	steep road	(16)
chéng	invite	(4)
chéng	please	(3)
chéng-mahn	please may I ask	(6)
chèuhng	cl: for performances, bouts, games	(13)
chèuhng	long	(22)
chèuhng-gok	corner	(8)
chèuhng-sai	detailed, fine, minute	(22)
chèuhn-lòh-chē	patrol car	(17)
chèuih-bín	as you please, feel free	(4)
chéui-sìu	to cancel	(10)
chēung-lím-bou	curtains	(25)
chēut	cl: for films and plays	(9)
chēut	out	(17)
chēut-bihn	outside	(12)
chēut-gāai	to go out into the street	(18)
chēut-nín	next year	(8)
chē-wái	parking space	(25)
chi	time, occasion	(6)
chi-fo	seconds	(5)
chi-gīk	exciting	(9)
chìh-dī	later	(2)
chìhn-bihn	front	(12)
chìhn-geí-nìhn	a few years ago	(18)
chìhng-fong	situation, circumstances	(16)
chìhn-máahn	the evening of the day before yesterday	(11)
chìhn-nín	the year before last	(10)
chìhn-yaht	the day before yesterday	(9)
chìh-sihn	charity	(13)
chīm-jing	visa	(15)
chín	light (coloured); shallow	(25)
chín	money	(5)
chìn	thousand	(11)
chìng-git	clean	(25)
chìn-kèih	whatever you do, don't	(16)
chín-làahm-sīk	light blue	(25)
chì-sin	crazy	(16)
chi-só	toilet	(10)
chit-beih	facilities, equipment	(15)
chit-gai	design	(11)
chìu-gwo	to exceed	(19)
cho	error	(19)

chóh	to travel by	(6)
chóh	sit	(3)
chóh-gāam	to be in prison	(18)
chóh-hòi-dī	sit further away	(17)
chóh-līp	to ride in a lift	(25)
chóh-màaih-dī	sit closer	(17)
chòhng	bed	(15)
choi	cuisine	(23)
choi-chē	motor racing	(16)
choi-chē-sáu	racing driver	(16)
choi-máh	to race horses	(13)
chò-kāp	elementary, first grade	(24)
chòuh	noisy	(25)
chóuh-yàuh-piu	to collect stamps	(24)
chúhng	heavy	(12)
chúhng-leuhng	weight	(15)
chùng	to rush, dash against	(12)
chùng-lèuhng	to have a shower	(25)
chùng-lèuhng-fóng	bathroom	(25)
chýuh-chuk	savings; to save	(19)
chỳuh-fóng	kitchen	(4)
chỳuhn-bouh	all, the whole lot	(23)
chỳuhn-jān	fax	(22)
chỳuhn-jān-gèi	fax machine	(22)
chýu-léih	to handle, deal with	(22)
dá	hit	(9)
daahn-haih	but	(6)
daahn-sing	flexible	(22)
daai	lead	(2)
daai	wear	(11)
daaih	big	(3)
daaih-dong	gambling den	(13)
daaih-fōng	tasteful, sophisticated	(11)
daaih-gáam-ga	sale	(5)
daaih-hohk	university	(6)
daaih-kwài-mòuh	large scale	(19)
daaih-mùhn-háu	main doorway	(20)
daaih-sèng	loud, in a loud voice	(11)
daaih-tòhng	lobby	(26)
daaih-wuih-tòhng	city hall	(6)
daaih-yeuk	approximately	(20)
Daaih-yràn	Your Honour, Your Excellency	(18)

dāan-chē	bicycle	(16)
dāan-yàhn-chòhng	single bed	(15)
daap	travel by	(3)
daap-dāk-dóu	able to catch	(18)
daap-m̀h-dóu	unable to catch	(18)
dá-bō	play ball	(9)
dá-dihn-wá	to make a phone call	(10)
dá-fó	to strike fire	(24)
dá-fó-gèi	cigarette lighter	(24)
dá-fùng	a typhoon	(8)
dá-gāau	fight	(18)
dá-gip	rob	(18)
dahk-biht	special	(23)
dahk-faai	express	(20)
Dahk-kèui	Special Administrative Region (SAR)	(20)
Dahk-sáu	Chief Executive of SAR	(20)
dá-hòh-bāau	purse snatching, to pick pockets	(18)
dái	worth it	(15)
daih-	(makes ordinal numbers)	(6)
daih-mēi	last in order	(22)
daih-yāt	the first	(6)
daih-yih	the second, the next	(6)
dá-jih	to type	(22)
dá-jih-gèi	typewriter	(22)
dāk	OK	(5)
Dāk-gwok	Germany	(19)
dāk-hàahn	at leisure	(13)
dá-léhng-tàai	to tie a necktie	(10)
dá-màh-jeuk	to play Mahjong	(13)
dáng	let, allow	(5)
dáng	wait	(4)
dāng	a light	(12)
dàng	to stare, open the eyes	(17)
dàng-daaih-deui-ngáahn	take a good look	(17)
dáng-dáng	etcetera	(15)
dáng-ngóh-béi	let me pay	(5)
dá-sou	sweep	(25)
dá-syun	intend	(8)
deih-fòng	place	(6)
deih-há	ground floor, the ground, the floor	(3)
deih-há-tit-louh	underground railway	(6)

deih-jí	*address*	(20)
deih-jīn	*carpet*	(25)
deih-léih	*geography*	(12)
deih-mín	*the floor*	(25)
deih-tit	*underground*	(6)
deih-tit-jaahm	*underground station*	(6)
déng	cl: for hats	(11)
deui	*exchange money*	(19)
deui	cl: a pair of	(16)
deui	*with regard to, towards*	(9)
deui-m̀h-jyuh	*sorry*	(1)
deui-mihn	*opposite*	(12)
deui-wuhn-léut	*exchange rate*	(19)
dī	cl: for plurals and uncountable things	(4)
dihn	*electricity*	(16)
dihn-chè	*tram*	(9)
dihn-dāan-chē	*motorbike*	(16)
dihng-haih	*or?*	(13)
dihn-jí	*electronic*	(25)
dihn-nóuh	*computer*	(22)
dihn-nýuhn-lòuh	*electric heater*	(8)
dihn-sih-gèi	*television set*	(15)
dihn-tòih	*radio station*	(13)
dihn-wá	*telephone*	(10)
dihn-yàuh	*petrol*	(16)
dihn-yíng	*film (cinema)*	(9)
diht-jeuih	*order*	(12)
dīk-sí	*taxi*	(3)
dīk-sih-gōu	*discotheque*	(24)
dím	*a point, spot, dot*	(23)
dím(-yéung)	*how? in what way?*	(5)
dím-gáai	*why?*	(4)
dím-sām	*dim sum*	(23)
diuh-tàuh	*turn to face the other way*	(16)
dò	*many, much*	(3)
dò-dī	*a little more*	(15)
dò-jeh	*thank you*	(5)
dò-jeh-saai	*thank you very much*	(15)
dong	*regard as*	(4)
dong-háu	*street stall*	(5)
dòng-yín	*of course*	(13)
dóu	*to gamble on, bet on*	(13)
dōu	*all, both*	(4)

dōu	*also*	(1)
dou	*arrive, arrive at, reach*	(6)
dóu-bō	*to bet on football*	(13)
dóu-chèuhng	*casino*	(13)
dóu-chín	*to gamble with money*	(13)
dóu-gáu	*to bet on dogs*	(13)
dōu-géi	*quite*	(3)
dóu-gú-piu	*to gamble on shares*	(13)
douh	*cl: for doors*	(25)
douh	*road, street*	(3)
dóu-máh	*bet on horses*	(13)
dóu-ngoih-wuih	*to gamble on foreign exchange*	(13)
dóu-pē-páai	*to gamble at cards*	(13)
dou-yìh-gā-wàih-jí	*up to now*	(18)
dò-yùh	*surplus*	(9)
duhk-laahp	*independent*	(22)
duhk-sỳu	*study*	(12)
dùng	*east*	(6)
dùng-bāk	*northeast*	(6)
dùng-bihn	*the east side*	(12)
dùng-nàahm	*southeast*	(6)
dýun	*short*	(22)
faahn	*rice, food*	(4)
faahn	*to offend, commit crime*	(18)
fáahn-duhk	*to peddle drugs*	(17)
faahn-tēng	*dining room*	(25)
fàahn-wìhng	*prosperous*	(13)
faahn-wún	*rice bowl*	(25)
faai	*fast, quick, quickly*	(15)
faai-dī	*get a move on!*	(17)
faai-jí	*chopsticks*	(16)
fàan	*return*	(3)
fàan-gùng	*go to work*	(22)
fāan-tāan	*fantan*	(13)
fáan-yìh	*on the contrary, despite this*	(19)
fáan-ying	*reaction*	(16)
Faat-gwok	*France*	(19)
faat-gwùn	*a judge*	(18)
faat-muhng	*to dream*	(25)
faat-sàng	*happen, occur, transpire*	(18)
fahn-jí	*element, member*	(12)
faht-chín	*to fine, be fined*	(18)

fai-yuhng	cost, fee	(15)
fan-gaau	sleep	(16)
fan-lihn	training, to train	(24)
fan-m̀h-jeuk	unable to get to sleep	(25)
fan-mihn	to give birth	(22)
fā-yéung	pattern	(11)
Fà-yùhn-Douh	Garden Road	(3)
fà-yún	garden	(2)
fēi	ticket	(15)
feì	to fly	(24)
feì-faat	illegal	(13)
fèi-gèi	aircraft	(6)
fèi-gèi-chèuhng	airport	(6)
fèi-gèi-piu	air ticket	(15)
fèi-lám	film (camera)	(25)
fō	a subject, a discipline	(12)
fo-bún	textbook	(12)
fó-chē	railway train	(6)
fó-gei	waiter	(4)
fō-geih	science and technology	(24)
fòhng-gāan	room	(15)
fō-hohk	science	(12)
fòng-bihn	convenient	(17)
fong-ga	holiday	(9)
fong-gùng	finish work	(22)
fòng-mihn	aspect	(12)
fuh-gahn	nearby	(4)
fuh-jaak	responsible	(22)
fuhk-mouh	service	(15)
fūi-sīk	grey	(12)
fūk	cl: for paintings	(24)
fūk-leih	benefits, welfare	(22)
fùng	cl: for letters	(20)
fùng	wind	(8)
fùng-fu	rich, abundant	(13)
fún-sīk	style	(5)
fùn-yìhng	welcome	(22)
ga	cl: for vehicles, aircraft, machinery	(12)
gá	false	(17)
ga? = ge + a?	fp	(2)
gāai	street	(3)
gāai-háu	road junction	(6)

gaai-siuh	*introduce*	(4)
gáam-síu	*reduce, cut down*	(9)
gàan	cl: for houses and rooms	(3)
gáan-dàan	*simple*	(20)
gaan-jip	*indirectly*	(22)
gaan-jūng	*occasionally*	(10)
gàau	*to hand over*	(15)
gaau-sỳu	*teach*	(12)
gàau-tùng	*traffic, communication*	(12)
gàau-tùng-dāng	*traffic light*	(12)
gaau-yuhk	*education*	(12)
ga-chìhn	*price*	(11)
ga-chìhn-páai	*price tag*	(11)
ga-fē	*coffee*	(3)
ga-fē-sīk	*brown*	(12)
gà-ga	*to increase price*	(23)
gahn *or* káhn	*close to*	(20)
ga-kèih	*holiday*	(22)
gám	*dare*	(18)
gám	*so, in that case*	(3)
gam	*so*	(4)
gàm-jìu-jóu	*this morning*	(4)
gàm-máahn	*this evening, tonight*	(11)
gàm-nín	*this year*	(8)
gam-noih	*so long a time*	(18)
gam-seuhng-há	*approximately*	(9)
gām-sīk	*gold, golden*	(12)
gàm-yaht	*today*	(4)
gám-yéung	*in that case, so*	(3)
gàn	*catty*	(5)
gán-yiu	*important*	(21)
ga-sái	*driving, to drive*	(16)
gáu	*dog*	(13)
gau	*enough*	(16)
gáu	*nine*	(2)
gauh	*old (not new), used*	(8)
gauh-nín	*last year*	(8)
gau-jai-gām	*relief money*	(18)
gau-jūng	*time's up*	(13)
gà-yahp	*to join, recruit into*	(17)
ge	fp: that's how it is!	(3)
ge	links adjectives to nouns	(4)
ge	shows possession; -'s	(2)
géi	*quite, rather, fairly*	(3)

gei	*to post, mail*	(20)
géi	*several*	(9)
géi?	*how many? how much?*	(9)
gèi-chèuhng	*airport*	(6)
gei-dāk	*remember*	(9)
géi-dō	*how much? how many?*	(5)
gèi-fùh	*almost but not quite*	(18)
géi-gam . . . laak	*how very . . . !*	(18)
gèi-hei	*machine*	(24)
géi-nihm	*memorial, to commemorate*	(20)
géi-noih	*how long?*	(20)
gèi-piu	*air ticket*	(15)
géi-sí *or* géi-sìh	*when?*	(8)
gèi-wuih	*chance*	(22)
gèi-yuhk	*muscle*	(9)
ge-la	fp: *strong emphasis*	(5)
géui-baahn	*to run, hold, conduct*	(15)
geuk	*foot, leg*	(16)
geuk-jai	*footbrake*	(16)
gihn	cl: *most clothing items*	(5)
gihn-hòng	*healthy*	(9)
gím-chàh	*to check, inspect*	(25)
gím-hung	*to accuse*	(12)
Gim-kìuh	*Cambridge*	(6)
gin	*see, meet*	(8)
gìn-chìh	*insist, insist on*	(25)
gíng-chaat	*policeman*	(12)
gìng-gwo	*to pass by, via*	(11)
gìng-jai	*economy*	(19)
gìng-léih	*manager*	(15)
gíng-yùhn-jing	*warrant card*	(17)
git-gwó	*result*	(16)
giu	*tell to do*	(17)
gó	*that, those*	(2)
go	cl: *for people and many objects*	(2)
gó-douh	*there*	(5)
gói	*alter*	(8)
gói-bin	*to change, alter*	(24)
gó-jahn-sìh	*at that time*	(10)
gok-dāk	*feel*	(9)
gō-kehk	*opera*	(24)
góng	*speak*	(9)
Góng-jí	*Hong Kong dollars*	(19)

gong-kàhm	*piano*	(24)
góng-siu	*to joke*	(16)
gón-jyuh	*hurrying*	(15)
gó-syu	*there*	(5)
gòu	*high, tall*	(10)
gú	*guess*	(2)
gú-dāk-dóu	*able to guess*	(18)
gù-duhk	*solitary*	(24)
gu-haak	*customer, client*	(23)
guhk	*bureau, office, department*	(16)
guih	*tired*	(24)
gú-m̀h-dóu	*unable to guess*	(18)
gùng-bou	*to announce*	(19)
gùng-fo	*homework*	(12)
gùng-guhng	*public*	(12)
gùng-gwàan	*public relations*	(15)
gùng-héi	*congratulations*	(23)
gùng-jok	*work*	(22)
gùng-jouh	*to work*	(22)
gūng-léih	*kilometre*	(23)
gūng-sī	*company*	(8)
gùng-yàhn	*worker, servant*	(25)
gú-piu	*stocks and shares*	(13)
gwàai	*'good boy', well behaved, obedient*	(13)
gwàan-haih	*relationship, relevance, connection*	(13)
gwa-houh	*to register*	(10)
gwái	*a ghost*	(21)
gwai	*expensive*	(1)
gwai-gwok	*your country*	(23)
gwaih-tói	*counter*	(15)
gwái-lóu	*ghost fellow* (westerner)	(10)
gwai-sing-a?	*what is your name?*	(1)
gwàn-deui	*army*	(17)
gwàn-fuhk	*military uniform*	(17)
gwàn-yàhn	*soldier, military personnel*	(17)
gwo	*past, across, by*	(6)
gwo	*than*	(12)
gwo-bóng	*to weigh*	(15)
gwo-chúhng	*overweight*	(15)
gwok-gà	*country, state*	(19)
gwóng-bo	*to broadcast*	(13)
Gwóng-dùng	*Guangdong* (province)	(23)

Gwóng-dùng-choi	*Cantonese food*	(23)
Gwóng-jàu	*Guangzhou* (Canton)	(13)
Gwóng-jàu-wá	*Cantonese language*	(23)
gwòng-máahng	*bright*	(25)
gwo-sìh	*overtime*	(22)
gwún	*control, be in charge of*	(12)
gwùn	*an official, an officer*	(16)
gwún-léih	*management, manage*	(25)
hā	*prawn, shrimp*	(5)
hà	*ha ha!*	(23)
hàahng	*to walk*	(15)
hàahng-gāai	*go out into the streets*	(15)
háahng-hòi-jó	*not here*	(17)
hàahng-louh	*walk*	(15)
hàahng-sàan	*walk in the country*	(15)
haak-hei	*polite*	(4)
haak-tēng	*living room, lounge*	(25)
hàan	*to save; stingy*	(8)
háau	*to examine, to test*	(16)
háau-síh	*examination*	(16)
hah-(yāt)-chi	*next time*	(15)
hah-bihn	*under, underside*	(12)
hah-go-láih-baai	*next week*	(10)
hah-go-yuht	*next month*	(17)
hah-jau	*afternoon, p.m.*	(15)
hahm-baah(ng)-laahng	*all told*	(20)
hàhng	*to journey, go towards*	(6)
hàhng-léih	*luggage*	(15)
hah-pàh	*chin*	(9)
hahp-kwài-gaak	*to qualify, meet requirements*	(17)
hái	*at, in, on*	(2)
hái-douh	*at the indicated place*	(11)
haih	*be*	(1)
hái-syu	*at the indicated place*	(11)
hāk-sīk (hāak-sīk)	*black*	(12)
háng	*willing*	(22)
háu-bouh	*the mouth*	(9)
hauh-bihn	*back*	(12)
hauh-lòih	*later, afterwards*	(25)
hauh-máahn	*evening of day after tomorrow*	(11)
hauh-nín	*year after next*	(10)
hauh-sāang	*young*	(12)

hauh-sāang-jái	*youngster*	(12)
hauh-yaht	*day after tomorrow*	(10)
hei-chè	*vehicle, car*	(12)
héi-dím	*start*	(22)
héi-fèi	*to take off* (aircraft)	(15)
hèi-mohng	*hope, to hope*	(10)
héi-sàn	*get up*	(10)
héi-yáuh-chí-léih	*how could that be?*	(16)
hèng	*light* (in weight)	(15)
heui	*go, go to*	(2)
hèung	*fragrant*	(23)
heung	*towards*	(6)
Hèung-góng	*Hong Kong*	(3)
hèung-há	*countryside*	(6)
héung-sauh	*enjoy*	(15)
hing-cheui	*interest*	(13)
hìng-daih	*brothers*	(3)
Hòh	a surname: *Ho*	(1)
hohk-haauh	*school*	(12)
hohk-sāang	*pupil, student*	(16)
hòhng-noih-yàhn	*insider, expert*	(15)
hòi	*run/start a business*	(23)
hòi	*open*	(19)
hói	*sea*	(25)
hòi-chē	*start/drive a car*	(16)
hòi-gùng	*start work, start a job*	(22)
hòi-sàm	*happy*	(8)
hói-sīn	*seafood*	(23)
hói-tāan	*the beach*	(8)
hó-nàhng	*possible that, possibility*	(16)
hó-sīk	*it's a pity that, unfortunately*	(11)
hóu	*good*	(1)
hóu	*very*	(1)
hóu-chíh	*just like*	(4)
hóu-chói	*lucky, fortunately*	(12)
hóu-dò	*a lot more*	(16)
hóu-gám	*favourable impression*	(23)
houh	*day of the month*	(20)
hóu-meih	*delicious*	(4)
hóu-noih-móuh-gin	*long time no see*	(3)
hóu-sihk	*delicious* (to eat)	(13)
hóu-tái	*good-looking, attractive*	(13)
hóu-tèng	*harmonious, melodic*	(13)
hóu-wáan	*good fun, enjoyable*	(13)

hóu-yám	*delicious (to drink)*	(13)
hó-yíh	*may, can*	(6)
hùhng-dāng	*red light*	(12)
hùhng-sīk	*red*	(5)
hùng	*empty*	(11)
hùng-yàuh	*airmail*	(20)
hyun	*advise, urge, plead with*	(24)
hyut	*blood*	(16)
jaahm-sìh	*temporary*	(20)
jaahp-gwaan	*accustomed to; habit*	(24)
jaahp-háu	*gate, gateway*	(15)
jaahp-jùng	*concentrated, centralized*	(23)
jaak	*narrow*	(16)
jaan	*praise*	(11)
jáan	cl: *for lamps and lights*	(12)
jáau(-fàan)-chín	*to give change*	(20)
jà-chē	*drive*	(6)
jái	*son*	(10)
jài	*to put, place*	(8)
jai-douh	*system*	(22)
jai-fuhk	*uniform*	(17)
jái-néui	*children*	(22)
jàm	*pour*	(25)
jàng	*hate*	(24)
jàng-gà	*to increase*	(13)
jàn-haih	*truly*	(4)
jāt-déi	*quality*	(5)
jáu	*alcoholic drink*	(8)
jáu	*run, run away*	(3)
jáu-dim	*hotel*	(15)
jáu-gā	*Chinese restaurant*	(23)
jauh	*then*	(4)
jauh-faai	*soon*	(23)
jauh-jàn	*that's for sure!*	(25)
jáu-làuh	*Chinese restaurant*	(4)
jáu-lóng	*passage, corridor*	(8)
jáu-naahn	*flee disaster; take refuge*	(6)
jáu-wúi	*reception, cocktail party*	(11)
jē	fp: *only, and that's all*	(3)
jek	cl: *one of a pair*	(16)
jek	cl: *for animals*	(5)
jēk	fp: *only, and that's all*	(3)
jeuhn-leuhng	*so far as possible*	(19)

jeui	*most*	(6)
jeui-gahn	*recently*	(19)
jeuih	*crime*	(18)
jeuih-mìhng	*charge, accusation*	(18)
jeuih-on	*criminal case*	(13)
jeui-síu	*at least*	(18)
jeuk	*a bird*	(24)
jeuk	*wear*	(11)
jéun	*permit*	(17)
jèun	*bottle, bottle of*	(10)
jeun-bouh	*progress*	(24)
Jèung	*a surname: Cheung*	(1)
jèung	cl: *for sheet-like objects*	(2)
jéung-bán	*prize*	(13)
jèung-lòih	*future*	(24)
jéun-tip	*allowance, grant*	(22)
jí	*paper*	(20)
jì	cl: *for stick-like objects*	(2)
jì	*to know (a fact)*	(8)
ji	*only then*	(10)
jí(-haih)	*only*	(4)
jì-chìhn	*before*	(10)
jì-dou	*know (a fact)*	(8)
jì-fōng	*body fat*	(9)
jih	*characters; 5 minutes*	(15)
jí-haih	*only*	(4)
jì-hauh	*after*	(6)
jih-géi	*self*	(24)
jihk-jip	*direct, directly*	(22)
jihm-jím	*gradually*	(8)
jihng	*quiet*	(25)
jih-òn	*law and order*	(18)
jih-yuhn	*voluntarily, willing*	(18)
jīk-haih	*that is to say*	(5)
jīk-yùhn	*staff, employee, clerk*	(22)
jī-máh	fp: *only*	(12)
jí-muih	*sisters*	(3)
jing	*certificate, pass*	(17)
jíng	*make, prepare*	(4)
jing-fú	*government*	(12)
jing-haih	*just happens to be*	(11)
jin-jàng	*war*	(19)
jín-láahm	*show, exhibition*	(11)
jì-noih	*within*	(6)

jì-piu	a cheque	(19)
jí-sīk	purple	(12)
jit-muhk	programme	(15)
jìu-jóu	morning	(4)
jì-yāt	one of the . . .	(6)
jí-yiu	so long as, provided that	(9)
jó-(sáu-)bihn	left side	(12)
joh	cl: for massive things	(25)
johk-jìu-jóu	yesterday morning	(4)
johk-máahn	last night, yesterday evening	(11)
johk-yaht	yesterday	(4)
johng	run into, knock into	(16)
joi	again	(4)
joi-chi	another time, a second time	(18)
joi-gin	goodbye	(1)
jōi-naahn	disaster	(19)
jok-áu	to retch, about to vomit	(10)
jóu	early	(4)
jóu-chāan	breakfast	(22)
jouh	do	(3)
jouh-gùng	to work	(22)
jouh-māt-yéh?	why? for what reason?	(3)
jouh-sàang-yi	to do business	(4)
jóu-sàhn	good morning	(1)
jó-yiuh-yauh-báai	shaking from side to side	(10)
juhng	still, yet	(3)
juhng	even more; furthermore	(8)
juhng-meih	still not yet	(16)
jūk-kàuh	soccer	(13)
jūk-kéi	play chess	(24)
jūng	clock	(15)
jùng-dím	finish	(22)
jung-fā	to cultivate flowers	(24)
jùng-gāan	in the middle of, in between	(12)
Jùng-gwok	China	(2)
Jùng-gwok-choi	Chinese food	(23)
Jùng-gwok-wá	Chinese language	(18)
Jùng-gwok-yàhn	a Chinese	(10)
jùng-hohk	secondary school	(12)
jung-léuih	type, kind, species	(23)
Jùng-màhn	Chinese language	(12)
jūng-tàuh	hour	(4)
Jùng-wàahn	central district	(6)
Jùng-yì	Chinese medicine	(10)

jùng-yi	like, fond of	(6)
jȳu	pig	(10)
jýu	cook	(4)
jýu-choi	main course	(4)
jyuh	live, dwell	(3)
jȳu-jái	piglet	(10)
jýun	turn, change	(6)
jȳun-gā	expert, specialist	(24)
jýu-sihk-lòuh	cooking stove	(25)
jýu-yàhn-fóng	master bedroom	(25)
jýu-yi	idea	(6)
jyu-yi	pay attention to	(15)
jȳu-yuhk	pork	(10)
káhn	near, close to	(20)
kā-lāai-ōu-kēi	karaoke	(24)
kāp-duhk	to take drugs	(18)
kāp-yàhn	to attract	(13)
kàu-tùng	to communicate	(24)
kéih	stand	(17)
kèih-gwaai	strange	(24)
kèih-tà	other	(5)
kèuhng-gàan	rape, to rape	(18)
kéuih	he, she, it	(1)
kìng-gái	chat	(11)
kwaang	to cruise	(25)
kwaang-gūng-sī	go window shopping	(25)
kwài-dihng	to regulate, lay down a rule	(17)
kỳuhn	right, powers, authority	(17)
kyut-dihng	decide	(25)
kyut-faht	lack	(24)
la	fp: that's how the case stands now	(3)
lā	fp: urging agreement or co-operation	(3)
làahm-sīk	blue	(12)
laahn	broken, damaged	(5)
láahng	cold	(8)
láahng-hei-gèi	air conditioner	(8)
láahng-tìn	winter, cold weather	(8)
laahp-saap	rubbish	(4)
laahp-saap-túng	rubbish bin	(4)
làai	arrest	(17)

làai	*pull*	(17)
laak	fp: that's how the case stands now	(3)
làih	*come*	(3)
láih-baai	*week*	(5)
làih-ge/ga?	fp: for identification	(19)
láu	*flat, apartment*	(3)
làuh	*flow*	(16)
làuh	*remain*	(24)
làuh-dái	*ceiling*	(25)
làuh-fàan	*to leave behind*	(24)
làuh-tài	*staircase*	(25)
léhng-tàai	*necktie*	(8)
Léih	a surname: *Li/Lee*	(1)
lèih	*distant from*	(25)
lèih-dóu	*outlying island*	(6)
lèih-hòi	*leave, depart from*	(9)
leih-sīk	*interest* (money)	(19)
léih-yàuh	*reason*	(25)
leng	*pretty, beautiful*	(1)
Lèuhn-Dēun	*London*	(6)
lèuhn-dou	*the turn of*	(16)
léuhng	*two*	(2)
lèuhn-pún	*roulette*	(13)
léuih-bihn	*inside*	(9)
léuih-yàuh	*tourism, travel*	(15)
lihk-sí	*history*	(12)
lìhn . . . dōu . . .	*even*	(17)
lihng	*cause*	(18)
lìhng	*zero*	(11)
lihn-jaahp	*practise*	(24)
lihn-jaahp-bóu	*exercise book*	(12)
lìhn-juhk	*in succession, consecutively*	(19)
līp	*lift*	(25)
lo	fp: agreement with previous speaker	(15)
ló	*take*	(15)
lohk	*alight*	(6)
lohk-hauh	*backward, old fashioned*	(25)
lohk-yúh	*rain*	(8)
lòih-wóhng	*coming and going; current* (account)	(19)
ló-tái	*naked, nude*	(17)
lóuh	*old, elderly*	(6)

louh-bīn	*the roadside*	(17)
louh-mín	*road surface*	(15)
lóuh-saht	*honest*	(13)
louh-tòih	*balcony*	(25)
lóuh-yàhn	*the elderly, the aged*	(18)
luhk	*six*	(2)
luhk-dāng	*green light*	(12)
luhk-sīk	*green*	(12)
lùhng	*dragon*	(26)
lùhng-hā	*lobster*	(4)
ma?	fp: makes questions	(1)
máahn	*evening*	(6)
maahn	*slow*	(16)
maahn	*ten thousand*	(11)
máahn-chāan	*dinner, supper*	(23)
máahn-faahn	*dinner*	(23)
máaih	*buy*	(2)
maaih	*sell*	(1)
máaih-choi	*food shopping*	(23)
màaih-dāan	*bill*	(23)
máaih-máh	*bet on horses*	(14)
máaih-sung	*food shopping*	(23)
māau	*cat*	(24)
máh	*horse*	(13)
máh-chèuhng	*racecourse*	(13)
màh-fàahn	*trouble*	(12)
Máh-hāak	*Deutschmark*	(19)
máh-louh	*road*	(6)
màh-mā	*mother*	(3)
mahn	*ask a question*	(2)
màhn-gín	*document*	(22)
mahn-tàih	*problem*	(15)
máih	*don't*	(4)
mān	*dollar*	(5)
māt-yéh	*what? what kind of?*	(2)
màu-dài	*squat down, crouch*	(10)
màuh-saat	*murder, to murder*	(18)
mē?	fp: do you mean to say that . . . ?	(5)
meih	*not yet*	(10)
méih	*tail, end*	(17)
mèih-bō-lòuh	*microwave oven*	(25)
Méih-gām	*American dollars*	(19)

Méih-gwok	*USA*	(1)
m̀h	*not*	(1)
m̀h gán-yiu	*never mind*	(2)
m̀h-cho	*not bad*	(11)
m̀h-dāk	*no can do*	(5)
m̀h-gin-jó	*lost*	(24)
m̀h-gòi	*thank you*	(2)
m̀h-gòi-saai	*thank you very much*	(15)
m̀h-gwaai-dāk	*no wonder*	(23)
m̀h-haih-géi	*not very*	(3)
m̀h-haih-hóu	*not very*	(3)
m̀h-hóu	*don't*	(4)
m̀h-jí	*not only*	(18)
m̀h-jì	*I wonder*	(11)
m̀h-sái	*no need to*	(4)
m̀h-síu-dāk	*not less than*	(15)
m̀h-sỳu-fuhk	*unwell, uncomfortable*	(10)
míhn-fai	*free of charge*	(5)
mìhng-baahk	*understand*	(12)
mìhng-seun-pín	*postcard*	(20)
míhn-seui	*tax free, duty free*	(15)
miht-fó-túng	*fire extinguisher*	(8)
mòhng	*busy*	(10)
móu	*hat, cap*	(11)
móuh	*have not*	(3)
móuh-mahn-tàih	*no problem!*	(15)
muhk-dīk	*aim, purpose*	(24)
mùhn	*door*	(20)
mùhn-háu	*doorway*	(20)
múih	*each, every*	(12)
mùih-hei	*town gas*	(25)
nàahm	*male*	(9)
nàahm	*south*	(6)
nàahm-bihn	*south side*	(12)
nàahm-chi(-só)	*gentlemen's toilet*	(17)
nàahm-gùng-yàhn	*male servant*	(25)
nàahm-hohk-sāang	*boy pupils/students*	(17)
nàahm-pàhng-yáuh	*boyfriend*	(17)
nàahm-yán	*man, adult male person*	(17)
nàahn	*difficult*	(17)
nàh!	*there! here it is, look!*	(5)
nám	*think about*	(20)
nàu	*angry*	(4)

Náu-yeuk	*New York*	(18)
nē?	*fp: for rhetorical questions*	(5)
nē?	*fp: repeats same question*	(1)
néih, néih-deih	*you*	(1)
néih-tái	*in your opinion*	(24)
néih-wah	*in your opinion*	(24)
néui	*daughter*	(17)
néuih	*female*	(17)
néuih-chi(-só)	*ladies' toilet*	(17)
néuih-gíng	*policewoman*	(17)
néuih-hohk-sāang	*girl pupils/students*	(17)
néuih-pàhng-yáuh	*girlfriend*	(17)
néuih-shìu-fòhng-yùhn	*firewoman*	(17)
néuih-yán	*woman, adult female*	(17)
ngáahn	*eye*	(11)
ngaahng	*hard, unyielding*	(5)
ngàahn-sīk	*colour*	(13)
ngāam	*correct*	(10)
ngāam-ngāam	*moment ago*	(11)
ngāam-ngāam	*exactly, precisely*	(20)
ngàhn-chín	*dollar*	(19)
ngàhn-hòhng	*bank*	(12)
ngàhn-sīk	*silver-coloured*	(25)
ngái	*low*	(24)
ngàih-hím	*danger*	(4)
ngàuh	*cow, ox*	(4)
ngàuh-yuhk	*beef*	(2)
ńgh	*five*	(15)
ńgh-sīng-kāp	*five star, top class*	(16)
ngh-wuih	*misunderstand*	(1)
ngóh	*I, me*	(12)
ngoih-bihn	*outside*	(18)
ngoih-gwok	*foreign country*	(19)
ngoih-hóng	*layman, outsider*	(11)
ngoih-tou	*jacket*	(13)
ngoih-wuih	*foreign exchange*	(2)
nī	*this, these*	(5)
nī-douh	*here*	(24)
nī-géi-nìhn	*these last few years*	(24)
nī-géi-yaht	*these last few days*	(17)
nī-go-yuht	*this month*	(8)
nìhn	*year*	(22)
nìhn-méih	*end of the year*	(16)
nìng	*bring*	

nī-syu	*here*	(5)
noih	*long time*	(3)
noih-hóng-yàhn	*insider, expert*	(15)
noih-yùhng	*contents*	(9)
nýuhn	*warm*	(15)
óh!	*oh, now I understand!*	(4)
òn-chỳuhn	*safe*	(25)
òu!	*oh!* (surprise)	(1)
Ou-mún	*Macau*	(13)
pa	*fear*	(8)
paak-wái	*to park a car*	(16)
páau-máh	*horse racing*	(19)
pàhng-yáuh	*friend*	(2)
pàh-sàan	*climb mountains, walk in the hills*	(9)
pèhng	*cheap*	(5)
pei-yùh	*for example*	(16)
pē-páai	*playing cards*	(13)
pìhng-gwàn	*average*	(12)
pìhng-yàuh	*surface mail*	(20)
póu-pin	*common (widespread)*	(18)
pou-táu	*shop*	(5)
póu-tùng	*common*	(18)
Póu-tùng-wá	*Putonghua (Mandarin)*	(18)
póu-tùng-yàhn	*an ordinary chap*	(18)
pùih	*to keep company with*	(25)
pun	*to sentence*	(18)
sàai	*waste*	(8)
saai-taai-yèuhng	*to sunbathe*	(8)
sàam	*three*	(2)
sāam	*clothing*	(8)
sāam-kwàhn	*dress*	(5)
sàan	*mountain, hill*	(9)
saan-bouh	*to stroll, go walking*	(24)
Sàan-déng	*The Peak, hilltop*	(22)
sàang-gwó	*fruit*	(4)
sàang-yaht	*birthday*	(23)
sàang-yi	*business*	(4)
saan-séui	*to scatter away*	(17)
sahp	*ten*	(2)
sahp-fàn	*totally*	(18)

sahp-go-baat-go	nine or ten	(10)
saht-joih	in fact, really	(11)
saht-yuhng	practical	(8)
sai	small	(5)
sái	wash	(15)
sài	west	(6)
sái	to drive	(16)
sài-bāk	northwest	(6)
sài-bihn	west side	(12)
sài-chāan	western food	(23)
sai-gaai	world	(6)
sai-mān-jái	children	(22)
sài-nàahm	southwest	(6)
sái-sàn	to bathe	(15)
sái-sàn-fóng	bathroom	(15)
sai-wún-gèi	dishwasher	(25)
Sài-yàhn	a westerner	(9)
Sài-yì	western medicine	(10)
sái-yì-gèi	washing machine	(25)
sà-jín	sergeant	(17)
sà-léut	salad	(4)
sàm	deep	(25)
sàm-gèi	mind, thoughts	(22)
sàn	new	(5)
sàn-chíng	apply	(17)
sàn-fán-jing	identity card	(17)
sàn-fú	hard, distressing	(12)
sàn-fún	new style	(11)
sàn-màhn	news	(13)
sàn-séui	salary	(22)
sàn-sìn	fresh	(4)
sàn-tái	body	(9)
sāt-baaih	a loss, a failure	(12)
sáu-bīu	wristwatch	(2)
sáu-chēung	handgun, pistol	(17)
sàu-dou	receive	(19)
sauh	to suffer	(24)
sáu-jai	handbrake	(16)
sáu-juhk-fai	handling charge	(20)
sáu-jūk	brothers (secret society)	(17)
sàu-léih	repair	(16)
sáu-sàn	conduct a body search	(17)
sáu-sìn	first of all	(20)
sáu-tàih	portable	(15)

sáu-tàih-dihn-wá	mobile phone	(15)
sáu-yaht	first day	(20)
sé	write	(19)
sèhng-	the whole	(9)
sèhng-yaht	the whole day	(9)
seh-wúi	society	(12)
séi	die, dead	(5)
sei	four	(2)
Sei-chỳun	Sichuan (Szechwan)	(23)
Sei-chỳun-choi	Sichuan food	(23)
séi-jái	deadbeats, bastards	(17)
sé-jih-làuh	office	(2)
sé-mìhng	written clearly	(19)
séng	wake up	(16)
séuhng	go up	(17)
seuhng-(yāt)-chi	last time	(15)
seuhng-bàan	go to work, go on shift	(22)
seuhng-bihn	on top of	(12)
séuhng-chē	get onto a vehicle	(17)
seuhng-go-yuht	last month	(17)
Seuhng-hói	Shanghai	(22)
seuhng-jau	morning, a.m.	(15)
séuhng-sàan	go up the hill	(17)
seuhng-sī	superior officer, boss	(17)
seuhng-sou	appeal to a higher court	(18)
séuhng-tòhng	attend class	(12)
séui	water	(5)
seui	year of age	(9)
sèui-teui	go into decline	(19)
sèui-yìhn	although	(18)
seun	believe	(4)
seun	letter	(19)
seun-fùng	envelope	(20)
sēung	cl: pair of	(16)
sēung	double	(9)
sèung	to wound, a wound	(16)
séung	would like to	(2)
sèung-fáan	on the contrary	(11)
séung-jeuhng	to imagine	(18)
seung-pín	photograph	(17)
sèung-sàn	double salary	(22)
sèung-seun	to believe, trust	(19)
sèung-yàhn-chòhng	double bed	(15)
seun-jí	letter paper	(20)

shàng-wuht	*to live, livelihood*	(18)
si	*try*	(11)
sī-gēi	*driver*	(12)
sih	*matter, business*	(2)
síh-chèuhng	*market*	(19)
sih-dō	*a store*	(25)
sìh-gaan	*time*	(3)
sìh-hauh	*time*	(8)
sih-hou	*hobby*	(24)
sìh-jōng	*fashion*	(11)
sihk	*eat*	(4)
síh-kèui	*urban area*	(6)
sihk-faahn	*to eat, have a meal*	(4)
sihk-maht	*food*	(23)
síh-màhn	*citizen*	(12)
sìhng-jīk	*result, score, report*	(16)
sìhng-laahp	*established, to establish*	(18)
sìhng-síh	*city, town*	(18)
sìhng-wàih	*to become*	(18)
sìh-sìh	*always*	(8)
sīk	*know how to*	(4)
sīk-hahp	*suitable to, fitting*	(13)
sīk-hèung-meih	*appearance, aroma and flavour*	(23)
sìn	*first*	(6)
sing	*surname*	(1)
sing-gaak	*temperament, disposition*	(24)
sìng-gong-gèi	*lift*	(25)
sìng-kèih	*week*	(5)
sìn-jeun	*advanced*	(22)
sìn-ji	*only then*	(10)
sìn-sàang	*teacher*	(12)
sìn-sàang	*Mr*	(1)
síu	*few, little*	(4)
siu	*smile*	(16)
Síu-	*Little* (name prefix)	(22)
síu-bā	*minibus*	(6)
sìu-fòhng-guhk	*fire brigade*	(17)
sìu-fòhng-yùhn	*fireman*	(17)
síu-hohk	*primary school*	(12)
síu-jé	*Miss*	(1)
síu-lèuhn	*ferry*	(6)
síu-sàm	*careful*	(16)
síu-sìh	*hour*	(25)

sìu-sīk	news, information	(23)
síu-síu	somewhat	(5)
si-yuhng-kèih	probationary period	(22)
só	lock	(25)
sō-fá-yí	sofa, easy chair	(11)
sou-hohk	mathematics	(12)
só-yíh	therefore	(4)
suhk-sīk	familiar with	(15)
sung	deliver, send	(6)
sung	food	(4)
sỳu	book	(12)
sỳu	lose	(13)
sỳu-faat	calligraphy	(24)
sỳu-fuhk	comfortable	(10)
syun	to be regarded as, to be reckoned	(8)
sýun-sāt	a loss	(23)
syut-gōu	ice cream	(8)
syut-gwaih	refrigerator	(15)
taai	too	(4)
taai-táai	Mrs	(1)
taam	visit a person	(3)
tái	look at	(5)
tái-dāk-dóu	able to see	(18)
tàih	to mention	(25)
tái-hei	see a play, go to the cinema	(9)
tái-m̀h-dóu	unable to see	(18)
tái-sỳu	read	(14)
tái-yī-shāng	see the doctor	(3)
tàuh	head	(10)
tàuh-jéung	first prize	(13)
tàuh-jyu	to stake, bet	(13)
tàuh-sìn	just now	(10)
tàuh-tung	headache	(10)
tàuh-wàhn	dizzy	(10)
tau-jì	overdraft, to overdraw	(19)
tàu-yéh	steal	(18)
tèng	listen	(6)
tèui	push	(17)
teui-yàu	retire	(22)
teui-yàu-gām	a pension	(22)
tìhm-bán	dessert	(4)
tìhng	stop	(11)

tìhn-sé	*fill in a form*	(20)
tìm	fp: *as well, what's more, also*	(8)
tìng-máahn	*tomorrow night*	(11)
tìng-yaht	*tomorrow*	(8)
tìn-hei	*weather*	(8)
tìn-màhn-tòih	*observatory*	(8)
Tìn-sīng máh-tàuh	*Star Ferry Pier*	(6)
tip-séuhng	*to stick on*	(20)
tiu-gòu	*to jump high; high jump*	(10)
tìuh	cl: *for long flexible things*	(8)
tiuh-gín	*conditions, terms*	(22)
tiu-móuh	*to dance*	(24)
Tòhng-chāan	*Chinese food*	(23)
Tòhng-yàhn	*a Chinese*	(10)
tòih	*carry, lift*	(16)
tòng	*soup*	(4)
tòng-wún	*soup bowl*	(25)
tou	cl: *set of, suit of*	(8)
tou-fóng	*en suite*	(25)
tóuh	*stomach, abdomen*	(10)
tùhng	*same, alike*	(24)
tùhng	*with, and*	(3)
tùhng-màaih	*and*	(2)
tùhng-sih	*colleague*	(16)
tùhng-yi	*to agree*	(8)
tung	*pain*	(10)
tùng(-fo-pàahng)-jeung	*inflation*	(19)
tùng-yùhng	*stretch a point*	(15)
ūk	*house*	(3)
ūk-ga	*house price*	(25)
ūk-kéi	*home*	(3)
wá	*language, speech*	(4)
wà!	*wow!*	(5)
waahk-gwái-geuk	*'draw a ghost's leg'*	(21)
waahk-jé	*or, perhaps*	(16)
waahk-wá	*to paint, draw*	(24)
waaih	*go wrong, break down*	(16)
waaih	*bad*	(12)
wàaih-gauh	*nostalgia, nostalgic*	(23)
wàaih-yìh	*to suspect*	(17)
wáan	*play*	(6)

wah	*say*	(6)
wah . . . jì/tèng	*tell*	(8)
wahn	*to transport*	(11)
wahn-duhng	*physical exercise*	(9)
wahn-fai	*transportation costs*	(25)
wahn-sỳu	*to transport*	(11)
wái	cl: (polite) for people	(17)
wái!	*hello!* (on the phone)	(10)
wai!	*hey!*	(17)
wàih-kéih	Go, *'surrounding chess'*	(24)
Wài-lìhm	*William*	(10)
wán	*look for*	(2)
wàn-jaahp	*to revise lessons*	(12)
wihng-chìh	*swimming pool*	(15)
Wòhng	a surname: *Wong*	(1)
wòhng-ngàuh	*a brown cow*	(12)
wòhng-sīk	*yellow*	(12)
wuh-háu	*bank account*	(19)
wuh-jiu	*passport*	(15)
wuhn	*exchange*	(25)
wúih	*it is likely that* (future	
	possibility)	(8)
wúih	*meeting; club, society*	(13)
wúih	*able to*	(5)
Wùih-gwài	*Handover* (1997)	(20)
wún	*bowl*	(25)
wún-gwaih	*cupboard*	(25)
wù-yíhm	*pollution*	(23)
yah-	*twenty-*	(13)
yahm-hòh	*any*	(17)
yàhn	*person*	(1)
yàhn-deih	*other people*	(Ap)
Yàhn-màhn-baih	*renminbi, RMB*	(19)
yàhn-sou	*number of people*	(13)
yàhn-yùhn	*personnel, staff*	(25)
yahp	*enter*	(5)
yahp-bihn	*inside*	(12)
yahp-dihn-yàuh	*refuel, put petrol in*	(16)
yaht	*day*	(6)
Yaht-bún	*Japan*	(1)
yaht-táu	*daytime*	(15)
yah-yāt-dím	*blackjack, pontoon*	(13)

yám	*drink*	(8)
yám-chàh	*'drink tea', have a dim sum meal*	(25)
yàn-waih	*because*	(4)
yāt	*one*	(2)
yāt . . . jauh	*as soon as*	(24)
yāt-bùn	*general, the general run of, common*	(12)
yāt-chāi	*every single one of*	(22)
yāt-chàih	*together*	(3)
yāt-dī	*a little bit*	(9)
yāt-dihng	*certainly*	(3)
yāt-go yàhn	*alone*	(18)
yāt-go-gwāt	*quarter*	(15)
yāt-guhng	*altogether*	(20)
Yāt-gwok-léuhng-jai	*'One country, two systems'*	(20)
yāt-háh	*a little bit, once*	(15)
yāt-heung	*all along, up to now*	(24)
yāt-jahn(-gāan)	*in/for a moment*	(24)
yāt-jihk	*straight*	(6)
yāt-làuh	*first rate*	(23)
yāt-sìh	*momentarily, briefly*	(16)
yāt-yeuhng	*same*	(11)
Yāt-yuht	*January*	(17)
yàuh	*from*	(6)
yàuh	*tour, to tour*	(15)
yauh	*furthermore*	(7)
yáuh	*have*	(2)
yauh-(sáu-)bihn	*right side*	(12)
yauh . . . yauh . . .	*both . . . and . . .*	(5)
yáuh-behng	*to be ill*	(10)
yáuh-chín	*rich*	(13)
yáuh-dī	*some, a little bit*	(10)
yàuh-fai	*postage*	(20)
yàuh-gáan	*airletter form*	(20)
yàuh-gúk	*post office*	(20)
yáuh-gwàan	*relevant*	(19)
yàuh-haak	*tourist*	(15)
yàuh-hei	*games*	(24)
yàuh-hei-gèi	*games machine*	(24)
Yàuh-jing-júng-gúk	*General Post Office*	(20)
yáuh-kèih-sih	*especially*	(12)
yáuh-māt-yéh-sih-a?	*for what purpose? why?*	(2)
yáuh-méng	*famous*	(6)

yàuh-piu	*postage stamp*	(20)
yáuh-sàm	*kind of you*	(1)
yàuh-séui	*swim*	(5)
yàuh-séui-fu	*swimming trunks*	(8)
yáuh-sìh	*sometimes*	(13)
yáuh-sih	*something is wrong*	(16)
yàuh-túng	*pillar box*	(20)
yáuh-yàhn	*somebody*	(11)
yáuh-yāt-dī	*somewhat, a little bit*	(10)
yáuh-yuhng	*useful*	(8)
yéh	*thing, object*	(8)
yeh-	*twenty-*	(13)
yeh-máahn	*nighttime*	(15)
yèhng	*win*	(13)
yeuhk	*medicine*	(10)
yeuhk-séui	*(liquid) medicine*	(10)
yeuhng	*kind, sort, type*	(13)
yéuhng	*to rear, keep (pets)*	(24)
yèuhng-jáu	*(non-Chinese) liquor*	(15)
yéuhng-sìhng	*inculcate, form, breed*	(24)
yeuhng-yeuhng	*all kinds of*	(13)
yí	*chair*	(11)
yí!	*hello, what's this?*	(5)
Yi-daaih-leih	*Italy*	(19)
yih, léuhng	*two*	(2)
yìh-ché	*moreover*	(9)
yìh-gā	*now*	(2)
yíh-gìng	*already*	(8)
yìh-màhn	*immigrate, emigrate*	(17)
yìhm-juhng	*serious, desperate*	(10)
yihn-gām	*cash, ready money*	(19)
yihng-jān	*serious, sincere*	(16)
yihng-sīk	*recognize; understand*	(23)
yìhn-hauh	*afterwards*	(10)
yiht	*hot*	(8)
yiht-séui-lòuh	*water heater, boiler*	(25)
yíh-wàih	*assume, think*	(11)
yīk	*hundred million, billion*	(13)
yí-laaih	*to rely on*	(24)
yì-lìuh	*medical*	(22)
yìng-bóng	*pound sterling*	(19)
Yìng-gwok	*UK*	(1)
yíng-héung	*influence*	(23)
yíng-seung	*to photograph*	(17)

yī-sāng	*doctor*	(3)
yi-sì	*meaning*	(17)
yiu	*must, need to*	(3)
yiu	*want*	(1)
yìu-chéng	*to invite*	(23)
yìuh-wàhn	*to shake up*	(10)
yi-yih	*meaning, significance*	(23)
yì-yún	*hospital*	(10)
yú	*fish*	(23)
yù-góng	*fishing port*	(6)
yuh-beih	*prepare*	(4)
yùh-gwó	*if*	(4)
yùh-gwó-m̀h-haih	*otherwise*	(12)
yuh-jì	*to predict*	(24)
yuhk	*meat*	(4)
yùhn	*dollar*	(13)
yúhn	*distant, far*	(25)
yuhng	*spend, use*	(4)
yùhng-yih	*easy*	(20)
yùhn-lòih	*originally*	(20)
yùhn-yān	*reason*	(23)
yuht	*moon, month*	(17)
yuht . . . yuht . . .	*the more . . . the more . . .*	(19)
yuht-git-dāan	*monthly statement*	(19)
yuht-méih	*end of the month*	(17)
yūk	*make a movement*	(17)

Numbers in brackets indicate the unit in which the entry is introduced.

able to	wúih	(5)
address	deih-jí	(20)
after	jì-hauh	(6)
afternoon	hah-jau	(15)
again	joi	(4)
aim, purpose	muhk-dīk	(24)
aircraft	fèi-gèi	(6)
airmail	hùng-yàuh	(20)
alcoholic drink	jáu	(8)
alight	lohk	(6)
all, both	dōu	(4)
all told	hahm-baah-laahng	(20)
almost	chà-m̀h-dō	(12)
alone	yāt-go yàhn	(18)
already	yíh-gìng	(8)
also	dōu	(1)
alter	gói	(8)
although	sèui-yìhn	(18)
altogether	yāt-guhng	(20)
always	sìh-sìh	(8)
and	tùhng-màaih	(2)
angry	nàu	(4)
any	yahm-hòh	(17)
apply	sàn-chíng	(17)
approximately	daaih-yeuk	(20)
arrest	làai	(17)
arrive	dou	(6)
as soon as	yāt . . . jauh	(24)

ask a question	mahn	(2)
assume, think	yíh-wàih	(11)
at least	jeui-síu	(18)
at leisure	dāk-hàahn	(13)
at, in, on	hái	(2)
average	pìhng-gwàn	(12)
back	hauh-bihn	(12)
bad	waaih	(12)
bank	ngàhn-hòhng	(19)
bathroom	chùng-lèuhng-fóng	(25)
be	haih	(1)
be forced to	beih-bīk	(11)
because	yàn-waih	(4)
bed	chòhng	(15)
beef	ngàuh-yuhk	(4)
before	jì-chìhn	(10)
believe	seun	(4)
bet on horses	dóu-máh	(13)
bicycle	dāan-chē	(16)
big	daaih	(3)
bill	màaih-dāan	(23)
birthday	sàang-yaht	(23)
black	hāk-sīk	(12)
blood	hyut	(16)
body	sàn-tái	(9)
book	sỳu	(12)
boss	bō-sí	(25)
both . . . and . . .	yauh . . . yauh . . .	(5)
bowl	wún	(25)
breakfast	jóu-chāan	(22)
bring	nìng	(16)
broken, damaged	laahn	(5)
brothers	hìng-daih	(3)
bus	bā-sí	(3)
bus stop	bā-sí-jaahm	(6)
business	sàang-yi	(4)
busy	mòhng	(10)
but	daahn-haih	(6)
buy	máaih	(2)
by (passive)	beih	(12)
car	chē	(1)
careful	síu-sàm	(16)

carry	tòih	(16)
cat	māau	(24)
catty	gàn	(5)
cause	lihng	(18)
certainly	yāt-dihng	(3)
chair	yí	(11)
chance	gèi-wuih	(22)
chat	kìng-gái	(11)
cheap	pèhng	(5)
children	jái-néui	(22)
China	Jùng-gwok	(2)
Chinese restaurant	jáu-làuh	(4)
chopsticks	faai-jí	(16)
city, town	sìhng-síh	(18)
clean	chìng-git	(25)
clock	jūng	(15)
close to	gahn, káhn	(20)
coffee	ga-fē	(3)
cold	láahng	(8)
colour	ngàahn-sīk	(5)
come	làih	(3)
comfortable	sỳu-fuhk	(10)
common	póu-tùng	(18)
company	gūng-sī	(8)
compare	béi-gaau	(19)
computer	dihn-nóuh	(22)
congratulations	gùng-héi	(23)
convenient	fòng-bihn	(17)
cook	jýu	(4)
correct	ngāam	(13)
country, state	gwok-gà	(19)
countryside	hèung-há	(6)
cow, ox	ngàuh	(4)
crazy	chì-sin	(16)
cuisine	choi	(23)
cup, glass	bùi, būi	(25)
danger	ngàih-hím	(24)
dare	gám	(18)
daughter	néui	(17)
day	yaht	(6)
daytime	yaht-táu	(15)
decide	kyut-dihng	(25)
deep	sàm	(25)

delicious	hóu-sihk	(13)
deliver, send	sung	(6)
die, dead	séi	(5)
difficult	nàahn	(17)
dinner	máahn-faahn	(23)
distant from	lèih	(25)
distant, far	yúhn	(25)
do	jouh	(3)
doctor	yī-sāng	(3)
dog	gáu	(13)
dollar	māan	(5)
don't	máih, m̀h-hóu	(4)
door	mùhn	(20)
dress	sāam-kwàhn	(5)
drink	yám	(8)
drive	jà-chē	(6)
driver	sī-gēi	(12)
each, every	múih	(12)
early	jóu	(4)
east	dùng	(6)
easy	yùhng-yih	(20)
eat	sihk	(4)
economy	gìng-jai	(19)
education	gaau-yuhk	(12)
eight	baat	(2)
electricity	dihn	(16)
empty	hùng	(11)
enjoy	héung-sauh	(15)
enough	gau	(16)
enter	yahp	(5)
envelope	seun-fūng	(20)
error	cho	(19)
etcetera	dáng-dáng	(15)
evening	máahn	(6)
examination	háau-sih	(16)
exchange	wuhn	(25)
expensive	gwai	(1)
express	dahk-faai	(20)
eye	ngáahn	(17)
false	gá	(17)
familiar with	suhk-sīk	(15)
famous	yáuh-méng	(6)

fashion	sìh-jōng	(11)
fast	faai	(15)
father	bàh-bā	(3)
fax	chỳuhn-jān	(22)
fear	pa	(8)
feel	gok-dāk	(9)
female	néuih	(17)
ferry	síu-lèuhn	(6)
few, little	síu	(4)
fight	dá-gāau	(18)
film (camera)	fēi-lám	(25)
film (cinema)	dihn-yíng	(9)
finish work	fong-gùng	(22)
first	sìn	(6)
fish	yú	(23)
five	ńgh	(2)
flat, apartment	láu	(3)
flow	làuh	(16)
food	sung	(4)
foot, leg	geuk	(16)
for example	pei-yùh	(16)
foreign country	ngoih-gwok	(18)
four	sei	(2)
fragrant	hèung	(23)
free of charge	míhn-fai	(5)
fresh	sàn-sìn	(4)
friend	pàhng-yáuh	(2)
from	yàuh	(6)
front	chìhn-bihn	(12)
fruit	sàang-gwó	(4)
furthermore	yauh	(7)
future	jèung-lòih	(24)
garage	chē-fòhng	(3)
garden	fà-yún	(2)
get up	héi-sàn	(10)
give	béi, sung . . . béi	(4)
go	heui	(2)
go to work	fàan-gùng	(22)
go up	séuhng	(17)
good	hóu	(1)
good boy	gwàai	(13)
good morning	jóu-sàhn	(1)
goodbye	joi-gin	(1)

government	jing-fú	(12)
gradually	jihm-jím	(8)
guess	gú	(2)
half	bun	(4)
hand over	gàau	(15)
happen	faat-sàng	(18)
happy	hòi-sām	(8)
hard, distressing	sàn-fú	(12)
hate	jàng	(24)
have	yáuh	(2)
have not	móuh	(3)
he, she, it	kéuih	(1)
head	tàuh	(10)
healthy	gihn-hòng	(9)
heavy	chúhng	(12)
help	bòng . . . sáu	(4)
here	nī-syu, nī-douh	(5)
history	lihk-sí	(12)
hit	dá	(9)
holiday	fong-ga	(9)
home	ūk-kéi	(3)
honest	lóuh-saht	(13)
Hong Kong	Hèung-góng	(3)
hope	hèi-mohng	(10)
hospital	yì-yún	(10)
hot	yiht	(8)
hotel	jáu-dim	(15)
hour	jūng-tàuh	(4)
hour	síu-sìh	(25)
house	ūk	(3)
how long?	géi-noih	(20)
how much?	géi-dō	(5)
how?	dím(-yéung)	(5)
hundred	baak	(11)
hurrying	gón-jyuh	(15)
I, me	ngóh	(1)
I wonder	m̀h-jì	(11)
idea	jýu-yi	(6)
identity card	sàn-fán-jing	(17)
if	yùh-gwó	(4)
illegal	fèi-faat	(13)
important	gán-yiu	(21)

influence	yíng-héung	(23)
inside	léuih-bihn	(9)
insurance	bóu-hím	(15)
intend	dá-syun	(8)
introduce	gaai-siuh	(4)
invite	chéng	(4)
Japan	Yaht-bún	(1)
just like	hóu-chíh	(4)
just now	tàuh-sīn	(10)
kilometre	gùng-léih	(23)
kind of you	yáuh-sàm	(1)
kitchen	chyùh-fóng	(4)
know a fact	jì-dou	(8)
know how to	sīk	(4)
lack	kyut-faht	(24)
language	wá	(4)
last in order	daih-mēi	(22)
last month	seuhng-go-yuht	(17)
last year	gauh-nín	(8)
later	chìh-dī	(2)
law and order	jih-òn	(18)
lead	daai	(2)
leave	lèih-hòi	(9)
left side	jó-(sáu-)bihn	(12)
let, allow	dáng	(5)
letter	seun	(19)
lift	līp	(25)
light (coloured)	chín	(25)
light (weight)	hèng	(15)
like, fond of	jùng-yi	(6)
listen	tèng	(6)
live, dwell	jyuh	(3)
lobby	daaih-tòhng	(26)
lobster	lùhng-hā	(4)
lock	só	(25)
long	chèuhng	(22)
long time	noih	(3)
look at	tái	(5)
look for	wán	(2)
lose	syù	(13)
lost	m̀h-gin-jó	(24)

low	ngái	(25)
luggage	hàhng-léih	(15)
machine	gèi-hei	(24)
make, prepare	jíng	(4)
male	nàahm	(9)
manager	gìng-léih	(15)
many, much	dò	(3)
market	síh-chèuhng	(19)
matter, business	sih	(2)
may, can	hó-yíh	(6)
meal	chāan	(4)
meaning	yi-si	(17)
meat	yuhk	(4)
medicine	yeuhk-séui	(10)
menu	chāan-páai	(23)
midday	aan-jau	(22)
minibus	síu-bā	(6)
Miss	síu-jé	(1)
misunderstand	ngh-wuih	(16)
moment ago	ngāam-ngāam	(10)
money	chín	(5)
moon, month	yuht	(17)
moreover	yìh-ché	(9)
morning	jìu-jóu	(4)
most	jeui	(6)
mother	màh-mā	(3)
motorbike	dihn-dāan-chē	(16)
Mr	sìn-sàang	(1)
Mrs	taai-táai	(1)
narrow	jaak	(16)
nearby	fuh-gahn	(4)
never mind	m̀h gán-yiu	(2)
new	sàn	(5)
news	sàn-màhn	(13)
newspaper	bou-jí	(18)
next year	chēut-nín	(8)
nighttime	yeh-máahn	(15)
nine	gáu	(2)
no need to	m̀h-sái	(4)
no wonder	m̀h-gwaai-dāk	(23)
noisy	chòuh	(25)
north	bāk	(6)

not	m̀h	(1)
not bad	m̀h-cho	(11)
not yet	meih	(10)
now	yìh-gā	(2)
occasionally	gaan-jūng	(10)
of course	dòng-yìhn	(13)
office	sé-jih-làuh	(2)
OK	dāk	(5)
old (not new)	gauh	(8)
old (elderly)	lóuh	(6)
on top of	seuhng-bihn	(12)
one	yāt	(2)
only	jí-haih	(4)
only then	sìn-ji	(10)
open	hòi	(19)
opposite	deui-mihn	(12)
or, perhaps	waahk-jé	(16)
or?	dihng-haih	(13)
originally	yùhn-lòih	(20)
other	kèih-tà	(5)
otherwise	yùh-gwó-m̀h-haih	(12)
outside	chēut-bihn	(12)
pain	tung	(10)
paper	jí	(20)
passport	wuh-jiu	(15)
past, across, by	gwo	(6)
pay attention to	jyu-yi	(15)
pen	bāt	(2)
permit	jéun	(17)
person	yàhn	(1)
petrol	dihn-yàuh	(16)
photograph	seung-pín	(17)
physical exercise	wahn-duhng	(9)
place	deih-fòng	(6)
play	wáan	(6)
play ball	dá-bō	(9)
please	chéng	(3)
please may I ask	chéng-mahn	(6)
policeman	gíng-chaat	(12)
polite	haak-hei	(4)
pollution	wù-yíhm	(23)
pork	jyù-yuhk	(10)

portable	sáu-tàih	(15)
possibility	hó-nàhng	(16)
post, mail	gei	(20)
post office	yàuh-gúk	(20)
pour	jàm	(25)
practical	saht-yuhng	(8)
practise	lihn-jaahp	(24)
praise	jaan	(11)
prawn	hā	(5)
prepare	yuh-beih	(4)
pretty, beautiful	leng	(1)
price	ga-chìhn	(11)
problem	mahn-tàih	(15)
programme	jit-muhk	(15)
prosperous	fàahn-wìhng	(13)
public	gùng-guhng	(12)
pull	làai	(17)
pupil, student	hohk-sāang	(16)
push	tèui	(17)
quality	jāt-déi	(5)
quarter	yāt-go-gwāt	(15)
quiet	jihng	(25)
quite	dōu-géi	(3)
railway train	fó-chē	(6)
rain	lohk-yúh	(8)
reaction	fáan-ying	(16)
read	tái-sỳu	(14)
receive	sàu-dóu	(19)
recently	jeui-gahn	(19)
red	hùhng	(5)
regard as	dong	(4)
relevant	yáuh-gwàan	(19)
remain	làuh	(24)
remember	gei-dāk	(9)
repair	sàu-léih	(16)
responsible	fuh-jaak	(22)
restaurant	chāan-tēng	(23)
result	git-gwó	(16)
retire	teui-yàu	(22)
return	fàan	(3)
rice	faahn	(4)
rich	yáuh-chín	(13)

right side	yauh-bihn	(12)
road surface	louh-mín	(15)
rob	dá-gip	(18)
room	fòhng-gāan	(15)
rubbish	laahp-saap	(4)
run, run away	jáu	(3)
safe	òn-chỳuhn	(25)
salad	sà-léut	(4)
salary	sàn-séui	(22)
sale	daaih-gáam-ga	(5)
same	yāt-yeuhng	(11)
say	wah	(6)
school	hohk-haauh	(12)
science	fō-hohk	(12)
sea	hói	(25)
seafood	hói-sīn	(23)
secret	bei-maht	(24)
secretary	bei-sỳu	(22)
see	gin	(8)
self	jih-géi	(24)
sell	maaih	(1)
service	fuhk-mouh	(15)
seven	chāt	(2)
several	géi	(9)
shares	gú-piu	(13)
shop	pou-táu	(5)
short	dýun	(22)
simple	gáan-dàan	(20)
sisters	jí-múih	(3)
sit	chóh	(3)
six	luhk	(2)
sleep	fan-gaau	(16)
slow	maahn	(16)
small	sai	(5)
smile	siu	(16)
so	gám	(3)
so	gam	(4)
soccer	jūk-kàuh	(13)
society	séh-wúi	(12)
solitary	gù-dūhk	(24)
sometimes	yáuh-sìh	(13)
somewhat	síu-síu	(5)
son	jái	(10)

soon	jauh-faai	(23)
sorry	deui-m̀h-jyuh	(1)
soup	tòng	(4)
south	nàahm	(6)
speak	góng	(9)
special	dahk-biht	(23)
speech	wá	(4)
spend	yuhng	(4)
stand	kéih	(17)
steal	tàu-yéh	(18)
still, yet	juhng	(3)
stop	tìhng	(11)
straight	yāt-jihk	(6)
strange	kèih-gwaai	(24)
street	gāai	(3)
street stall	dong-háu	(5)
study	duhk-sỳu	(12)
style	fún-sīk	(5)
surname	sing	(1)
sweep	dá-sou	(25)
swim	yàuh-séui	(5)
system	jai-douh	(22)
take	ló	(15)
take part in	chàam-gà	(11)
taxi	dīk-sí	(3)
tea	chàh	(4)
teach	gaau-sỳu	(12)
telephone	dihn-wá	(10)
television set	dihn-sih-gèi	(15)
tell	wa . . . jì	(8)
tell to do	giu	(17)
temporary	jaahm-sìh	(20)
ten	sahp	(2)
ten thousand	maahn	(11)
thank you	m̀h-gòi	(2)
thank you	dò-jeh	(5)
that is to say	jīk-haih	(5)
that, those	gó	(2)
then	jauh	(4)
there	gó-syu, gó-douh	(5)
therefore	só-yíh	(4)
think about	nám	(20)
this, these	nī	(2)

thousand	chìn	(11)
three	sàam	(2)
ticket	fēi	(15)
time	sìh-gaan	(3)
time, occasion	chi	(6)
time's up	gau-jūng	(13)
tired	guih	(24)
today	gàm-yaht	(4)
together	yāt-chàih	(3)
toilet	chi-só	(10)
tomorrow	tìng-yaht	(8)
too	taai	(4)
totally	sahp-fàn	(18)
tourism, travel	léuih-yàuh	(15)
tourist	yàuh-haak	(15)
towards	heung	(6)
traffic light	gàau-tùng-dāng	(12)
tram	dihn-chè	(9)
travel by	daap	(3)
trouble	màh-fàahn	(12)
truly	jàn-haih	(4)
try	si	(11)
turn, change	jýun	(6)
two	yih, léuhng	(2)
typewriter	dá-jih-gèi	(22)
UK	Yìng-gwok	(1)
under	hah-bihn	(12)
underground	deih-tit	(6)
understand	mìhng-baahk	(12)
university	daaih-hohk	(6)
USA	Méih-gwok	(1)
use	yuhng	(4)
useful	yáuh-yuhng	(8)
very	hóu	(1)
visa	chìm-jing	(15)
visit a person	taam	(3)
visit a place	chàam-gwùn	(6)
wait	dáng	(4)
waiter	fó-gei	(4)
wake up	séng	(16)
walk	hàahng-louh	(15)

want	yiu	(1)
warm	nyúhn	(15)
wash	sái	(15)
waste	sàai	(8)
water	séui	(5)
wear	daai	(11)
wear	jeuk	(11)
weather	tìn-hei	(8)
week	láih-baai, sìng-kèih	(5)
welcome	fùn-yìhng	(22)
west	sài	(6)
what?	māt-yéh	(2)
when?	géi-sí *or* géi-sìh	(8)
where?	bīn-syu, bīn-douh	(3)
which?	bīn	(2)
white	baahk-sīk	(12)
who?	bīn-go	(2)
why?	dím-gáai	(4)
willing	háng	(22)
win	yèhng	(13)
wind	fùng	(8)
within	jì-noih	(6)
work	gùng-jok	(22)
world	sai-gaai	(6)
worth it	dái	(15)
would like to	séung	(2)
wrap up	bàau	(20)
wristwatch	sáu-bīu	(2)
write	sé	(19)
year	nìhn	(8)
year of age	seui	(9)
yellow	wòhng-sīk	(12)
yesterday	johk-yaht	(4)
you	néih, néih-deih	(1)
young	hauh-sāang	(12)
zero	lìhng	(11)

chinese language, life & culture
kenneth wilkinson

- Why was the Long March so long?
- How does Chinese medicine work?
- Is China the world's last communist superpower?
- What is the mysterious force called 'qi'?

This book answers these questions, and many more, in a concise and lively overview of China: the country, its heritage and its people. It gives the student and the enthusiastic traveller the means to talk and write confidently about all aspects of Chinese life.

The book looks at: government, arts, language, work, leisure, education, festivals, food – and much more besides! This is your key to understanding China's past, present and future, with plenty of suggestions for further study and background reading.

chinese
elizabeth scurfield

- Do you want to cover the basics and progress fast?
- Do you want to be confident in a range of situations?
- Do you want to know how Chinese characters work?

Chinese starts with the basics but moves at a lively pace to give you a good level of understanding, speaking and writing. You will have lots of opportunity to practise the kind of language you will need to be able to communicate with confidence and understand Chinese culture.

teach
yourself

beginner's chinese script
elizabeth scurfield & song lianyi

- Are you interested in the Chinese script?
- Are you planning a business trip or holiday?
- Do you want to understand simple signs and notices in China?

Beginner's Chinese Script will help you get to grips with reading and writing simple Chinese, whether you are studying the language or planning a trip for business or pleasure. The step-by-step approach will build your confidence to read and write mainly simplifed characters in a variety of real contexts.

teach yourself®

the A-Z of teach yourself language titles

Afrikaans
Arabic
Arabic Script, Beginner's
Bengali
Brazilian Portuguese
Bulgarian
Cantonese
Catalan
Chinese
Chinese, Beginner's
Chinese Language, Life & Culture
Chinese Script, Beginner's
Croatian
Czech
Danish
Dutch
Dutch, Beginner's
Dutch Dictionary
Dutch Grammar
English, American (EFL)
English as a Foreign Language
English, Correct
English Grammar
English Grammar (EFL)
English, Instant, for French Speakers
English, Instant, for German Speakers
English, Instant, for Italian Speakers
English, Instant, for Spanish Speakers
English for International Business
English Language, Life & Culture
English Verbs
English Vocabulary
Finnish
French
French, Beginner's
French Grammar
French Grammar, Quick Fix
French, Instant
French, Improve your
French Language, Life & Culture
French Starter Kit
French Verbs

French Vocabulary
Gaelic
Gaelic Dictionary
German
German, Beginner's
German Grammar
German Grammar, Quick Fix
German, Instant
German, Improve your
German Language, Life & Culture
German Verbs
German Vocabulary
Greek
Greek, Ancient
Greek, Beginner's
Greek, Instant
Greek, New Testament
Greek Script, Beginner's
Gulf Arabic
Hebrew, Biblical
Hindi
Hindi, Beginner's
Hindi Script, Beginner's
Hungarian
Icelandic
Indonesian
Irish
Italian
Italian, Beginner's
Italian Grammar
Italian Grammar, Quick Fix
Italian, Instant
Italian, Improve your
Italian Language, Life & Culture
Italian Verbs
Italian Vocabulary
Japanese
Japanese, Beginner's
Japanese, Instant
Japanese Language, Life & Culture
Japanese Script, Beginner's
Korean

Latin
Latin American Spanish
Latin, Beginner's
Latin Dictionary
Latin Grammar
Nepali
Norwegian
Panjabi
Persian, Modern
Polish
Portuguese
Portuguese, Beginner's
Portuguese Grammar
Portuguese, Instant
Portuguese Language, Life & Culture
Romanian
Russian
Russian, Beginner's
Russian Grammar
Russian, Instant
Russian Language, Life & Culture
Russian Script, Beginner's
Sanskrit
Serbian
Spanish
Spanish, Beginner's
Spanish Grammar
Spanish Grammar, Quick Fix
Spanish, Instant
Spanish, Improve your
Spanish Language, Life & Culture
Spanish Starter Kit
Spanish Verbs
Spanish Vocabulary
Swahili
Swahili Dictionary
Swedish
Tagalog
Teaching English as a Foreign Language
Teaching English One to One
Thai
Turkish
Turkish, Beginner's
Ukrainian
Urdu
Urdu Script, Beginner's
Vietnamese
Welsh
Welsh Dictionary
Welsh Language, Life & Culture
Xhosa
Zulu

available from bookshops and on-line retailers